The Living Voice of the Gospels

Francis J. Moloney

HENDRICKSON
PUBLISHERS

The Living Voice of the Gospels
Hendrickson Publishers, Inc.
P. O. Box 3473
Peabody, Massachusetts 01961-3473

ISBN 978-1-59856-065-7

Printed in the United States of America

First Printing — June 2007

Cover Art: Donald J. Forsythe. "Burning Lights." 2002. Gouache monotype collage with photo serigraph on artist-made and market papers, joss paper. Courtesy of the collection of Lois M. Paine.
Photo Credit: Andrew Bale. Used with permission.

Library of Congress Cataloging-in-Publication Data

Moloney, Francis J.
    The living voice of the Gospels / Francis J. Moloney.
      p. cm.
    Rev. ed. of: The living voice of the Gospel : the Gospels today. 1986.
    ISBN-13: 978-1-59856-065-7 (alk. paper)
    I. Moloney, Francis J. Living voice of the Gospel. II. Title.
    BS2555.52.M65 2007
    226'.061—dc22
                     2007012736

For the Salesians of the Australian Province
1960-2006

Acknowledgements

All the material in this book has been freshly written, or re-written from earlier publications by the author. Earlier studies that have contributed to the following texts are:

The Gospel of Mark. A Commentary (Peabody: Hendrickson, 2002).
Mark. Storyteller, Interpreter, Evangelist (Peabody: Hendrickson, 2004).
This is the Gospel of the Lord. Year A (Homebush: St. Paul Publications, 1992), 13-49.
This is the Gospel of the Lord. Year B (Homebush: St. Paul Publications, 1991), 82-91.
The Gospel of John (Sacra Pagina 4; Collegeville: The Liturgical Press, 1998).
"The Function of Prolepsis for the Interpretation of John 6," in *The Gospel of John. Text and Context* (Biblical Interpretation Series 72; Boston/Leiden: Brill, 2005), 169-92.

Note on quotations

Unless otherwise stated, all quotations from the Biblical texts are the author's own translations, largely guided by the fine traditional translation of the Revised Standard Verson (RSV). Occasionally, where more inclusive language is called for, my translation has been further guided by the New Revised Standard Version (NRSV).

Quotations from the Second Vatican Council are taken from A. Flannery (ed.), *Vatican Council II. The Conciliar and Post Conciliar Documents* (Dublin: Dominican Publication, 1975).

Abbreviations

LXX   The Septuagint: the pre-Christian Greek Translation of the Hebrew Bible.

MT   The Masoretic Text: the pointed text of the Hebrew Bible.

NRSV   The New Revised Standard Version.

PL   *Patrologiae cursus completes, series Latina,* ed. J. P. Migne

RSV   The Revised Standard Version

YHWH These four letters respectfully represent the name for God in the Hebrew Bible. I use them throughout to indicate the God of Israel.

CONTENTS

PREFACE

THE FIRST EDITION OF THIS INTRODUCTION to a contemporary reading of the four Gospels was published in 1986. I signed off on the script on the Feast of Saint John Bosco, the founder of my Religious Congregation, the Salesians of Don Bosco, on January 31, 1986. The first edition was published in Australia by the then Collins Dove, in Great Britain by Darton, Longman and Todd, and in the United States of America by Paulist Press. It has obviously served a need, as it is nowadays impossible to obtain a copy of that edition. I am pleased to present a complete rewriting of this introduction to a contemporary reading of Mark, Matthew, Luke and John. I am grateful to Garry Eastman, formerly of Collins Dove, but now the Director of John Garratt Publishing, who has encouraged me for some years to republish this volume. What follows has the shape of the original edition, but its contents have changed very markedly.

A great deal has happened in Gospel studies over those years, especially the development of more literary and narrative readings of these texts. These methods of interpretation were in their infancy in 1986. They now occupy center-stage, and I have been deeply influenced by them. However, if the book that follows is somewhat different from the original version of *The Living Voice of the Gospel*, it has been written for the same purposes and the same audience. The Gospels resonate deeply in the minds and hearts of the many people who have followed lectures, courses, seminars and days of reflection dedicated to some form of study of these narratives. The problem enunciated twenty years ago, however, remains. Some of us have been equipped to read these texts in their original language, aware of the socio-cultural, historical and religious setting that produced them. We are well schooled in the rhetorical and literary techniques that determine the spirit and the shape of the narratives as a whole, and the formative parts of each narrative. But most Christians have not been equipped with these tools. What follows is an attempt to bridge that gap somewhat for the interested lay reader of the Gospels of Mark, Matthew, Luke and John.

After more than forty years since the close of the Second Vatican Council, and the restructuring of the Weekly and Sunday Lectionaries, too few people have captured the intention of the post-conciliar commission that led to this restructure. There are still many who are unaware that the Church asks us to meditate, week by week, on a cursive reading of the Gospel of Matthew (Year A), the Gospel of Mark (Year B) and the Gospel of Luke (Year C). No year is dedicated to a reading of the Gospel of John. However, this profound text is regularly used during certain high periods of the Liturgical Year, especially during the Easter and Christmas Seasons.

The Roman Lectionary has served as a model for Lectionaries that have developed within other Christian communities and Churches across the past forty years, and also the Common Lectionary. Identical readings are not found across all Lectionaries, and some lectionaries offer alternative selections from time to time. However, the principle that guided the formation of all Lectionaries was the same: to provide both preacher and faithful the opportunity to move through Lectionary cycles that made possible a Gospel catechesis that reflects the four-fold Gospel tradition. The Christian life is based upon an acceptance of the person and teaching of Jesus of Nazareth that come to us from the Gospels. The aim of this presentation of the four Gospels is to assist all committed Christians in their receptivity to the Word, as it is proclaimed in the Liturgy, and in their following of Jesus of Nazareth as Gospel-inspired believers.

The structure of the book that follows is simple, and strives to follow a didactic model that leads from the general to the particular. The first chapter deals with the development and the nature of a Gospel, and the uniqueness of each of the four Gospels. With these general principles in mind, the reader will find eight chapters that deal with each Gospel in turn: Mark, Matthew, Luke and John. Two chapters are devoted to each Gospel. In the first of these two chapters I outline the general and overall theological message and literary structure of the Gospel under consideration. The second chapter is devoted to a closer reading of a discrete literary section from that Gospel. This closer reading should introduce the reader into a contemporary method of reading a Gospel text. The choice of the passages for a closer reading, however, has been determined by another criterion. As we will see in the introductory chapter, the Gospels contain a number of so-called "literary forms." I will attend to four different literary forms in the four close readings of Gospel texts: the prologue to the Gospel of Mark (Mark 1:1-13), the infancy of Jesus in the Gospel of Matthew (Matt 1-2), the death and resurrection of Jesus in the Gospel of Luke (Luke 22-24), and the miracles, the bread of life discourse and consequent response to the word of Jesus in the Gospel of John (John 6:1-71). At the end of each section devoted to one of the Gospels I will provide a list of valuable single-volume commentaries on that Gospel. Many major commentaries upon the Gospels run into two or even three volumes. These fine commentaries are generally too technical, and at times too expensive, for the intended audience of the book that follows.

Both the more general chapters on the message and structure of each Gospel, and the chapters dedicated to a detailed reading of a text should be read with the Gospel texts open at your side. Most modern translations are adequate, but I personally prefer the RSV and the NRSV. The book will close with a chapter describing the important developments in the interpretation of the Gospels that led to the current approaches to the Gospel narratives and also into research into the figure of the historical Jesus. Every attempt is made to avoid technical language, and the book is written in the spirit of words that Paul wrote to the Thessalonian Christians almost two thousand years ago: "When you received the word of God that you heard from us, you accepted it not as the word of human beings but as it really is, the word of God" (1 Thess 2:13).

There are many fine introductions to the New Testament, ranging from the scholarly to the very simple, and the many possible shades of difficulty between these two extremes. To my mind, the best contemporary scholarly introduction to the New Testament is Udo Schnelle, *The History and Theology of the New Testament Writings* (trans. M. Eugene Boring; Minneapolis: Fortress, 1998). Well-informed and well written, but less scholarly, are two books that I would recommend. Bart D. Ehrman, *The New Testament. A Historical Introduction to the Early Christian Writings* (2d ed.; New York/Oxford: Oxford University Press, 2000) contains a lucid and beautifully presented setting of the books of the New Testament within their historical, literary and cultural setting. Ehrman's main concern is, however, the setting of the books. Robert A. Spivey and D. Moody Smith, *Anatomy of the New Testament. A Guide to Its Structure and Meaning* (5th ed.; Upper Saddle River, NJ: Prentice Hall, 1994) have inspired the work that follows, as an earlier edition inspired this book's first appearance. Spivey and Moody Smith approach each book of the New Testament with a long introductory chapter, providing general background to the book, the message and meaning of the book, and an indication of its overall literary structure. They then take a section from the document under consideration, and subject it to closer analysis, to show how the more general principles help the reader to understand the detail of a specific text. A sixth edition of this book is in preparation. I have always found the approach adopted by Robert Spivey and Dwight Moody Smith singularly helpful for my own reading and teaching of the New Testament. For this reason alone, this more modest introduction to the Four Gospels was originally written, and now appears in a second edition.

The years between 1986 and 2006 have been, for me, years of intense academic and teaching activity. After seven years as the Katharine Drexel Professor of Religious Studies and two years as the Dean of the School of Theology and Religious Studies at the Catholic University of America, Washington, DC, USA, I have returned to my home Salesian Province of Australia. As a sign of my gratitude to my Salesian confreres who have always supported me, and never failed to make me most welcome in their communities when I returned from overseas, I am dedicating this second edition of *The Living Voice of the Gospel* to the Salesians of the Australian Province I have known and with whom I have shared so much over the past 46 years. May we all learn to live in a way that more closely reflects the way of Jesus, as traced out for us in the Gospels.

Salesian Province Centre
Ascot Vale, Victoria, Australia

PART I

Reading a Gospel

CHAPTER ONE

Reading a Gospel Today

This chapter is concerned with the development, nature and function of a Gospel, and the uniqueness of each of the four Gospels as theologically motivated narratives. The Gospels are neither factually accurate records of what Jesus said and did, nor are they literary inventions. Originally the stories of Jesus were told and retold in many settings (oral tradition) and in the earliest liturgies (liturgical tradition). The inspired writers of the Gospels looked backward to the Jesus traditions they received and forward to the present and future needs of their own communities. Eventually, the Christian Churches adopted these texts as Sacred Scripture, as they continued to speak eloquently of what God had done and continues to do in and through Jesus Christ. Not only in the Incarnation, but also in the Gospels "the Word has become flesh and dwells among us" (John 1:14).

Chapter 1
summary

THE FIRST OBSTACLE A CONTEMPORARY READER of the Gospels must overcome is the inclination to read the Gospels as if they were history books. We are products of the Enlightenment, a period when reason was enthroned, and the only acceptable "truths" were those that could be proved to be *factually* true.[1] This generates two problems among our contemporaries. Many read the succession of events reported in the Gospels from the life of Jesus uncritically, accepting them as accurate reports of events and words of Jesus and other characters in the story. Everything is *factually true*. Others, however, see that such an interpretation is impossible. There are too many contradictions across the four Gospels, impossible juxtapositions of events, time sequences and shifts in geography. Such readers conclude that the reports are not *factual*, and run the danger of regarding the Gospels as irrelevant mythical inventions of the early Church, probably written to substantiate its own existence.

The Gospels are neither factually accurate records of what Jesus said and did, nor are they literary inventions. The authors of these inspired texts were fundamentally concerned to communicate what we would call "theological truths." To do this, they reached back into the historical origins of the Christian Church and its traditions. This must never be lost from view, as we must avoid a contemporary subjective reading of the texts, searching for "what this says to me today." There is a close link between the historical origins of the Christian Church in the life and teaching of Jesus, and in the founding experiences of his death and resurrection. Subjective readings are based on the relevance of a book or a passage for an interpreter and his or her particular life-situation and religious point of view. The events reported in the Gospels, and many of the words spoken by Jesus reach back to the events and words of his own lifetime. We will consider this aspect of the Gospels in the final chapter of this book (Chapter Ten: *Modern and Contemporary Gospel Study*).[2] But the Evangelists never imagined that their accounts of the life and teaching, death and resurrection of Jesus would ever have been read as a "history book" in the way we understand "history" at the beginning of the third Christian millennium. The most important single contribution that modern Gospel interpretation has contributed to the history of the interpretation of the Bible is an emphasis on theological, rather than historical questions. Closely associated with this *theological* approach to the Gospels is the very recent turn among scholars to a greater appreciation of the fact that each of the Gospels is a deliberately contrived *narrative*. What is meant by these claims calls for further explanation, and indeed the readings of the Four Gospels that follows this introductory chapter presupposes that Mark, Matthew, Luke and John are *theologically motivated narratives*. Some introductory reflections, using the Gospels themselves, on what this means in practice are called for.

The Gospels and a "Life of Jesus"

An attentive reading of the four Gospels, especially when they are read side by side, makes it clear that it is impossible to trace a simple historical account of the life of Jesus, to summarize what he said, to trace his day-to-day movements across a week, a month, or a year.[3] We speak of "the Gospel," as if there were one Gospel, a unified story of the life of Jesus, but this is not the case. Even though the four Gospels have a great deal of material that is similar, and even identical, there are many passages that may appear the same, but when read carefully betray confusing differences. Mark, Matthew and Luke have much in common. They are generally called "Synoptic Gospels." The word "synoptic" comes from the Greek word for the eye, and the expression *sun-opsis* literally means "with the eye." The term came from the practice of placing the texts of Mark, Matthew and Luke side by side on a page, in parallel columns. Such a presentation of the texts shows the close similarities and the sometimes surprising differences. These similarities and differences are a good first indication that three Evangelists use the same tradition, but sometimes in slightly different ways.[4] John can hardly ever be fitted into the Synoptic scheme, but even here there are surprises. The Johannine account of the multiplication of the loaves and fishes is followed by a sea journey, and culminates in a confession of faith from Simon Peter (6:1-71). This report largely repeats the events and the sequence of events that one finds in Mark (8:1-33), Matthew (15:32-16:23) and Luke (9:10-22). One must not simply discount anything in any of the Gospels as not having roots in the historical events upon which the Christian Church was founded. Nor can we, however, ignore that each Evangelist is shaping the tradition in a slightly different way as he writes his story of Jesus.

Matthew 5:1-7:28 contains what is popularly called the Sermon on the Mount. Matthew sets the scene for the discourse by telling his readers: "Seeing the crowds, he *went up the mountain*, and when he sat down *his disciples* came to him. And he opened his mouth and taught *them*, saying ..." (Matt 5:1-2).[5] Jesus then begins his sermon with the beatitudes (vv. 3-11). The sermon then proceeds uninterrupted until 7:28. No-one interrupts Jesus, as he moves from one issue to another. Marking the end of the sermon, Matthew again remarks, "And when Jesus finished these sayings, *the crowds* were astonished at his teaching" (7:28). He appeared to leave the crowds in 5:1, so that he could sit with his disciples at his feet in 5:2. But they are still present, amazed at his teaching, in 7:28. We have uncovered an initial narrative tension in this carefully composed story.

The Gospel of Matthew devotes three lengthy chapters to the Sermon on the Mount. It is a memorable collection of Jesus' teachings, with particular focus upon the way a person must live, and pray, to belong to the Kingdom that Jesus has come to establish. His disciples, and/or the crowd are told what is demanded of them, if they are to follow Christ: witness, patience, marriage, swearing oaths, retaliation, praying, almsgiving, fasting, money, judging, and many other teachings that have become central to a Christian life and practice based upon the Gospels. In sum, disciples are to be perfect, as their heavenly Father is perfect (see 5:48). This significant discourse, delivered solemnly on the top of a mountain (the original Greek says "*the* mountain"), must have marked a memorable day in the public ministry of Jesus. One would think that this event would have left an indelible mark on the tradition. But a search through the Gospel of Mark and the Gospel of John will provide no trace of such a day, or even of the message of that day. This lack of evidence from two of the other major witnesses to Jesus leaves us somewhat perplexed, if we are hoping to discover in Matthew 5-7 a "history" of a day in the life of Jesus, in the twenty-first century sense of that word.

At first glance, it looks as though there may be some consolation for the contemporary historian in Luke 6:12-49. In verse 12, Jesus goes up onto a mountain to pray. He prays through the whole night, and then chooses his twelve apostles (vv. 13-16). Two important elements that are unique to the Gospel of Luke have already appeared in vv. 12-16. Before major events in the life of Jesus, he devotes himself to long hours of prayer, and only in Luke are twelve of the disciples called "apostles."[6] Having established a group of twelve followers who will be his apostles, he sets out with them. The Lukan text continues:

And he *came down with them* and stood on a *level place*, with a great crowd of his disciples and a *great multitude of people* from all Judea and Jerusalem and the seacoast of Tyre and Sidon. They came to hear him and be healed of their diseases. And those who were troubled with unclean spirits were cured. And all the crowd sought to touch him, for power came forth from him and he healed them all (vv. 17-19).

The scene for the sermon that follows is set. Jesus, with his Twelve Apostles, after *descending* from the mountain is sought out by a multitude of disciples and both Jews (Judea and Jerusalem) and Gentiles (Tyre and Sidon). The text resumes: "And he lifted up his eyes on his disciples and said…" (v. 20a). The Lukan version of the beatitudes follows in vv. 20b-26. Luke has arranged the tradition in a carefully balanced statement of three beatitudes, matched by three woes. The beatitudes are followed, as in Matthew, with a discourse on the quality of life demanded by those who wish to enter the Kingdom, during which Jesus is never interrupted. However, the discourse is much shorter, occupying only 33 verses in the Gospel of Luke (6:17-49). Nevertheless, everything found in the Lukan sermon *on the plain* is also found in the Matthean sermon *on the mount*. What is also intriguing is that while Luke does not gather everything from Matthew 5:1-7:28 into his 6:20-49, many of the passages found in the Matthean Sermon on the Mount are found elsewhere in Luke. Matthew and Luke had access to the same traditions, but the former gathered them all into one long sermon while the latter used some of the same traditions in a shorter sermon. He sensed that he could better enhance the message of his story of Jesus by using some of those traditions elsewhere.

But the twenty-first century historian must face a number of problems. Was the original sermon on a mountain, or on a level place? Was it delivered to the disciples, or to an unspecified crowd, or to a multitude of disciples, Jews and Gentiles? What motivated the presence of the crowd: wonder (Matthew) or were they seeking to hear his word and be cured (Luke)? Did he say all that we find in the three chapters of Matthew, or only what we find in the thirty-three verses in Luke? Why is there no trace of this important discourse in the Gospels of Mark and John? If readers look to the Gospels determined to find in them the raw data for a "life of Jesus," as historians of the third millennium understand the life-story of any great person, the texts themselves present insurmountable difficulties. But this is not our only interpretative option.

The Gospel as Good News

We are fortunate to find in the very first line of the first Gospel to be written, the Gospel of Mark, a bold-faced statement of the intentions of the Evangelist as a story-teller. The Gospel of Mark begins with the following statement from the narrator of the story: "The beginning of the Good News of Jesus Christ, the Son of God" (Mark 1:1). The reader is not told that the book that this verse prefaces is a life story, but Good News. The Greek word I have translated "Good News" is *evangelion.* It is made up of two parts, the prefix "*eu*" which always is associated with "good" and the main word "*angelion*" which has as one of its meanings "news."[7] This Greek word has never been associated with a biography. It has a long history in the Greek language, and is associated with the joyful proclamation of glad tidings: victory in battle, the arrival of the king, the birth of a son to the king, and similar great and joyful events for the people to whom the news is announced.[8] The original Evangelists had no intention of writing an objective, modern "life of Jesus." They had something quite different to do. Mark opens his story with the explosive "good news" that the man known as "Jesus" is the Christ and the Son of God. The story that follows will be his attempt to persuade his readers that this is the case, despite the fact that Jesus of Nazareth was cruelly executed.[9] Mark begins a bold new literary form: he tells a story of the life, teaching, death and resurrection of Jesus of Nazareth, in order to persuade his readers that Jesus of Nazareth was the Christ, the Son of God. Matthew, Luke and John join Mark in this project. All four Gospels were written to proclaim, by means of a narrative reporting the life, teaching, death and resurrection of Jesus, that he is the Christ, the Son of God. All four Evangelists will further attempt to persuade by means of their stories that salvation is now possible for all humankind because of his death, resurrection, and the subsequent community of faith, built upon that death and resurrection. This is not "history" nor is it "myth" in the generally intended negative sense of that expression.[10]

No doubt each of the Evangelists and the members of early Christian communities for whom they wrote, were conditioned by many factors. The way each Gospel story is told reflects the major religious and social problems each community needed to face. The Evangelists were also pastors, addressing the needs of believers in the early decades of the life of the Christian Church. But one must also recall another important fact, too often neglected by modern scholars. In compiling their various versions of the "good news" about Jesus who was the Christ the Son of God, the Evangelists looked back to the earlier Christian traditions that had their origins in the life, teaching, death and resurrection of Jesus. Some of Jesus' words had been faithfully remembered, and were passed on from generation to generation by word of mouth. This is generally called *oral tradition*. We must not underestimate the importance of the memories of Jesus kept alive in the oral tradition of the early generations. They belonged to a non-literary culture. Very few read and wrote, and those who did found it hard to purchase the papyri and parchment necessary for the practice of written communication. The New Testament contains several hymns (for example, the prologue to the Gospel of John [John 1:1-18] and the hymn that Paul cites for the Philippians [Phil 2:5-11]). These passages are an indication that traditional material was also gathered at liturgical celebrations. These traditions could be called *liturgical traditions*. Finally, there were probably written documents that pre-dated the written Gospels, but which we no longer have. Once these traditions were incorporated into the Gospels, they fell into disuse, and were eventually lost. We probably have traces of one of them in a theoretically reconstructed pre-Gospel document we call "Q" (from the German word *Quelle*, which means "source"). But we will see more of that in the next section. Each Evangelist used prior traditions in his own way, but the memory of the life and teaching, death and resurrection of Jesus was very much alive in the earliest Churches, for whom the Evangelists wrote. The Gospels *do* tell us about the life, the person and the activity of Jesus of Nazareth, but they were never written to be *the* life of Jesus.

The Relationship between the Four Gospels

Nineteenth-century post-Enlightenment criticism wanted to know "what had actually happened" so that the "real Jesus" could be identified. The best way to discover that information was to trace the "source" of the three so-called Synoptic Gospels. Thus, early Gospel criticism developed what came to be known as "source criticism." It did not take long to decide that Mark, the shortest and least used of the Gospels, was the major source for Matthew and Luke. Ongoing work on the three Synoptic Gospels continues to lead most contemporary scholars to agree with the majority position from the nineteenth-century: Mark was the first of all the Gospels. Not all agreed then, and there are still several vocal scholars who regard the theory of Markan priority a scholarly imposition that does not resolve all the problems. It is certainly true that Markan priority does not resolve *all the problems*. Thus theories concerning the relationships among the three Synoptic Gospels have become more complex, with greater attention given not only to the antiquity of the Markan material, but also to the material that is only found in Matthew (sometimes called "M"), the material found only in Luke (sometimes called "L"), and a large amount of material common to Matthew and Luke that does not appear in Mark, generally called "Q" (after the German word for "source" [*Quelle*]). Most problematic are the so-called "minor agreements": those passages where Matthew and Luke should be depending upon Mark (in the classical theory of Markan priority), but which agree almost word for word with one another, over against the Markan rendition of the same episode, or words of Jesus.

The majority of contemporary scholars adopt what is called "the two source theory." They accept that Mark was the first to write a Gospel, one of the sources used by Matthew and Luke. But Matthew and Luke used a second source: "Q." However, the classical expression "two source" is too limited. As I have already indicated, Matthew had sources of his own that provided him material found only in his Gospel (called M), and Luke also had such material (called L). Thus, we are already talking about "four sources."[11] A number of contemporary scholars question what is, after all, a "theory" that still leaves a number of questions unresolved. The probable solution to these difficulties, especially the "minor agreements," is the dynamic and ongoing nature of the oral tradition. Writing in the second half of the second-century, Papias (as cited by Eusebius) can still rate oral traditions about Jesus more important than written books (see Eusebius, *Ecclesiastical History*, 3.39.3-15). These oral traditions must have played an important part in the development of the Synoptic tradition, independent of the strictly literary dependence of Matthew and Luke upon Mark and Q, and they necessarily generate a fluidity that scholarly accuracy finds difficult to catalogue. We are, therefore, talking about "five sources," and they were all interacting in a time of exciting telling and re-telling the story of Jesus. All these sources reached back into a time in the literary history of the early Christian communities where *oral tradition* dominated the story-telling practice. It is here that the earliest Jesus-traditions were formed, and it is also from here that all four Gospels, Matthew, Mark, Luke *and* John, receive the bulk of the traditions they have shaped to produce their story of Jesus.

Most discussions of the sources for the Gospels provide readers with a simple diagram, showing how Mark and Q dominate the tradition. The following diagram follows that general pattern, but attempts to show that there was more involved than "two sources."

Throughout this scheme, however, one must imagine (as it cannot be rendered schematically) the ongoing oral preaching and story telling. The Evangelists did not cut and paste material from their sources. They received them in a living tradition, and many of the technical details that often disturb scholars (e.g. the minor agreements) should be explained by the dynamic ongoing presence of the oral tradition as the preaching and story telling practices of the Church developed, and began to take

Figure 1: Sources influencing the Gospels

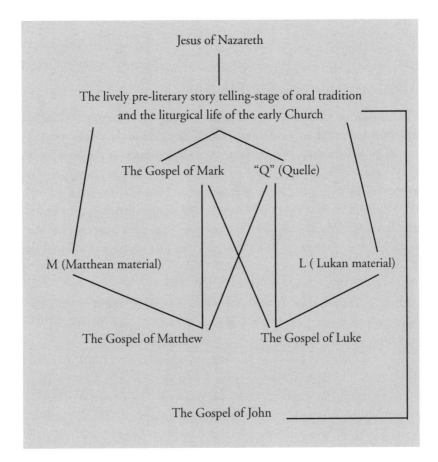

a written shape.   In the end, factors in the transmission of the Jesus-material found in the Four Gospels, lie outside scientific control. They were the result of the imaginative preaching and story telling that has been lost to us. We thus have Gospels that reach back to stories of Jesus (one source), that first appeared in a written form in Q (whose date we cannot determine) and Mark, that appeared about 70 AD (two further sources). Matthew and Luke used Mark and Q, and also reached back into the oral traditions for material of their own (M and L, two further sources). These Gospels probably first appeared in the middle of the 80's of the first century. The Gospel of John also reached back into the earliest oral traditions, but emerged as a unique story of Jesus, told in the largely Greco-Roman world, but faithful to the traditions about Jesus, in the 90's of the first century. One could claim that in the Gospel of John we see the manifestation of yet another source. The similarities yet differences that one senses between the Synoptic Gospels and the Gospel of John comes from their common dependence on the same original traditions, and the creative genius of John's presentation of those traditions.

The Mountain or the Plain?

Once we are prepared to accept that the Gospels are primarily theological documents, written to proclaim the Good News about what God has done for us in and through Jesus Christ, then the problem of the Sermon on the Mount or the Sermon on the Plain is eased. Contemporary scholars agree that, among other issues, the Gospel of Matthew is concerned with the relationship that exists between the emerging Christian community and Israel as a People of God. Matthew has shaped his story to show that Jesus had not severed the link between Israel as a people of God and the Matthean community as a people of God. There could be no denying that the Christian community, of which Matthew was a member, was "different" from the Synagogue, to which they all belonged in their pre-Christian days. Yet, Matthew wishes to insist, the new people of God had inherited the ancient promises made to Israel.[12]

In order to make this clear, the Matthean Jesus is sometimes presented as the new and perfect Moses. This is already apparent in the infancy stories where, as at the birth of Moses in Egypt, the slaying of innocent male children accompanies the birth of Jesus (Exod 1:15-22; 2:1-10; Matt 2:13-15). Still in the infancy story, a passage from Hosea, originally referring to the Exodus, is applied to Jesus: "Out of Egypt I have called my son" (Matt 2:15, citing Hosea 11:1). However, Moses' greatest act in the creation of Israel as God's people was his reception of the Covenant on Mount Sinai and his troubled transmission of the law to a recalcitrant people (Exod 19:10-20:21). With this background in mind, we are able to read Matthew 5:1-7:28, with its solemn setting of Jesus' going up to the top of *the* mountain, and his careful instruction of his disciples (see 5:1-2) as a new and perfect Moses giving a new and perfect law to a new people of God. This is particularly clear across 5:17-48. Jesus tells his audience that he has come to bring the law to perfection (v. 17). He then proceeds to quote from the law, as it was given on Mount Sinai, beginning each citation with such words as, "You have heard that it was said to the men of old." Various laws are cited (see vv. 22, 27, 31, 33, 38, 43). These laws had been handed down by Moses, and taught by the Rabbis (see Exod 20: 13, 14; Deut 24:1; 23:22; Exod 21:24-25; Lev 19:18). But Jesus reinterprets these sacred and time-honored laws. What is more, the authority for this bold reinterpretation is his own word: "But I say to you!" He generally does not negate the law of old, but he internalizes it. It is not enough to refrain from active sexual sinfulness; one must not even create a lustful relationship between a man and a woman (Matt 5:27-28). It is often said that the Matthean Jesus calls his followers to a "higher righteousness."

One must be careful in interpreting Jesus as a new and perfect Moses. For Matthew, he is not just "another Moses" or a "second Moses." The law given by Jesus is not *received* on the mountain, as Moses received the law. Jesus gives the new law, perfecting the old law, by virtue of his own word and person. Jesus is the *perfection* of the old law. For this reason, Jesus can ask his followers to be perfect as their heavenly Father is perfect (5:48). Once this *theological* and literary link with Moses is in place, the use of "the mountain" for the setting of the famous sermon is something more than a geographical place that we may be able to identify by the Lake of Galilee. It is a symbol of a new Sinai. Upon this new Sinai Jesus, a new and perfect lawgiver bringing to completion the original gift of the law made by God through Moses, promulgates a new law for a new people of God. The ascent to the top of the mountain is not an indication of some historical moment in the life of Jesus. To read the passage in this way would be to miss a most important theological element in Matthew's attempt to tell a story that shows that the Christian community had not broken with the authentic traditions of God's People. Indeed, Jesus' teaching summons them to the perfect living of those traditions (see 5:48). God's covenant with Israel has not been lost, but perfected.

Turning to a closer analysis of the Lukan setting of the sermon, we acknowledge that Luke's situation and the problems it generated were different. New Testament scholars agree that Luke was most likely a Gentile, writing for a Gentile audience, a long way from the land, religion and culture that had produced Jesus and the Jesus-movement. Indeed, as the years passed, Luke and his communities find themselves a long way from the foundational events of the life, teaching, death and resurrection of Jesus. They were suffering from their own "tyranny of distance." As Luke and his communities lived and preached Christianity within the context of this distance of time, space, religion and culture, a Gospel emerged that addressed those issues. One of the many important messages that Luke had to generate through his story of Jesus was to insist that – however distant – this community belonged to those origins. However, the members of the community faced another problem. Having reached this far into the Gentile world, was it not time to stop? They had done enough, and in the midst of some suffering and confusion, the Lukan Christians ran the danger of sinking into a solid mediocrity, staying where they were. The preaching of the message would stop, and the community might run the risk of stagnation and death.

The clearest indication (among many) that Luke was writing into such a situation is found in the fact that he is the only story-teller in the New Testament to write two volumes. He wrote the Gospel that had its beginnings in the Old Testament (Zechariah, Elizabeth, Anna, Simeon and John the Baptist in the infancy stories). During his ministry, Jesus states this agenda: "The law and the prophets were until John; since then the good news of the kingdom is preached" (Luke 16:16). The rest of the Gospel tells the story of Jesus' ministry, journey to Jerusalem, his death, resurrection and ascension. Only in Luke's Gospel all the events of Jesus' suffering, death, resurrection and ascension take place in the city of Jerusalem. The second volume, the Acts of the Apostles, begins where the first concluded, in Jerusalem with the risen Jesus. He tells them that they must wait in the city, and not depart until they are empowered from on high (Acts 1:4). At the end of the Gospel he had already instructed his disciples: "Repentance and forgiveness of sins should be preached in his name to all nations. You are witnesses of these things" (Luke 24:47-48).

Jesus' final words to his disciples constitute a renewal of that commission: "You shall receive power when the Holy Spirit has come upon you. You shall be my witnesses in Jerusalem and in all Judea and Samaria, and to the ends of the earth" (Acts 1:8). The earlier chapters of Acts are set in Jerusalem. In a new Pentecost the Spirit is given to the community (2:1-13), and its numbers increase as they gather in peace and increasing strength and union. However, and especially through the journeys of Paul (which match the journey of Jesus in the Gospel), the message is preached in Jerusalem, all Judea, Samaria, and to the ends of the earth. The book closes with Paul in the city of Rome fearlessly preaching the kingdom of God and the Lord Jesus Christ (20:31).

For Luke this was the beginning of a journey that would come to a close only at the end of time. His two volumes voice a message to Christian communities, telling their members that the journey of the Church through history, whatever this might cost them, is never over. There can be no settling for what they have already attained. The genius of Luke is found in the fact that, as time passed, and distances opened up, he was able to remind the Churches, through his two volumes, that they had their beginnings in Jesus but they had to commit themselves to the task, and the discipline, of a mission that still lay in the future. Jesus was not about to return in glory in the near future to win over all opposition and to reward the faithful, as one suspects Mark seemed to think (see Mark 9:1; 13:1-37). The Jesus of Luke's Gospel takes on a special character. In his exhortation of his community to continue their mission into an unpredictable future, he tells of Jesus who initiated such a mission. At the beginning of the Gospel, after appointing the founding Apostles, those who would be sent out to continue Jesus' mission (6:12-16), he descends to a level place where the multitudes gather (vv. 17-19). For Luke, Jesus' sermon, although primarily addressed to the disciples (see v. 20), is spoken in the presence of people from Israel (Jerusalem and all Judea) and from the Gentile world (the seacoast of Tyre and Sidon) who are longing to hear his word, and to experience his healing touch (vv. 17-19). The mission of the Lukan Churches was to continue what Jesus had done, to be witnesses of repentance and forgiveness (Luke 24:47), empowered by the Spirit (Acts 1:4) to bring Jesus' word to the ends of the earth (Acts 1:8). Jesus' sermon to his disciples (Luke 6:20-49), in the presence of the multitudes who waited to hear his word, is an instruction for all who have been called to that task. The plain is not some geographical "level place" in Palestine where a multitude of Jews and Gentiles once gathered to listen to Jesus. It is an important *theological* indication that Jesus descends from his hours of prayer, accompanied by his future Apostles, to set the agenda for the future missionary activity of the Christian Churches, reaching out till the end of time and to the ends of the earth.

If we claim that the Gospels are primarily historical documents, in the contemporary sense of that expression, then either Matthew or Luke had their "facts" wrong. These brief reflections, on the mountain and the plain as the setting for Jesus' sermon in Matthew and Luke respectively, show that such is not the case. The Gospels are not *historical documents* in that sense. Both Matthew and Luke make use of the same material (which would have come to them from Q) to make two equally "true" presentations of what God has done for humankind in and through Jesus Christ. For Matthew and subsequent Christian belief, Jesus is the new and perfect Moses, providing in his word and person a new law for a new people of God. For Luke and subsequent Christian belief, Jesus is the founder of a universal mission that must be continued by all who claim to be his disciples.[13] They are to bring his word and his healing touch to all who seek him. The "truth" of these narratives does not come from our ability to find the exact hill or plain where these events took place, or to be able to reconstruct precisely what Jesus said, and to whom. Nor should we try to harmonize the Matthean and the Lukan account as in both Matthew and Luke we have an inspired use of earlier traditions that proclaim what God has done for us in and through Jesus. These are *theological truths*, and each Evangelist told the story of Jesus in order to communicate such truths to the Church.

The Gospels and Literary Forms

The expression "literary form" has already appeared in these pages. The study of literary forms has played an important role in Gospel criticism. Before the first Gospel appeared (the Gospel of Mark, about AD 70), Paul had already been executed (about AD 64), and left to the Christian Church the remarkable theological synthesis that one can trace in his Letters. For Paul, the life, death and resurrection of Jesus unleashed a radically new understanding of God's ways with the world. Paul saw humankind now offered the possibility of living a new creation, drawing back into history the promised restoration of a fallen world. Within a classical Jewish understanding of history, this was to take place at the end of time, when God's original order would return. For Paul, Jesus' obedient response to God, culminating in his death and resurrection, draws the "new creation" (see 2 Cor 5:17; Gal 6:15) into history. The destruction wrought by the sin of Adam continues in history, but something greater than Adam has reversed that situation. Humankind now has a choice, as both sin and grace play out their roles in history. Humankind is called to recognize that "where sin increased, grace abounded all the more" (Rom 5:20. See 5:12-21).[14] This vision, already in place only thirty years after the death of Jesus, was expressed by means of what we have come to call "letters." While some of Paul's writings may be called letters, most of them were rhetorical tracts that sought to persuade.[15] For our purposes, all we need to notice is that they are not "narratives." There are a few places, however, where Paul uses a narrative form. For example, he reports that Jesus was "born of a woman" (Gal 4:4). He also reports the meal that Jesus celebrated with his disciples the night before he died (1 Cor 11:23-26) and he provides a brief narrative summary of Jesus' death and resurrection (1 Cor 3-8). Thus, although Paul certainly had a "gospel," the Good News of what God did for us in and through Jesus Christ (he uses the expression *evangelion* over fifty times in his letters), he did not use the literary form that we have come to call a "Gospel."

I am stressing this as the literary form that we call a "Gospel" appeared on the scene later than Paul. It was the author behind the Gospel of Mark who created a new literary form, that we call a "Gospel." We do not use the expression "literary form" in our every-day language, but we take literary forms for granted. Some examples may help to make this point clear. Each morning we take a daily paper, and glance at the major headline on the first page. Most headlines are not an English sentence, but they simply express clearly in a few words the main news item of the day. Spectacularly, it may even be only one word, for example: WAR! That one word is a "form" of literature. It is a written word that effects a communication with a reader. That reader may turn from the front page to the editorial to find what the editor of the newspaper in question thinks about the outbreak of warfare, its causes, its consequences, and so on. Elsewhere in the newspaper one could find pages dedicated to the response of the national economy, the impact of the recent events upon the stock market, and other such crucial matters, understandable only to those who know how to read that particular "literary form." Any newspaper contains many different "literary forms," from news items to the comic strips to the sports page. Only an Australian living in Victoria toward the end of winter has sufficient expertise to understand what is meant by a headline on the sports page: "Sheedy shuts gate on flag."[16]

These few examples, taken from the familiar world of the daily press, indicate that different forms of literary communication are taken for granted. We subconsciously accept and respond to the impact of each literary form. This needs to be appreciated in the reading of the New Testament. There are several "forms" of literature there. It is impossible to list them all here. For our purposes, it is sufficient to indicate that there is a "gospel form" (Matthew, Mark, Luke and John), an "epistle form" (the letters of Paul) and an "apocalyptic form" (Revelation). Of course, each document may contain many different forms. For example, it could be argued that Mark 13 is also an apocalypse, and that Revelation 2:1-3:22 is a collection of epistles to various Churches in Asia. To the best of our knowledge the earliest form of literature produced in the early Christian Church was the epistle. We have many of them in the letters of Paul which were written across the years from 50-64 AD.[17] But if we only had Paul's writings, then we would know very little about the story of Jesus: he was born of a woman, he celebrated a new ritual the night before he died, and he was slain, buried and was raised and seen (Gal 4:4; 1 Cor 11:23-26; 1 Cor 15:3-8).

What is interesting, however, about these rare reports of "facts" from the life of Jesus is that before two of them he tells the Corinthians he is passing on to them something he has received:

> For I *received* from the Lord what I also *delivered* to you (1 Cor11:23).

> For I *delivered* to you as of first importance what I also *received* (1 Cor15:3).

Even in our earliest written documents we see that the reporting, in a narrative form, of major moments in the life story of Jesus came from something that was "handed down."

The Latin word for something that is handed down is *traditio*, and this provides an expression in English that is of major importance for a serious reading of the Gospels: *tradition*. As is obvious from 1 Corinthians 11 and 15 (and elsewhere) "traditions" about Jesus were already important to Paul.[18] As we have already seen in discussing the relationship between the four Gospels, traditions lie behind all the Gospels. All four Evangelists built the story of Jesus upon the traditions they received. A brief analysis of a section at the center of the Gospel of Mark will serve as an indication of the importance of this fact.

Mark 8: A Story Formed from Stories

The Matthean and the Lukan renditions of the same sermon, one situated on the mountain and another situated on a plain, served well as an example showing the primacy of theology, over against history and geography, as a major interpretative principle. However, as we noted in passing, Matthew and Luke used the same traditions, even though they used them differently. They reached back into a collection of sayings of Jesus. We now know that this collection of sayings is commonly called Q (from the German word *Quelle*: source). Matthew placed many of them side by side in the Sermon on the Mount, while Luke used some of them in his Sermon on the Plain, and used others elsewhere in his story of Jesus. A study of Mark 8 shows that "traditions" can also be found in the earliest of the Gospels. Various traditional elements from the life of Jesus and from the memory of the earliest Church are placed side by side to present what is, in the end, a very impressive and unified theological message to all who wonder who Jesus might be, and what it means to follow him.

I have chosen Mark 8:1-9:8 because of its central place in the Gospel of Mark, and because it is an excellent example of the way the Evangelist worked, by gathering together into a coherent narrative sequence what were originally independent traditions.[19] The following series of events is narrated:

- The miracle of the loaves and fishes (8:1-9)

- A dispute with the Pharisees who, after the miracle, ask for a sign (vv. 10-13)

- A journey in a boat during which Jesus discusses the presence of bread with his disciples. Despite the two miracles (see also 6:31-44), they do not understand because their hearts are hardened. He asks if they are deaf and blind (vv. 14-21)

- The gradual curing of a blind man at Bethsaida (vv. 22-26)

- ◻ The question of Jesus' identity, and Peter's confession at Caesarea Philippi (vv. 27-30)

- ◻ The first prediction of the oncoming passion, and Peter's inability to accept a suffering Son of Man (vv. 31-33)

- ◻ Jesus teaches the disciples and the crowd on the necessity to take up one's cross and follow Jesus, if one wishes to be his disciple (8:34-9:1)

- ◻ The transfiguration (9:2-8).[20]

Across this hectic series of events, the only indication of time is that the transfiguration took place "after six days" (9:2). If all the events placed side by side in the reporting of events from 8:1-9:1 took place without any time interval, that must have been an exhausting day! But we have already seen that such a "historical" reading of this sequence of events would be a misreading. We must trace what the author is attempting to communicate to a reader by means of this gathering of what were originally independent traditions: a miracle story, a conflict story, a teaching story, a miracle story, a confession of faith, a passion prediction, a theophanic story.[21] What is the message that Mark wishes to communicate?

After a careful and detailed setting of the scene (8:1), we find a feeding of "about four thousand" people (v. 8) with loaves and fishes, on the Gentile side of the lake. This is the second time Mark has reported a story of such a miraculous feeding. In 6:31-44 he told of a feeding of a Jewish crowd, on the Jewish side of the lake.[22] Bread is at the center of the story, and much of the language sounds Eucharistic (see v. 6). The story tells of Jesus' feeding Gentiles, as he had earlier nourished Jews. Twice in 6:31-44 and once in 8:1-10 Jesus associates the disciples with this ministry (see 6:37: "You give them something to eat"; v. 41: "gave them to the disciples to set before the people"; 8:6: "gave them to his disciples to set before the people"). Despite the greatness of this miracle, it is immediately followed by a dispute between Jesus and the Pharisees over the need for a sign, and Jesus refuses to give one (v. 12).[23] In v. 14 Jesus and his disciples set out in a boat. In the discussion that takes place during their voyage together the disciples show that, despite a warning from Jesus (v. 15), they are like the Pharisees, unable to understand who Jesus is. He recalls the two bread miracles, when they express concern over their lack of bread (see vv. 16-17). Jesus explains their inability to understand in terms of their deafness and blindness (v. 18).

On Jesus' arrival at Bethsaida, a blind man is led to him. He leads the blind man out of the village, makes spittle and puts it on his eyes, and asks him if he can see. The man receives sight, but it is an imperfect sight: men look like walking trees (8:24). He has only partially recovered his vision. In a second moment, Jesus lays his hands upon the man, and total sight is restored. He sees clearly (v. 25). The blind man has gone through a journey from blindness (v. 22) to partial sight (v. 24) to a fullness of sight (v. 25). The Evangelists Matthew and Luke, who follow Mark closely at this stage of their accounts, have omitted this strange miracle, where Jesus appears to have to make two attempts to perform the miracle. However, as the story unfolds, we will find that this journey from blindness to sight is not a sign of Jesus' limitations, but a narrative preparation for the crucial scene that follows, and on the faith experience of the disciples across the rest of the Gospel. The man who comes progressively to perfect vision is a comment upon the disciples' journey of faith.

In the events reported thus far, the miracle of the loaves and fishes, the encounter with the Pharisees and the discussion with the disciples in the boat, no character in the narrative has understood who Jesus is and what he is doing. They too, like the blind man in the miracle story, are completely without sight, but the miracle story shows that a progressive recovery of sight is possible. This journey of sight, from no faith to the fullness of faith is made very clear in the episode that follows, the confession of Peter at Caesarea Philippi (vv. 27-29). The disciples journey with Jesus to Caesarea Philippi, and on the way, Jesus asks them: "Who do men say that I am?" (v. 27). They respond that most people think he is one of the expected messianic precursor figures: John the Baptist, Elijah or one of the prophets (v. 28).[24] He turns to his followers and asks: "But who do you say that I am?" and Peter confesses: "You are the Christ" (v. 29). This passage has rightly been regarded as a central moment in the Gospel of Mark. For the first time in the story, someone confesses that Jesus is the Christ (see 1:1).

But the confession is followed by a command from Jesus, insisting that they say nothing about this to anyone (8:30). This is so because they have not genuinely understood the confession of faith they have just made and heard. Jesus is the Christ, but he immediately begins to teach them that the Son of Man must go to Jerusalem, suffer, and be rejected and slain by the elders, the chief priests and the scribes (v.

31). Only now, in Jesus' further spelling out of what it means for him to be the Messiah, have we come to a fullness of sight. Jesus' own words reveal the true identity of Jesus. The disciples have moved from their blindness in the boat (8:18, 21) to the partial vision confessed by Peter (v. 29). Jesus has now revealed the full truth to them. The difficulty with Peter's confession, no doubt expressing the messianic hopes of the disciples, lies in the fact that they hope Jesus will be a messianic figure *as they understand the Messiah.* They seem to expect the Christ to be a royal, political figure, and hope they are following a person who will place them in seats of authority when he comes to his glory in Jerusalem (see 9:33-37; 10:35-45). They cling to this view until, in the end, they flee from Jesus, and he goes to his cross alone (see especially 14:50-52). The disciples' false messianic hope is already made clear in Peter's response to Jesus' self-identification as a suffering, dying and rising Son of Man. He refuses to accept that Jesus should face such a destiny, but Jesus tells him to take his correct place where all disciples should be: behind him, following him down *his* way.

The discourse that follows (8:34-9:1) enlarges upon what has happened in Jesus' command to Peter to take up his correct place as a disciple: following Jesus. It is addressed to all his disciples, and to the crowd (v. 34). If they wish to be followers of Jesus, his disciples, they must take up their cross and follow him. They must be prepared to tread the same path as Jesus, and in this way eventually come to the glory of the resurrection, also with Jesus (see v. 38; 9:1). Notice how the flow of the story has moved gently away from the person of Jesus toward the disciples. Mark has assembled a series of originally independent traditions to instruct the reader on the person of Jesus and the nature of true discipleship. But one can join the original readers of this story, who have only just heard, for the first time, that Jesus is the Christ (v. 29), wondering what sort of Christ this can be. Is it possible that the Christ must suffer and die? What is more incredible is that he asks all who wish to be his disciples to follow him down this same path, if they wish to join him in his glory (8:34-9:1). Who is this man who has called them into this way of suffering and death?

The answer is found immediately in the Markan account of the transfiguration. The glorious transformation of Jesus provides the background. It presents Jesus, in the company of two figures who had ascended to heaven, as a heavenly figure. What really matters, however, is the voice from heaven that explains this heavenly appearance: "This is my beloved Son; listen to him" (9:7). What Mark has proclaimed through the narrative made up of the series of events found side by side in Mark 8 can only make sense in the light of what the reader is told in 9:2-8. It is absurd to ask followers to commit themselves to a life-style that is leading to death, in the light of a vague promise that such a loss of self will lead to the saving of one's life (8:35). But because of the authoritative words of God, the voice that comes from heaven, it makes sense. The readers must pay attention to the story they are hearing; they must listen: "This is my beloved Son; listen to him!" (v. 7). The origin of the traditional narrative that originally reported the transfiguration of Jesus is hard to identify. Some scholars have suggested that it has its roots in a deep spiritual experience that disciples had with Jesus during his ministry. Others suggest that it comes from post-resurrection traditions, while others suggest that it is entirely the creation of the early Church, as it began to articulate its belief that Jesus was the presence of the divine in the human story. For Mark, its exact chronological location in Jesus' own time, or its origins in the growing expressions of faith in the early Church, is unimportant. He uses the tradition in a way that enables him to instruct his readers that Jesus, the one who has called them to follow him into a life of self-gift, suffering and death (8:34-9:1), is the Son of God. This alone is sufficient for all readers to "listen to him" (9:7).[25]

Mark's use of prior traditions, setting them side by side in the way outlined above, may not offer us a day-to-day life-story of Jesus of Nazareth. Mark offers us a narrative that makes two basic theological affirmations. In the first place, he instructs the reader that Jesus is the Christ, the Son of Man and the Son of God. Secondly, he calls those who would be disciples of Jesus to take up their own cross and follow him. We are at the heart of the message of the Markan Gospel, written about 70 AD for a Christian community suffering its own experience of crucifixion and death. Mark's Gospel presents a suffering, yet victorious Jesus of Nazareth, Messiah, Son of Man and Son of God. The story attempts to call the struggling members of that community to take up their cross – a day to day physical possibility in a world dominated by Rome and its legal procedures. They must not be ashamed to follow a suffering Son of Man, because that same Son of Man will have the last word (8:37-38, 9:1. See 14:61-62). They must listen to the word of the Son of God (9:2-8).

Four Stories Read in the Church

The comparative reading of the Sermons on the Mount and on the Plain, along with the above reading of Mark 8:1-9:8 serve as an initial indication that the Evangelists never intended to write twenty-first century style biographies.   Mark created the literary form we call "Gospel," and Matthew, Luke and John adopted that literary form.   They use a narrative about the life, teaching, death and resurrection of Jesus to communicate to their readers their inspired understanding of what God has done for us in and through him.   Many of the traditions the Evangelists used to develop this literary form may have had their origins in the life of Jesus, but the Gospels cannot be understood as a simple collection of remembered episodes from the time of Jesus.   The Gospels are what that word means: the "good news" proclaimed in and for a community of faith: Jesus is the Christ, the Son of God, and through his life, teaching, death and resurrection God has offered us the possibility of salvation.

This chapter has insisted that a correct reading of any Gospel must focus upon the situation of the community for which it was written, and the literary and rhetorical techniques used by the author to communicate his theological message by means of a narrative.   However, this generates a problem for those of us who want to read the Gospels today.   Once I have done all my careful reading of this first-century text, what have I discovered?   We must avoid the danger of remaining with a text that addresses first century problems that can only be understood in terms of a first century Christian community.   The Christian Churches have proclaimed the Gospels as a living word of God for almost two millennia. They have never been allowed to become dusty pages from a long-forgotten and irrelevant past.

The liturgical use of the Scriptures is a privileged place for the reading of the Gospels.   This age-old practice reflects the Church's commitment to the efficacy of the word of the Gospels today.   Within the Catholic tradition, the Fathers of the Second Vatican Council addressed the question of the word of the Gospels in the life of a Christian:

> Among all the inspired writings, even among those of the New Testament, the Gospels have a special place, and rightly so, because they are the principal source of the life and teaching of the Incarnate Word, our Savior (*Dei Verbum* 18)

> The Church has always venerated the divine Scriptures as she venerated the Body of the Lord, in so far as she never ceases, particularly in the sacred liturgy, to partake of the bread of life and to offer it to the faithful from the one table of the word of God and the Body of Christ (*Dei Verbum* 21).

> Christians share the belief that the Scriptures are sacred: inspired by God and committed to writing once and for all time, they present God's own word in an unalterable form, and they make the voice of God sound again and again in the words of the prophets and apostles. *(Dei Verbum* 21*)*.

The conviction that a link existed between the Word of God, committed to writing in the distant past, and that same word, addressing men and women in the Christian Church through all its history and across the many cultural and geographical distances, is something the Church came to appreciate through experience. The early Church did not dream up the notion of a New Testament to be read beside an Old Testament. Nor was there an executive Christian decision that we needed a holy book as the Jewish people, among whom Christianity had its birth, had their holy book. Very early in the existence of Christian communities one senses a respect for certain Christian books. Paul's letters are already spoken of with respect in 2 Peter 3:14-18, and there is evidence of a tradition of the scribal transmission of certain books from the second century. But no one *imposed* a Christian New Testament.[26] The documents that eventually emerged as the New Testament emerged from the many early Christian documents that circulated in the early centuries because they continued to address the fundamental questions raised by the Christian tradition. They "spoke" to the faithful, and thus were read, and re-read until they became part of the Church's collection of inspired books. The Gospels, read and interpreted within the life of the Christian Church, offer an inspired and inspiring insight into what God has done for us in and through Jesus Christ. This is what has given them their privileged place in the life of the Church. They are "the principal source for the life and teaching of the Incarnate Word, our Savior" (*Dei Verbum* 18).

Conclusion

In the beginning was the person of Jesus of Nazareth. After the impact of the resurrection, a belief in the risen Christ was born, and an oral tradition communicated his story. The first Christian writings that we have came from the pen of Saint Paul. He did not "tell the story" of Jesus, but presupposed it, and built his theology upon the bedrock events of his death and resurrection and communicated it by means of his epistolary literary form. Nevertheless, the stories were told and retold in many settings (oral tradition) and in the earliest liturgies (liturgical tradition). Some of the sayings of Jesus were probably also written down, but we no longer possess any such document (Q, for example). The Jesus tradition grew, but in time the generation which had lived those early decades began to die away, and communities saw the need to preserve its heritage from their *past* as it addressed the pastoral and theological problems of their *present* and looked toward the *future*. Thus the theologically motivated narratives of the life of Jesus, the literary form of the Gospel, begun by Mark about 70 AD, emerged.

The few examples that we have seen in this chapter are a first indication that Mark, Matthew and Luke looked *backward* to the Jesus traditions they received and *forward* to the present and future needs of their own communities. The chapters that follow, dedicated to a closer reading of Mark, Matthew, Luke and John, will demonstrate this in more detail. Eventually, the Christian Churches adopted these texts as Sacred Scripture, as they continued to speak eloquently of what God had done and continues to do in and through Jesus Christ. The Gospels are living witness to the wisdom of God who chooses men and women to address other men and women in their human and thus limited way. Not only in the Incarnation, but also in the Gospels "the Word has become flesh and dwells among us" (John 1:14).

Notes

[1] For further reflection on this "setting" for our interpretation, see below, pp. 310-314.

[2] See below, Chapter 10.

[3] In fact, the span of time for Jesus' ministry and death in Mark, Matthew and Luke may be a little more than a year. There is mention of only one Passover (see Mark 14:1; Matt 26:2; Luke 22:1). In the Gospel of John, Jesus' ministry spans the celebration of three Passovers (John 2:23; 6:4; 11:55-56).

[4] The most used English language "synopsis" (using the text of the Revised Standard Version) is B. Throckmorton, *Gospel Parallels. A Synopsis of the First Three Gospels* (London/New York: Nelson, 1979).

[5] Throughout this book I will refer to Matthew, Mark, Luke and John as the authors of the Gospels that bear their names. We cannot be sure that people bearing those names actually wrote the original Gospels. No author signed off on any of the Gospels, and only the Gospel of John tells us that the Beloved Disciple "has written these things" (John 20:24). But the Gospel of John never identifies the Beloved Disciple with a person whose name was "John." The Gospels were ascribed to the Apostles Matthew and John, and two lesser figures from the Acts of the Apostles, Mark and Luke, in the second century. For the sake of clarity and simplicity, I will continue to refer to the Evangelists by their traditional names, without wishing to indicate that someone by that name did, or did not, write a Gospel.

[6] These issues will be discussed further in our treatment of the Gospel of Luke as a whole (Chapter Six). For the moment, it should be noted that all four Gospels know of a group of disciples called "the Twelve," but only Luke calls them "the Twelve Apostles." On the Twelve, the Apostles, and various named members of the Twelve, see J. P. Meier, *A Marginal Jew. Rethinking the Historical Jesus* (3 vols.; Anchor Bible Reference Library; New York: Doubleday, 1991-2001), 3:125-285.

[7] The English word "Gospel" comes from the Old English rendition of the Greek as "god-spel," i.e., good news.

[8] See W. Marxsen, *Mark the Evangelist. Studies on the Redaction History of the Gospel* (trans. J. Boyce, D. Juel and W. Poehlmann; Nashville: Abingdon, 1969), 117-50.

[9] This point will be more fully developed in Chapter Two, dedicated to the message and structure of the Gospel of Mark. For more detail on Mark 1:1, see also Chapter Three, a close reading of 1:1-13, the prologue to the Gospel of Mark.

[10] As modern scholars rightly point out, narratives that may be based on historical events, but which are not told primarily to report the details of the events from the past, but in order to persuade readers of the saving action of a divine power are rightly called "myth." This is a very positive meaning of a narrative "myth." A narrative that attempts to communicate what God has done for humankind, in any religious tradition, may draw on historical events from the life of its founder, but the heart of the message is about the action of God, and not about the human events. In this sense, the Gospels could fall under the general literary classification of "myth." One must be careful in the use of this expression, however, as for most people "myth" means "untrue." One of the most creative Christian scholars in the nineteenth century was disgraced by his use of "myth" in this sense: David Friedrich Strauss [D. F. Strauss, *The Life of Jesus Critically Examined* [translation of the 4th German edition; London: Allen & Unwin, 1906]). On this question, see J. Macquarrie, *Jesus Christ in Modern Thought* (London: SCM Press, 1990), 224-30. In fact, a narrative myth may be the best way to communicate what is otherwise incommunicable – God's saving action.

[11] More skeptical scholars often regard the material designated as M and L (material unique to the Gospel of Matthew and Luke) as creations within the Matthean or Lukan tradition, and thus not a "source." Such skepticism is uncalled for, as one can see from some of the parabolic material in Matthew and Luke. Much of this material may be traced back to Jesus.

[12] After the Jewish War (66-70 AD), the land of Israel, the Temple and its cult, and the Priesthood no longer existed. This was a difficult time for the Jewish people. Under the direction of the Pharisees, who had survived the war, a very pastoral, domestic and mobile form of Judaism emerged. It was focused upon the Synagogue, the reading and interpretation of Torah (the Law), and directed

by the Rabbis. It was also a difficult time for the Christians, who were gradually separated from the Synagogue as their belief in Jesus of Nazareth as the Christ of God became more obvious (to them and to others). This appears to have been an important pastoral problem in the Matthean community.

[13] Chapters 4-7, below, will be devoted to a more detailed analysis of the Matthean and the Lukan stories of Jesus. A very helpful survey of the theology and purpose of the Gospels of Matthew and Luke can be found in E. A. Laverdiere and W. G. Thompson, "New Testament Communities in Transition: A Study of Matthew and Luke," *Theological Studies* 37 (1976): 567-97.

[14] For a clear presentation of this central feature of Paul's thought and theology, see B. J. Byrne, *Reckoning with Romans. A Contemporary Reading of Paul's Gospel* (Good News Studies 18; Wilmington: Michael Glazier, 1986), 20-26. For an analysis of Romans 5:12-21, see Idem, *Romans* (Sacra Pagina 6; Collegeville: The Liturgical Press, 1996), 173-87.

[15] See Byrne, *Romans*, 13-26.

[16] This headline, from a Melbourne newspaper in 1985, commented on the fact that the coach of the Essendon football club, coached by Kevin Sheedy, had won the Grand Final match of the Australian Football League. A premiership "flag" is awarded to the winning club. Such "explanations" are not needed by the initiated.

[17] It is possible that Q emerged about the same time as the Pauline letters. If that is true, then a collection of the sayings of Jesus also circulated very early. However, we do not have any such document. We reconstruct Q from the material common to Matthew and Luke that most likely came from this collection of sayings. That the earliest Church would quickly collect sayings of Jesus should not surprise us.

[18] On this, see the well documented study of J. D. G. Dunn, *The Theology of Paul the Apostle* (Grand Rapids: Eerdmans, 1998), 182-206.

[19] For a more detailed study of Mark 8:1-9:8, see F. J. Moloney, *The Gospel of Mark. A Commentary* (Peabody: Hendrickson, 2002), 152-82. What follows is a simple example of "narrative criticism." For a discussion of different

contemporary approaches to the Gospels, see Chapter Ten.

[20] I have argued elsewhere that the transfiguration scene encompasses the whole of 9:1-13 (see Moloney, *Mark*, 177-82). For the purposes of this reflection, however, the scene on the mountain (9:1-8) is sufficient.

[21] Note that the various "stories" also have different "literary forms." This is often a good indication that they once existed independently of one another.

[22] On the details that point to a Jewish (6:31-44) and a Gentile (8:1-9) feeding, and the theological and pastoral purpose of the repetition, see F. J. Moloney, *Mark. Storyteller, Interpreter, Evangelist* (Peabody: Hendrickson, 2004), 167-81.

[23] The historically improbable presence of Pharisees on the Gentile side of the lake also points to the fact that this tradition of Jesus' angry encounter with Pharisees who asked for a sign was originally independent of the bread miracle. Mark links them, and thus transports them to the Gentile side of the lake. The point of view being communicated by means of the narrative sequence takes priority over geographical considerations.

[24] On John the Baptist, Elijah and one of the prophets as messianic precursors, see Moloney, *Mark*, 165-66.

[25] For a stimulating recent study of the Transfiguration, see D. E. Lee, *Transfiguration* (New Century Theology; London/New York: Continuum, 2004). On the discussion of the origin of the tradition, see pp. 1-8. On the Transfiguration in Mark, see pp. 9-37.

[26] Many people accept that this was the case because Dan Brown regularly affirms it in his best selling novel, *The da Vinci Code* (New York: Doubleday, 2003). He insists that the New Testament was imposed upon the early Church by the Emperor Constantine for political reasons. The development of a New Testament was already well under way, although not finally established, before Constantine even came on the scene. See D. L. Bock, *Breaking the Da Vinci Code* (Foreword by F. J. Moloney; Nashville: Nelson, 2004), 99-124. Unfortunately, *fiction* often determines public opinion. See also F. J. Moloney, "What Came First: Scripture or Canon? The Gospel of John as a Test Case," *Salesianum* 68 (2006), 7-20.

Select New Testament Introductions

Achtemeier, P. J., J. B. Green and M. M. Thompson. *Introducing the New Testament. Its Literature and Theology.* Grand Rapids: Eerdmans, 2001.

Barr, David, L. *New Testament Story. An Introduction.* Belmont: Wadsworth Publishing Company, 1995.

Brown, R. E. *An Introduction to the New Testament.* The Anchor Bible Reference Library. New York: Doubleday, 1997.

Collins, R. F., *Introduction to the New Testament.* Garden City: Doubleday, 1983.

Ehrman, D. B. *The New Testament. A Historical Introduction to the Early Christian Writings.* New York/Oxford: Oxford University Press, 2004.

Freed, E. C. *The New Testament. A Critical Introduction.* Belmont: Wadsworth Publishing Company, 1991.

Harris Stephen L. *The New Testament. A Student's Introduction.* 5th ed. Mountain View/London: Mayfield Publishing Company, 2005.

Johnson L. T. *The Writings of the New Testament. An Interpretation.* Philadelphia: Fortress, 1986.

Kümmel W. G. *Introduction to the New Testament.* Translated by H. C. Kee. 2d ed. Nashville: Abingdon, 1984..

Perkins, P. *Reading the New Testament. An Introduction.* 2d ed. New York: Paulist, 1988.

Perrin, N. *The New Testament. An Introduction. Proclamation and Parenesis, Myth and History.* 2d ed. Edited by D. C. Duling. New York: Harcourt Brace Jovanovich, 1982.

Schnelle, U. *The History and Theology of the New Testament Writings.*

Translated by M. E. Boring. Minneapolis: Fortress, 1998.

Spivey, R. A. and D. Moody Smith. *Anatomy of the New Testament. A Guide to Its Structure and Meaning.* 5th ed. Upper Saddle River, NJ: Prentice Hall, 1994.

PART II

The Gospel of Mark

CHAPTER TWO

Reading the Gospel of Mark

This chapter offers a guide to the literary and theological skill that produced Mark's radical arrangement of his relatively brief and – at first sight – simple story of Jesus. Mark, now established as the earliest of the Gospel writers, wrote a new account of Jesus from a theological viewpoint. At the start he invites the question "Who is Jesus?" and responds by defining Christ as the Messiah, the son of God and the son of Man. By masterfully employing literary devices Mark guides his audience to discovering biblical truths behind this definition. He structures his text in four sections, and employs "textual markers" to render his interpretation of the story of Jesus as a theological narrative. This often differs to our modern expectations of how either history or literature works.

Chapter 2
summary

I
N THE NINETEENTH CENTURY SCHOLARS CAME TO ACCEPT that Mark was the first Gospel to be written. As it was the oldest, many thought it would be the best place to look for an accurate record of the life of Jesus. But after an initial burst of interest in Mark as an historian, scholars increasingly agreed that Mark was little more than an editor who had clumsily stitched together older stories. In 1921 Ruldolf Bultmann claimed: "Mark is not sufficiently master of his material to be able to venture on a systematic construction himself."[1] The decades since Bultmann have shown how wrong he was! Over the past twenty years, much has been done to uncover the literary and theological skill that produced Mark's arrangement of his relatively brief and – at first sight – simple story of Jesus.[2]

It is often said that a successful story has a good beginning, a good middle, and a good end. This can be said for the Gospel of Mark. The story begins with a solemn confession concerning the good news of Jesus as the Christ and the Son of God (Mark 1:1), God's prophetic word (vv. 2-3), John the Baptist (vv. 4-8), the witness of God, in a voice from heaven (vv. 9-11), and Jesus' victory over Satan (vv. 12-13). This "prologue" brings Jesus to the center of the story. He bursts onto the scene, proclaiming the advent of the reigning presence of God (vv. 14-15). In the middle of the Gospel, after a series of encounters with characters from the world of Israel, with his own family, and with his disciples, during which he has worked wonders and taught by means of parables, Jesus asks his disciples who they think he is. In the name of the disciples, Peter confesses: "You are the Christ" (8:29). At the end of the story, after the instruction of his disciples on the need to follow him, cost what it may, his final bitter encounters with the leaders of Israel, his arrest, trials and violent death on a cross, the reader finds proof that Jesus' story did not end with his death. He has been raised. The women find an empty tomb and hear the Easter proclamation from the young man at the tomb (16:1-8).

These crucial turning points in the Markan narrative catch the ambiguity of the story. Who Jesus is and what he does are spelt out for the reader in the prologue (1:1-13). Peter, in the name of the disciples, confesses at least a partial understanding of who Jesus is in 8:29: "You are the Christ" (see 1:1). But a warning that this may not be the whole truth follows the confessions, as the disciples are to say nothing about this to anyone (8:30). This shadow across the performance of the disciples reaches tragic dimensions at the end of the Gospel as they flee (14:50), betray him (14:43-46) and deny him (14:66-72). Jesus goes alone to the cross, abandoned by all except the women who watch his death and burial from afar (see 15:40-41, 47). The young man at the empty tomb will command these women to tell Peter and the disciples that Jesus is going before them into Galilee. But the women run away in panic, and say nothing to anyone. Like the disciples, they flee in fear (16:7-8).

Attentive reading of the Gospel reveals that Mark left other signs of his handiwork in what I call "textual markers." These markers suggest to the reader that the storyteller is "up to something." The most obvious textual marker in any narrative is a summary, wherein an author pauses to open a new section in his story, to draw a conclusion, or to pass a critical comment upon events just reported. There are many summaries in Mark (see, for example, Mark 1:14-15, 39, 45b; 3:7-12; 4:33-34; 6:6b, 53-56; 9:30-31; 10:1). Other markers can take the form of a repetition. For example, there are two bread miracles in Mark 6:31-44 and 8:1-9. The passion predictions are found three times, in 8:31, 9:31 and 10:32-34. Two stories tell of the cure of a blind man (8:22-26; 10:46-52). Another form of "repetition" in the Gospel of Mark is his favored practice of what has come to be known as a "sandwich construction." Two separate incidents are knitted together by beginning one report, introducing the story of another event on the way, and then resuming and concluding the original report. Well-known examples of this are the story of Jairus and his daughter (5:21-24, 35-43) with the cure of the woman with the flow of blood, and the "framing" of the cleansing of the Temple (11:15-19) with the cursing of the fig tree (vv. 12-14, 20-25). Other textual markers are shifts in the action from one place to another (a change in the geography of the story), from one period of time to another (a change in the time frame of the story), or from one set of characters to another (a change in the author's focus upon characters). The Gospel of Mark has many such signposts (see, for example, 1:35; 2:1; 2:23; 3:7; 4:35; 7:24, 31). On the basis of these textual markers, clear hints emerge. The story is changing direction or beginning to develop another point of view. A narrative "plot" can be traced for the Gospel.

Plotting the Gospel of Mark

A single-minded desire on the part of the Evangelist to communicate a message about Jesus, the Christ, the Son of God, dominates the plot (see

1:1). "The beginning" of the story is announced in 1:1, and it runs from vv. 1-13. We regard this section of the Gospel as a genuine prologue, just as the Gospel of John has its famous prologue (John 1:1-18), and Matthew and Luke have prologues to their narratives in their respective birth and infancy stories (Matt 1-2; Luke 1-2). Jesus appears on the scene, proclaiming the good news of the impinging presence of God as king (1:14-15). This event signals a turning point. Peter's confession and Jesus' command to silence (8:29-30) close the first half of the Gospel. These are followed by the first passion prediction (8:31), as Jesus sets off on his journey to Jerusalem, asking his disciples to follow him (8:34-9:1), and the second half of the Gospel has begun. The end of the story reports the morning after the Sabbath, as women go to anoint the body of the crucified Jesus and discover an empty tomb (16:1-8). We can thus suggest that there are four major sections to the Gospel of Mark:

1. The Gospel begins (1:1-13).

2. Jesus opens his ministry in Galilee (1:14-8:30).

3. Jesus announces his journey to Jerusalem, forms disciples on the way, is arrested, tried, crucified and buried (8:31-15:47)

4. Women discover an empty tomb (16:1-8).

Mark tells his story of Jesus carefully, and we can trace clearly defined literary "sections" to uncover the shape of the narrative.

1. Mark 1:1-13 serves as a prologue, providing the reader with vital information about God's beloved Son.

2. Through Mark 1:14 to 8:30 the words and deeds of Jesus' ministry increasingly force the question: who is this man (see 1:27, 45; 2:12; 3:22; 4:41; 5:20; 6:2-3, 48-50; 7:37)? Some accept him, some are indifferent, and many oppose him, but the question behind the story is: can he be the Messiah? In 8:29 Peter, in the name of the disciples, resolves the problem by confessing: "You are the Christ." The guessing has come to an end but the first half of the story can be entitled: "Who is Jesus?" An answer has been provided, but in the last verse Jesus warns Peter not to tell anyone of his being the expected Messiah (8:30). Peter's confession may not contain the whole truth about Jesus.

3. Mark 8:31-15:47 opens with the first passion prediction (8:31: "And he began to teach them that the Son of Man must suffer many things, and be rejected by the elders and the chief priests and the scribes,

and be killed, and after three days rise again"). Jesus is setting out on a journey to Jerusalem. He will suffer, be crucified and rise in that city. One can sense that this part of the story forms a "second half" of Mark's story of Jesus showing that Jesus is the Messiah who will be revealed as Son of God on the Cross, a suffering and vindicated Son of Man (8:31; 9:31; 10:32-33; 13:26; 14:61-62; 15:39). In 15:39 a Roman centurion confesses: "Truly this man was God's Son!" The suffering Christ is truly the Son of God, and thus the mystery of Jesus' identity has been resolved. Mark 8:31-15:47 can be called "The suffering and vindicated Son of Man: Christ and Son of God."

4. Many questions raised by the story remain unresolved. The disciples have fled (see 14:50) and Jesus has cried out: "My God, my God, why have you forsaken me?" (15:34). In 16:1-8 the reader learns that God has not forsaken his Son. He has been raised (see 16:6). But a solution to the problem of failing disciples lies in the future. They are to go into Galilee; there they will see him (v. 7). The women, frightened by all they have seen and heard, flee and say nothing to anyone (v. 8).

The first Christian Gospel features a careful ordering of a succession of events. The feature shows that the story as a whole is permeated by a storyteller's desire to proclaim something about God, the Christ, and the followers of Jesus. The first chapter of this book strove to point out that the order of events as they are now found in any of the Gospels was not fortuitous. It was largely determined by the desire of the Evangelists to communicate a message about what God has done for us in and through the teaching and person of Jesus of Nazareth. The authors of the Gospels reached back into older traditions about Jesus, but they told the story in their own way. The Gospel of Mark, which began the literary form of "gospel" within world literature, was a bold venture, and the story carries a bold message. *Whatever the first readers knew of the life-story of Jesus of Nazareth was seen as subverted by the Markan story. This account of Jesus' presence in Galilee, his single journey to Jerusalem to be rejected, tried and crucified, the resurrection and the surprising silence of the women at the empty tomb was not familiar.* Mark told the story of Jesus in this way for the first time and his narrative was a new and original way of reporting events from the life of Jesus.[3]

The Markan Literary Design and Its Theological Message

Reading Mark 1:1-13

Three "voices" dominate the prologue to the Gospel of Mark. For the most part, the narrator of the story is informing the reader. The voice of the storyteller reports most of vv. 1-13. In 7-8, however, John the Baptist takes center-stage, and the reader hears his "voice" describing the one who is to come after him. But there is also another "voice" echoing across vv. 2-3. Even though, at first glance, it may appear that the narrator is generally speaking, this is not always the case. The narrator steps aside, and God speaks through Israel's Scriptures. What must be noted, however is the fact that vv. 1-13 are directed only to the reader. Characters will appear in the story of the life and death of Jesus, who are not present in vv. 1-13. The crowds, the leaders of Israel, the disciples, and various other characters that populate the pages of the Gospel do not know what the reader was told in the prologue. This literary technique privileges the reader. Throughout the Gospel of Mark, the one who has read or heard vv. 1-13 knows the secret of who Jesus is and what he has done.

In vv. 1-3 the readers or listeners hear the voice of the narrator, initially announcing the beginning of a book that will tell them the good news: Jesus is the Christ, the Son of God. In the first line, the narrator has nailed his colors to the mast. However, in the following two verses (vv. 2-3), although reported by the narrator, one hears the voice of God. By citing the Hebrew Scriptures, the narrator steps aside. God's voice announces the sending of a messenger to prepare the way of the Lord. Thus, in the opening verses of the prologue two authoritative voices have spoken to the reader, the narrator (who knows what he wants) and God (who knows and plans everything!). Jesus is the Christ, the Son of God and the Lord, and God will send a messenger to prepare his way.

The narrator takes complete control in vv. 4-6 and describes the messenger whom God promised to send. In these verses John the Baptist does nothing, but the one who will prepare the way of the Lord (see vv. 2-3) is portrayed. However, in vv. 7-8 the voice of the Baptist takes over. He is no longer a third person, described by the narrator, but he speaks for himself. He speaks of the coming of "the stronger one," one before whom he is unworthy even to untie the sandal. The figure to come "will baptize with the Holy Spirit." What God promised about a figure that would prepare the way for the Lord, is fulfilled.

In vv. 9-11 the narrator takes over again. He introduces Jesus into the story for the first time. Jesus does not *do anything*, but things happen to him. John baptizes him, and the Spirit descends upon him. A voice announces that Jesus is God's beloved Son. In vv. 12-13 dramatic events surround the person of Jesus. The Spirit drives him into the desert and Satan tempts him. But angels minister to him, and he is with the wild beasts.

The prologue has moved rapidly from one affirmation about Jesus to another. He is the Christ, the Son of God, the Lord, "the stronger one," he will baptize with the Holy Spirit, he is taken over by the Spirit, and then driven by the Spirit to be tested by Satan. In the desert he lives a life that parallels the lives of Adam and Eve *before the entry of sin*. He is nourished by angels, and "with the wild beasts." The reader has been offered crucial information about who Jesus is, and some of the things he will do. However, *only the reader* knows this, and sets off into the experience of reading the narrative. The reader's knowledge will be sorely tested by the story that follows. Can all that happens to Jesus in this story really be about God's beloved Son? Jesus' life, teaching and cruel death, vindicated by the action of God at an empty tomb reveal him as the Christ, the Son of Man and the Son of God.[4]

Reading Mark 1:14-8:30

This section can be given the title: "The Mystery of Jesus." Many are stimulated by his words and actions and ask questions of Jesus' identity. But the Gospel of Mark is not only about Jesus, Christ and Son of God (see 1:1, 11). It is equally about the challenge of "following" a suffering Son of Man to Jerusalem and beyond. As the first half of the Gospel comes to an end, the identity of a true disciple also begins to emerge. This theme will dominate the second half of the story (8:31-15:47), but it is not altogether absent from 1:14-8:30.

Further textual markers indicate that 1:14-8:30 can be sub-divided. The first half of the Gospel establishes relationships, and raises questions concerning the person of Jesus. Across 1:14-8:30 the main textual markers are the "summaries." The storyteller slows down his fast moving narrative to summarize Jesus' ministry. These summaries of Jesus' activities cannot be easily tied to a time or a place. They offer, in a more general fashion, illustrations of that activity (see 1:14-15; 3:7-12; 6:6b). The Gospel of Mark contains other similar summaries of Jesus' ministry (see, for example, 1:39, 45b; 4:33-34; 6:53-56; 9:30-31; 10:1). What is unique about the general descriptions of Jesus' ministry in the three summaries that I have singled out (1:14-15, 3:7-12 and 6:6b) is that each summary is followed by material that deals with disciples and discipleship (1:16-20: Jesus calls the first disciples; 3:13-19: Jesus appoints the Twelve and names them; 6:7-30: Jesus sends out the Twelve on their first mission). The summaries, and the following report of Jesus' association with his disciples, introduce a series of episodes during which different audiences respond to the words and deeds of Jesus.

After the first summary and the vocation of the disciples (1:14-20), Jesus demonstrates, in word and deed in his teaching and healing, that the reigning presence of God (the Kingdom of God) is breaking into the human story. But antagonism to his person and message increases, and at 3:6 the Pharisees and the Herodians gather together to plan how to eliminate him. Subsequent to the second summary statement and Jesus' appointing the Twelve to be with him and to share in his life and mission in a special way (3:7-19) Jesus continues to work wonders and proclaim the coming of God's reign. But Mark focuses upon the lack of understanding that he meets from his own family, from the people of Israel, and in his own home town. In 6:1-6a the people from his own country regard him as a charlatan; they know his mother and brothers and sisters. The third summary, followed by Jesus' sending of the disciples on their first mission (6:6b-30) pays growing attention to the association of the disciples with Jesus, and their increasing inability to understand who he is. But this section closes with a glimmer of hope, as Peter confesses the faith of the disciples that Jesus is the Christ. However, as we have already seen, there is a shadow over this confession. The disciples' understanding of Jesus' messiahship may not be altogether correct, as they are warned not to say anything about this to anyone (8:29-30). [5]

The three summaries leading directly into passages that deal with disciples, and concluding with a response to Jesus indicate Mark's careful writing of 1:14-8:30. A more detailed reading of these three literary sections shows the following gradual emergence of the issue of the mystery of Jesus.

1. *Jesus and the leaders of Israel* (1:14-3:6). The first key summary appears in 1:14-15: "Now after John was arrested, Jesus came to Galilee, proclaiming the good news of God, and saying, 'The time is fulfilled and the kingdom of God has come near, repent and believe in the good news.'" This summary is followed by the account of the vocation of the first disciples (1:16-20). They respond to him spontaneously, following down his way without question, leaving behind all that could be judged as the signs of their success: the boats, their nets, their hired servants and their father. Jesus then exercises his ministry in Galilee, chiefly at Capernaum (1:21-3:6). In a very carefully plotted story, the Kingdom comes with power. Jesus conquers an unclean spirit (1:21-28), he overcomes sickness and taboo as he heals Simon Peter's sick mother-in-law by touching her, he prays to God, the source of all he is doing (1:32-24, 35-39), and again vanquishes sickness and taboo as he heals a leper. The power of the reigning presence of God sweeps all powers of evil before it: sickness, taboo and the demonic. But human beings are more difficult, and they gradually increase in their opposition to Jesus and the Kingdom.[6] Jesus cures the man with palsy, and is questioned (2:1-12). He calls Levi from the tax house, and shares his table with sinners, and is questioned (vv. 13-17). He is interrogated over the lack of proper fasting practices among his disciples (vv. 18-22). He is questioned over the Sabbath law, as his disciples pluck the grain (vv. 23-28). Finally, he works a further miracle on a Sabbath, watched by his enemies, who gather to plot his death (3:1-6). In this fashion, tension steadily mounts until this carefully assembled series of encounters between Jesus and those in opposition to him ends with the comment from the narrator: "The Pharisees went out and immediately conspired with the Herodians against him, how to destroy him" (3:6).

2. *Jesus and his new family* (3:7-6:6a). A summary of Jesus' Galilean ministry follows in 3:7-12. It concludes: "He had cured many so that all who had diseases pressed upon him to touch him. Whenever the unclean spirits saw him, they fell down before him and shouted, 'You are the Son of God!' But he sternly ordered them not to make him known" (3:10-12). This summary leads into the account of Jesus' institution of the Twelve. He appoints them to a special intimacy: to be with him so they might do all he has done (3:13-19). But Jesus' ministry meets opposition from his family. They think he is insane, and try to prevent him from caring for the needy. The leaders of Israel oppose him, suggesting he

does his powerful deeds by the authority of the devil, Beelzebul (3:20-30). In the face of these failures from his natural and his national "family," he responds to the presence of his mother and brothers, who are "outside" asking for him by pointing to those gathered around him "inside." He establishes new principles for belonging to his family: "Here are my mother and my brothers. Whoever does the will of God is my brother, and sister and mother" (vv. 34-35). He proceeds from these situations to teach through parables (4:1-34) and a stunning series of miracles (4:35-5:43). As he teaches through his parables, he singles out his "new family," the disciples, and indicates how blessed they are to have the secret of the reigning presence of God, as those "outside" fail to understand. But even the disciples show signs that they do not understand the parables of the Kingdom (4:10-13). Similarly, during miracles in which Jesus shows his authority over nature (4:35-41), the demonic (5:1-20), illness and death (5:21-43), the disciples ask: "Who then is this, that even the wind and the sea obey him?" (4:41. See also 5:16, 31). Jesus returns to his hometown, but his own people reject him: "Is not this the carpenter, the son of Mary and brother of James and Joses and Judas and Simon, and are not his sisters here with us?' And they took offence at him" (6:3). Jesus was "amazed at their unbelief" (6:6a).

3. *Jesus and his disciples* (6:6b-8:30). Rejected in his hometown, Jesus' ongoing ministry in Galilee is summarized: "Then he went about among the villages teaching" (6:6b). Jesus sends out the Twelve on a mission that parallels his own (6:6b-13). While they are on the mission, the execution of John the Baptist is a sign of the destiny of those who give everything for the Kingdom (vv. 14-29). But the disciples return to Jesus, and tell him, the source of all they are able to do, of their successes, as if they were the fruits of their newly acquired personal authority over demons and sickness (v. 30). Jesus feeds a Jewish crowd, drawing into service the disciples who want Jesus to send the crowd away, and a large amount of the meal remains (vv. 31-44). After the miracle, he comes to his frightened and unbelieving disciples on the water (vv. 45-51). The issue of eating continues, marked by increasing hostility between Jesus and the Jews, especially in his conflict with the Pharisees who object to his lack of observance of the laws of purity. He turns on them and warns them that true cleanliness comes from inside, not from the outside (see 7:1-23). He leaves Israel, journeying into the region of Tyre and Sidon.

There he nourishes the humble believer, the Syrophoenician woman, with the crumbs that fall from the table (vv. 24-30). After a further miracle in a Gentile land (vv. 31-37) he nourishes Gentiles, and again draws his unwilling disciples into his ministry to both Jew and Gentile. The gathering of the fragments at the end of this meal leaves the table of the Lord open to all who may long to approach it (8:1-10).

Another boat trip reveals that the disciples are drawing closer to the attitude of the Pharisees and the Herodians (see 8:11-13), as they do not recognize who is in the boat with them in their concern that they have no bread. He accuses them of blindness, deafness, hardness of heart and lack of understanding (vv. 14-21). Still, there is hope. A blind man comes to sight by stages (vv. 22-26), and the disciples show that they too are on a similar journey into sight and faith. The first half of the Gospel draws to a close as Jesus broaches the question that has been lurking behind the narrative since 1:14: "Who do people say that I am?" (8:27). Many think that Jesus is one of the expected messianic precursors. Jesus asks the disciples "Who do you say that I am?" (v. 28). Peter responds: "You are the Christ" (v. 29). The reader, informed by the storyteller at 1:1, has known from the outset that Jesus is the Christ. Part of the question "who is Jesus?" has been answered for the disciples. There is a sense in which Peter is correct, but Jesus' words to the disciples sound a warning bell, and open the door to the second part of the Gospel: "He charged them to tell no one about him" (8:30). Jesus is the Christ, but there is more to his being the Christ than Peter and the disciples imagine, as becomes immediately obvious.

Reading Mark 8:31-15:47

Jesus' command to silence in 8:30 closes the first half of the story, and points toward the second half which opens with a prediction, spoken openly, of his future death and resurrection in Jerusalem (8:31). Textual markers across 8:31-15:47 point to a further three stages in the story of the suffering and finally vindicated Son of Man, Messiah and Son of God. Obvious changes of place, characters and situations occur across this second half of the story.

1. *Jesus and the disciples' journey to Jerusalem* (8:31-10:52). The first passion prediction marks the opening of the first major section of the second half of the Gospel. Jesus' destiny as the suffering and vindicated

Son of Man is stated without compromise (8:31). A steady literary pattern will emerge across this section of the story. Jesus indicates that he is going to be slain and raised from the dead in the *first passion prediction* (8:31). Peter *fails* as he refuses to accept this central element in Jesus' messianic response to God (vv. 32-33). Jesus thus turns to the disciples and the crowd and *teaches* them on the need to follow him, to *take up their cross* and follow him (vv. 34-37). Only as "followers" will they join Jesus in the victory that God will grant (8:38-9:1). The disciples are further instructed by the event of the transfiguration (9:2-13), where Jesus' demand that disciples join him on his way of the Cross is supported by no less a figure than God. The voice from heaven insists: "This is my beloved Son, *listen to him*" (9:7). But the disciples still languish, as they wonder why they cannot cure the possessed boy (vv. 14-29).

The *second passion prediction* follows (9:30-31), but again the disciples *fail* as they discuss along the way which of them would be the greatest (vv. 32-34). Jesus *teaches* the disciples of the necessity of *service and receptivity,* by the example of the child (vv. 35-50, 10:13-16), and then by instructing them on those areas of the life of the disciple that find service and receptivity most difficult: marriage (10:1-12) and possessions (vv. 17-31).

The *third passion prediction* follows immediately (10:32-35), but James and John *fail* by their request for positions of honor. Jesus *teaches* them that they will embrace *the Cross* (vv. 36-40). The other disciples *fail* as they think James and John have gained an edge in jockeying for power, and Jesus *teaches* them on the need for *service and receptivity* (vv. 41-44). The model of Jesus closes his teaching on discipleship. He points to himself as the one they must *follow*: "For the Son of Man also came, not to be served but to serve, and to lay down his life as a ransom for many" (10:45). He asks his disciples for *Cross* and *service*. The Son of Man also came to serve and to give his life on the Cross. The Markan narrative has led the reader to the crucial and fundamental statement from Jesus about his own mission in 10:45 by a threefold repetition of a passion prediction (8:31; 9:30-31; 10:32-25), followed by failure among the disciples (8:32-33; 9:32-34; 10:36-44), to which Jesus always responds with teaching on their vocation to cross and service. *Jesus never fails the failing disciples.* Matching the blind man's three-fold stumbling to sight at Bethsaida (8:22-26), this section of the story closes with Bartimaeus' unconditional acceptance of Jesus, cost him what it may, and he followed

Jesus down his way (vv. 46-52). The first blind man stumbles gradually to full sight (8:22-26). In this, he models most of us who read and listen to the Gospel of Mark. The response of the second blind man to Jesus indicates what it means to believe without conditions (10:46-52).

2. *Endings in Jerusalem* (11:1-13:37). In 11:1-25, Mark describes three major events. Jesus enters Jerusalem in the first episode (vv. 1-11). He then brings to an end the commercial and cultic activities of the Temple (vv. 12-21). Finally, alone with his disciples, he replaces Israel's cult with a new approach to God, elaborating the need for faith, prayer and forgiveness (vv. 22-25). In 11:1-11, on arrival at villages that lie on the outskirts of the city, Jesus prepares to enter Jerusalem (vv. 1-7a). He tells two of his disciples where they are to go, what they will find, and what they must say and do. It happens exactly as Jesus said, and the stage is set for Jesus' entry, riding the colt brought by the disciples. Jesus is lavishly welcomed as he approaches the city. The spreading of garments and laying of leafy branches accompany a cry *from those who followed and those who went before* that welcomes Jesus as the Messiah: "Hosanna! Blessed is he who comes in the name of the Lord! Blessed is the kingdom of our father David that is coming! Hosanna in the highest" (vv. 9-10). These words go no further than the confession of Peter in 8:29, and the false expectation of the disciples from 8:31-10:45. Indeed, it is "those who followed" who utter this cry, as is recalled by the use of this expression across the earlier parts of the Gospel (see, for example, 1:16-20). It is the disciples of Jesus who continue to misread Jesus' messianic program. He has not come to bring the kingdom of David, but the kingdom of God. Only after this false acclamation does Jesus enter Jerusalem, go to the Temple, and look round at everything (v. 11). There is something ominous about this survey of the Temple, and his anger will burst forth in the next scene. For the moment, he leaves the city, and goes to Bethany.

In vv. 12-21 Jesus brings the Temple cult to an end. On the way from Bethany to Jerusalem, Jesus sees the fig tree in leaf, seeks its fruit, and curses it. The fig tree is cursed because it was not the "proper time" for fruit (vv. 12-14). Jesus brings to an end the money-dealings that went on at the entry to the Temple. But these deals were essential to the cultic activity of the Temple. On the one hand, people who carried coins with effigies had to exchange them for coins bearing no image in order to respect the holiness of the place they were entering. On the other hand, the pigeons were the sacrificial victims used by the very poor. The storyteller then adds: "And he would not allow anyone to carry any sacred vessel (Greek: *skeuos*) through the Temple" (v. 16). This translation catches the meaning of the episode.[7] All cultic activity within the Temple comes to a standstill, as Jesus takes over and insists that his house is to be a house of prayer for all the nations. It has been reduced to a den of robbers. The next day the fig tree has died and withered (vv. 20-21). The fig tree is a symbol of an Israel that did not recognize its "proper time" and thus has lost its life-giving authority, and has withered. Jesus solemnly indicates that the cult of Israel may have been symbolically brought to a standstill in 11:12-21, but in its place, the new community will worship in faith (v. 22-23), with prayer (v. 24), and finally, lest prayer become mere words, not reflected in action, he adds the need for forgiveness (v. 25). In place of the cultic practices of Israel, Jesus teaches the way of faith, prayer and forgiveness.

Another "ending" takes place in 11:27-12:44: the end of Israel's religious leadership. Jesus' encounters with the leaders of Israel take place within the temporal context of a single day and the never-changing geographical location in the Temple in Jerusalem. In 11:27 Mark announces that Jesus came again to Jerusalem, and was walking in the Temple (see 11:11, 15). He does not move from the Temple until 13:1a: "And as he came out of the Temple." Jesus debates with the chief priests, the scribes and the elders (vv. 27-33), and tells a parable that these same interlocutors recognize as "against them" (12:1-12). Three public conflicts follow: with the Pharisees, whom he reduces to silence in the debate over rendering to Caesar what is Caesar's and to God what is God's (vv. 13-17), the Sadducees, who are silenced over the question of the resurrection, as they understand neither the Scriptures not the power of God (vv. 18-27), and finally, he instructs a Scribe, who responds by accepting Jesus' teaching (vv. 28-34). Jesus has reduced the religious leaders of Israel to silence: "And after that no one dared to ask him any question" (v. 34c). The section closes with a reflection on the relationship between the Christ and the Son of David, arguing that the scribal interpretation is incorrect (vv. 35-37). The Scribes are denounced (vv. 38-40), and Jesus points to the contrasting example of a poor widow, who gives her whole life (vv. 41-44).

Not only are the leaders of Israel reduced to silence, but the disciples, leaders of a new people of God (see 3:34-35), are challenged to recognize the need to give one's all. This is spelt out for them in the related attack on the false religion of the Scribes and the story of the widow's mite (vv. 38-44). The theme of "widows" locks together the storyteller's closing presentation of Jesus' encounter with the leaders of Israel. Public acclaim covers evil men who publicly make long prayers, "for a pretense," but privately exploit the poor and suffering, as they "devour widows' houses" and they are condemned. The scene changes, as Jesus and his disciples watch as a poor widow comes, and puts in the two copper coins that made up a penny, in the midst of showy generosity from the wealthy. Turning to his disciples, Jesus, who has brought the leaders of Israel to silence and condemned false religion (11:27-12:40), points to her as the model of a disciple. While many give out of their abundance, and thus lose nothing in their gift, the woman gives her all. The Greek phrase used (*holon ton bion autēs*), placed emphatically at the very end of the sentence and the passage as a whole, has two meanings. The woman has put in "her whole livelihood," and thus given all her possessions. But she has also given her very life. This is precisely what Jesus asked of his disciples as he instructed them in 8:34-9:1.

Finally, Jesus tells of the end of Jerusalem (13:1-23) and the end of the world (vv. 24-37). On the Mount of Olives and looking across toward Jerusalem and its Temple, the disciples admire its wonder, and Jesus tells them that soon all will be destroyed. He sits down with them on the Mount of Olives, and Peter, James, John and Andrew, the first disciples to be called (1:16-20), ask two questions: when will this be and what will be the sign of its final accomplishment. These questions set the agenda for the discourse. In vv. 1-23 Jesus will answer the first question, telling them of the end of Jerusalem and its Temple. In vv. 24-37 he will speak of other signs leading to the final end of human history. Mark has carefully arranged Jesus' teaching on the end of Jerusalem, focusing upon the experiences of the city and its people, and the need to recognize that the disaster of the destruction of Jerusalem by Titus and the Roman armies in 70 AD was not the end of the world. First, the Gospel had to be preached to all the nations.

(See over the page for Table1: The Structure of the End of Jerusalem)

Table 1:The Structure of the End of Jerusalem, 13:1-23

a) False prophets (vv. 5-6): Jesus warns the disciples against those who will arise among them, and claim that the return of the Messiah is taking place. They will claim, "I am he!" and they will lead many astray. This must be prevented.

b) Wars and rumors of wars (vv. 7-8): The readers of the Gospel hear of wars and rumors of wars, as reports of the tragic events of Jerusalem come to their ears. But this must not be understood as the end of time. There will be many wars, earthquakes and famines between now and the end of time. This is but the beginning.

c) Preach the Gospel to all nations (vv. 9-13): A long experience of trial and suffering, at the hands and in the courts of both Jews and Gentiles, lies ahead of the readers of the Gospel. They must not fear betrayal and death, as they will be guided by the Spirit, and those who endure to the end will be saved. All this is necessary because before the end of the world "The Gospel must first be preached to all the nations" (v. 10).

b¹) Wars and rumors of wars (vv. 14-20): Jesus now describes events that can be reconstructed from existing reports about the Jewish War. Titus and his standard bearers in the Holy of Holies (v. 14: the abomination of desolation that the reader must understand), the need to flee in haste, and the tribulations for mothers and those with child, as they flee into a beginning wintertime. They will survive only because of God's care for those he has called.

a¹) False prophets (vv. 21-23): Jesus returns to warn the disciples against any acceptance of the many voices who may be crying out that this is the end of time. They have now been told that first the Gospel must be preached to all nations (v. 10). False prophets will come and go, like wars and rumors of wars. None of this should shake them in their mission as Jesus comforts them: "I have told you all this beforehand" (v. 23).

The Structure of the End of the World (13:27-37)

Once the end of Jerusalem has been foretold, Jesus then tells of the end of the world, in two stages (vv. 24-37). First he tells them of the signs for the accomplishment of all things including the sign of the coming Son of Man, in vv. 24-27, and in vv. 28-31, the many signs of the inevitable and imminent end time. In vv. 32-37 he exhorts his disciples to watch and wait for the unknown day and hour. The suffering Son of Man, to whom authority has been given over the Sabbath and to forgive sins (see 2:10, 28), but whose authority is always questioned or rejected, will come as the final judge. He will send out angels, to gather the elect from the four corners of the earth. First the Gospel had to be preached to all the nations (13:10). Only when that has been done, will the Son of Man be able to gather the elect "from the four winds, from the ends of the earth to the ends of heaven" (v. 27). There will be signs of the inevitable and imminent end of time (vv. 28-31). There can be no doubt that everything will change and the world as the disciples know it will come to an end, and that end will be very soon. However, one thing will remain, and the disciples who have been with Jesus, as well as disciples to whom this Gospel is addressed, must take comfort: "Heaven and earth will pass away, but my words will not pass away" (v. 31).

They must watch for the unknown day and hour (vv. 32-37). The exact time of the end remains unknown. No one knows when it will be: not the angels in heaven, not even the Son, and certainly not the disciples. Jesus changes his tone. He no longer tells them of the events that are coming, nor does he continue to insist they should take heed (Greek: *blepete*). He has used this warning verb throughout the discourse (see vv. 5, 9, 23, 33). From now on, even though he insists that his disciples "watch," warning becomes exhortation. He uses another Greek verb that insists they act in a way that shows a preparedness to accept one's responsibilities. They are "to be on the watch" as a good doorkeeper must do as his master leaves (v. 34: Greek: *grēgoreite*). This final part of the discourse, therefore, suggests that Jesus is about to leave the disciples, and they must perform their task in his absence with diligence and care.

The reader knows that Jesus' departure will be through the Cross. The disciples should also know, as on three occasions Jesus has told them of his imminent death and resurrection in Jerusalem (8:31; 9:31; 10:33-34). Thus, Jesus' final warnings and recommendations to his disciples match the time-periods that mark his passion and death. The disciples are told that they do not know whether the master of the house will come in the evening (see 14:17), at midnight (see 14:32-65), at cockcrow (see 14:72), or in the morning (see 15:1). He will come suddenly, and find them asleep (see 14:32-42). The fragile first disciples hear Jesus' words as he enters into his passion: "What I say to you I say to all: Watch" (v. 37).

3. *The Passion and Death of Jesus.* Mark tells the passion and death of Jesus in two coherent sequences: Jesus, the disciples and the Jewish leaders (14:1-72), and the Roman trial, crucifixion, death and burial (15:1-47). Mark often uses the practice of "interlacing" episodes (see 3:20-35; 4:1-34; 5:21-43; 6:7-30; 11:12-26; 13:5-23). The Markan passion narrative (14:1-15:47) continues this literary practice. A twofold use of a simple, but effective literary presentation of the events of Jesus' passion and death render this account extremely effective. The pattern can be described as the steady reporting of scenes, shifting systematically from a focus upon other characters in the story [A] to a focus upon Jesus [B].

In 14:1-72 the "other characters" are always the disciples. In several of these episodes (see vv. 17-21, 26-31) Jesus is present, and is the speaker. However, he speaks of the future failures of Judas, Peter, and all the disciples. Similarly, Peter, James, and John are present (although absent as they are not able to "watch") in Gethsemane (vv. 32-42). The focus of the episode is the prayer of Jesus to the Father. In this sequence, the disciples move dramatically toward their final failure in 14:50. Full of fear they flee, and in vv. 51-52 the narrator adds a parable to comment upon their fear and flight. As a group they do not reappear in the story. The sequence unfolds as follows:

[A] 14:1-2: The plot of the Jewish leaders
   [B] vv. 3-9: The anointing *of Jesus*
[A] vv. 10-11: Judas, *one of the Twelve*, joins the plot of vv. 1-2
   [B] vv. 12-16: *Jesus* sees to the preparation for a Passover meal
[A] vv. 17-21: Jesus predicts the betrayal *of Judas, one of the Twelve*
   [B] vv. 22-25: *Jesus* shares the meal, giving bread and wine to *the disciples*
[A] vv. 26-31: Jesus predicts the future denials *of Peter* and the flight *of all the disciples*
   [B] vv. 32-42: The prayer *of Jesus* in Gethsemane
[A] vv. 43-52: *Judas, one of the Twelve*, along with representatives of the Jewish leaders arrest Jesus, and *all the disciples* flee
   [B] vv. 53-65: The self-revelation *of Jesus* at the Jewish hearing
[A] vv. 66-72: *Peter* denies Jesus three times.

The eleven brief scenes in this arrangement shift systematically from portrayals or predictions of disciples' failures to a presentation of the person of Jesus. Poignantly, and importantly for the Markan understanding of discipleship, at the very center, in the sixth scene (vv. 21-25), the failing disciples and Jesus share a meal.[8]

The same pattern is repeated in the second half of the narrative where the action plays itself out in a Roman world (15:1-47). It is dominated by Roman process, from the trial to the crucifixion. However, the chief priests and the scribes, leaders of the Jews, are always present, lurking in the background, inciting the crowd against Jesus. The disciples, having left the scene in 14:50, never appear. The ongoing narrative, continuing from 14:66-72 [A], requires that the Roman sequence open with a focus upon Jesus [B]. It unfolds as follows:

[B] 15:1-5: The self-revelation *of Jesus* as the Roman hearing begins

[A] vv. 6-11: The question of Barabbas

[B] vv. 12-15: Pilate ironically proclaims *Jesus* innocent and King as the Roman hearing closes

[A] vv. 16-20a: The Roman soldiers ironically proclaim the truth as they mock Jesus

[B] vv. 20b-25: The crucifixion *of Jesus*

[A] vv. 26-32: Passers-by and the Jewish leaders ironically proclaim the truth as they mock Jesus

[B] vv. 33-39: The death *of Jesus*, proclaimed Son of God

[A] vv. 40-41: The women at the Cross

[B] vv. 42-47: The burial *of Jesus.*

In a way that parallels the eleven scenes across 14:1-72, in which the central (sixth) scene was the meal with Jesus (14:21-25), the central (fifth) scene of the nine episodes that form the Roman process is the crucifixion of Jesus (15:21-25). As we have seen, 14:1-72 focused strongly upon the disciples, their failure, and Jesus' unconditional commitment to them. One of them is present, denying Jesus, in the final scene (14:66-72). The Roman process brings Mark's Christological proclamation to its high point. The disciples do not appear, and thus at its center is the crucified Christ.

This rapid movement from one brief scene to another adds urgency to the narrative. It enables Mark to describe the never-failing presence of Jesus, Messiah, Son of the Blessed, Son of Man (14:61b-62), and Prophet (v. 65), to an ever-failing group of disciples. Nowhere is this more poignantly highlighted than in the final meal he shares with them before they betray him, deny him and flee, as he said they would (14:1-72. See vv. 17-31). The pattern continues to throw into relief the Christological climax of the Gospel in the description of the unrelenting suffering of the innocent Jesus, King of the Jews (15:2, 9, 12, 14, 18, 26), the Christ, the King of Israel (v. 32), and Son of God (v. 39). Paradoxically, on the Cross the claims made by the narrator for Jesus in 1:1-13 are shown to be true (15:1-47). In the midst of the rejection and the suffering, new characters appear, "outsiders" like Simon of Cyrene (15:21), the centurion at the cross (v. 39), the women (vv. 40-41, 47) and Joseph of Arimathea (vv. 43-46). They are the first hint of a newer generation of disciples whose following (v. 21), commitment (vv. 40-41, 47), belief (v. 39) and courage (vv. 43-46) have their beginnings at the Cross.

Reading Mark 16:1-8

Mark brings his Gospel to a close in a remarkable fashion in 16:1-8. The setting of the first Easter morning is provided in vv. 1-4. Links are made with the passion story: the Sabbath has now passed, and the women who were at the cross and at the tomb bring spices to anoint Jesus' body. Light is dawning on this "first day of the week" as they approach the tomb, asking who will roll away the stone (vv. 2-3). There are some strange things happening here. Why anoint a dead body after three days? Why did they not think of the stone before they left home? Indeed, the stone was very large, but it had already been rolled back (v. 4). The passive use of the verb in the sentence "the stone was rolled back" indicates that someone else has entered the story. Who might that be? There are more questions than answers in these opening verses.

The answers are provided at the empty tomb (vv. 5-7). As the women enter it, they see a young man sitting on the right side, dressed in a white robe (v. 5). His description recalls the symbolic sign of the failing disciples, the young man who was dressed in a linen cloth and fled naked in his nothingness (see 14:51-52). Discipleship will be restored, despite fear and flight (see 14:50). The words of the young man in v. 6 tell them they are looking in the wrong place. They are seeking Jesus, the Nazarene, the crucified. They are told to look at the place where the dead body had been laid. He is not there, because *he has been raised!* The question concerning the rolling back of the stone is answered: God has entered the story, and has raised Jesus (v. 6). Jesus' question from the Cross, "My God, my God, why have you forsaken me" (15:34) has also been answered. God has not forsaken Jesus. The Father has not abandoned the Son, in whom he is well pleased (see 1:11). The final words of the young man recall Jesus' promise of 14:28. The women are told to announce the Easter message: "But go, tell his disciples and Peter that he is going before you to Galilee; there you will see him, as he told you" (v. 7). In 14:28 Jesus promised that, despite the failure of the disciples, he *would go* before them to Galilee; in 16:7 the young man announces he *is going* before them into Galilee. But the women run away from the tomb, associating themselves with the fear, trembling, astonishment and flight of the disciples (see 14:50-52). They say nothing to anyone, for they were afraid (v. 8), and thus the Gospel of Mark comes to a close.

Even the first readers of Mark knew of the tradition found in the other canonical Gospels: women were the recipients of the Easter message, and they delivered it to the disciples (see Matt 28:7-10; Luke 24:8-9; John 20:1-2). Mark the storyteller has deliberately changed a well-known tradition. He does this because he wishes to lead his readers back to the point where they began. In 1:1-13 the storyteller challenged readers by means of his Christological prologue. His main focus in 16:1-8 is again his readers, called to discipleship. Mark's epilogue makes clear that God's action is not the result of human initiative, but rests entirely with God. As with the promises of Jesus' forthcoming death and resurrection (8:31; 9:31; 10:33-34), the promises of 14:28 and 16:7 will be fulfilled. What Jesus said would happen, will happen. Challenged by his enemies to prophesy (14:65), the failure of the disciples (14:50; see v. 27), the betrayal of Judas (14:43-46; see 17-21) and the denials of Peter (14:66-72; see vv. 30-31), his arrest, his trials and his crucifixion have all shown that Jesus' predictions come true. The reader has every reason to believe that the promises of 14:28 and 16:7 have already come true. But Jesus' meeting with the disciples and Peter in Galilee does not take place within the limitations of the story. It cannot, because the women do not obey the word of the young man. They, like the disciples, fail. As with the disciples, they flee in fear (16:8). When and how does Jesus' meeting with the failed disciples, women and men, take place? The answer to that question cannot be found in the story; but the very existence of the story tells the reader that what Jesus said would happen, did happen.

The Gospel of Mark, with its faith-filled prologue telling of God's design for the human situation in the gift of his Son (1:1-13), addresses a believing community in its epilogue (16:1-8). This indicates that the disciples and Peter did see Jesus in Galilee, as he had promised (14:28; 16:7). As Jesus' prophecies came true (see 8:31; 9:31; 10:32-34; 12:11-12; 14:17-21, 27-31), the believing reader accepts that the promises of 14:28 and 16:7 also came true. For Mark, the consummate storyteller, there can be no record of any such encounter within the narrative. It is not required, as the believing community has the word itself: "Jesus has been raised" (16:6). Jesus' words to his disciples on the Mount of Olives ring out: "Heaven and earth will pass away, but my words will not pass away" (13:31). For this reason, the voice from heaven tells all disciples, readers and listeners to the story of the Gospel of Mark: "Listen to him" (9:7). If the promise of 14:28 and 16:7 had been thwarted, there would be no Christian community, and thus no Gospel of Mark, read and heard within the community. "This is the end of Mark's story, because it is the beginning of discipleship."[9]

Conclusion

It is noticeable that the storyteller designed the first half of his Gospel asking the question, "Who is Jesus?" The second half is designed to respond: "the suffering and vindicated Son of Man, the Christ and Son of God." However, these two "halves" of the plot overlap. Brick walls have not been erected between narrative units. One episode flows into the other, looks back to issues already mentioned, and hints at themes yet to come. Peter's confession of faith in Mark 8:29 might mark the closure of "The Mystery of the Messiah," but a theme of "blindness" has emerged in 8:22-26 in the strange story of a blind man at Bethsaida, who has his sight restored in stages. This theme will be resumed in 10:46-52 where a further story of a man coming to sight is reported: the story of blind Bartimaeus. Between these two miracle stories, where blind men are cured, Jesus speaks of the oncoming death and resurrection of the Son of Man (see 8:31; 9:31; 10:32-34), an issue hidden behind the events reported in 1:14-8:30 (see 3:6; 7:14-29; 8:11-15). After each of the passion predictions, Jesus instructs increasingly obtuse disciples who will not or cannot understand what it means to follow him (see 8:32-33; 9:33-37; 10:36-45). An earlier accusation of blindness also comes into play. After the second multiplication of the loaves and fishes (8:1-9) Jesus asks his dull disciples: "Do you not yet perceive or understand? Are your hearts hardened? Having eyes do you not see, and having ears do you not hear?" (8:18). This is but one example of Mark's ability to overlap, to look forward and to glance back, as he tells his story. [10]

Mark takes readers who are already familiar with the story through a new telling that transforms its well-known ending. Mark faced a problem stated some 20 years before the Gospel appeared: "For Jews demand signs and Greeks seek wisdom, but we preach Christ crucified, a stumbling block to Jews and folly to Gentiles, but to those who are called, both Jews and Greeks, Christ the power of God and the wisdom of God. For the foolishness of God is wiser than human wisdom, and the weakness of God is stronger than any human strength" (1 Cor 1:22-25). Mark also attempts to solve the scandal of the Cross by means of a story that begins as "the Good News" that Jesus is the Christ, the Son of God (1:1, 11), and ends with a scream from a Cross and an agonizing death, an empty tomb, and an Easter message that is not delivered (15:33-16:8). A story of the Christ and the Son of God that ends in this fashion is a narrative repetition of the Pauline message: "the foolishness of God is wiser than human wisdom, and the weakness of God is stronger than any human strength" (1 Cor 1:25). [11]

The Gospel's narrative structure can now be summarized, to offer a "road map" for the journey through Mark's story. Only a personal and/or shared reading of the Gospel itself can nourish a fuller understanding of the way the story unfolds. [12]

1. Prologue: The beginning (1:1-13).

2. The Mystery of Jesus (1:14-8:30).
   a) Jesus and the leaders of Israel (1:14-3:6).
   b) Jesus and his new family (3:7-6:6a).
   c) Jesus and the disciples (6:6b-8:30).

3. The suffering and vindicated Son of Man: Christ and Son of God (8:31-15:47).
   a) On the way from blindness to sight (8:31-10:52).
   b) The symbolic end of Israel and the world (11:1-13:37).
   c) The crucifixion of the Son of Man, Christ and Son of God (14:1-15:47).

4. Epilogue: A new beginning (16:1-8).

I conclude with a word of caution that should be kept in mind in all four "readings" of the Gospel that this book introduces. Having discovered the roadmap, the journey from this point on will not be easy. There are places in the Gospel of Mark where a reader finds the logic of the movement from one episode to the next hard to follow. We have become used to stories that flow smoothly, and tend to judge them according to the author's ability to lead the reader gently from one episode to the next. Such an easy passage is not always the case in the Gospel of Mark. For example, in 9:42-48, a series of sayings of Jesus that may have originally been independent, have been placed side by side on the basis of the repetition of the same words in the sayings ("cause to sin" [see vv. 42, 43, 45, 44], and "salt" [vv. 49, 50]). But the link between each saying is hard to trace, and one must strain one's imagination to follow the logic of vv. 42-48. These moments of obscurity in the narrative indicate the respect that the early writers in the Christian Church had for the traditions that came to them. Mark was a creative writer, but he respected words and events from the life of Jesus that he received. Mark's story must not be judged by the criteria we use to judge an enjoyable novel.

The tensions in the narrative should be resolved by the application of two principles. In the first instance, we need to understand that each Gospel storyteller attempted to write an account of the ministry, death and resurrection of Jesus that coherently communicated what he wanted to say to his original readers. We are historically, culturally, and even religiously distant from those original readers. We must allow ourselves to be challenged by the strangeness of this ancient text. Secondly, every reader strives "even if unconsciously, to fit everything together in a consistent pattern."[13] Inevitably a reader traces literary and theological connections across the Gospel that may be judged as the striving of that particular reader to impose her or his consistent pattern. That is an inevitable and perfectly acceptable part of the reading and listening process. It is true that, in some respects, we shape the meaning of what we read in the light of our own experiences and understanding.

But the text also shapes us. It is respect and admiration for a text that has been read again and again by many Christian individuals and within the life of the Christian Church that inspires our striving to understand the message of the Gospel of Mark. Despite Bultmann,[14] Mark was master of his material, and he used it to tell a striking tale that has stood the test of time.

Notes

[1] R. Bultmann, *History of the Synoptic Tradition* (tr. J. Marsh; Oxford: Blackwell, 1960), 350.

[2] A good introduction to this "change of direction" in reading the Gospel of Mark is D. Rhoads, J. Dewey and D. Michie, *Mark as Story: An Introduction to the Narrative of a Gospel* (2d ed.; Minneapolis: Fortress, 1999).

[3] See the important essay by E. Schweizer, "Mark's Theological Achievement," in *The Interpretation of Mark* (ed. W. Telford; Issues in Religion and Theology 7; Philadelphia: Fortress, 1985), 42-63.

[4] For more detailed analysis of Mark 1:1-13, and the function of a prologue in a Gospel, see Chapter Three: *Reading Mark 1:1-13: A Prologue to the Gospel.*

[5] For this proposal, which many have followed, see Schweizer, "Mark's Theological Achievement," 46-54.

[6] For a more detailed description of the narrative art used in assembling 2:1-3:6, see F. J. Moloney, *The Gospel of Mark. A Commentary* (Peabody: Hendrickson, 2002), 45-48.

[7] Most translations render this as he would not allow anyone "to carry anything" through the Temple. The word *skeuos* has a wide range of meanings, but it is regularly attested, especially in the LXX, as meaning a vessel to be used in cultic activity. For more detail, see Moloney, *Mark*, 223-24.

[8] See F. J. Moloney, *A Body Broken for a Broken People* (2d ed.; Peabody: Hendrickson, 1997), 31-56.

[9] M. D. Hooker, *The Gospel according to St. Mark* (Black's New Testament Commentaries; Peabody: Hendrickson, 1991), 394.

[10] For extensive consideration of this phenomenon in the Gospel of Mark, see J. Dewey, "Mark as Interwoven Tapestry: Forecasts and Echoes for a Listening Audience," *Catholic Biblical Quarterly* 53 (1991): 225-36; E. S. Malbon, "Echoes and Foreshadowings in Mark 4-8: Reading and ReReading," *Journal of Biblical Literature* 112 (1993): 211-30.

[11] On Mark 16:1-8 and the failure of the women, see Moloney, *Mark*, 239-54 and, more theologically, Idem, *Storyteller*, 191-95.

[12] For my attempt to "read the whole story," see Moloney, *Mark* and more briefly in Idem, *Storyteller*, 59-121.

[13] W. Iser, *The Implied Reader: Patterns of Communication in Prose Fiction from Bunyan to Beckett* (Baltimore: Johns Hopkins University Press, 1978), 283.

[14] See above, and note 1.

Reading Mark 1:1-13:
A Prologue to the Gospel

All four Gospels have a prologue, and their purpose is the same: to inform the reader of the story of Jesus that follows, of the fundamental truths about who he is and what he does. Mark uses three voices to establish the authority of Jesus as the Messiah: the Scriptures, John the Baptist, and God. However, at the end of the prologue the reader is well informed about who Jesus is, but as yet unaware of how Jesus fulfils his identity and how in his person God's original creative design has been restored. The prologue lays down this challenge. Once the reader knows who Jesus is, they must be prepared to read through a story which will show how Jesus pleases his Father.

Chapter 3
summary

ALREADY IN ANTIQUITY, CERTAIN CONVENTIONS were established for beginning a story. It has therefore long been recognized that "placing an item at the beginning or at the end may radically change the process of reading as well as the final product."[1] Even an uninitiated reader will notice that the Gospels of Matthew, Luke and John have a "beginning" that is different from the body of the Gospel. Matthew and Luke have a birth narrative (Matt 1-2; Luke 1-2), and John has a hymn that summarizes the christological proclamation of the Gospel which follows (John 1:1-18). Although not so immediately obvious, the Gospel of Mark's account of the activity of John the Baptist (Mark 1:1-13) also serves as a prologue to the story that follows.[2]

Most commentators see vv. 1-13 as made up of a superscription from the hand of the author (v. 1), a description of the person and activity of John the Baptist (vv. 2-8), the baptism of Jesus (vv. 9-11), and his temptation (vv. 12-13). This division of the text respects the intense presentation of both Jesus and John the Baptist. It is determined by the characters involved in these verses, but other narrative criteria could be used. If one pays attention to changes in character and action, time and place, and especially to the eyes through which the events reported are seen, generally called the "focalization" present in a story, five discrete sections emerge.[3]

1. *Verses 1-3*: The voice of the narrator opens the story, but what he announces reflects an omniscience that associates his words with the design of God. The narrator speaks with a "godly authority" which the reader cannot question. With the exception of Mark 13:14 ("Let the reader understand"), the narrator does not enter the story actively, and God only rarely (see 1:2-3, 11; 9:7), but God determines it and the narrator shapes it. A story of "good news" is at its "beginning," and the news is that a man called Jesus is Christ, Son *of God*.[4] Only a narrator at one with God's omniscience can tell the story of the "Son of God." The words that follow (vv. 2-3) are "Words of God." They are taken from the Prophets Malachi 3:1 and Isaiah 40:3, with some help from Exodus 23:20, and God speaks in the first person. The narrator and the voice of God utter a divine message, announcing the beginning of the Good News that Jesus is the Christ, the Son of God, and that God is sending a messenger to prepare the way of "the Lord." The divine message is the focus of the opening verses, announcing that the good news that follows will have to do with Jesus, Christ, Son of God, Lord.

2. *Verses 4-6*: The narrator takes over and tells of the partial

fulfillment of God's promise. Although he performs no actions, the one who will prepare the way (vv. 2-3) appears and is described.
3. *Verses 7-8*: The Baptist now becomes the focal person in the narrative. He is no longer described, as he speaks in the first person, announcing the coming of "the stronger one," one before whom he is unworthy who "will baptize with the Holy Spirit." He is preparing the way for "the Lord."
4. *Verses 9-11*: As with the introduction to the Baptist (vv. 4-6), the narrator again takes over and presents Jesus. Jesus does nothing, but things happen to him. John baptizes him, the Spirit descends upon him, and a voice from heaven describes him. What Jesus might think of this is not told. God makes things happen to Jesus.
5. *Verses 12-13*: Described by an omniscient narrator, the actions of Jesus and promises made to him dominate this final section. Although God's design continues to unfold, things still happen to him (the Spirit drives him into the desert, he is tempted by Satan, and ministered to by angels), for the first time in the narrative, Jesus becomes the active agent: "He was with the wild beasts" (v. 13).

God dominates this prologue, mentioned by name in v. 1, and present in direct speech in vv. 2-3. In vv. 4-5 and 6-8 the Baptist is the subject of most of the verbs, but his activity fulfills what God had promised in vv. 2-3. The Baptist points away from himself and eventually fades from the scene as Jesus of Nazareth is introduced as a third person figure. God and the Spirit are the main actors in Jesus' initial experiences until, at the close of vv. 1-13, Jesus is *with* the wild beasts and served by the angels. This prologue establishes an important truth for the reader: the chief agent in the action which follows is God. The Gospel of Mark may read like the story of "Jesus of Nazareth" (see 1:24; 10:47; 14:67; 16:6), but its prologue suggests that an omniscient narrator tells the story of how God acts among us through the death and resurrection of the Messiah and Son.[5] This is a strange way for a God to deal with his Son, but the reader is made aware from the first page of the story that the events of the life and death of Jesus of Nazareth are determined by the pleasure of God (v. 11: "You are my beloved Son; with you I am pleased").

Reading Mark 1:1-13
Now that we have established the narrative structure of vv. 1-13, carefully following the voice of the figure reporting each sub-section of the account, we can turn to a reading of the passage.

1. Verses 1-3

The first word echoes the opening of Genesis: "the beginning," but it also indicates the beginning of a long story. Both meanings are involved. The Gospel of Mark "begins" with an echo of God's original creative design (Gen 1:1). But it is "the Gospel" which begins, not the creation. The link with creation is left on hold as the person of Jesus is introduced. It will reappear later in the prologue, catching the reader and the listener somewhat by surprise. The expression "the good news" was used in the LXX and the Greco-Roman world. Second Isaiah used it to proclaim the "good news" of God's rule, salvation or vindication (see LXX Isaiah 40:9; 41:27; 52:7; 60:6; 61:1). The Greek writers used it to announce a military victory, a royal birth, or a political triumph.[6] The newness of the Markan usage in 1:1 is the noun, describing the story of a human being. The good news is: Jesus is the Christ, the Son of God. The Evangelist Mark introduced a new literary form into world literature: a narrative of the life, death and resurrection of Jesus that did not pretend to recount the brute facts of history. It was written to proclaim that Jesus was the Christ, the Son of God. He called this narrative form "the Good News."

The two expressions "Jesus" and "Christ" had become the proper name Jesus Christ before Mark wrote his Gospel, but the rapid succession of the name of a man "Jesus," and then the further descriptions of him as "Christ, the Son of God" proclaim who he is. The Good News is that Jesus of Nazareth is the Christ, the Son of God. Accepting, provisionally, a reading including "Son of God," Jesus' being the Son of God will become increasingly important as the narrative unfolds (see 1:11; 3:11; 5:7; 9:7; 14:61; 15:39). The notion will develop a character of its own which will stretch the traditional understanding of the expression. However, as the Gospel opens the reader is informed that, like the ideal King of Israel (see 2 Sam 7:14; Psalm 2:7; 89:26-29) and the chosen people of Israel (see Exod 4:22; Isaiah 63:16; Hos 11:1), Jesus can be regarded as "Son of God," and thus "Messiah," because of his relationship with God. This relationship will have some strange twists as the story unfolds, and much still lies ahead of the reader before the full significance of what "Christ, Son of God" might mean will be finally unveiled.

God enters the narrative, by means of the words of his prophet,[7] and two further elements are added to the story: there will be a God-appointed forerunner, and the one who is to come is called "the Lord"

(vv. 2-3). In v. 1 the narrator spoke with divine omniscience, but in vv. 2-3 God speaks directly. This is made clear by the use of the passive: "as it has been written" and the voice of God speaking in the first person through the words of the prophet. The author is God and the voice is God's. God speaks as "I" to "you": "I send *my* messenger before *your* face." God announces that a messenger will precede the coming of the one addressed. The prophetic passages report words of God to someone who is addressed. The one addressed is to make a journey down his "way." The theme of "the way" will have its place later in the story, but for the moment it is introduced as part of God's design for the coming one.[8] The one addressed as "you" ("before *your* [singular] face") in v. 2b becomes "the Lord" in v. 3b. A messenger will cry out in the wilderness: "prepare the way of the Lord." The "you" addressed by God in v. 2 is "the Lord" in v. 3. The combination of prophecies from Malachi, Exodus and Isaiah to provide words of God to begin the narrative, witnesses to the coming one as "the Lord." This expression (Greek: *ho kyrios*) is used systematically in the LXX to translate YHWH, the sacred name for God.[9] God names a figure, yet to appear actively in the story, *by God's own name.* But there is a third person involved in these words of God, a messenger who will prepare the way of the Lord. God has set the agenda. Jesus Christ, Son of God has not only been announced in v. 1, but the word of God has described him as "the Lord" who must go down a God-directed way, prepared by another character yet to appear.

2. Verses 4-6

The first figure announced by the voice of God is described in vv. 4-6. What had been promised in v. 3a: "a voice crying *in the wilderness,*" happens in v. 4a, John the Baptist "appeared *in the wilderness.*" This is the messenger God sends before the face of the one addressed in v. 2b, whose divinely ordered task was to prepare the way of "the Lord" (v. 3b). What God says will happen does happen. Thus it will be throughout the entire story. The Baptist's preaching of repentance has its roots in the prophetic call for a wholehearted return to YHWH (see, for example, Jer 18:11; Isaiah 55:7; Zech 1:4) through a "turning back" toward Israel's unique God.[10] The brief description of the Baptist's appearance and diet enhance his association with similar prophetic figures. Jesus will later identify John with Elijah (see 9:11-13) marking a similarity between the dress and life style of Elijah and the Baptist (see 2 Kings 1:8). Yet the description of his dress is nothing more than "the nomadic attire of the wilderness in general and ... the prophetic dress in particular."[11]   He lives as an ascetic, neither eating meat nor drinking wine. Such behavior is typical of late Jewish prophets (see, for example, Dan 1:18). For the moment, John the Baptist appears as one sent by God to announce a message of God.

The practice of a baptism for the forgiveness of sins is more difficult to locate within the religious culture and practice of the time. In historical terms, John's name, "the baptizer," "the plunger" or "the immerser," reflected a memorable aspect of his ministry. However familiar the Christian tradition is with this practice, it was rare in the pre-Christian period. There is newness about the baptismal activity of John, linked with the Baptist's preparing for the crucially important event of the one who is to come. Evidence exists for a use of baptism for proselytes by the Pharisees, and it was part of the rituals performed at Qumran. Both groups regarded it as an external sign of a serious commitment to "turning back" to God, but the Baptist's activity appears closer to proselyte baptism than to the rites practiced at Qumran. The effectiveness of John's preaching is enhanced by the rhetorical statement that "all the country of Judea and all the country of Jerusalem" went out to him at the Jordan. This is hardly likely, but the author makes his point: John the Baptist made a great impression, and "the fact that everything was astir indicated that the special salvation-time had begun when the gospel would reach out to the whole world (13:10)."[12] Many submit themselves to John's baptism to acknowledge their sins and turn back to God, but the reader is aware that this is not the main event. God's words have pointed forward to the coming of "the Lord" (v. 3), but someone would prepare this "coming" (vv. 2-3). The storyteller is ultimately interested in the action of God. The Baptist belongs to a long line of God's prophets. Although merely the one sent before the face ... to prepare the way of the Lord (vv. 2-3), his person (v. 6) and activities (vv. 4-5) are God-determined, and look forward to the coming of "the Stronger One" (see v. 7).

3. Verses 7-8

The direct speech of John the Baptist's proclamation changes the focus of the prologue at v. 7. While vv. 4-6 reported a description of the Baptist, he announces his message in vv. 7-8. A prophet of Israel traditionally recalled YHWH's *past* saving intervention, but the Baptist fulfills God's *future* promise of v. 3. He points *forward* to the future coming of "the Stronger One." This expression may not summon up directly messianic claims, but God has regularly been called "the Mighty One" in the LXX (see Deut 10:17; Judges 6:12; 2 Sam 2:32-33, 48; Jer 27:24; 32:18; Dan 9:4; Neh 1:15; 9:31-32; 2 Sam 22:31; 23:5; Ps 7:12. See also Isaiah 9:6). The term "the Strong One" is often found in the Book of Job (see Job 22:13; 33:29; 36:22, 26; 37:5). It always refers to God. The words of the Baptist shift the focus from himself (see vv. 4-6) to the mightier one who will come after him (vv. 7-8). As in v. 3b, where God spoke of the coming one as "the Lord," the forerunner uses another expression associated in the LXX with God. Before he has appeared in the narrative, the reader has already been told of Jesus, the Christ, the Son of God (v. 1), the Lord (v. 3), the Stronger One (v. 7). The use of "the Lord" and "the Stronger One" even suggest that the claims made only for the God of Israel, Lord and Mighty One, are being shifted to the one who is to come.

For all the greatness of the Baptist, the messenger of God sent to prepare the way of "the Lord," a gulf lies between the messenger and the one he announces. Untying the master's sandals was the one demeaning task never required of a Hebrew servant. "To be unworthy of such a task would be to lower oneself below the status of a slave."[13] The Baptist's final words in the Gospel of Mark look back to his practice of baptizing: "I have baptized (past tense) you with water," and forward to the future activity of Jesus: "He will baptize (future tense) you with the Holy Spirit" (v. 8). The narrator has already described John's baptism in vv. 4-5, and the idea of a baptism with the spirit is not entirely new. The prophet Ezekiel had promised, in the name of YHWH:

> I will sprinkle clean water upon you, and you shall be clean from all your uncleannesses, and from all your idols I will cleanse you. A new heart I will give you, and a new spirit I will put within you; and I will take out of your flesh the heart of stone and give you a heart of flesh. And I will put my spirit within you, and cause you to walk in my statutes and be careful to observe my ordinances (Ezek 36:25-27)

The Qumran sectarians and later Judaism spoke of a spirit-baptism in which the Spirit was a gift of God to the faithful, and his promises for them would be realized through this gift.[14] It is not so much the idea of a gift of a "holy spirit" which is new, but the proclamation that the coming one would dispense this gift. Not only are the names of God

("Lord" and "Mighty One") taken over by the coming one, but also one of God's functions as the giver of the Spirit.

4. Verses 9-11

To this point in the prologue, Jesus the Christ, the Son of God (v. 1) has not appeared in the narrative. God has been the main actor, through his word (vv. 1-3) and the partial fulfillment of that word (vv. 4-8). Jesus' entry is solemnly announced in a Greek version of a heavily Semitic introduction (see Exod 2:11; Judges 19:1; 1 Sam 28:1) of an important character into a story: "And it came to pass in those days that Jesus came from Nazareth of Galilee." John the Baptist had been introduced with the simple "it came to pass" (v. 4), but Jesus' active involvement has a more solemn biblical introduction: "and it came to pass in those days." The formula "in those days" also highlights the eschatological or definitive nature of Jesus' "coming" (see Jer 31:33; Joel 3:1; Zech 8:23). The significant claims made for Jesus earlier in the prologue are coming to resolution, but are momentarily left aside as the reader is told that he comes from a little known village, Nazareth, which calls for further identification: "of Galilee."[15] John the Baptist baptizes Jesus by immersing him in the river Jordan. But as Jesus *comes up* (v. 10a) from the water, a series of events are reported during which divine signs *come down* (v. 10b). Jesus has a vision: "He saw heaven opened and the Spirit descending upon him like a dove." The tearing open of the skies marks the beginning of a new era. "God has ripped the heavens apart irrevocably at Jesus' baptism, never to shut them again. Through this gracious gash in the universe, he has poured forth his Spirit into the earthly realm."[16]

In a world where God abides above the firmament and the human story takes place below, the opening of the heavens promises a communication from above to below (see Gen 7:11; Isaiah 24:18; 64:1; Ezek 1:1; Rev 4:1; 11:19). The messenger has performed his God-given task: going before the face and preparing the way for the Lord. We read of Jesus' experiences in vv. 9-11, but God's action is reported. The Spirit descends upon Jesus, a hint of the older promise of the gift of the Spirit in the new creation, especially as it had been announced by the prophet Isaiah (see especially Isaiah 42:1-5, but also 11:1-3; 61:1; 63:10-14). It is as one gifted with the Spirit (v. 10) that Jesus will baptize with the Spirit (v. 8). The appearance of creation themes recalls the adumbration of the creation story by means of the word "beginning" in v. 1 (see Gen 1:1). In

Gen 1:3 the Spirit of God was hovering over the face of the waters, and in Mark 1:10 the Spirit of God descends upon Jesus "like a dove." There is no precedent for the Markan link between the Spirit and the dove. The use of the symbol is to be taken at its face value. The Spirit of God, who cannot be *seen*, gently descends upon Jesus like a dove, which he can see. Jesus, Christ and Son of God (v. 1), the Lord (v. 3) and the Stronger One (v. 7) who will dispense the Holy Spirit (v. 8), has now been gifted with the Spirit (v. 10).[17]

Jesus' vision of the gift of the Holy Spirit, through the medium of the gently descending dove, is paired with an aural experience: he *hears* a voice from heaven. The Rabbis often spoke about a voice from above which indicated God's mind (the *bath qōl*), but this is merely a sound, sometimes little more than a shadowy hint. What Jesus hears is a "voice" coming from heaven. What has already been made clear in the prologue to this point is authoritatively re-stated by the voice of God: "You are my Son, the Beloved, with you I am well pleased." The claim made by the omniscient narrator in v. 1 ("the Christ, the Son of God") is confirmed by the voice of God in v. 11. The words from heaven are close to words of God reported in Psalm 2:7: "You are my Son." But the Markan voice of God insists further on the uniqueness of the Son by describing him as "the beloved." The same expression was used to describe the special relationship that existed between Abraham and Isaac; his "beloved son" (see LXX Gen 22:2, 12, 16). Perhaps this suggestion of the love between Abraham and Isaac, whom he was asked to sacrifice as a sign of his unconditional allegiance to YHWH, is a first subtle hint of Jesus' destiny.[18] The final words of God indicate the quality of the relationship between the Father and the Son: "with you I am well pleased." As the Gospel will show, through the Son's encounter with the forces that oppose God and God's original design for humankind, God's pleasure works itself out in surprising ways.

5. *Verses 12-13*

Thus far Jesus has come from Nazareth (v. 9), risen from the water (v. 10a), and seen the dove (v. 10b). These actions, however, have put him in the right place so that others (the Baptist and God) might do things *to* him and *for* him. The final section of the prologue continues Jesus' fundamentally passive role: "The Spirit immediately drove him out into the wilderness" (v. 12). The promises of earlier parts of the prologue continue to be fulfilled. The Baptist promised that Jesus would baptize with a holy spirit (v. 8), the heavens have opened and the Spirit has descended upon him (v. 10). The Spirit has taken possession of Jesus, and is now the driving force of his actions. A strong verb ("drove out") associated with the famous Markan use of "immediately" (Greek: *euthus*) illustrates the divine urgency which determines the actions of Jesus.[19] Jesus is still the subject of the actions of God, driven out "into the desert," as God's words had earlier predicted (vv. 2-3). The desert wilderness has a number of meanings in the Old Testament, Judaism and early Christianity. Above all, however, it is a place of ambiguity. This ambivalence has its origins in the experience of the Hebrew people after their liberation from Egypt and their crossing of the Reed Sea. The desert was for Israel a place of refuge against aggression, a place of privileged encounter with God, but also a place of physical and moral trials, of temptation and sin. The theme continues into the experiences of many Old Testament personalities (for example, Abraham, Elijah and David).[20] Against this background the authors of Genesis present the fallen state of humankind divided against itself, expelled from a garden where creation was in harmony, into a place where the land and its animal inhabitants rebel against a man and a woman, who are themselves in conflict (see Gen 2:15-25; 3:14-21).[21]

Moses was forty days and forty nights on Mt Sinai without bread or water (see Exod 34:28; Deut 9:9, 18), and Elijah fled through the desert for forty days without food (1 Kings 19:4-8). Jesus is in the wilderness for forty days (v. 13a). Like Moses and Elijah, he experiences the ambiguity of the desert, and in this ambiguity he is exposed to the experience of the man and woman in Eden, tempted by Satan (v. 13b). But here the parallel falters. Adam was tempted by Satan, fell, and was driven out of the garden (LXX Gen 3:24: "He [YHWH] *drove out* Adam"). Jesus, filled with the Spirit (v. 10), is *driven* by that Spirit into the wilderness (v. 12). The reader is not told explicitly of Jesus' fall or victory (unlike Matt 4:1-11//Luke 4:1-13). Jesus is tempted by Satan, and "he was with the wild beasts; and the angels ministered to him" (v. 13b). For the first time in the narrative Jesus is alone, and takes the initiative: "he was with the wild beasts." This may appear irrelevant, something expected if one spends too much time in the wilderness (!), or even a note which links this Gospel to the experience of the Roman Christians thrown to the wild beasts during the Neronic persecution.[22] Yet, "[t]his phrase, distinctive to Mark's account, holds the key to his temptation narrative."[23]

In the Genesis story Satan's victory over Adam led to hostility and fear in creation (see Gen 3:14-21; Psalm 91:11-13). In the Markan story that situation is reversed: he is *with* the wild beasts. Prophetic tradition surrounding the new creation has been fulfilled (see Isaiah 11:6-9. See also Isaiah 35:3-10; Ezek 34:23-31). One of the dreams of first century Judaism has been realized in the coming of Jesus: what was in the beginning has been restored.[24] This link with the creation myths is further enhanced by the final remark of the narrator: "and the angels ministered to him." Once again Exodus, Elijah and creation motifs are present in this lapidary statement. Repeatedly throughout the desert experience of Israel angels help and guide the wondering people (see Exod 14:19; 23:20, 23; 32:34; 33:2). During Elijah's experience of despair and hunger in the wilderness, he is served by the angels (1 Kings 19:5-7). Although not present in the Genesis account, Jewish documents wonder about the nourishment of Adam and Eve in the Garden of Eden. They were fed by the angels.[25]

Only toward the end of the prologue does the hint return of the link with the original creation, provided by the "beginning" of v. 1. Jesus is "with the wild beasts" and "waited on" by the angels. His coming has repeated the experience of the original people of God in the desert, but above all, it has restored the original order of God's creation. The promise of "the beginning" in v. 1 (see Gen 1:1), and the coming of the creative presence of the Spirit of God in v. 10 (see Gen 1:3) indicate that the prologue to the Gospel of Mark is linked to the prologue to the human story, as it was told in Genesis 1-11. God has been the most active figure in Mark 1:1-13. Jesus has been *presented* to the reader. He is the Christ, the Son of God (v. 1), the Lord (v. 3), the Stronger One (v. 7), one who will baptize with the Holy Spirit (v. 8).[26] God's voice has assured the reader that he is the beloved Son of God, and that God is well pleased with him (v. 11). He is filled with the Spirit (v. 10), and driven into the desert to reverse the tragedy of the Adam and Eve story, to re-establish God's original design (vv. 12-13).

Conclusion

The story-teller has provided a dense prologue for the reader/listener. Nothing should allow the reader to doubt *who Jesus is*. However, hints throughout the prologue point to a ministry, if he is to baptize with a holy spirit (v. 8). There is perhaps even a hint that he will accept total and unconditional self-sacrifice as God's "beloved" (v. 11). The reader comes to the end of the prologue well informed about *who* Jesus is, but as yet unaware of *how* Jesus is the Christ, the Son of God, the Lord, the Stronger One who baptizes with the Holy Spirit, and *how* in his person God's original creative design has been restored. The readers of this Gospel know that Jesus of Nazareth was crucified, and they may well wonder how such an end could be pleasing to God (see v. 11).[27] The prologue to the Gospel lays down this challenge. Now the reader knows *who Jesus is*, and must be prepared to read through a story which will show *how Jesus pleases his Father.*

Only the reader of (or listener to) the Gospel is aware of what has been said in the prologue. The various characters in the story: the Pharisees, the crowds, the Romans, and *especially* the disciples, have not read the prologue. By informing the reader – on the very first page of the story – of *who* Jesus is, the author issues a challenge. *In what way* does Jesus, the Son, respond to God's understanding of him? *How* does he live a life, preach a message and die a death which restore God's original design and make the Father delight in him (v. 11)?[28] Answers to these questions can only be found by reading or listening to the story that follows. The prologue has *told* the reader and the listener *who* Jesus is and *what* he does; but the story is needed to *show* the reader and the listener *how* this took place.[29]

There is little in the Gospel of Mark explicitly directed to the reader (see, however, 13:14).[30] But the reader has been the unique focus of the words of 1:1-13. However, at the end of the story (16:1-8) the author will return to the readers. They will be asked where they stand as they hear: "And they went out and fled from the tomb; for trembling and astonishment had come upon them; and they said nothing to anyone, for they were afraid" (16:8). The Gospel of Mark has both a prologue and an epilogue during which the author focuses intensely upon those who will read and who have read the intervening narrative of 1:14-15:47.

This first close reading of a Gospel text introduces the literary form of a "prologue." As I mentioned at the beginning of the chapter, all four Gospels have a prologue. The purpose of all four prologues is the same: to inform the reader of the story of Jesus that follows of the fundamental truths about *who he is* and *what he does.* "Informed readers" set out on the experience of the Markan story of the life of Jesus. But the characters in the story, who have not read the prologue, will struggle to come to grips with Jesus' person and mission. There may be some surprising turns in the story, but the readers are challenged to hold fast to what they have been told in the prologue.

Mark tells of John the Baptist, Jesus' baptism and temptation. Matthew (Matt 1-2) and Luke (Luke 1-2) tell of Jesus' infancy, while John opens his Gospel with a christological poem (John 1:1-18).[31] Despite the differences in literary form, each of these prologues performs the same task, drawing the reader into the story of Jesus. As the story unfolds, informed readers are aware of who Jesus is and what he has done. However, as the rest of the Gospel of Mark is told, the readers will be challenged by the strangeness of God's ways, especially in the mystery of the crucifixion of the beloved Son.[32]

Notes

[1] S. Rimmon-Kenan, *Narrative Fiction: Contemporary Poetics* (New Accents; London: Methuen, 1983), 120. On the use of prologues in antiquity, see the survey of D. E. Smith, "Narrative Beginnings in Ancient Literature and Theory," *Semeia* 52 (1991): 1-9.

[2] A number of recent critics have argued that Mark's prologue is vv. 1-15, rather than vv. 1-13. Especially important for this case was the study of L. Keck, "The Introduction to Mark's Gospel," *New Testament Studies* 12 (1965-66): 352-70. For more detail, and a defence of vv. 1-13 as the prologue, see F. J. Moloney, *The Gospel of Mark. A Commentary* (Peabody: Hendrickson, 2002), 27-28.

[3] The expression "focalization" is used in narrative criticism in reference to the eyes through which the reported events are seen. On this, see G. Genette, *Narrative Discourse. An Essay in Method* (Ithaca: Cornell University Press, 1980), 189-221, and Idem, *Narrative Discourse Revisited* (Ithaca: Cornell University Press, 1988), 72-78. See also Rimmon-Kenan, *Narrative Fiction*, 71-85.

[4] Many ancient manuscripts do not contain the words "of God." I am tentatively accepting it. Along with most who regard it as secondary, in the light of the use of "Son" and "Son of God" through the Gospel, John Painter (*Mark's Gospel: Worlds in Conflict* [New Testament Readings; London: Routledge, 1997] remarks: "The title is entirely appropriate" (p. 25). Whether or not "Son of God" should be read as authentic in v. 1 is not crucial. The use of the expression "my beloved Son" in the description of Jesus in v. 11 makes clear that the prologue leaves the reader with no doubt that Jesus is "the Christ" (v. 1) and "the Son of God" (v. 1?; v. 11).

[5] On the centrality of God in the Gospel of Mark, see J. R. Donahue, "A Neglected Factor in the Theology of Mark," *Journal of Biblical Literature* 101 (1982): 563-94.

[6] Both in the LXX and in the Greco-Roman documents, the verb-form "to proclaim the gospel" is mostly found. Paul uses the noun "gospel" to announce his gospel message of God's victory won in the death and resurrection of Jesus.

[7] The narrator only mentions Isaiah, but, as noted above, the text of vv. 2-3 is a

conflation of Exod 23:20 and Mal 3:1 (v. 2), and Isaiah 40:3 (v. 3).

[8] For a rich understanding of "the way" in the Gospel, and the possible allusion to this meaning for the Marcan community in 1:3, see J. Marcus, *The Way of the Lord. Christological Exegesis of the Old Testament in the Gospel of Mark* (Louisville: Westminster/John Knox Press, 1992), 29-47.

[9] J. Marcus, *Mark 1-8* (The Anchor Bible 27; New York: Doubleday, 2000), 147-48, rightly warns against identification between God and Jesus. He correctly suggests the interpretation: "where Jesus is acting, there God is acting" (p. 148).

[10] The Greek verb *metanoeō* translates the Hebrew *shûb*, which means to "turn back" or to "return." It implies a complete turning back from one's present direction.

[11] R. Guelich, *Mark 1-8:26* (Word Biblical Commentary 34a: Dallas: Word Books, 1989), 21.

[12] E. Schweizer, *The Good News According to Mark* (London: SPCK, 1971), 33.

[13] Guelich, *Mark*, 24.

[14] See Guelich, *Mark*, 24-26, for a discussion of the Qumran and other pre-Christian Jewish material. For J. P. Meier, *A Marginal Jew. Rethinking the Historical Jesus* (3 vols.; Anchor Bible Reference Library; New York: Doubleday, 1991-2001), 2:53-56, Mark records the distinction between the baptism "for the forgiveness of sins" which is preparatory, and the baptism in the Holy Spirit which marks the arrival of the eschatological age.

[15] C. Myers, *Binding the Strong Man. A Political Reading of Mark's Story of Jesus* (Maryknoll: Orbis Books, 1990), 128, comments: "tantamount to announcing him as 'Jesus from Nowheresville'."

[16] Marcus, *Mark*, 165.

[17] On the possibility of the descent of the Spirit upon Jesus as the moment on his becoming Messiah and Son of God, see Marcus, *Mark*, 160.

[18] See Marcus, *Mark*, 162.

[19] Mark uses this adverb more times in his 664 verses (47 times) than the rest of the New Testament put together. It is often omitted in translation, but the rhythmic appearance of this word is deliberate. It indicates the urgency of what God is doing in and through Jesus.

[20] On this theme, see Meier, *A Marginal Jew*, 2:43-46. The ambiguous nature of the desert wilderness continues into the early Church. See Athanasius, *Life of Anthony* (trans. R. C. Cregg; The Classics of Western Spirituality; London: SPCK, 1980), 33-65; P. Brown, *The Body and Society. Men, Women and Sexual Renunciation in Early Christianity* (London: Faber & Faber, 1988), 213-40.

[21] With this paragraph I am suggesting that the use of "the desert" in Mark 1:12-13 (prepared in 1:2-3) is linked with the fall in Genesis, rather than with the Exodus. This does not exclude the possibility of the presence of Exodus themes here. On the primacy of the story of Adam (and Jewish reflection upon Adam) in vv. 12-13, see Marcus, *Mark*, 169-70.

[22] See, for example, W. L. Lane, *Commentary on the Gospel of Mark* (The New International Commentary on the New Testament; Grand Rapids: Eerdmans, 1974), 38.

[23] Guelich, *Mark*, 38.

[24] See also Waetjen, *A Reordering of Power: A Socio-Political Reading of Mark's Gospel* (Minneapolis: Fortress, 1989), 74-77. On Jewish hopes for the restoration of the Adamic situation, see R. Scroggs, *The Last Adam. A Study in Pauline Anthropology* (Oxford: Blackwell, 1966); W. D. Davies and D. C. Allison, *A Critical and Exegetical Commentary on the Gospel according to Saint Matthew* (3 vols.; ICC; Edinburgh: T. & T. Clark, 1988-98), 1:356-57.

[25] For extensive documentation in support of this position, see Davies and Allison, *Saint Matthew*, 1:356-57. For a more detailed presentation of the final verses of the prologue as a return to God's original creative design for humankind, in Adam and Eve, see Moloney, *Mark*, 37-40.

[26] Waetjen, *Reordering*, 22, speaks of Jesus in the prologue as "God's surrogate."

[27] The reader still has a great deal to learn and experience via the story of Jesus. On this, see F. J. Matera, *New Testament Christology* (Louisville: Westminster John Knox Press, 1999), 6-10. On the role of "telling" and "showing" in narrative, see W. C. Booth, *The Rhetoric of Fiction* (2nd Edition; Chicago: University of Chicago Press, 1983), 3-20.

[28] See Marcus, *The Way of the Lord*, 75-77.

[29] J. Drury, "Mark," in *The Literary Guide to the Bible* (ed. A. Alter and F. Kermode; London: Collins, 1987), 405, puts it well: "Between the understanding given us in its first verse and the radical insecurity and incomprehension of the subsequent tale, Mark's book gets its energy."

[30] This rare but important comment from the narrator, "Let the reader understand" (Mark 13:14), is an indication that, despite the fact that the narrator does not regularly address the reader through the narrative, the reader is the focus of the narrator's story-telling.

[31] The literary form of an infancy narrative will be the subject of Chapter Five, a close reading of Matthew 1-2.

[32] The literary form of a passion and resurrection narrative will be the subject of Chapter Seven, a close reading of Luke 22:1-24:53.

Commentaries on the Gospel of Mark

The following list of single-volume commentaries on the Gospel of Mark is not exhaustive. An interested reader will find any of the below commentaries useful. I have listed the single volumes of R. A. Guelich and C. A. Evans in the Word Commentary series, even though together they form one commentary. Full reference to the as yet unfinished two volume outstanding commentary of Joel Marcus in the Anchor Bible series can be found in the footnotes of the preceding chapters.

Anderson, H. *The Gospel of Mark*. New Century Bible. London: Oliphants, 1976.

Dowd, S. *Reading Mark: A Literary and Theological Commentary on the Second Gospel*. Reading the New Testament Series; Macon, GA: Smyth & Helwys, 2000.

Edwards, J. R. *The Gospel According to Mark*. Pillar New Testament Commentary. Grand Rapids: Eerdmans, 2002.

Evans, C. A. *Mark 8:27-16:20*. Word Biblical Commentary 34b. Nashville: Thomas Nelson, 2001. This volume completes the work of R. A. Guelich (see below).

France, R. T. *The Gospel of Mark: A Commentary on the Greek Text*. New International Greek Testament Commentary. Grand Rapids: Eerdmans, 2002.

Guelich, R. A., *Mark 1-8:26*. Word Biblical Commentary 34a. Dallas: Word Books, 1989.

Hooker, M. D.. *The Gospel according to St. Mark* (Black's New Testament Commentary. Peabody: Hendrickson, 1991.

Lane, W. L. *Commentary on the Gospel of Mark*. The New International Commentary on the New Testament. Grand Rapids: Eerdmans, 1974.

Malbon, E. S. *Hearing Mark: A Listener's Guide*. Harrisburg, PA: Trinity Press International, 2002.

Moloney, F. J. *The Gospel of Mark. A Commentary*. Peabody: Hendrickson, 2002.

Myers, C. *Binding the Strong Man: A Political Reading of Mark's Story of Jesus.* Maryknoll: Orbis Books, 1990.

Nineham, D. E. *The Gospel of St. Mark.* Pelican New Testament Commentaries. Harmondsworth: Penguin Books, 1963.

Painter, J. *Mark's Gospel: Worlds in Conflict.* New Testament Readings. London: Routledge, 1997.

Schweizer, E. *The Good News according to Mark.* Translated by D. E. Madvig. London: SPCK, 1971.

Wright, N. T. *Mark for Everyone.* London: SPCK, 2001.

PART III

The Gospel of Matthew

Reading the Gospel of Matthew

Matthew is judged as the Church's Gospel yet is often thought of as the most Jewish. How does Matthew juggle this contradiction and why?

The Matthean community understood itself in terms of the sending of the disciples into the Gentile mission (28:16-20). On a new Sinai a new and perfect Moses gives a new People of God a new Law. But earlier Jesus says:

"Think not that I have come to abolish the Law and the Prophets; I have not come to abolish them, but to fulfill them." (Matt. 5:17).

Matthew deliberately structures his narrative of Jesus to resolve the seeming contradiction. He gives his account so that his community might see the perfection of the old, through the death and resurrection of Jesus, in the newness which they are living, a challenge we share today.

Chapter 4
summary

O F ALL FOUR GOSPELS IN THE EARLIEST CHRISTIAN centuries the Gospel of Matthew was the most respected. The Gospel of Mark, a briefer account of the life, teaching, death and resurrection of Jesus, most of which can be found in Matthew, was neglected. The Gospel of Luke took longer than the Gospel of Matthew to assume a central role in the liturgy and preaching of the emerging Christian communities. The Gospel of John was quickly adopted by Gnostic sectarians, and assumed its place as a genuinely Christian book late in the second century because of its association made by Irenaeus (c. 180) with the more sedate teaching of the First Letter of John and the identification of the Apostle John, the Son of Zebedee, as the Beloved Disciple. The Gospel of Matthew probably first appeared in its present form some time in the 80's of the first century. It was already being cited by other Christian books that may have appeared before the end of the century, or early in the second century (the *Didache*, Ignatius of Antioch). By the middle of the second century it was being cited by an increasing number of early Christian writers (Polycarp, Barnabas, Justin Martyr, 2 Clement).[1] This popularity has been sustained over the centuries.

There are good reasons for this preference. The life and practices of the Christian Church are well served by Matthew. Only Matthew provides extended teachings on Christian behavior in the Sermon on the Mount (Matt 5-7). The most widely used form of the Lord's Prayer appears in Matt 6:9-13, even though a parallel, though shorter (and possibly more primitive), version of the prayer is found in Luke 11:2-4. Only in Matthew does Jesus appoint Peter the "rock" upon which the Church was founded (16:16-18), and insist upon the teaching authority of his newly founded community (18:18-20). Other important early Christian doctrines were discovered within the pages of Matthew, for example, the virgin birth of Jesus (1:18-25) and the Trinity (28:19). This Gospel closes with Jesus' comforting promise that he would be with his community till the close of the age (28:19). From 650 to 1000 AD thirteen major commentaries were written on Matthew, and four on Mark.[2] In the Roman Catholic tradition, prior to the revision of the Lectionary that followed the Second Vatican Council, Matthew dominated the Sunday Gospel readings.

Matthew has long been rightly judged as the Church's Gospel.[3] Our contemporary approach to the Gospel of Matthew must ask the question that is posed of all texts that we regard as Sacred Scripture. Can this text, which was written to address a largely Jewish-Christian Church in the 80's of the first century, still be a word of life for us in the third millennium? Like the Gospel of Mark, which served Matthew as a source and model for his story of Jesus, the Gospel of Matthew has its plot, designed to address a readership both in its single parts, and as a whole utterance. For the purposes of this book, the present chapter will strive to outline the theological and literary features of the whole utterance of the Matthean story of the life of Jesus. As throughout this book, and in agreement with a majority of contemporary interpreters of the Gospels, what follows presupposes that the story of the Gospel, from 1:1-28:20, has a design, a plot that communicates the author's point of view to the reader. But before turning to an analysis of Matthew's plot, there are some conundrums in this Gospel that have long bothered interpreters. Let us begin with them.

A Starting Point: Matthew 28:16-20

Strange as it may seem, all biblical scholars recognize that the most logical place to begin a search for the purpose and message of the Gospel of Matthew, its "point of view," is at its conclusion. In Matthew 28:16-20 the risen Jesus gathers his disciples on a mountain in Galilee and sends them out to the whole world. A good story often reaches its climax on the last page. The Gospels are no exception to this, as we have already seen in the literary tension generated by Mark 16:1-8 (see further, Luke 24:44-48; John 20:30-31). The Matthean community understood itself and its apostolic task in terms of a commission given by the risen Lord. This commission is explicitly stated in 28:16-20. It is so important that we will consider this text in some detail.

> Now the eleven disciples went to Galilee, to the mountain to which Jesus had directed them. And when they saw him they worshipped him; but some doubted. And Jesus came and said to them: "All authority in heaven and on earth has been given to me. Go therefore and make disciples of all nations, baptising them in the name of the Father and of the Son and of the Holy Spirit, teaching them to observe all that I have commanded you; and lo, I am with you always, to the close of the age" (Matt 28:16-20).

After the Easter events (see Matt 28:1-15), the disciples return to Galilee, to the mountain indicated by Jesus (v. 16). This is not the first time that Jesus has summoned his disciples to the top of a mountain to give them important instructions. Earlier in the Gospel (5:1-7:28) he began his ministry of teaching by gathering his disciples on a mountain (see 5:1) to give them a new Law (see 5:17-20, 21-22, 27-28, 31-32, 33-34, 38-39, 43-44). On a new Sinai a new and perfect Moses gives a new People of God a new Law.[4] As the situating of the giving of the new Law on a mountain was important, so is it also important for the risen Lord's commissioning of his Church.[5]

Both uses of a mountain, of course, have their origins in the importance of mountains, beginning with Sinai, in the biblical tradition (see Exod 19). We are about to witness a significant communication of God's ways and teaching to the disciples. One senses a community well-versed in, and full of respect and appreciation for, the traditional religious symbols of Israel behind these indications. Yet, as we will see, the details of the commission of Jesus to his disciples appear to contradict that respect and appreciation. The Jewish world is essential to Matthew's story, but it reaches beyond that world.

The reaction of the disciples to the sight of Jesus is ambiguous. Some worship him. The Greek verb used here (Greek: *proskunein*) is used extensively in the Gospel of Matthew to show a correct understanding of who Jesus is and how one should relate to him (see, for example, Matt 2:2, 11; 4:9-10; 8:2; 9:18; 14:33; 15:25; 18:26; 20:20; 28:9, 17). But despite the fact that some of the disciples worship Jesus, and despite the climactic significance of this final scene, Matthew still reports: "but some doubted" (v. 17). The hesitation of the disciples in the presence of the risen Lord, one of the hallmarks of each of the synoptic resurrection accounts (see Mark 16:8 and Luke 24:10-11, 13-35, 36-37), is also an important part of Matthew's theology of the Church. All the Gospels have a realistic understanding and presentation of the disciples of Jesus. They believe, yet they falter in their belief.

Jesus opens his final instructions with a declaration about himself, and then spells out the consequences of such a declaration for his disciples and their mission. The man whom they had known as Jesus of Nazareth claims that all authority on heaven and earth has been given to him (v. 18). This is nothing less than to claim that Jesus has taken over the authority and dignity that traditional Israel allowed only to YHWH. Passages indicating this are innumerable. An example, and perhaps the most important Old Testament passage on the oneness of God and his complete authority, is found in Deuteronomy 6:4-9 which begins: "Hear, O Israel, the Lord our God, the Lord alone" (Deut 6:4). Behind Jesus' claims to absolute authority, there is probably also a reference to the giving of all authority to the "one like a son of man" in Dan 7:14: "To him was given, dominion and glory and kingship, that all peoples, nations and languages should serve him."

On a mountain with his hesitant disciples, Jesus claims to have been given all the authority that, according to traditional Judaism, belonged to YHWH alone. This is a bold claim. It would not have been well received by the Jews of the 80's of the first century. After the destruction of the Temple-city Jerusalem and Israel as a political entity in 70 AD, Judaism had to struggle through a period of religious reconstruction. The Jews no longer had a capital city with its Temple; they no longer had a Land. Judaism gradually established its identity after the disastrous effects of the Jewish war of 70 AD. A universal (although still varied) approach to YHWH, the unique and traditional God of Israel, was developed from the earlier Pharisaic form of pre-War Judaism. It later came to be called Rabbinic Judaism. It was broadly based on the synagogue as a place of worship and upon the Law as a way of life.

Within this religious context, Matthew's Gospel develops a very exalted idea of Jesus. Some of the exalted Christological claims of the Fourth Gospel (see, for example, John 5:17-18; 10:30) parallel this understanding of Jesus, to whom all authority in heaven and on earth has been given, reflected in Matt 28:17. Over against the synagogue's attempts to re-establish YHWH and his Law at the center of post-war Judaism, this Gospel presents Jesus as having been given the authority and privilege allowed only to YHWH.

Flowing from the uniqueness and universality of his authority, the Matthean Jesus then breaks through three further elements basic to post-70 AD Jewish belief and practice.

1. He commands his disciples to "Go therefore and make disciples of all nations" (v. 19a). This is in direct opposition to the belief in Israel's exclusive place among the nations of the world as God's chosen people. Once again, this would have been hard for post-war Judaism to accept. Although there had been openness to the idea of a universal salvation in the prophets (see, for example, Isaiah 2:1-4), it had always meant a movement from the Gentile world towards Sion. Here this is reversed:

the new people of God, founded by Jesus of Nazareth, are to "go out" to make disciples of all nations.

2.   The disciples are further instructed to "baptize" in the name of the Father and of the Son and of the Holy Spirit (v. 19b), thus introducing a new initiation rite for the new people of God, setting out on its mission. It is to replace the centrally important Jewish rite of circumcision. The Jewish tradition insisted on circumcision as the central act of initiation to YHWH's unique people. In seeking an identity, barriers that separate one group from another are important. Initiation rites are fundamental to this separation, and the traditional rite of circumcision provided it. But the Christian missionary is told to replace the initiation of circumcision with baptism.

3.   As if what had been commanded so far was not enough, the final command demolishes the very basis of traditional Jewish faith, built upon the teaching and the learning of the Torah. The Torah had become even more central for post-war Judaism. Without the Temple with its priesthood and its cultic actions, Torah alone remained as the heart of the Jewish understanding of God's ways among his people and his people's approach to him. But even the Torah is replaced. Jesus uses words commonly found in passages on the importance of the Torah: "to teach," "to observe," "commandments" (see, for example, Deut 5–6, esp. 6:1, where all these terms appear) to indicate a new teaching: "teaching them to observe all that I have commanded you" (v. 20a). No longer does the command to teach and observe look to the Torah, but to the teaching of Jesus. The Law of Moses has been replaced by the teaching of Jesus.

4.   Jesus' final words are not words of departure, but words assuring that he will always be with his disciples (v. 20b). In the Gospel of Luke the idea of ascension is a pictorial image of Jesus actually leaving this earth and returning to his Father but in Matthew there is no trace of any such event. In fact, one could say that the opposite is the case. Matthew's Gospel ends with Jesus' promise that he will never leave them. Of course, theologically, Luke is saying exactly the same thing through his message of a return to the Father and his eventual sending of the Spirit. But whether it is Jesus' Spirit sent by the Father (Luke) or the abiding presence of Jesus who will never leave his Church (Matthew), the message of God's purposes to found and sustain a holy people in and through Jesus rings true.

From these last few verses of the Gospel of Matthew (28:16-20) one could argue that we are dealing with a Gospel that is extremely hostile to the traditional ways of Judaism, especially as they were being forged in the post-70 AD situation of what eventually came to be Rabbinic Judaism. They could be read as the charter of a Christian Church that had broken definitively from its origins in Judaism. We are clearly in touch with a community being strongly exhorted to set out on a journey away from the confines of Israel into the new world of a universal Church where Jesus, his ways and his teachings are to be the measure of one's "belonging." But from these first indications should we conclude that the traditions of Israel are now a thing of the past, valueless? This would be a partial and incorrect reading of the Gospel of Matthew as a whole.

A Strange Contradiction

Matthew's Gospel is often regarded as the most Jewish of all Gospels. How can it be that the author disregards all that is traditional and sacred to Judaism? Is Matthew's Gospel only concerned with the new? What is the author's attitude to the old, the ways of God in the history of Israel? Matt 28:16-20 is found at the end of the Gospel. Matthew's story of Jesus concludes with the sending of the disciples into the Gentile mission, a mission to all the nations. Naturally, tension between the missionary Church and the historical origins of Christianity from within Judaism will be sensed. But there is an equally important passage much nearer the beginning of the story of Jesus:

> Think not that I have come to abolish the Law and the Prophets; I have not come to abolish them, but to fulfill them. For truly, I say to you, till heaven and earth pass away, not an iota, not a dot will pass from the Law until all is accomplished (Matt. 5:17-18).

In the light of 28:16-20 we seem to be faced with a strange contradiction. The Gospel concluded in a way that indicated a radical breach between the Christian Church setting out on a mission to all the nations and Israel; but these words of Jesus, as he begins his preaching, mark a close bond between the Church and the Law.

The matter becomes more complex as we read further into the Gospel. On two occasions during his public ministry Jesus speaks about the exclusiveness of his mission to Israel. He similarly limits his disciples' mission to Israel alone. In the light of the universalism of the missionary command in 28:16-20 they are very puzzling. At the beginning of a long discourse that deals with the mission of the Church (10:1-11:1), we read:

> These twelve Jesus sent out, charging them: "Go nowhere among the Gentiles, and into no town of the Samaritans, but go rather to the lost sheep of the house of Israel" (10:5-6).

Some time after this discourse, he responds to the pleas of a Canaanite woman, that he heal her daughter: "I was sent only to the lost sheep of the house of Israel" (15:24). These passages from the public ministry of the Matthean Jesus appear to limit the mission of Jesus and his disciples to Israel (10:5-6; 15:24), and exhort the followers of Jesus to live and teach the traditional law of Israel (5:17-18). How can we reconcile this with the boldness of the thrust into the Gentile mission that is at the heart of the risen Lord's closing mandate (28:16-20)?

The Gospel of Matthew is marked by two points of view. One is open and enthusiastic about the newness of the Christian Church, along with the challenge of the Gentile mission; another presents Jesus and his disciples involved in a mission limited to Israel (10:5-6, 15:24), and a perfect living of the Law (5:17-18).

Jesus among the Gentiles

The impression gained from our reflections thus far is only slightly weakened by the two miracles which Jesus performs for Gentiles during his public ministry, one of which I have already mentioned: the curing of the daughter of the Canaanite woman. In 8:5-13 Matthew reports the story of the healing of the Gentile centurion's servant. Although Jesus cures the servant of a Gentile soldier, the miracle is worked within the context of the lack of belief that Jesus finds in Israel (see 8:1-27) and is used, ultimately as a teaching for Israel:

> Truly, I say to you, not even in Israel have I found such faith. I tell you, many will come from east and west and sit at the table of Abraham, Isaac and Jacob while the sons of the kingdom will be thrown into the outer darkness; there men will weep and gnash their teeth (vv. 10-12).

These words on the lips of Jesus formed part of the experience of the members of the Matthean community. Respectful of their roots within ancient Jewish traditions, they were now inevitably involved in the Gentile mission. In that situation their experience as Christians corresponded to what Jesus had said. Despite Jesus' personal mission to Israel alone, he had already spoken of the later experience of the Matthean Church itself: refused by "the sons of the kingdom," but sent on a mission to peoples "from east and west." Strangely, it will be those to whom the kingdom had been given who will be cast into darkness, while many "from east and west" will be seated at the table of Abraham. The Christians in Matthew's community had experienced expulsion from the synagogue, and they were now moving into the Gentile mission. These words of Jesus gave them courage, as they wondered about their historical and religious origins within Judaism, a way of approaching God that had refused Jesus and his followers.

A similar point is made in Matt 15:21-28, the story of the "Canaanite" woman. At the end of Jesus' encounter with the Gentile woman Jesus explains why this particular woman has been granted her request: "O woman, great is your faith! Be it done for you as you desire" (v. 28). However, this point is not reached until the woman herself has placed her understanding of herself and her request within the context of Jesus' unique mission to Israel (see vv. 23-27). The greatness of her faith has created an exception that proves the rule! A Gentile is used to instruct the true Israel (the Matthean Church) on authentic faith.

A Tension Resolved

The apparent contradiction between Jesus' program to fulfill the Jewish Law found at the beginning of the Gospel (5:17-18) and its conclusion, as the risen Jesus sends his disciples to all nations (28:16-20), is reinforced by a consideration of the two miracles that Jesus performs for Gentiles (8:5-13; 15:21-28). They may be directed towards Gentiles, but they instruct Israel. Yet the contradiction is a key to understanding the situation of the Matthean community, the Evangelist's appreciation and presentation of Jesus, his mission and the mission of the Church.

An important feature of any narrative is the way Matthew uses the time-line of the story as it unfolds.[6] Generally, the events in a narrative are reported in the chronological order in which they happen in a human story. This means that the events follow one another down an acceptable and understandable time line. In more technical language, which is not hard to understand, this use of time is generally called "narrative time." In reading through narrative time the reader moves simply from one event to another, from one day to another, one year to another, until the end of the story is reached.

But sometimes events or words are reported which look back to an earlier happening, throwing light on the story as it is being reported. Something from the past is recalled, and is drawn into the story to add meaning to the events of "narrative time" as they unfold. A well-known example of this can be found in the story in the Gospel of John that tells of a blind man (John 9). Through a series of events, following one another chronologically (narrative time), he is healed, and subsequently interrogated, until he comes to prostrate himself before Jesus and confess that Jesus is the Son of Man (see John 9:35-37). But, at the start of the story, the reader is told that this man was "born blind" (v. 1). The unfortunate past event of his being born blind enables the disciples to ask who must bear the guilt for this man's affliction. Who, in the past, committed some sin that led to a child being born blind?[7] This question gives Jesus the chance to set the agenda for the story: the man's blindness will lead to the revelation of the glory of God (see 9:2-5). This practice of looking back into a time before the "narrative time" of the regular passing of events in a story is called "analepsis."

But if clarifications can enter into the narrative time of a story by means of this looking back (analepsis), tension and interest also enters a story when the storyteller gives a hint of something that will happen in the distant future. In all the Gospels, Jesus' predictions of his oncoming passion and resurrection (see, for example, Mark 8:31, 9:31, 10:32-34) are excellent examples of this technique. As Jesus pursues his mission, he sometimes tells his disciples that he will one day be slain in Jerusalem, and he will be raised from the dead. This sort of inserted information creates a sense of expectancy in a reader, who reads on into the events reported in the narrative, waiting for the accomplishment of some future event which has promisingly (or threateningly) already been mentioned. The technical term used for these interruptions into "narrative time" is prolepsis. The general term used to refer to both of these interruptions into narrative time, looking either backwards into events happened earlier (analepsis), or forecasting future events (prolepsis), is "plotted time."

Focusing our attention on the temporal element in the passages which highlight the contradiction between the accepted ways of Judaism and the new openness to "all the nations," we notice that the passages which limit Jesus' and his disciples' activities to Israel are located at the beginning, and then during the public ministry of Jesus (5:17-18; 10:5-6; 15:24). The mission to "all the nations" is the final scene of the Gospel (28:16-20). The events of the life of Jesus follow one another in regular succession, from his birth to his death and resurrection (narrative time). But the narrative time of the life, teaching, death and resurrection of Jesus is bracketed between two crucial uses of plotted time. The passages that appear to contradict one another, Jesus' insistence upon the fulfillment of the Law in 5:17-18 and his final commissioning of the Church to go out to the whole world in 28:16-20, form this bracket.

Let us look again at the programmatic words of Jesus, found at the beginning of the Sermon on the Mount (5:17-18). The temporal element of these words calls for a closer examination. Although they come at the beginning of Jesus' ministry in the narrative time of the story, they contain words that look outside the unfolding time line of the narrative, into the plotted time of the future (prolepsis).

> Think not that I have come to abolish the law and the prophets; I have come not to abolish them but to fulfill them. For truly, I say to you, *till heaven and earth pass away*, not an iota, not a dot, will pass from the law *until all is accomplished.*

I have stressed two different expressions in the passage: they are both references to some future "time." There is the "now" of Jesus' preaching during his public ministry (narrative time), but there is a moment "yet to come" when the present order of things will be changed (plotted time). These expressions refer to a time in the future when the perfection of the law will be completed: "till heaven and earth pass away ... until all is accomplished." When might that future time be? In the light of our general understanding of Jesus' eschatological teaching (still found in Matt 24) we are immediately led to regard these words of Jesus as referring to the end of all time. Indeed, many scholars continue to read Matt 5:17-18 as a reference to the traditional Jewish notion of the end of time.[8]

This understanding of the future events referred to in 5:17-18, however, renders Matt 28:16-20 very difficult to understand. In 28:16-20 Matthew reports words of the risen Jesus that once again use plotted time to reach outside the narrated events of the Gospel. The disciples are sent on a mission to the ends of the earth, and Jesus promises that he will be with them till the close of the age. If the future time of 5:17-18 referred to the end of all time, the command of Jesus that the Jewish Law be perfectly observed, without changing even the tiniest detail, would still be in force in the Christian Church, as we await Jesus' final coming. But Jesus abandons the perfect observance of the Jewish Law in 28:16-20 when he sends his disciples on a mission. As we have seen, Jesus' commission to his disciples transcends much that is central to Jewish law and thought.

There may have been different points of view within the community, and some of its members may have claimed that the Church must still live under the Law (5:17-18), while others argued that they must go out to all the nations armed only with the teaching of Jesus (28:16-20). Indeed the traditions that Matthew uses to report these words of Jesus may reach back to these different points of view. But the Gospel must be read as a single utterance that made sense to an author. Matthew did not leave these contradictory understandings of the Christian Church to stand unresolved in the Gospel. The author has written a story of Jesus to resolve the seeming contradiction. Indeed, that was one of the practical, pastoral reasons for the writing of the Gospel of Matthew. An understanding of the uniqueness of this particular Gospel will show that such is the case. It is the responsibility of the interpreter to see these apparent contradictions, and to come to understand why Matthew inserted them into his well-crafted story.

Between Jesus' insistence on the mission to Israel at the beginning and during the course of his public ministry (5:17-18; 10:5-6; 15:24), and his final commission as the risen Lord to the Matthean disciples to go out to the whole world (28:16-20), something happens which dramatically changes the future roles of both Jesus and his disciples.[9] The events from the narrated time of the story that stand as a watershed between the opening of the ministry of Jesus (5:17-18), his continued insistence upon the limitation of his mission to Israel (10:5-6; 15:24), and his final missionary command, are his death and resurrection (chapters 26-27).

The words sending the young Church out to the whole world in the service of a new universal Lord, teaching his commandments, come from the lips of the risen Jesus (28:16-20). Something happens in the Matthean story of the death and resurrection of Jesus that transforms the ministry of Jesus and his disciples. During the life of Jesus it was limited to the lost sheep of the house of Israel. However, 28:16-20 instructs the disciples, and the all subsequent followers of Jesus, forever accompanied by the risen Jesus, to reach out to all nations. Later in the Gospel, there are two events - reported only in Matthew - where there are descriptions that could be regarded as "heaven and earth passing away" (see 5:17-18). The first of these moments is at the death of Jesus:

> From the sixth hour there was darkness all over the land until the ninth hour. The veil of the temple was torn in two from top to bottom; the earth quaked; the rocks were split; the tombs opened and the bodies of many holy men rose from the dead (27:45, 51-53).

The second of these moments is found in the Matthean description of the events surrounding the resurrection of Jesus:

> All at once there was a violent earthquake, for the angel of the Lord, descending from heaven, came and rolled away the stone and sat upon it. His face was like lightning, his robe white as snow (28:2-3).

Heaven and earth are passing away. Matthew has taken some of the imagery used here from the Christian tradition concerning Jesus' death. It is found in Mark's report of the tearing of the veil, the darkness at the death of Jesus, and the whiteness of the robe of the angel at the tomb, although he was a "young man," not an angel (Mark 15:38; 16:5). When the overall context is put together, however, it is obvious that Matthew has changed the scenario considerably. He has drawn upon some traditionally "apocalyptic" symbols from Jewish thought but has shifted their timing. The events described: darkening of the skies, splitting of the rocks, earthquakes, lightning, the rising of the dead and the appearance of angels are events which were expected to happen at the final end of all time when YHWH would return as Lord and Judge (see Amos 8:9; Jer 15:9; Ezek 37:12-13; Isa 26:19; Dan 7:9; 10:6; 12:2). Matthew indicates that these events will not only take place at the very end of history, as was held by Jewish traditions. They already have happened at the death and resurrection of Jesus.[10]

The plotted time of the prolepsis involved in the future time indicated by the words of Jesus 5:17-18 ("till heaven and earth pass away ... until all is accomplished") has now become narrated time in the actual succession of the events of the passion of Jesus. The promise has been fulfilled. Only Matthew's story of the life of Jesus makes this point. This is his way of saying that the death and resurrection of Jesus is a single event that marks the turning point of the ages. It is the paschal mystery of Jesus that alters everything. Yet, as we have seen from the Gospel itself, Matthew is anxious to show that Jesus himself lived out the perfection of the Old Law (for example, read 3:13-17 in the light of what we have just uncovered), as well as becoming, through his death and resurrection, the foundational figure of the new Law.

We would do Matthew an injustice if we did not see the great care he takes to show that Jesus does not abolish the old Law. Rather, Jesus perfects the Law, not only in what he does, but also in who he is. This is made particularly clear in Matt 1-2. The events of the birth and infancy of Jesus, bridging the time between the former covenant into the days of Jesus are a fulfillment of the promises of old. Almost every scene in the Matthean infancy narrative indicates that the events of Jesus' birth and infancy are "to fulfil what was said by the prophet ..." (see 1:22-23, 2:5-6, 15, 17-18, 23). The same theme also flows into the ministry of Jesus (see 3:3; 4:6-7, 14-16). Matthew was convinced that Jesus was the perfection of all the promises of the Old Testament. The Gospel of Matthew begins in the Old Testament, through the genealogy of Jesus (1:1-17) where God's providential handling of the history of a chosen people is already obvious. Nevertheless, the promise of the Old Testament is fulfilled in the events of the birth and the public life of Jesus. Yet, Jesus appears to be extremely anxious that his life and ministry be the perfection of the Old Law. He himself attempts to live the Law perfectly, and he exhorts his followers to do the same.

However, after his death and resurrection, those same followers are instructed to reach out to the Gentile mission, commanded by a new Lord to teach a new Law, to forge a new community with a new initiation rite (28:16-20). This is possible only because the death and resurrection of Jesus are understood by the Gospel of Matthew as the 'turning point of the ages." The members of Matthew's Church are caught up in the Gentile mission. Nevertheless, they are still very aware that they are the product of the perfection of the old Law in the person and teaching of Jesus. As this is the case, the Evangelist can claim that it is his community, the followers of Jesus of Nazareth, who can regard themselves as the "true Israel." The synagogue-centered religion of post-war Judaism, which rejected and expelled the followers of Jesus, could not claim to be Israel. The Matthean Church was living out God's saving history, from Abraham to Jesus (see 1:1-17) into the Gentile mission (28:16-20). The historical Israel had lost its way, and the true Israel was to be located in the missionary Church, the continuation of Jesus' perfection of the Law, transformed by the turning point of his death and resurrection.

The Matthean Literary Design and Its Theological Message

With this underlying understanding of the way God has acted through Jesus for the perfection of Israel and the bringing of Jesus' saving teaching to the ends of the earth, I will now consider how the plot of Matthew's Gospel, from 1:1 to 28:20 unfolds. The whole utterance of Matthew's Gospel can be read as a single story. It was written to communicate a point of view that is best understood through an analysis of literary design, otherwise known as its "plot." The plot of this Gospel can be described as the way the author has told the words and actions of Jesus, and the order in which they are told, so that a desired impact might be made upon the reader.

One of the features of the Gospel of Matthew is the presence of five lengthy discourses in the story of Jesus (5:1-7:28: the sermon on the mount; 10:1-11:1: the missionary discourse; 13:1-53: the parable discourse; 18:1-35: the discourse on Church life and order; 24:1-25:46: the discourse on the end of time and the final judgment). Many scholars have taken the five discourses as the main indication of the internal structure of the Gospel.[11] Such a structure, however, fails to give sufficient attention to the blending of the discourses with the narratives of Jesus' infancy, his preaching and healing, his instruction of disciples, his passion, death and resurrection.

Recent interest in the Gospel of Matthew as a narrative with an identifiable plot has shown that the discourses, although important, form part of larger narrative blocks. I would like to propose the following design of the narrative of this Gospel, in the hope that it will serve as a guide to a more fruitful reading of the text itself.[12]

My explanation of the seeming contradiction which exists between the beginning (5:17-18) and the end (28:16-20) of the Gospel of Matthew is fundamental to my understanding of the overall theological and Christological argument of the Gospel. It leads me to conclude that this Gospel has the following major concerns:

1. Matthew wants to insert the story of Jesus into the history of God's saving plan, begun in the promises to Israel, perfected in the life and ministry of Jesus. His death and resurrection marked a turning point in that history, and from that moment on the Church has been sent out, as the true Israel, to the ends of the earth.

2.   He understands and presents Jesus as the Messiah and the Son of God. In Matthew's story, this understanding of Jesus is rejected by traditional Israel.

3.   The unfortunate rejection of Jesus by Israel leads to the establishment of the true Israel, now to be identified as the followers of Jesus, called for the first time in the Gospel of Matthew "the Church" (16:18; 18:17 [twice]).

4.   But the Christian community cannot remain content with its role in salvation history as the true Israel. The risen Jesus commissions it to preach the Gospel to the Gentiles.

5.   At the heart of the unfolding plan and argument of the Gospel stand Jesus' death and resurrection as the turning point of the ages, and the great commission which sends the Church into the Gentile mission.

However, these theological themes are embedded in a plot, and plots are formed by a series of narrative units marked by a central scene which is the focus of the unit (sometimes called "the kernel"), surrounded, supported and further explained by other narratives (sometimes called "satellites"). The overarching theme of each narrative unit can be gleaned from the major thrust of the key episode and the way in which other episodes flow from it, further explain it and are dependent upon it. But narrative units are never self-contained ends unto themselves. They also contain crisis moments that lead the reader further into the story. There are always hints in the unit that look forward to the end of the story. In a good story the reader is told enough to be made curious, without ever being given all the answers. Narrative texts keep promising the reader the great prize of understanding — later.[13]

On the basis of these simple principles for the understanding of the gradually emerging plot of a narrative, the story line of the Gospel of Matthew can be divided into six units.

1. *The First Narrative Unit: The Coming of the Messiah (1:1-4:16).*
The kernel of this unit is the birth of Jesus (2:1a). In a unit that makes its central theme the coming of the Messiah, his birth is crucial, no matter how briefly the event is mentioned. Indeed, the physical birth of Jesus is only alluded to, rather than described, in 2:1a. Nevertheless, it is the foundation for what precedes: the genealogy of Jesus (1:1-17) and the description of how his birth came about (1:18-25). It is also

the foundation for what follows: the coming of the Wise Men from the East and Israel's response (2:2-12), the flight into Egypt, the slaying of the innocents and the return from Egypt, which leads to a further flight to Nazareth (2:13-23), the preaching of John the Baptist (3:1-12), the baptism of Jesus (3:13-17), and, finally, the temptation of Jesus (4:1-11). This unit closes with Jesus' withdrawal to Capernaum, enabling Matthew to see this withdrawal as the fulfillment of Isaiah 8:23-9:1. Jesus enters the territory of Zebulun and Napthali, the Galilee of the Gentiles. The openness to the Gentiles that opened this section in 1:1, returns as it closes in 4:12-16.[14]

The genealogy (1:1-17) indicates that the birth of Jesus is the fulfillment of God's promises, and this is further strengthened in the annunciation to Joseph (1:18-25). Without this event the story cannot begin and 1:1-25 prepare for such a beginning. Although the appearance of John the Baptist (3:1-12), the baptism of Jesus (3:13-17), and the temptations in the wilderness (4:1-11) occur several years later, they depend upon Jesus' coming. Because Jesus of Nazareth has been born (see 2:23), because he has come, the question can now be asked: is he the Messiah or not? John testifies that he is (3:11, 14). God proclaims that Jesus is his beloved son (3:17). Satan tests Jesus to see if he is God's son (4:1-11).

From the beginning of the story several events foreshadow the ultimate outcome of the plot. The identification of Jesus as "the son of David, the son of Abraham" (1:1) suggests that the Jewish Messiah will have meaning for all Abraham's children, Jew and Gentile (see Gen 12:1-4). The homage of the Magi (2:11) points to the coming of the Gentiles, as does John's warning to the Pharisees and the Sadducees that "God is able from these stones to raise up children to Abraham" (3:9). On the other hand, Jerusalem's inability to accept what the Scriptures proclaim, that the Messiah will come from Bethlehem, and Herod's persecution of the infant King of the Jews prefigure the passion. Satan's messianic temptations show that Jesus' messiahship will be misunderstood in terms of power and authority (see the mockery found in the passion story 27:39-44 where many of the terms used by Satan re-appear). Thus the birth of Jesus (2:1a) initiates a crisis in Israel that will not be resolved until Jesus' death and resurrection.

2. *Second Narrative Unit: The Messiah's Ministry to Israel of Preaching, Teaching and Healing (4:17-11:1).*

The kernel of this unit is found at 4:17, the beginning of Jesus' ministry. The arrest of John the Baptist (4:12) leads Jesus to return to Galilee and begin his mission (4:12-17), limited exclusively "to the lost sheep of the house of Israel" (10:6). No longer is Jesus a figure in the background. He is actively present to the story, preaching: "Repent, for the kingdom of heaven is at hand" (4:17). This section of the Gospel contains the beginnings of Jesus' ministry in Galilee (4:12-25), the discourse of the sermon on the mount (5:1-7:28), a series of nine miracles, separated by brief episodes, which are related to the vocation of a disciple of Jesus (8:1-9:38), and the discourse on the mission of the disciples (10:1-11:1).

Jesus' messianic ministry of preaching, teaching and healing dominates the entire section. This theme is repeated several times in the narrator's commentaries upon his story, at the beginning, in the middle, and at the end of the section: "And he went about all Galilee, teaching in their synagogues and preaching the gospel of the kingdom and healing every disease and every infirmity among the people" (4:23. See also 9:35; 11:1). He preaches and teaches through the Sermon on the Mount (5:1-7:28) and his discourse on mission (10:1-11:1). Between the two discourses he works a series of nine miracles to show that he is mighty not only in word but also in deed (8:1-9:38). In brief narratives located between the nine miracle stories, he associates disciples with his ministry of teaching, preaching and healing (8:14-22; 9:9-17; 9:35-38). Jesus has compassion for the crowds, "harassed and helpless, like sheep without a shepherd" (9:36), and he invites his disciples to pray the Lord of the harvest to send laborers into the harvest (9:37).

However, Jesus does not only exhort to prayer. His compassion and his concern that the Gospel of the kingdom be preached leads him to call his twelve disciples, to give them authority to do all the things which he has done so far in the story, and to send them out on a mission "to the lost sheep of the house of Israel" (10:1-15). In the discourse that follows, Jesus describes how they are to behave toward others and toward one another, as they share the mission (10:1-11:1).

This section of the plot, read carefully, shows that from its very inception, the mission of Jesus to Israel already produces crises. On the one hand the crowds are astonished at Jesus' teaching (7:28-29), and after the healing of a deaf-mute they are led to say, "Never was anything like this seen in Israel" (9:33). The disciples respond generously to Jesus' call (4:20-22), and he sends them on his mission (10:1-11:1). On the other hand, the Pharisees complain that "he casts out demons by the prince of demons" (9:34), and Jesus suggests that their ethical behavior is not in line with their teaching (see 5:20). The disciples are warned that their mission, like Jesus' mission, will cause division and hatred (10:16-25, 34-36). The mixed reception that greets the teaching and healing ministry of Jesus already tells the reader that the Messiah may be rejected.

Other events in this section foreshadow the ultimate outcome of the plot. The faith of a centurion points to the coming of the Gentiles, and leads Jesus to say: "I tell you, many will come from east and west and sit at table with Abraham, Isaac and Jacob in the kingdom of heaven, while the sons of the kingdom will be thrown into the outer darkness" (8:11-12). An accusation, leveled at Jesus during his passion (see 26:65), is aimed at Jesus for the first time when he forgives the sins of a man who is paralyzed: "This man is blaspheming" (9:3). Jesus' ministry to Israel will not be accepted.

3. *The Third Narrative Unit: The Crisis in the Messiah's Ministry (11:2-16:12).*

After the conclusion of the first phase of Jesus' ministry (4:12-11:1), John the Baptist, still in prison, sends messengers to enquire: "Are you he who is to come, or shall we look for another?" (11:3). This question hangs over the whole narrative unit. "The Coming One" is an expression used to speak of the Messiah (see 3:11; 21:9). Jesus uses the question of the Baptist to review his ministry so far: people are healed and the Good News is preached (see 11:4-5), but John's question raises another problem that Israel must answer. On the basis of Jesus' ministry of preaching, teaching and healing, now amply displayed in the story so far (especially in the previous narrative section, 4:12-11:1), will Israel recognize Jesus as the Coming One, or will Israel be offended by this activity of the Messiah?

A chain of events responds negatively and positively to the question raised by John the Baptist: "Are you he who is to come, or shall we look for another?" Some will decide that he is the one who is to come, while others will decide, once and for all, that they must look for another. Jesus will take appropriate action in each case. A rift opens between Jesus and traditional Israel, while a close bond between Jesus and his disciples develops. They are the nucleus of the new people of God.

On the negative side, Jesus points to the disappointing reception his ministry has received from "this generation" (11:6-19) and from the unrepentant cities of Chorazin and Bethsaida (11:20-24). But Jesus then issues an unforgettable invitation: "Come to me, all who labor and are heavy-laden" (11:28). Jesus offers a yoke and a burden that are easy and light, in contrast to the yoke and the burden of a people who refuse to accept their Messiah. This challenge leads to a series of episodes through which the Pharisees either question or test Jesus' authority. The relationship between Jesus and the leaders of Israel is one of anger and distrust (12:1-45), but he establishes a new family of God, not built upon bonds of blood or nation: "Whoever does the will of my Father in heaven is my brother, and sister, and mother" (12:50).

No longer able to speak directly to the crowds, he must turn to a parabolic form of speech, "because seeing they do not see, and hearing they do not hear, nor do they understand" (13:13). In the parable discourse of 13:1-52 Jesus turns decisively away from Israel, to make himself known to those to whom it has been given to know the secrets of the kingdom of heaven (13:11). After the discourse, as if in answer to his distancing himself from his own people, Jesus is rejected at his hometown, Nazareth (13:54-58).

Throughout this section, the Pharisees (sometimes with the scribes) attack Jesus for violating the Sabbath (12:1-14), for casting out demons (12:22-24), and for transgressing the traditions of the elders (15:1-2). They also demand signs (12:38; 16:1). After Jesus cures an afflicted demoniac (12:22), even the crowds ask in disbelief if Jesus can really be the Son of David (12:23).

Positively, Jesus' disciples maintain their faith. Immediately before the parable discourse, he identifies the disciples as his true family (12:48-50). In the parable discourse, he tells them: "To you it has been given to know the secrets of the kingdom of heaven" (13:11). At the end of the discourse the disciples say they have understood all that Jesus has said, and Jesus identifies them as scribes who have been trained for the kingdom of heaven (13:51-52). Yet even the faith of the disciples is not perfect. It is described as "little faith" (14:17). They do not understand the parable about clean and unclean (15:16), and they are annoyed by the Canaanite woman (15:23). But they still confess that Jesus is the Son of God (13:33), and they understand that the leaven of the Pharisees and the Sadducees refers to their teaching (16:12).

A clear line of demarcation is now emerging in the narrative between Israel and its leaders who have become increasingly hostile to Jesus and the believing but fragile disciples who accept and understand him. The story has arrived at a major crisis. Israel is blind to Jesus' teaching, and the religious leaders attack him. Jesus responds by speaking in parables, a speech which Israel cannot understand. As in the narrative section which dealt with Jesus' preaching and healing in Israel, where the storyteller summarized his activity, once again, on three occasions the reader finds that "Jesus, aware of this, withdrew from there" (12:15. See 14:13a; 15:21). The narrator remarks that Jesus "withdraws" himself from Israel.

A section of the Gospel (14:1-16:12), highlighted by the two bread miracles of 14:13-21 and 15:32-39, now follows. Jesus deals with his fragile disciples, and their equally fragile leader, Peter (14:22-33). He instructs and argues with the leaders of Israel (15:1-20), and feeds both Israel (14:13-21) and the Gentiles (15:32-39), who have glorified the God of Israel for the miracles he does among them (15:29-31). Jesus has not abandoned Israel and he continues to instruct and nourish the people. However, he increasingly focuses his attention upon his disciples. They are the nucleus of the new nation which will believe in him, and they must be wary of the leaven of the Pharisees and the Sadducees (see 16:1-12).

As in the earlier parts of the Gospel's plot, there are further hints of the end of the story throughout this unit. Jesus is identified with Isaiah's suffering servant (12:17-21), but to the text of Isaiah 42:1-4, 9, the author adds another passage from Isaiah (11:10): "and in his name will the Gentiles hope" (Matt 12:21). Although initially refusing to reach beyond the boundaries of Israel (15:24), Jesus eventually responds to the requests of the Canaanite woman because of the Gentile woman's great faith, in contrast to the little faith of the disciples (15:28). Because Israel is blind to Jesus' messiahship and the religious leaders attack him, Jesus will turn to all disciples who believe, even Gentiles.

4. *The Fourth Narrative Unit: The Messiah's Journey to Jerusalem (16:13-20:34).*

One of the most quoted, and memorable, of all Gospel stories forms the kernel event that controls this narrative unit. The very first scene is Peter's confession of faith at Caesarea Philippi (16:13-28). In this scene:

i. In response to Jesus' question about public opinion concerning his person, Peter confesses, in the name of the disciples, that Jesus is the Messiah, the Son of God (vv. 13-16)

ii. Jesus announces his death and resurrection (v. 21)

iii. Jesus associates his disciples with his own passion (vv. 23-28).

The previous section of the Gospel (11:2-16:12) involved struggle with the question raised by John the Baptist: "Are you the one who is to come" (11:2). The encounter between Jesus, Peter and the disciples provides the answer to John the Baptist's question (11:3): Jesus is the Coming One, the Messiah, the Son of God. But this public proclamation of Jesus' messiahship is only half the story. Although there have been hints for the reader that Jesus is destined to be rejected and suffer, the scene at Caesarea Philippi explicitly opens a new direction for the narrative. "From that time on Jesus began to show his disciples that he must go to Jerusalem and suffer many things from the elders and the chief priests and the scribes, and be killed, and on the third day be raised" (16:21). The explicit linking of the proclamation of Jesus' messiahship with his suffering produces a further crisis. From this point on Jesus' disciples must decide if they can follow a Messiah who calls them to suffering and even death.

The controlling texts in this narrative unit are Jesus' predictions of his passion and resurrection. After the first of these predictions there are a further two passion predictions, strategically placed through this part of the story (17:22-23; 20:17-19). They further develop the key event of Caesarea Philippi by regularly reminding the reader of Jesus' destiny at Jerusalem. However, the reader is not only faced with the information provided by Jesus' regular predictions of his death. The reader also responds to the reaction of the disciples in this section. Although there are encounters with the Pharisees and other characters in the story, they only serve to highlight Jesus' instruction of the disciples, as he calls them to follow their Messiah to a cross. The disciples, in turn, demonstrate that they do not completely understand the nature of Jesus' messiahship and the demands it entails.

The disciples witness, but misunderstand the Transfiguration (17:1-8) and immediately show the littleness of their faith in their inability to cure the epileptic boy (17:14-21). The second prediction of the passion re-orients the narrative towards the Cross (17:22-23), and the strange story of the payment of the temple tax associates Peter with Jesus (17:24-

27). The discourse on Church order then follows (18:1-19:1). This detailed discourse on how the community is to treat the sinners and the frail within their midst is created by a question raised by the disciples: "Who is the greatest in the kingdom of heaven?" (18:1). The Pharisees' question about divorce leads to Jesus' instruction of his disciples on the sacredness of what God has joined together (19:1-12), and the encounter with the rich young man is the springboard for Jesus' instruction of his disciples on wealth and possessions (19:16-30). Throughout, the disciples are taught that, like little children, they must be open and receptive to the ways of God (see 19:13-15).

The counter-cultural nature of this teaching is reinforced by the parable of the master of the vineyard who calls whomever he wishes to work in his vineyard, whenever he wishes to call them, and pays whatever he decides. After all, he is the Lord of the vineyard (20:1-16). The third passion prediction (20:17-19), however, does not lead to the disciples' conversion to the way of Jesus. The sons of Zebedee, through their mother, seek positions of authority, and when the other ten hear of it, they are indignant (20:20-28). This narrative unit closes with the story of the two blind men who proclaim their faith in Jesus as he comes out of Jericho. Abandoning all because of their belief in him, "they received their sight and followed him" (20:29-34). The reader, who has followed fragile disciples through this section, learns from the blind men how to commit oneself to the following of Jesus without any conditions or expectations of human success.

Thus, the event of Caesarea Philippi confronts the disciples with a vision of messiahship and discipleship that they cannot fully integrate at this stage of the story. Nevertheless, the disciples do not abandon Jesus, and he continues to instruct them. At the transfiguration, the Father confirms that Jesus is his beloved son (17:5), and later Jesus explains that Elijah has returned in the person of John the Baptist (17:13). Jesus helps Peter to pay the temple tax (17:24-27) and then delivers a major discourse on the kind of relationships that should mark his new community (18:1-35). Peter is able to boast that the disciples have left everything in order to follow Jesus (19:27), and Jesus promises that they will sit on "twelve thrones, judging the twelve tribes of Israel" (19:28). The parable of the workers in the vineyard (20:1-16), which follows this promise, suggests that the disciples are among the last who will be first (19:30; 20:16).

As Jesus approaches Jerusalem, two blind men call him the Son of

David (20:30-31). Their confession of Jesus' messiahship, coming at the end of the unit (20:29-34), forms an inclusion with Peter's confession at Caesarea Philippi, which began it (16:13-28).[15] The blind are among the insignificant people who accept Jesus' messiahship. The events of this part of the story lead Jesus to Jerusalem, the city of his destiny. The virtual elimination of the crowd, which only appears incidentally throughout this section of the story (see 17:14; 19:2; 20:29, 31), and the emphasis upon Jesus' teaching the disciples suggests that the disciples will form the nucleus of Jesus' new community, despite their inability to accept completely Jesus' way to resurrection, by means of the cross.

5. *The Fifth Narrative Unit: The Messiah's Death and Resurrection (21:1-28:15).*

The kernel event in this section of the Gospel is the cleansing of the temple. It happens after Jesus enters Jerusalem as its messianic king (see 21:9), and as a consequence of that fact (21:1-17). The event serves as a crisis because it confronts the inhabitants of Jerusalem with the question of Jesus' person and authority. This question plays out in the rest of the story, leading inevitably to his final rejection and death on the one hand, but to his victory and resurrection as God's anointed one on the other. Only in Matthew's story of the cleansing of the temple do the Jewish leaders question Jesus' authority for such outrageous action (see 21:15-16).

The event of the messianic purification of the temple, powerfully commented upon by the insertion of the destruction of the barren fig tree, supplies the proximate occasion for Jesus' death. A theme emerges at the cleansing of the temple that will be repeated on two further occasions as the account draws to its dramatic conclusion. At Jesus' trial, witnesses make the accusation: "This fellow said, 'I am able to destroy the temple of God, and to build it in three days'" (26:61). During the crucifixion, Jesus is mocked: "You who would destroy the temple and build it in three days, save yourself!" (27:40). At his death the prophetic gesture of Jesus which began this narrative section becomes a reality: "And behold, the curtain of the temple was torn in two, from top to bottom" (27:51).

After Jesus cleanses the temple, the chief priests and elders of the people ask, "By what authority are you doing these things, and who gave you this authority?" (21:23). When the religious leaders refuse to answer Jesus' counter-question about the baptism of John, Jesus utters three parables against them (21:28-22:14). In the second of them, he announces: "the kingdom of God will be taken away from you and given to a nation producing the fruits of it" (21:43).

After the parables, the bitter invective against the leaders of Israel continues through a series of controversies with them: with the Pharisees, over the payment of taxes (22:15-22); with the Sadducees, over the resurrection from the dead (22:23-33); and with a Scribe, over the greatest commandment (22:34-40). These debates reduce Jesus' opponents to silence: "And no one was able to answer him a word, nor from that day did anyone dare to ask him any more questions" (22:46).

As if this were not enough, Jesus next denounces the scribes and Pharisees in a series of seven woes (23:13-36) and pronounces an oracle of doom over Jerusalem (23:37-39). The old world, represented by the established authorities in Israel and the city of Jerusalem, can no longer claim the allegiance of the true people of God: "The Scribes and Pharisees sit on Moses' seat; so practice and observe whatever they tell you, but not what they do, for they preach, but do not practice" (23:2). Having disposed of the traditional leaders of God's people, Jesus next turns to his disciples, the nucleus of the true people of God. He warns them not to be led astray. Many things must happen before God's plan is ultimately achieved. Jesus foretells the destruction of the temple and his return as the Son of Man (24:1-51). However, between the "now" of Jesus' final days with them and the "end time" when the Son of Man will come in glory, there will be a long "in between time." This will be the time of the Church, the new people of God. Therefore, Jesus instructs the disciples to produce works of righteousness during the period of his absence (25:1-46).

The passion opens with a comment from the narrator indicating that the teaching is over, and words from Jesus that look back to his earlier passion predictions. The turning point of the ages has arrived: "When Jesus had finished all these sayings he said to his disciples, you know that after two days the Passover is coming, and the Son of Man will be delivered up to be crucified" (26:1-2). But the events of the passion of Jesus follow as a result of events initiated by the cleansing of the temple. Anger and animosity broke out on that occasion which has gone on unabated ever since.

Rather than analyze Matthew's passion narrative passage by passage, I will limit myself to an indication of the way the main thrust of the plot is achieved through Matthew's passion. The sequence of events, and the major thrust of Matthew 26:1-27:66, matches that of the Gospel of Mark. They can be traced in my earlier summary of the Markan passion narrative.[16]

Ironically, those who condemn him to death proclaim Jesus' messianic status. This happens at the Jewish trial, where the messianic terms used at Caesarea Philippi are repeated in the question of the high priest and the response of Jesus: "'I adjure you by the living God, tell us if you are the Christ, the Son of God'. Jesus said to him, 'You have said so. But I tell you, hereafter you will see the Son of Man seated at the right hand of Power, and coming on the clouds of heaven'" (26:63-64). The proceedings of the Roman trial insist that Jesus is "King of the Jews" (see 27:11, 29) and "Christ" (27:17, 22).

During the passion, the people who have been passive through all the angry encounters between Jesus and the leaders of Israel, under the influence of their leaders, reject Jesus as the Messiah, and choose a false messianic pretender, Barabbas, in his place (27:15-23). Indeed, they support their demand that Jesus be crucified with terrible words indicating that the former people of God has made its choice: "His blood be on us and on our children" (27:25). But a Gentile soldier and those with him confess that Jesus was truly the Son of God (27:54).

In accordance with Jesus' predictions, God raises him on the third day, despite the efforts of the Jewish leaders to make "the sepulcher secure until the third day" (26:62-66). Matthew's resurrection account moves from the negative report of the guarding of the secured sepulcher (26:62-66), to the positive experience of the women who discover the empty tomb, and encounter Jesus (27:1-10), to the lies that are spread abroad when the guards report the events at the tomb to the Jewish leaders (vv. 11-15), to the final climactic positive experience of Jesus' encounter with the disciples, and their final commission (vv. 16-20). The fifth narrative unit is the climax of Israel's opposition to the Messiah. As Israel rejects Jesus, the Gentiles in the person of the Roman soldiers begin to accept him, and the risen Lord encounters his fragile, but believing, disciples. Thus, as the plot moves towards its conclusion, the Gospel moves from Israel to the nations.

6. *The Sixth Narrative Unit: The Great Commission (28:16-20).*
This concluding scene stands alone. It is an ending that opens to the future. For the first time, Jesus allows the disciples to teach and to proclaim the Gospel to the Gentiles. Earlier, as we had occasion to see, he limited their mission to the lost sheep of the house of Israel (see 10:5-6; 15:24).

Although the story ends here, the reader knows what will take place after the great commission, thanks to Jesus' parable discourse (13:1-52) and his eschatological discourse (24:1-25:46). In these discourses Jesus tells several parables which explain what will happen in the period between his resurrection and his return as the Son of Man at the close of the age. There will be periods of persecution when many will fall away (13:21). There will be a mixture of good and bad within the Church (13:24-30). Many will grow weary waiting for his return (25:1-13), but at the end of the age Jesus will come as the royal Son of Man to judge the nations (25:31-46). Thus the great commission (28:16-20) is not an ending but a beginning that invites the reader to discipleship and to the evangelization of the nations.

The Experience of the Matthean Community

If this is the story of Jesus as it has been told in the Gospel of Matthew, one further question needs to be raised before we turn to a closer reading of the story of Jesus' birth and infancy. Is it possible for us to recapture the experience of the Christian community for which the Gospel of Matthew was written? Given the very clear understanding which the author and his readers appear to have had of the Jewish world and its traditions, the community was obviously largely Jewish in origin. The Jewish background and religious formation of this early Christian community led its members to recognize the greatness of God's ways with his people of old. But it was not only the God of Israel who continued to be at the center of their belief; they also struggled to understand how they related to the chosen people of old, the people of Israel. In fact, one could say that the crisis which produced the Gospel of Matthew could be called "an identity crisis."

We may lose sight of how much it would have cost the earliest Christians — mostly Jewish people — to leave their traditional faith and practice to enter a Christian community, such as the one that eventually produced the Gospel of Matthew. This was a most difficult journey for believing Jews to make, even though they may have come to believe that Jesus Christ was the Messiah. Their faith in Jesus of Nazareth as the Christ, the Son of the living God (see 16:16) was causing them great suffering, as their long-time friends from the synagogue in the town (probably Antioch in Syria) could no longer abide the presence of these renegades in their community. In fact, it is possible that their old friends eventually came to pray, each day:

> For apostates may there be no hope and may the Nazarenes and the heretics suddenly perish (Twelfth Blessing of the synagogue prayer, the *Shemoneh Esreh*).[17]

To be separated from their former way of life, so closely associated with the synagogue, meant that almost every aspect of their day-to-day life was changed. They were snubbed by their former friends from "the synagogue across the road."[18] They could no longer marry their sons and daughters within a community whose faith they shared and whose way of life they had always respected and also attempted to live. In a non-Jewish city (like Syrian Antioch), they were not able to go into the confusion of the market place and buy their food from places where they had always been welcome, and where they knew it had been prepared in the time-honored and sacred ways.

Although these practical difficulties were many, they would have labored under an even greater problem. They were now separated from what was the heart of the life of a good Jew in the time when Matthew was writing his Gospel. They were excluded from the synagogue celebration of the Torah and its authoritative transmission by the Rabbi, the teacher, the authentic interpreter of the greatest of all teachers: Moses. Cut off from the world they knew and loved so much, they had to find a new "Teacher" and a new authority. If the synagogue "across the road" possessed Moses' Law and its authentic interpreter in the Rabbi (see, for example, 19:7 and 22:24), to whom could this struggling Jewish Christian Church now turn? The Matthean Jesus provides the answer to that question:

> The Scribes and the Pharisees sit on the seat of Moses. So practice and observe whatever they tell you, but not what they do. For they preach but do not practice. ... You are not to be called teacher, for you have one Teacher and you are all brethren. And call no one on earth your Father, for you have one Father, who is in heaven. Neither be called masters, because you have one Master: the Christ (23:2-3, 8-11).

The members of Matthew's community are further instructed that they are, in their own turn, to teach all nations to observe all the things that Jesus had taught them (see 28:20). The Gospel of Matthew exists because this particular early Christian community took those words seriously and acted upon them. Jesus was their one teacher, and they taught what he had taught them. This is the other side of the Matthean experience that must not be forgotten in reading this Gospel. As they "went out" from traditional synagogue Judaism, they found themselves immersed in a large city that was dominated by powerful Roman culture and practices.[19] This story of Jesus, as reported in the Gospel of Matthew, had to face two major environments. On the one hand, the Matthean community was located in a place where there was a strong Jewish presence, and the members of the community had to come to understand how the events of the life, teaching, death and resurrection of Jesus Christ determined their relationships with Judaism. On the other hand, this same community had to recognize that it was now living in a world populated by people who were Gentiles, predominantly Romans, and that the message had to be preached to "all the nations" (28:19).

Conclusion

Matthew has told his story of Jesus to a community which had been forcibly separated from Judaism, and which probably had members longing for the old and trusted ways. They were hesitant, and perhaps unwilling, to go out into the Gentile mission, to cross the bridge into the Gentile world. He was aware of the fragility of his own community, some of whom were tempted to slip back into the ways of the synagogue, yet certain in his faith that God had broken into human history irrevocably in the birth, life, death and resurrection of Jesus. To bridge the gap between the old and the new, Matthew draws out of his story his central theme: during his life Jesus lived and asked for the perfection of the old ways, and then, through his death and resurrection the turning point of the ages came to pass. The past, the present, and the future can be explained in terms of Jesus Christ.[20]

Matthew tells his largely Jewish community that despite the hostility and the ridicule of the synagogue across the road, they have lost nothing. God's ways in the world have now been fulfilled, as the Old Testament has led to and been perfected in Jesus. The old ways are now perfected further in the universal presence of Jesus, through his Church, to the whole world. For Matthew, the true Israel is not to be found in the post-War synagogue stoutly defending its traditions to maintain its identity, but in the Christian community, now irrevocably committed to the Gentile mission.

Many of the Jewish people in Matthew's community were wondering if perhaps they had lost their way by becoming Christians, but Matthew's message dispels that doubt. He builds a bridge between the Old and the New, and that bridge is the person of Jesus. The puzzled members of Matthew's Church are told that they now belong to the new and perfect Israel, which has been given its new and perfect law by a new Moses on a new Sinai (see Matt 5:1-48).

Matthew never destroys the old. He has a deep respect for 1,000 years of sacred history. In fact, he rewrites Mark 2:22 which spoke of the uselessness of the "old" wineskins. He wishes to show the ongoing value and importance of the "old," side by side with the "new."

> Neither is new wine put into old wineskins; if it is the skins burst, and
> the wine is spilled, and the skins are destroyed; but new wine is put into
> fresh wineskins, and so both are preserved (Matt 9:17).

As he leads a traditional Jewish Christian community into the challenge of the Gentile mission he looks back to Jesus. He tells his story so that the community might see the perfection of the old, through the death and resurrection of Jesus, in the newness which they are living.

The Christian Church can never evade the challenge of the risen Lord questioning us and leading us into our "Gentile mission." We too face the new ways and cultures that surround us, teaching them all that Jesus has taught. In our situation Matthew's Gospel tells us that we must allow ourselves to be led into a future that only God can create. Jesus will be with us until the close of the age. We are called to leave the securities of old and safe ways, yet always respecting those ways. They came into existence as the fruit of accumulated wisdom and experience. They are not simply to be discounted, as an appreciation of them prepares us for the newness of God's plans. God does not come to us "new" in every new situation; he is always among us in a "history of salvation," however much the turns of this history may surprise us. Little wonder that Matthew described himself — and consequently all dedicated Christians — in a tiny biographical insertion which both gives his secret away and challenges all who follow him as disciples of Jesus:

Every scribe who becomes a disciple of the kingdom of heaven is like a householder who brings out of his treasure things both new and old (13:52).

Notes

[1] For a thorough study of the earliest use of the Gospel of Matthew by Christian writers, see E. Masseaux, *The Influence of the Gospel of Matthew on Christian Literature before Saint Irenaeus* (trans. N. J. Belval and S. Hecht; ed. A. J. Bellinzoni; New Gospel Studies 5; Macon: Mercer, 1993).

[2] For a review of this period, see S. P. Kealy, *Mark's Gospel: A History of Its Interpretation* (New York: Paulist Press, 1982), 7-57.

[3] Among the Gospels, only in Matt 16:18 and 18:17 (twice) does the Greek word *ekklesia* (assembly, congregation, church) appear. On the origins and the significance of this expression, see E. W. Stegemann and W. Stegemann, *The Jesus Movement. A Social History of Its First Century* (trans. O. C. Dean Jr.; Minneapolis: Fortress, 1999), 262-87.

[4] See above, pp. 15-24.

[5] For an excellent study of the use of the theme of "the mountain" in the Gospel of Matthew, see T. L. Donaldson, *Jesus on the Mountain. A Study in Matthean Theology* (Journal for the Study of the New Testament Supplement Series 8; Sheffield: JSOT Press, 1985). For a briefer, but also excellent, treatment, see D. A. Lee, *Transfiguration* (New Century Theology; London/New York: Continuum, 2005), 43-46.

[6] For more detailed discussion of the narrative theory that follows, see G. Genette, *Narrative Discourse. An Essay in Method* (trans. J. E. Lewin; Ithaca: Cornell University Press, 1980), 33-85, and the excellent summary of Genette's contribution in S. Rimmon-Kenan, *Narrative Fiction: Contemporary Poetics* (New Accents; London: Methuen, 1983), 43-58.

[7] It appears strange to us that some sort of "blame" has to be laid at the feet of either the parents or even the child in the womb. But this way of thinking starts with the sound theological principle that God does not make mistakes. In John 9:3-5 Jesus points out that this birth was not a mistake, as it serves God's greater design.

[8] See, for example, the authoritative interpretation of W. D. Davies and D. C.

Allison, *The Gospel According to Saint Matthew* (3 vols.; International Critical Commentary: Edinburgh: T. & T. Clark, 1988-1997), 1:482-503.

[9] For what follows, on the "salvation history" perspective in Matthew, see J. P. Meier, *Law and History in Matthew's Gospel* (Analecta Biblica 71; Rome: Biblical Institute Press, 1976), 12-25.

[10] See J. P. Meier, *Matthew* (New Testament Message 3; Wilmington: Michael Glazier, 1980), 142-48. Notice, however, that Jesus' death and resurrection only draw eschatological events into the human story. This marks the "turning point of the ages." It is not the end of time. The Matthean Christians were firmly located in a time and a place, awaiting the final end of all history (see Matt 24).

[11] This suggestion was first made by B. W. Bacon, "The 'Five Books' of Matthew against the Jews," *The Expositor* 15 (1918): 56-66. It has been repeated many times since then. See, for example, the valuable popular commentary of Meier, *Matthew*, vii-viii, xii.

[12] What follows depends on the rich study of F. J. Matera, "The Plot of Matthew's Gospel," *The Catholic Biblical Quarterly* 49 (1987): 233-253.

[13] These terms (kernel, satellite, etc.) have been taken by Matera (see previous note) from the influential work on narrative by S. Chatman, *Story and Discourse. Narrative Structure in Fiction and Film* (Ithaca: Cornell University Press, 1978), 53-56.

[14] In this I differ from Frank J. Matera (see above, note 12) who closes the first unit at 4:11, and regards 4:12-17 as the beginning of Jesus' ministry.

[15] An "inclusion" is another literary expression. It is used to indicate a narrative, or a section of a narrative, which begins and ends in much the same way. The inclusion acts as a type of "frame" around the intervening material. In this case, Peter confesses Jesus as the Christ, the Son of the living God (16:13-28) as the passage opens, while the two blind men at Jericho confess Jesus as the Son of David (20:29-34). This "inclusion" closes the narrative unit by the repetition of a confession that was found at its beginning.

[16] See above, pp. 61-64.

[17] This twelfth benediction, the so-called *Birkat ha-minim*, the blessing of the heretics, has long been regarded as originating in the same post-war setting as the Gospel of Matthew, some time in the 80's of the first Christian century. For this position, and its importance for the formation of the Gospel of Matthew, see W. D. Davies, *The Setting of the Sermon on the Mount* (Cambridge: Cambridge University Press, 1966), 256-315. However, the dating and the wording of the so-called "blessing" is now the subject of considerable discussion. See P. W. van der Horst, "The *Birkat ha-minim* in Recent Research," *The Expository Times* 105 (1994): 363-68. It should not be dated so early, and we cannot be sure of its wording, but it expresses the sentiments that the "parting of the ways" may have generated among Jews. Similar disrespect for the Jews was also shown by early Christians, and there are traces of this in the Gospel of Matthew, who claims that the followers of Jesus have become the true Israel.

[18] This expression, which helps localize the experience of the Matthean Christians, is taken from K. Stendahl, *The School of St. Matthew and Its Use of the Old Testament* (Acta Seminarii Neotestamentici Upsaliensis XX; Lund: Gleerup, 1968), xi.

[19] A scholar who has done a great deal to bring discussion of the the Roman world into an understanding of the Gospel of Matthew is Warren Carter. See his important studies, W. Carter, *Matthew and the Margins. A Sociopolitical and Religious Reading* (Maryknoll: Orbis Books, 2000), and Idem, *Matthew. Storyteller, Interpreter, Evangelist* (Peabody: Hendrickson, 2004).

[20] As Meier, *Law and History*, 89, puts it: "It is Jesus in whom all prophecies are fulfilled, Jesus who authoritatively interprets, radicalizes, and rescinds the Mosaic Law, Jesus who by his death-resurrection brings about the turning of the ages, Jesus who now rules the cosmos as exalted Son of Man."

Reading Matthew 1:1-2:23:
The Infancy Narrative

Matthew 1:1-2:23 acts as a classical "prologue" to the narrative. The stories surrounding the build-up toward Jesus' birth and its aftermath provide information for the reader of the Gospel that the characters in the story do not have. This allows the reader to interpret the narrative with hind-sight, which helps in interpreting the Gospel's in-vestigation into the identity and mission of Jesus.

There are two major sections in Matthew 1:1-2:23. In the first the origins of Jesus, both human and di-vine in fulfilment of the Scriptures, are established. In the second his grim but divine destiny is fore-shadowed: Herod rejects him even as he is revealed to and accepted by the Gentiles in the form of the wise men, and his identity as a Nazarean is accom-plished, again showing Jesus fulfilling his Scriptural mission.

Chapter 5
summary

THE OPENING PAGES OF THE GOSPEL OF MATTHEW report a number of "beginnings." In Matt 1:1-17, the Gospel *begins* by delving into the history that led to the birth of Jesus, the Christ. The life of Jesus *begins* with the annunciation to Joseph, explaining the divine origin of his betrothed's expected child (vv. 18-25). A double response to Jesus *begins* once Jesus is borne. In Jerusalem, he is sought out by wise men from the East and rejected by a king (2:1-12). Suffering and even death at the hands of the powers in Israel *begins* as Jesus is taken to Egypt, innocent children are slain, and Joseph must flee again, unable to return to his home, the place of Jesus' birth, Bethlehem. They must go to Nazareth (2:13-23). Matthew 1:1-2:23 acts as a classical "prologue" to the narrative. The stories surrounding the buildup toward Jesus' birth and its aftermath provide information *for the reader of the Gospel* that the *characters in the story* do not have.[1]

The Literary Shape of Matthew 1:1-2:23

Matthew 1-2 opens in 1:1, introducing and summarizing the genealogy that follows ("the book of the genealogy"). The genealogy closes in v. 17 with an inclusion, repeating the theme and the words of v. 1 ("all the generations"). The list of generations does more than provide Jesus' pre-history; it also serves to introduce the reader to the Christology of the Gospel as a whole. The data of the genealogy provided by vv. 2-17 confirms the statement of v. 1: "Jesus Christ, Son of David, Son of Abraham." This story of Jesus' pre-history leads into the way Jesus was born: the description of Joseph's dilemma and decision concerning Mary's pregnancy and the dream-annunciation that concludes with Joseph taking Mary as his wife (vv. 18-25). The story of how Jesus came to be born is closely connected to the genealogy by means of the word "the birth" (Greek: *genesis*) in v. 18. The first major section of Matthew 1-2 is thus carefully bound together (v. 1: "the book of the genealogy" [*geneseōs*]; v. 17: "generations" [*geneai*]; v. 18: "birth" [*genesis*]). A shadow of impending threat also hovers over the narrative: a threat to the continuation of the line of Israel in the genealogy (1:1-17) and the threat to Mary and her child (vv. 18-23).

A wider world and further important Matthean themes enter the narrative in 2:1-12. However, a literary link is maintained between 1:1-25 and 2:1-23 by the announcement of Jesus' birth in Bethlehem. The expression "Jesus was born" looks back to the parallel expressions in vv.

1, 17 and 18. This birth brings wise men from the East seeking out Jesus. They come to Jerusalem, broodingly fearful at the news of the birth of someone "born king of the Jews" (v. 2), in Bethlehem (vv. 5-6, 8). Jesus is born in the city of David. As the Gentile visitors adore the newly born king, Herod plots his death. In vv. 13-23, Joseph experiences another dream-encounter with an angel of the Lord. He flees with his wife and Jesus to Egypt, and Herod slays the young males from the region of Bethlehem. On the death of Herod, Joseph is summoned to return to Israel, but unable to settle in Archelaus' Judea, he does not go back to Bethlehem. He and his family flee a second time, to dwell in a city called Nazareth (2:13-23). Opposition and even the threat of violent death are foreshadowed in the episodes of 2:1-23.[2]

There are two major sections in Matthew 1:1-2:23, each one articulated in two further episodes.[3]

1:1-25: The origins of Jesus are described: Who is Jesus?

> 1:1-17: The book of the genealogical pre-history of Jesus, the Christ, the Son of David, the Son of Abraham

> 1:18-25: The divine origin of Jesus, the Emmanuel who will save his people from their sins.

2:1-23: The destiny of Jesus is foreshadowed.

> 2:1-12: Jesus, rejected by Herod, is revealed to Gentiles

> 2:13-23: Jesus comes from Egypt, and will be known as a Nazarene.

Matthew 1:1-25: Who is Jesus?

The Genealogy of the Son of David (1:1-17)

Biblical genealogies explain the rights of belonging to a certain family or tribe (see, for example, Gen 6:14-25), they undergird status (see, for example, Ezra 2:62-63; Neh 7:64-65), they structure history into epochs (see, for example, Gen 5:1-32; 10:1-32), and they link the personality at the center of the narrative with a significant past (see, for example, Gen 11:10-32).[4] There is a strong sense of continuation with this biblical tradition in the Matthean genealogy of Jesus. Matthew 1:1 affirms that Jesus' genealogy traces the pre-history of the Christ, the son of David, the Son of Abraham. The coming of Jesus as "Christ" fulfills Jewish messianic hopes, made more explicit in the description of the Christ as the Son of David.[5] Among the various expressions of messianic hope in Israel, one of the more important was the return of someone from the house of David, to restore God's people with the re-establishment of a royal authority, answerable only to God. The claim that Jesus is the son of David is important for Matthew's infancy story, especially 1:18-23. It is central to the annunciation to Joseph. Joseph is a son of David, and he is told that he must respond to God's design by accepting Jesus as his son (see 1:20). Jesus is the fulfillment of Jewish hopes.

But Jesus is also described as "son of Abraham." Abraham (Abram), the father of Israel, is also a gift of God to all nations. The words of God to Abram/Abraham across his story, reported in Genesis, make this clear. In his call to leave his father's home to become, in his own turn, the father of a great nation, he is also promised: "I will bless those who bless you, and him who curses you I will curse; *and by you all the families of the earth shall be blessed*" (Gen 12:3). Before the strange rite by which God establishes a covenant with him (Gen 15:7-20), Abram is promised: "'Look toward heaven and number the stars, if you are able to remember them.' Then he said to him, 'So shall your descendents be'" (vv. 5-6). In another crucial context, associated with the shift from the name Abram to Abraham, God makes another promise: "Behold my covenant is with you, and you shall be the father of a multitude of nations" (Gen 17:4).[6] Jesus' origins lie in Abraham. He is the Christ, and he fulfills the promises of God to Israel, and to all the nations. Matthew addresses one of the fundamental issues that drives his story of Jesus in the very first line of the Gospel. Jesus is heir to the promises made to David and kept alive in Judaism, but he is also heir to the wider promise of blessings made to the Gentiles through Abraham. As Jesus' Davidic origins are further ratified by his becoming the supposed son of Joseph (1:20, 24), so also is his fulfillment of the promises made to Abraham ratified by the coming of the wise men from the Gentile world of the East to pay homage to the king of the Jews (2:2, 11). Three personal names appear in 1:1: Jesus Christ, David, and Abraham. These names reappear, in reverse order, across the genealogy: Abraham (v. 2), David (v. 6), and Jesus Christ (v. 16).

Everything in the genealogy indicates that it should be read as an articulation of God's providential plan. There are three turning points in the list, and these turning points mark major moments in Israel's history.

David appears in v. 6, the exile to Babylon is reported in v. 11, and the birth of Jesus, who is called Christ, is announced in v. 16. In v. 17 the genealogy closes recalling v. 1, making explicit the tri-partite structure based on three epochs in Israel's history. In doing so, the Evangelist adds a further detail, as the number "fourteen" may have gone unobserved in a first reading: "So all the generations from Abraham to David were fourteen generations, and from David to the deportation fourteen generations, and from the deportation to Babylon to the Christ fourteen generations" (v. 17). The shaping of three generations of fourteen can hardly reflect the *facts of history*. Perhaps seven to eight hundred years passed from Abraham to David (fourteen generations), a little more than four hundred years from David and the Babylonian exile (fourteen generations), and almost six hundred years from the exile to the birth of Jesus (fourteen generations). Many (but not all) of the names can be traced in records of Israel's past. Material that came to him from the Old Testament and popular traditions (*historical data*) has been used by Matthew to show God at work (*theological truths*).[7]

The first period, a sacred history based upon the biblical story, leads to David (vv. 2-6a). He does not receive the seed of Abraham through the older Ishmael, but through the divinely chosen Isaac (v. 2; Gen 16-17). A similar divine action makes Jacob, not Esau, the one who continues the line from Isaac (v. 2; Gen 27). Among the twelve sons of Jacob, it is Judah who continues the line (v. 3; see Gen 49:10). Finally, within the house of Judah, it is to the least indicated but divinely chosen David that the scepter is given (v. 6; 1 Sam 16:1-13). Only a selection of the kings in the Davidic line is found in the second group of fourteen (vv. 6b-11). It closes with Jechoniah who, despite the exile, is reported at the head of the final section (v. 12) as having had a son. Thus the line passing from Abraham, through David, and eventually to Jesus, is divinely ordered. The final section (vv. 12-16) connects the end of the monarchy through a series of largely unheard of names, descendents of the biblical Zerubbabel, who rebuilt the temple in 520-515 B.C.E. (Ezra 3:2-8; Neh 12:1; Hag 1:1, 12, 14; 2:2-23). From this line appears the anointed king, Jesus the Christ. Jesus is a product of the action of God who has providentially directed history toward the birth of the Messiah.

Scholarly speculation upon the symbolic possibilities of the number "fourteen" is never-ending.[8] The most likely explanation for the use of fourteen comes from the fact that in Hebrew, where the letters of the alphabet also have numerical value, links can be forged between numbers and names (*gematria*). In this case, the sum of the letters that form "David" (*dalet [4]-waw [6] –dalet [4]*) is fourteen. The perfect (three-fold) repetition of a number that also means "David" produces Jesus, the anointed Messiah.

The final puzzle that has been a source of speculation across the centuries is the naming of women in Matthew's genealogy of Jesus: Tamar (v. 3), Rahab (v. 5), Ruth (v. 5), Bathsheba (v. 6a: "the wife of Uriah"). Vv. 1-17 read aloud makes it obvious that the names of the women break the typical rhythm of a genealogy, where father begets son, and son becomes father: "A was the father of B, and B was the father of C," and so on. As it is most unusual in biblical genealogies to mention mothers, long reflection upon 1:1-17 has rightly claimed that Matthew's insertion of the women's names was done for a purpose. But what was that purpose?[9] Some, following Jerome, suggest that the women in the genealogy were sinners, and their presence in the generations is to foreshadow the words of the angel of the Lord to Joseph, in explanation of the name "Jesus": "for he will save his people from their sins" (1:21; see Jerome, *In Mattheum* 9 [PL 26.21-22]). Others, following Martin Luther, point to their being foreigners, and thus their presence continues the theme, already present in v. 1, that Jesus' coming is marked by an openness to the Gentile world.

Even though the women are all associated with sexually questionable activities, they are not presented in the biblical tradition, nor in later Jewish and Christian speculation, as sinners. Their assessment as sinners is an anachronistic judgment of their roles within the biblical accounts. The second suggestion, at first sight, appears more likely, but what if one includes the mother of Jesus among the women in vv. 1-17? The figure of "Mary, of whom Jesus was born" (v. 16) must be part of the equation. The following passage (vv. 18-23) will point to the suspicion that she was a sinner, but there is no hint that she is not Jewish. These suggestions play into the solution to this puzzle, once Mary is included among the women mentioned in the genealogy. Three features can be attributed to all five women.

1. Each of the women mentioned plays a fundamental role at turning points in Israel's sacred history. Tamar continues God's appointed line after the death of Er and Onan (Gen 46:12). Rahab, called a prostitute, is nevertheless the hero at Jericho, as Israel enters the promised land (Josh

2:1-21; 6:17-25). Ruth is the mother of Obed, the grandfather of David (Ruth 4:18-22). Bathsheba conceives Solomon by David, and with the guidance of the prophet Nathan establishes her son as the continuation of the Davidic line (1 Kings 1:11-2:9). Mary is the women "of whom Jesus was born, who is called Christ" (Matt 1:16).

2. In every case, even though not judged as sinful, there was something irregular in the sexual situation of the women. It appears odd that such people could be part of the unfolding of God's design. Joseph's resolution of his dilemma in vv. 18b-19 indicates that this is also the case with Mary.

3. Despite the surprising association of such women, with their compromising situations or backgrounds, with the unfolding of God's history, all of them, including Mary, showed initiative and courage when summoned by God to preserve the line from Abraham, through David, that would eventually lead (through Joseph) to the Messiah (v. 16). But there is more at stake than the sexual irregularities lurking behind the stories of the five women. In a genealogy that follows an accepted patriarchal transmission from one generation to another, these women emerge from the margins of society and culture to show that God works through people who are generally denied status and privilege. Their presence shows God's working over against prevailing cultural absolutes, and each of these women, in her own way, is threatened by those absolutes.

God called all five women to play an integral role in the unfolding of the messianic promise. In the cases of the women from the pre-monarchical period, God has overcome the moral irregularity of human parents. However, in the case of Mary, something more spectacular takes place. The careful description of Mary as "of whom Jesus was born" (v. 16) detaches the maternity of Mary from the paternity of Joseph. To these three elements which all five women share, the fact that four of the women are not only associated with a dubious sexual situation, but are also from the world outside Israel, must be added. The presence of the women in Jesus' genealogy, therefore, reflects "the strange righteousness of God,"[10] and the risky consequence of responding to that righteousness. The genealogy, therefore, addresses the situation of the members of the Matthean community, composed of both Jew and Gentile. They did not share a racial heritage, but they were united by their faith in Jesus Christ,

Messiah, Son of David and Son of Abraham. In his own turn, he was the perfection of promises made to both Abraham and David.[11]

How the Son of David was Born (1:18-25)

The careful description of Mary as the woman "of whom Jesus was born" in v. 16 raises a question concerning Jesus' birth which is answered in vv. 18-23. A link with the genealogy is created by means of the words, "Now the birth (*genesis*) of Jesus Christ (see also v. 1) took place in this way" (v. 18a). But the broader notion of generations narrows, to become more focused upon *how* the birth of Jesus Christ took place. The situation described in v. 18b reflects Jewish marriage practice, and Jewish law regarding infidelity. Mary is already in a situation of betrothal to Joseph, but they have not yet had sexual relations. Betrothal could take place some time before a husband led his wife to his home. However, even in the time of the betrothal, the woman was regarded as his wife (see the use of "wife" in vv. 20 and 24), already under the jurisdiction of the man. Although not widely practiced, it was legitimate for a man to have sexual relations with his betrothed, even before he formally led her to his home.[12] Thus, if the woman had sexual relations outside the betrothed relationship, she was to be dealt with according to the legislation of Deuteronomy 22:23-25. A betrothed woman who was attacked could cry out, and be heard. If this has not happened, it is taken for granted that she has been disloyal to her betrothed partner, and both she and her male partner are to be stoned to death, to "purge the evil from among you" (v. 25). Matthew makes it clear that Mary and Joseph had not yet had sexual relations. He describes them as "betrothed" (v. 18a), reports that this was the time "before they came together" (v. 18b), and by the further clarification of the nature of their relationship in v. 25: "He knew her not until she had borne a son."

In this situation, Mary is described as "found with child of the Holy Spirit" (v. 18c). No explanation of how this situation came about is offered.[13] For Matthew, Joseph's response to the action of God is more important than Mary's experience. The action of God is indicated by the passive "she was found." No further explanation is required, except that this pregnancy is the result of the action of the Holy Spirit. The Spirit plays only a minor role in the Gospel of Matthew (see 3:16-17; 28:19), and "[t]he Spirit's role here at the origin of Jesus' life is reminiscent of the function of the Spirit in Genesis at the beginning of creation (Gen 1:1-

2)."[14] A new era begins, and – as in Genesis – God is the active agent. There is no suggestion in the text that the Spirit somehow impregnates Mary. The reader, and not Joseph, is bluntly informed that a betrothed girl is found to be with child, and that God, by means of the Holy Spirit, is the one from whom this child comes. No male agent is involved in the generation of the child that Mary is carrying. Jesus is born in a way that is marked by the continuity of the Davidic line, by means of Joseph, and discontinuity, because this child is the result of God's action in and through a virginal conception.

Joseph, who is at the center of all the action from this point on, is described as a "just man." This expression indicates that Joseph is a man who lives in an upright way, according to the Law. This description promises he will make a decision that is obedient to the Law. Joseph had the right to have Mary stoned publicly at the gate of the city (see Deut 22:24), but he decides not to shame his wife in this fashion. The point of the legislation was to "purge the evil from among you" (v. 25). This leaves open the possibility of a lenient interpretation of the law, to divorce her quietly, and in this way eliminate the evil. Joseph decides to adopt the practice of divorce as a sufficient "purging of the evil."[15]

Joseph is considering this possibility (v. 20a) when a communication from God takes place (v. 20b). Like his namesake, Joseph, known to his brothers as a dreamer, and the interpreter of dreams for the Pharaoh (see Gen 37:5-7, 9, 19-20; 40:5-19; 41:1-36), he is visited by "an angel of the Lord." An angel of the Lord is not simply a heavenly messenger, but the bearer of a communication that comes directly from God.[16] The encounter between Joseph and the angel of the Lord takes the form of an annunciation scene across vv. 20-21 (see also Gen 16:7-12 [Ishmael is announced]; 17:1-21; 18:1-15 [Isaac is announced twice]; Judges 13:3-22 [Samson is announced]; Luke 1:11-20 [John the Baptist is announced]; Luke 1:26-37 [Jesus is announced]).[17] In v. 20 an angel of the Lord appears, and the visionary is addressed by name, "Joseph." A qualifying phrase describes the visionary, "son of David." He is urged not to be afraid, as his wife is with child by the Holy Spirit. The use of the divine passive, "which is conceived" stresses that Mary's pregnancy is the result of the action of God through the Holy Spirit. Of foremost importance is the fact that Mary is carrying a child not generated by human means. The dilemma faced by Joseph, "the just man," has been resolved. The Law has not been broken. There is no need to resort to a lenient observation of the law because God, the giver of the Law, is the source of this pregnancy. Joseph is thus free to take his wife to his home. If Joseph were to dispense with her, or even have her executed, would frustrate God's design of raising up Jesus as a Son of David (see 1:1). This possibility has been overcome by God.

The growing recognition in the early Church that Jesus was the Son of God lies behind this carefully articulated presentation of a virginal conception.[18] The annunciation experience draws Joseph into God's design. Jesus Christ has already been described as "the Son of David" (v. 1), but it is only through Joseph that Jesus can be a son of David. It is essential to sacred history that Joseph, belonging to the line of David, make his own the child at present being carried by his wife, Mary. It is through Joseph that Jesus will be known as a son of David, and will show himself to be the messianic "Son of David" (v. 20c). Thus, in vv. 18-20 Matthew tells *how* the as yet unborn Jesus is both "Son of God" and "Son of David."

The annunciation to Joseph continues into v. 21. Mary will give birth to a male child, and the angel tells Joseph he must call the child "Jesus." The Hebrew origins of the name "Jesus" means "the one who saves." Thus, his name explains future accomplishments: "for he will save his people from their sins." Jesus' future, which will be more fully developed in 2:1-23, is revealed in this name. There are already sufficient indications in the genealogy ("Son of Abraham" in v. 1, and the presence of the women in vv. 2-26), but further elements in the infancy story (especially 2:1-12) and the story of Jesus' life, death and resurrection (see 8:17; 9:2-8; 26:28) will show that, for Matthew, this means that both Jews and Gentiles will be liberated from the slavery of sin by Jesus, Son of God and Son of David.

Matthew 1:18-25 draws to a conclusion with the first use of a so-called "fulfillment citation." More than any other Evangelist, Matthew looks back to the Old Testament as an explanation for what God has done in and through the person and ministry of Jesus. This is an important indication of a largely Jewish community that looked to its Scriptures to explain the new situation in which they found themselves in their acceptance of Jesus of Nazareth as the Christ. Jesus Christ is the "fulfillment" of the promises to Israel. The narrative of Joseph's annunciation, with its command to take Mary to his home (vv. 20-21) and his wordless obedience to the command of the Lord (vv. 24-25), is interrupted by the citation in

vv. 22-23. The passage comes to its conclusion as Matthew inserts his interpretation of Jesus as the fulfillment of the Scriptures. The formula itself is stereotypical, but makes Matthew's point well: "*All this* took place to fulfill what the Lord had spoken by the prophet" (v. 22). However, the expression "all this took place" is found in only one other fulfillment citation in Matthew (26:56). It "indicates that Matthew adduces the quotation not only for the sake of the name Immanuel but because the *entire* story of the birth announcement is important to him. ... Thus our text is for Matthew not only an explanatory note to the genealogy; it also indicates new Christological themes to be unfolded further in the gospel."[19]

The biblical citation itself is a sophisticated early Christian reflection upon Isaiah. The passage was originally directed by Isaiah to King Ahaz (ca. 735-715 BC) as a sign that God would provide if he would abandon his plan to form military alliances with Syria and the Northern Kingdom (Ephraim) in an attempt to resist Assyria. As a sign, a young woman who may or may not have been a virgin, but was physically ready to bear a child (the meaning of the Hebrew word *'almah*) would fall pregnant. This child would continue the Davidic line, but there is no suggestion that he would be an expected Messiah. The birth of the child would be a sign that there was no need to form alliances and conduct war, because God was still "with us" (Emmanuel).[20] The Greek translation (LXX) makes some important alterations to the Hebrew. The most significant is the alteration of the translation of the Heberew ' *almah* with *parthenos*, a Greek word that means "virgin." There can be no doubt that this was a deliberate ploy on the part of the LXX translator to render more spectacular the sign that would be given to Ahaz. There is no suggestion in the LXX, however, of a *virginal conception*. All that is said is that a woman at present a virgin will, by the usual sexual procedures, become pregnant.

Matthew seizes upon this text. Isaiah 7:1-17 is directed to a son of the House of David (see v. 13: "O house of David!"), and the LXX introduces a virgin who will bear a son. Matthew reshapes the passage to see its fulfillment (v. 22) in "how" Jesus Christ was born (v. 18), Son of David, from a virgin mother, a child who is "of the Holy Spirit" (v. 20). The LXX tells of a virgin *who will conceive*, i.e. she will receive male seed and conceive. Matthew eradicates all possible reference to male intervention by altering the LXX to a virgin who *will be with child and bear a son.* The LXX prophesied that "you (singular = Ahaz) will call his name Emmanuel." For Matthew, this becomes "they will call his name Emmanuel." Matthew steers away from the uniquely Davidic line produced by this birth. The reference to "they" will lead directly into the story of the wise men from the East. Jesus is not only a "Son of David," and the fulfillment of Jewish hopes, but also "Son of Abraham" in whom all nations shall be blessed (see 1:1; Gen 12:1-3). Finally, the LXX offers no interpretation of the transliterated Hebrew word "Emmanuel." Matthew explains it by adding an explanation of "Emmanuel" to the passage from Isaiah 7:14: "which means God with us."

As the description of the identity of the person of Jesus continues to unfold, the reader senses climax as prophecy is fulfilled (vv. 22-23). By means of this short passage, shaped in the form of a typical annunciation from the Lord, the reader has been told and shown that Jesus is the Christ (v. 18), the Son of David (v. 20), the Son of Abraham (vv. 21, 23), the Son of God (vv. 18, 20), and the presence of God with us (v. 23). The theme of the Emmanuel will return as the Gospel closes with the promise from Jesus: "I am *with you always*, to the close of the age" (28:16). Scripture confirms the extraordinary story told in 1:18-25.

The passage closes by resuming the story of Joseph, who wakes from the sleep during which he has had his dream (v. 24. See v. 20). Described earlier as a just man, his obedience to the law is prolonged into his obedience to the word of God that has come to him from the angel of the Lord. For Matthew, the two are not at odds, as what is happening in the story of the birth of Jesus is the fulfillment of Scripture (v. 22). Matthew does exactly as the angel had commanded: "He took his wife" (v. 20). Everything that has been revealed about the identity of Jesus depends upon this unconditional obedience. Joseph is able to lead Mary to his home, as the Law has not been broken. The giver of the Law is responsible for the son his wife is carrying. Once established in his home, Joseph must guarantee what has been said about the divine origin of the child. There can be no doubt about the paternity of the son that Mary will bear. Therefore, he and his wife do not have sexual relations "until she had borne a son" (v. 25).[21] The promise of the word of God, communicated by the angel of the Lord, is brought to a conclusion in Joseph's further obedient response to the design of God. He called the child by the name Jesus. All that has been promised by this name in v. 21 awaits its own fulfillment.

The Destiny of Jesus (2:1-23)

The theme of Jesus as a royal Son of David was present across 1:1-25. This becomes explicit in 2:1-23, but points beyond Jesus' beginnings toward the end of his story. The wise men come to Jerusalem, seeking "he who has been born king of the Jews" (v. 2). Herod, the king, accompanied by all Jerusalem, is troubled (v. 3) by the search for a new-born king. Herod inquires of "all the chief priests and scribes of the people" (v. 4). At Jesus' trial and crucifixion, the secular ruler in Jerusalem and "all the chief priests and the elders of the people" assemble in opposition to Jesus (27:1), and "all the people" accept responsibility for his blood (27:25). The title "the king of the Jews" will be nailed over the head of Jesus as he hangs on a cross (27:37). Much that appears in 2:1-23 anticipates Jesus' passion and resurrection. The use of the expression "the king of the Jews" in 2:2 is the only place outside the passion narrative where it appears in the Gospel of Matthew. In 2:1-23 this king will be rejected by Herod (and implicitly by those who advise him and all the people), but accepted by the wise men. In the crucifixion Jesus dies, but is brought back to life through the resurrection. In 2:1-23 he is taken away to another land and returns. In both the infancy narrative and the passion narrative God confounds the kings and rulers who assemble against him and his Messiah.[22]

In 2:1-12, the first half of 2:1-23, the reader initially encounters the report of the experience of the wise men from the East, developed against the backdrop of troubled Jerusalem and a threatening Herod. Although the story continues against the backdrop of Herod's violence, in vv. 13-23 Joseph returns to dominate the action, as he did in 1:18-25. Not only does he reappear as the major agent in the flight to Egypt, the return to Israel, and the further decision to settle in Nazareth; he continues to respond with wordless obedience to an angel of the Lord (vv. 13-14, 19-21, 22-23), who appears to him in dreams (vv. 13, 19, 22). The figure of Joseph holds the narrative of 1:1-2:23 together although he is completely absent in 2:1-12. The figure of Herod does the same across 2:1-23. His actions, anticipated in vv. 1-12, draw Joseph back into the story in vv. 13-23. The threat of Herod lurks behind each episode (see vv. 3-6, 7-8, 12, 13, 15, 16, 19, 22).

There is a concentration on geography in 2:1-23 that is absent from 1:1-25. With the exception of the mention of Babylon in vv. 11 and 17, a period in Israel's history rather than a place, no geographical location is mentioned in 1:1-25. Jesus' birth in Bethlehem is announced in 2:1, as wise men from the East come to Jerusalem. They are directed to Bethlehem (vv. 5-6). Jesus flees to Egypt (vv. 13-14). Herod slays the male children under two years old in Bethlehem (v. 16), and a voice is heard in Ramah (v. 18). On the death of Herod, Joseph brings his family from Egypt to Israel (vv. 19-21), and finally locates them in Galilee (v. 22), in a city called Nazareth (v. 23). Matthew 2 opens in Bethlehem and closes in Nazareth. Across 2:1-23 Matthew uses traditions that came to him to generate a geographical journey. Matthew 1:1-2:23 has been shaped to produce a unified proclamation of Jesus' divine and human origins, his person, and his destiny.

2:1-12: Two Responses

There are two parts to vv. 1-12, each one marked by movement from one place to another, and concluding with a fulfillment citation.

1.   vv. 1-6: The wise men come from the East to Jerusalem, and are directed to Bethlehem. This fulfills what was written by the prophet (Micah 5:1, with help from 2 Sam 5:2).

2.   vv. 7-12: The wise men travel from Jerusalem to Bethlehem. There they find the child with his mother, and they worship him. The passage ends with an implicit citation of Psalm 72:10-11 and Isaiah 60:6, concerning foreigners bringing gifts of gold and frankincense to give homage to God's royal son (see Ps 72:1).

1. The Wise Men in Jerusalem (vv. 1-6)

Matthew locates Jesus' birth in a place and a time in v. 1. In so doing, he introduces the reader to the main figures in the action: Jesus (present [v. 1] but never active), Herod and the wise men. The reader is informed of Jesus' birth in the Davidic city of Bethlehem. Subtly, this continues the Christological theme of 1:18-25, where Joseph, from the line of David, must take Jesus as his son. Matthew will clarify the importance of the place where Jesus was born in v. 5, as Herod will be informed that, according to Micah 5:1, the Messiah would be born in Bethlehem. Jesus is born "in the days of Herod the king." Herod, known as "the Great," ruled Jewish Palestine, in collaboration with Rome, from 37 to 4 B.C.E. Only partly Jewish (the son of an Idumean), he was a remarkable figure. He cruelly maintained his authority by violence and murder, even (perhaps especially) within the inner circle of his own family.[23] During his long rule he was supported by the Romans, yet he demonstrated an outward allegiance to the great symbols of Israel, especially by means of his famous restoration of the Jerusalem Temple.

The remaining characters, the magi (Greek: *magoi*), wise men from the East, came to Jerusalem responding to the sign in the sky and seeking information from the Jewish traditions and authority (v. 2). They worship Jesus (v. 11), and respond unquestioningly to the warning they receive in a dream (v. 12). The role of the star in the story indicates that they are to be regarded as astrologers, men who gaze into the heavens to trace indications of God's designs. Matthew's indication that they are "from the East" does not point to any identifiable place, but singles these men out as non-Jews. They are Gentiles who come to Jerusalem to find the new born "King of the Jews" (v. 2). The indication of 1:1 that Jesus was the Christ, the Son of David, has been developed in 1:1-25. Now his being the Son of Abraham, in whom all peoples will be blessed, emerges.

The question posed by the wise men from the East in v. 2 is a confession of faith that looks back to 1:1-25. They ask "Where is he who has been born the King of the Jews?" Gentiles, the wise men do not have the traditions that would lead them to the newborn king. They believe that a king of the Jews has been born, and the reader knows that this is true, as these events have been foretold in the genealogy and taken place in the description of how Jesus came to be born in 1:1-25. The wise men come to Jerusalem, the center of Jewish Scriptures, traditions and worship, seeking an answer to their question concerning the King of the Jews. The motivation for their belief that a king has been born to the Jews comes from their having seen his star. There is no indication in the text that the wise men have followed a moving star from their Gentile world into Jerusalem. The star they have seen is to be understood in the light of the widespread idea that great people are born under a star. There are many ancient witnesses to the appearance of a star in the sky to mark significant births and events (e.g. the association of Aeneas with Rome [Virgil, *Aeneid*, 2.692-704], the fall of Jerusalem [Josephus, *War*, 6.284], the births of Alexander the Great [Cicero], Nero (Dio Cassius, 61.2,1-4) Augustus, Mithridates, and Alexander Severus [Suetonius, *Augustus*, 94.2; *Tiberius*, 14.2]). The idea that one is born under a certain star can still be found in contemporary popular myths and their expressions.[24] The wise men have come to Jerusalem to seek out the newborn king of the Jews because they saw his star "in its rising." The event of the rising of the star that marked the birth of a king of the Jews led them to Jerusalem. Their presence in Jerusalem is determined by their desire to know "where" this king was to be found. They come to the center of the Jewish world to seek knowledge from those who know Israel's Scriptures and its prophecies about the Messiah, not because a moving star has led them there.

Matthew's use of the star looks back to Numbers 23-24: the story of Balaam and Balak. The basic account is found in the Bible, but it has been used and developed by others. In Numbers 23-24 Balak, a king from the Transjordan region, seeks to destroy Moses. He enlists the support of a famous seer, Balaam, that he might put a curse upon Israel. Balaam is a non-Israelite, a visionary who practices magical rites and who, like the wise men in Matthew 2, comes from the East (LXX Num 23:7). But the plans of the hostile Balak are foiled. Filled by the spirit, no longer master of his own oracle, Balaam prophesies the future greatness of Israel, and the rise of its royal ruler. The presentation of the future leader of Israel begins in LXX Num 24:7: "There will come a man out of his (Israel's) seed, and he will rule many nations … and his kingdom will be increased." However, the passage that impinges most upon the Matthean text is found in Numbers 24:17. A comparison between the Hebrew text (MT) and its Greek translation (LXX) shows the direction of the reinterpretation that appears in Matthew:

> I see him, though not now;
> I behold him, though he is not near;
> a star will come forth from Jacob,
> And a scepter will rise from Israel (MT).

> I will point to him, though not now;
> I bless him, though he has not drawn near;
> a star will rise from Jacob,
> and a man will stand forth from Israel (LXX).

The background to this reinterpretation is an attempt to render more specific the emergence of the Davidic dynasty, over two centuries after Moses' time: David was the star and the scepter ruling over a united Judah and Israel. Matthew has drawn close links between the magician, Balaam, who appeared in the story of Moses, and the wise men who came to Jerusalem in search of the king of the Jews in 2:1-2. Both come from the East, see a star that hails the arrival of a messianic king, and foil the evil designs of a wicked king (Balak, Herod). Balaam tells of the future destruction of Edom, Seir, Ir and Amalek, as Israel and the house of Jacob rise (Num 24:18-19). Although not explicit in Matt 2:1-12, the threatening rejection of the newly born King of Israel by Herod, all Jerusalem (v. 3), the chief priests and the scribes (v. 4) forecasts Israel's rejection of Jesus, and reflects the hostility between Matthew and the Judaism of his time. After Balaam has acknowledged the coming king of Israel, he departs: "Balaam went off to his own home" (Num 24:25), just as the wise men, after recognizing the newborn king of the Jews at Bethlehem "went away to their own country" (Matt 2:12).

On arrival in Jerusalem, they announce that they "have come to worship him." Matthew uses the verb *proskuneō* thirteen times, more frequently than Mark (twice) and Luke (three times). He regularly uses it to indicate a correct approach to Jesus, and the action of God in and through Jesus, an acceptance of who Jesus is and does. In the episode of the coming of the wise men, Matthew uses the verb three times: twice to indicate the correct response of the wise men (vv. 2, 11) and once to show the perversity and falseness of Herod (v. 8). For Matthew, the wise men from the East are Gentile believers who have reacted in faith to the Christological proclamation of the conception and birth of Jesus (1:18-25). They fulfill the promise made in 1:1, that Jesus is not only the Davidic Christ, but also the Son of Abraham, in whom all nations are blessed. One of Matthew's major concerns, the proclamation of the Gospel to the Gentiles (see 28:16-20), lies behind their presence at the beginning of Jesus' story.

Herod enters the scene in v. 3. All readers of the Gospel of Matthew know of Herod. Even if they do not know his full story, they do know of his role in the execution of John the Baptist (14:1-12). In v. 3 Herod is described as "the King." The wise men have come to Jerusalem seeking a newly born King (v. 2). Before the action even begins, the reader has every reason to suspect that the suggestion of the presence of another King will lead to violence: there cannot be two Kings! Thus, on hearing of another king, Herod was troubled (v. 3a), and "the whole of Jerusalem" is troubled along with him (v. 3b). There is both irony and imagination in this presentation of the response of Herod and all Jerusalem. The verb behind the troubled response of all Jerusalem (*tarassō*) indicates a profound emotional reaction, a mixture of shock, surprise and fear. The only other occurrence of the verb in the Gospel of Matthew is in 14:26, where the frightened disciples see Jesus coming to them across the stormy waters. In their case, his appearance leads to their worship (14:33). Herod's response will be different.

It is unlikely that "the whole of Jerusalem" was privy to the question of the wise men, but Matthew draws the people into the story, along with "all the chief priests and the scribes" (v. 4). These same personalities will assemble as Jesus' enemies in the passion story (see 26:3, 57; 27:17, 27, 62). As Pilate pleads Jesus' innocence, "all the people" will accept the responsibility for his blood (27:25), just as at his birth, all Jerusalem is deeply moved, and associate themselves with the plotting of Herod (2:3). The theme of suffering will become explicit in vv. 16-18, and Jesus' destiny will be foreshadowed there. However, it is already present in the rapid association of the wise men's search for "the King of the Jews" (2:2; 27:11, 29, 37) and the gathering of all the people, the high priests and the scribes (2:3-4; 26:3, 57; 27:17, 25, 27, 62). Herod inquired of the high priests and the scribes: "where the Christ was to be born" (v. 4b). There is reason to wonder about the motivation for Herod's search for the birthplace of the Messiah, but his inquiry to those entrusted with the interpretation of the sacred tradition of Israel renders explicit the theme of the *place* of Jesus' origins.

The *correct* answer to this question is provided for Herod. The wise men have done well to read the star as a sign leading them to Israel, to the city of Jerusalem, and to those entrusted with the interpretation of God's word. The high priests and the scribes are able to provide Herod with the answer to his question of v. 4, and, at the same time, the answer to the query of the wise men: "Where is he who has been born King of the Jews?" (v. 2). Israel and its God-given traditions possess the Word of God, and thus the high priests and the scribes are able to read it correctly. This intensifies the problem of their inability to accept what that Word tells them. They have the Word of God, but they are unable to accept its promise.[25] They respond to Herod's (and also the wise men's) question about the place of the birth of the King of the Jews (v. 2), the Messiah (v. 4), by citing Micah 5:1 (2) and 2 Samuel 5:2.[26] Two important statements are made in these two citations, and both are called for. In the first place, Micah 5:1 (2) states that one who is a ruler in Israel will come from the Davidic city of Bethlehem. The association with David is made more explicit by means of the addition of 2 Samuel 5:2: "you will shepherd my people Israel." These words are taken from a passage in 2 Samuel addressed to David who was, at that stage, the King of Judah. The tribes of Israel ask him to extend his sovereignty over them as well. The shepherd image of the 2 Samuel passage links the Davidic city of Bethlehem to the Davidic task of ruling over the whole of God's people.

However, Matthew has reworked the Old Testament texts to reflect better his understanding of Bethlehem, and the child born there, especially in the text from Micah. A comparison of translated versions of the MT (Hebrew), the LXX (Greek) and Matthew's use of the passages makes this clear.[27]

> And you, O Bethlehem Ephrathah, small to be among the clans of Judah;
> from you there will come forth for me one who is to be a ruler in Israel (MT: Mic 5:1).
> You will shepherd my people Israel (MT: 2 Sam 5:2).

> And you, O Bethlehem, house of Ephrathah, are too small to be among the thousands of Judah;
> from you there will come forth for me a leader of Israel (LXX: Mic 5:2).
> You will shepherd my people Israel (LXX: 2 Sam 5:2).

> And you, O Bethlehem (in the) land of Judah, are by no means least among the rulers of Judah;
> For from you will come forth a ruler
> who will shepherd my people Israel (Matt 5:6).

Matthew has eliminated all reference to Ephrathah, and replaced it with "in the land of Judah." He has adapted the text to respond to the promise made in 1:2-3: the Messiah was to descend from Judah. There can be no suggestion (as in the MT and the LXX) that Bethlehem is a place of little significance. Jesus, the Christ, was born there. Finally, Matthew eliminates the reference to "Israel" in the Micah passage, as it appears in the closing statement from 2 Samuel. Matthew's reinterpretation of Micah, guided by his understanding of the centrality of the person of Jesus, works creatively with this Old Testament passage.[28] His reworking of the passage points to his attempt to make his audience aware of the fact that Jesus, the Christ (see 1:1, 17), was born in Bethlehem. This was the place foretold in the Jewish Scriptures (Mic 5:1 [2]) as the birthplace of the Messiah. A theme central to the Matthean Christology lies behind the author's use of Micah 5:1 (2): Jesus fulfills the hopes of Israel.

2. *The Wise Men Travel to Bethlehem (vv. 7-12)*

Matthew subtly introduces Herod's duplicity in the report of his encounter with the wise men (vv. 7-8). Less than honest motives appear to lie behind his summoning of them "secretly," and the verb used to speak of his questioning of them goes beyond mere questioning. It indicates a concerned careful enquiry about the time of the rising of the star. As yet, there is no suggestion of a moving star, but Herod wants to know *when* this child was born. His careful and secret investigation of the wise men will lead to his decision to destroy all the young boys "of two years of age and under" in the region of Bethlehem (2:16). They are commanded by Herod to join his concern, and to go to Bethlehem to "search diligently" for the child. Once they have discovered the newborn king, they are to report back to Herod, so that he too might come and worship him. Herod's falseness lies behind this request. He is King in Jerusalem, and he will certainly not be searching out a newborn King to prostrate himself before him in an act of worship. There would be other motivations for such a search. The verb *prokuneō* is used by Matthew to indicate two responses to the birth of Jesus. The wise men come to worship the newborn king (v. 2), and will eventually do so (v. 11). Herod claims that he wishes to worship him (v. 8), but his request reflects his rejection of Jesus, and will lead to the murder of innocents (vv. 16-18).

The opening words of v. 9 indicate that wise men set out for Bethlehem with every intention of obeying the command of Herod. Their journey is motivated by their having been spoken to by Herod, who is able to point them toward Bethlehem in the light of Israel's Scriptures (see v. 6). Only now does the star that they had seen at its rising, marking the birth of the Messiah, begin to move. It goes ahead of them, until it comes to rest upon the place where the child was (v. 9).[29] The sight of the star, leading them to their desired goal arouses great joy in the wise men. In v. 10 Matthew uses their exaggeratedly enthusiastic expression of joy to mark the first vision of the Christ child. Up to this point in Matthew 1-2, the reader has only read *about* the child; he has never appeared in the story. Exceedingly great joy marks their discovery of the place where the child is (v. 10b). The positive outcome of the search of the wise men to find the newly born king of the Jews (v. 2) is anticipated in this expression of great joy.

In v. 11 they enter the house where the child is found with Mary his mother.[30] The mother of Jesus has played no active role in the narrative thus far. Unlike Luke 1-2, where Mary is the leading figure, in Matt 1-2, Joseph is at the center of the story. Nevertheless, the mother of Jesus was mentioned by name in 1:16 as the fifth and final significant woman in a series of women who have preserved the line of Israel from Abraham, through David, to the Messiah. Although not a major player, Matthew refers to her four times in speaking of "the child with his mother" (2:11, 13, 14, 21). These allusions serve to remind the reader of the virginal conception of the child, a divine action in which Joseph plays no role but to accept the manifestation of God's will. The wise men fall down and worship the child. The joy of v. 10 and the act of obeisance of the wise men before the child shows they believe that they have found the royal Messiah. They recognize Jesus as the universal king, a recognition further reinforced by the gifts of gold, frankincense and myrrh. After the genealogy (1:1-17), each scene of the narrative to this point (1:18-23; 2:1-6) has closed with an *explicit* use of the Old Testament (1:22-23; 2:5-6).

The third scene, the encounter between the wise men and Jesus, closes with an *implicit* reference to scripture. The Balaam story in Numbers acknowledges the greatness of an Israelite ruler, who is symbolized by the rising of a star. There is nothing in that episode about the offering of gifts. However, the mention of the rising star suggested to Matthew an amalgam of passages from Isaiah 60 that speak of a rising light and the bringing of gifts:

> Be enlightened, O Jerusalem, for your light has come;
> and the glory of the Lord has risen upon you (Isa 60:1).
> The wealth of nations will come to you …
> All those from Sheba will come bringing gold and frankincense,
> and proclaiming the salvation of the Lord (LXX Isa 60:5-6).

The figure of Balaam provides background for the presentation of the wise men, responding to a star rising in the East, and this background is filled out by the implicit use of Isaiah 60. The star now moves and comes to rest over the place of the birth of the Messiah (Matt 2:9. See

Isa 60:1). Representatives of the nations bring gold and frankincense to Bethlehem (not Jerusalem, as in Isa 60:1), because the light and glory of God have risen upon that place. In Jerusalem, its king and all the people have been deeply troubled by the news of the birth of the Messiah. The Davidic city of Bethlehem replaces the city of Jerusalem as the place of God's favor, despite the fact that in Jerusalem, at the heart of Israel and the bearer of its sacred traditions, the wise men discover the truth about the birth place of the Messiah, revealed in Israel's Scriptures.[31] The Isaian reference further underlines the Gentile character of the wise men. However, the mention of Sheba in Isaiah 60:5 guides Matthew to another Old Testament passage, linking the two themes of gifts and homage:

> May the kings of Sheba and Saba bring gifts;
>
> may all kings pay homage (Ps 72:10-11).

Later Christian identification of the wise men as kings from the East shows an early awareness of Matthew's implicit use of this Psalm. The implicit use of Isaiah 60:1-6 and Psalm 72:10-11 continues Matthew's development of his Christological statement in 1:1: "Jesus Christ, son of David, son of Abraham." In 1:22-23 his use of Isaiah 7:14 insisted upon Jesus' messianic status (Jesus *Christ*). In 2:6 he used Micah 5:1 and 2 Samuel 5:2 to emphasize and develop the fact that Jesus is a Davidic king who will rule over Israel (son *of David*). The use of Isaiah 60:1-6 and Psalm 72:10-11 picks up the insistence that Jesus brings blessing upon all the nations of the earth (son *of Abraham*). The star that rose in the East was hailed by the wise men as the star that announced the birth of the king of the Jews (v. 2), but the use of the Scriptures in v. 11 shows that this king rules over all the nations.[32]

The sinister plans of Herod are thwarted, as the result of the action of God (v. 12). Throughout the narrative, God makes his design known by means of dreams (see 1:20; 2:13, 19, 22). The wise men are warned by God that they must not go back to Herod. The warning explicitly states that they are "not to return to Herod." This is a deliberate reversal of Herod's command: "Bring me the word" (v. 8), which the wise men were initially prepared to obey (v. 9). Like Joseph, they respond without question to the divine command, and "depart to their own country by another way." Within a context of widespread disturbance (v. 8) and veiled threats of danger to the newly born King (vv. 3, 7-8), Jesus Christ, son of David and son of Abraham has been identified and worshiped. Matthew has imaginatively drawn upon well-established ideas of "magi" as wise men who are able to read the signs that manifest themselves in the skies, and described their journey, culminating in the worship of the newly born Messiah, against the rich Old Testament background of Numbers, Isaiah and the Psalms.

A Future Foreshadowed (2:13-23)

The presence of Herod across vv. 1-12 was threatening. The threat becomes reality in the remaining three sections, found in Matthew 2:13-23. Herod now seeks to kill the newly born King. But through God's intervention and Joseph's obedience, the Messiah escapes death, emerges from Egypt alive and settles in Nazareth. Each of the three sections concludes with a formula leading into the citation of Old Testament passages that focus upon a place, significant to the story of God's people, and the story of the Christian community.

1. vv. 13-15. Joseph, obedient to the word of God revealed in a dream, flees with the child and his mother to Egypt. This first scene closes with a formula, and the citation of Hosea 11:1, mentioning *Egypt*.

2. vv. 16-18. By order of Herod, the male children under two years of age are massacred in Bethlehem. The second scene closes with a formula, and the citation of Jeremiah 31:15, mentioning *Ramah* (thought to be close to *Bethlehem*).

3. vv. 19-23. On the death of Herod, again responding to a dream, Joseph returns with the child and his mother to Israel, not to Bethlehem, but to Nazareth. The final scene closes with a formula and the citation of words stemming from Isaiah 4:3 and Judges 16:17, mentioning Jesus' origins in *Nazareth*.

The close association between Moses and Jesus continues into this section of the narrative.[33] As innocent Hebrew children were slain at the birth of Moses, so also innocent Hebrew children are slain at the birth of Jesus (vv. 16-18). As Moses and the original people of God were led out of Egypt to take possession of the promised land, so also Jesus comes out of Egypt to establish a new people of God (vv. 13-15). However, the earlier insistence that Jesus, the Son of David, was accepted by Joseph as his son (1:18-23), and born in the city of David as the King of the Jews and son of Abraham (2:1-12), belies the fact that Jesus was known as "Jesus of Nazareth." Jesus' presence in Nazareth is shown to be the result of the action of God, leading him from Egypt to Nazareth (vv. 19-23).

1. *The Flight to Egypt (vv. 13-15)*

Matthew links the account of the journey of the Wise Men to Bethlehem with the following episode. They have already departed (v. 13a) when the events that follow take place. Repeating the divine intervention that determined Joseph's decision to take Mary as his wife, an angel of the Lord appears to him in a dream (v. 13b. See 1:20a). The divine command first instructs Joseph on what he must do: take the child and his mother and flee to Egypt. It further informs him of the reason why this flight is necessary: Herod is planning to search and find the child so that he might destroy him. The sovereignty of God is indicated by the knowledge of future events: Herod is "about to" destroy the "other" King. As in 1:18-25, Joseph's response is immediate and wordless. Described as a "just man" the first time he appeared in the story (1:19), he continues to respond without hesitation to the revelation of God. The fact that he departs "by night" makes the point that the moment he hears the word of God in a dream, he rises. The stress is not on secrecy, but unconditional obedience to the command of God.

In response to the command of God, Joseph, the child and his mother flee to Egypt. The response of Joseph and the response of Herod and his entourage are at odds. The latter have been instructed by the Scriptures of Israel on the birth of the Messiah at Bethlehem (2:5-6), but they reject the promise of those Scriptures. This rejection will lead to the following episode (vv. 16-18), but God will have the last word. This truth is indicated by the proleptic introduction of the death of Herod in v. 15a. Joseph, the child and his mother remained in Egypt until the death of Herod. Herod's anger will produce violence and death, but he will die, and the child will live beyond that death.

Further proof that the will of God has been done by the response of Joseph to the word of the angel of the Lord is provided by the formula that introduces the citation of Hosea 11:1. The presence of Jesus in Egypt fulfills what the Lord had spoken by the prophet. As throughout Matthew, the use of the verb "to fulfill" assures the reader that in the fulfillment of the Scriptures, God's plan is made manifest. The citation from Hosea shifts the original focus of the prophecy away from *Israel* as the "son" whom the Lord called forth from Egypt, to *Jesus* as the "son" whom the Lord called forth from Egypt. The association between the experience of Jesus and the experience of Israel under the leadership of Moses has been introduced into the text. The people of Israel, under the leadership of Moses, came from Egypt. The citation of Hosea promises that a new "son" comes from Egypt, a "son" whose life, death and resurrection will establish the new people of God, and thus bring to perfection the promises of God. This is the first time that Jesus has been called "son" in Matthew 1-2. His divine origins have been indicated by the virgin birth, and thus the expression is fitting. The Lord summoned *Israel* from Egypt into the freedom of the promised land as an expression of the relationship that existed between God and the people. How much more so is this the case for the relationship between God and the person who "will save his people from their sins" (1:21). The theme of the sonship of Jesus is certainly present, but it will not reach its complete articulation until later in the narrative. At Jesus' baptism the voice from heaven will announce: "This is my beloved son" (3:17).

2. *The Slaying of the Innocents (vv. 16-18)*

A close link with the response of the wise men to the warning not to return to Herod opens vv. 16-18. Herod moves on Bethlehem and its neighboring regions when he finds that he has been mocked and thwarted by the wise men (v. 16a). The same word is used in Exodus 10:2. God promises Moses that the threats of Pharoah will be thwarted. "The verb will appear again in Matt 20:19; 27:29, 31, 45. When Herod is *mocked*, death follows. When Jesus is mocked, death and life follow."[34] The angel's prediction of v. 13 is fulfilled. In the light of his question to the wise men in v. 7 (at what time the star had appeared), he calculates the possible age of the infant King. As the wise men were exceedingly joyful at the sight of the newborn Messiah (v. 10), Herod is exceedingly angry (v. 16a) because his plans have been frustrated. The reader knows, in the light of the dream warning of v. 12, that God has frustrated his plans. There is no other evidence, outside of vv. 16-18, for the senseless slaying of "all the male children in Bethlehem and in all that region who were two years old or under" (v. 16b). But it is perfectly in character with Herod's performance in his final years.[35] What is more important for an appreciation of Matthew's message, however, is the parallel between the story of the slaying of the male children by Pharoah at the birth of Moses, and Moses' escape in Exodus 1-2. Herod's final years were filled with violence. The slaying of innocent males at the time of the birth of Jesus, paralleling the slaying of innocent male Hebrew children that accompanied the birth of Moses, could easily be attributed to Herod.

Another biblical theme is introduced by means of the fulfillment formula and the citation of Jeremiah 31:15 in vv. 17-18. Matthew, reflecting an already established biblical tradition, mistakenly associates Ramah with Bethlehem. Genesis 35:16-19 and 48:7 say that Rachel died "on the way to Ephrathah" and Ephrathah is linked with Bethlehem (see Micah 5:1 [2]),[36] but the more likely location for Ramah was near Bethel, about eleven miles north of Jerusalem, mentioned by Jeremiah as a marshalling place for exile to Babylon (Jer 40:1). Jeremiah 31:15 addresses the weeping of the mother of the nation (Rachel) as Israel was led off, past Ramah, into the Babylonian captivity. However imprecise the geography may be, the introduction of the text from Jeremiah extends Matthew's background beyond traditions associated with Moses. It points to the Exile, a theme already exploited in the separation of the generations that led to the birth of the Messiah in 1:2-12. As at the Exile, Rachel wept for her lost children, she weeps again as the children of Israel suffer persecution. But, just as God broke the power of the tyrants who persecuted Israel – first in Egypt, and then in the Exile – so will he also frustrate the designs of Herod. Jesus, who is to save God's people (1:21), relives two watershed moments in Israel's sacred history: the Exodus and the Exile. Matthew's use of Scripture leads from Bethlehem, the birthplace of the Messiah, to Egypt, the land from which God led Moses in the Exodus, to Ramah, the mourning place of the Exile. "Just as Jesus sums up the history of the people named in his genealogy, so his early career sums up the history of these prophetically significant places."[37]

3. The Return to Nazareth (vv. 19-23)

The promise of v. 15a is fulfilled in v. 19a. Herod died in 4 BC. Matthew situates the following episodes in a historical setting in which they are possible. At the death of Herod, his kingdom was divided between his three sons. Archelaus, ruler of Judea, Idumea and Samaria, proved to be so cruel that he was denounced to Augustus, and exiled to Gaul (France) in 6 AD.[38] It was therefore a prudent decision not to return to Bethlehem in Judea, where a tyrant still ruled, but to go to Nazareth, a village in Galilee ruled by Herod Antipas, a foolish but more benevolent younger brother of Archelaus who ruled from 4 BC – 39 AD In the end, however, he too was exiled to Gaul.

The stereotypical account of a dream appearance of the angel of the Lord appears for the third time (v. 19).[39] The words in the account are exactly the same as those of v. 13, except the names of the places are different. It is now time to return: "Rise, take the child and his mother" (see v. 13). But they are not to flee to Egypt: "Go to the land of Israel" (v. 20). In Exodus, the Pharoah was the enemy of Jesus; in Matthew it is the King in Israel. In Exodus, Moses fled for safety *out of Egypt*, and returned only to lead his people into the promised land. In Matthew, Jesus is taken *into Egypt* for safety. The rejection of Jesus by the leadership of Israel, so important in the passion narrative, has shaped this rewriting of the Moses traditions in this reversal of the location of hostility to God's design. But Jesus will return to Israel, a new Moses, perfecting the original exodus from Egypt to Israel for the foundation of a new people of God. The intended link with Exodus is made clear in the use of the plural in v. 20b. In v. 19 the death of Herod was announced, but in v. 20b the angel tells Joseph: "for those who sought the child's life are dead." Matthew depends upon Exodus 4:19: "The Lord said to Moses: Go back to Egypt, for all those who were seeking your life are dead." This close parallel points to the link between Jesus (2:19-21) and Moses (Exod 4:19-20) that is so important for the Christology of the Gospel of Matthew.

Matthew		*Exodus*	
2:19:	But when Herod died,	4:19	After these many days the king of Egypt died (LXX).
	the angel of the Lord appeared in a dream		The Lord said
	to Joseph in Egypt.		to Moses in Midian
2:20	saying, "Rising, take the child and his mother		
	and go		Go back
	to the land of Israel.		to Egypt
	For those seeking		for all those seeking
	The life of the child		your life
	Have died		have died.
2:21	Rising, he took	4:20	Moses, taking his wife
	the child and his mother		and his children, mounted them on asses

and went unto	and returned to
	Egypt
the land of Israel	(MT: the land of Egypt)

The reader is not surprised to find that Joseph, the "the just man" (see 1:19), responds without a word to the divine command, issued by an angel of the Lord. The words used in the command of the angel in v. 20 are repeated in the description of the response of Joseph in v. 21.

As we have already seen, the description of the political situation in Judea in v. 22 is accurate. Joseph is described in v. 21 as taking the child and his mother back *to Israel*, in accordance with the command of the angel, again recalling God's leading the people to the promised land by means of the Exodus (see Exod 25; Num 32:9; Deut 4:21) and after the Exile (see Ezek 20:36-38). However, guided by a final dream warning, he avoids a return to his hometown of Bethlehem, in the region of Judea, governed by the tyrant Archelaus. He returns *to Galilee*. More than geography, politics and prudence are involved here. Not only does this journey *to Galilee* set the scene for Jesus' dwelling in Nazareth, and the further indication of the fulfillment of the Scriptures in v. 23, but it keeps Matthew's insistence before the reader: Jesus is the son of Abraham. Reliving Israel's experience under the guidance and leadership of Moses, Jesus is to go *to Israel* (vv. 20-21). But, more specifically, he is to go "to the district of Galilee" (v. 22). This region was called "Galilee of the Gentiles" by Isaiah (9:1-2), a citation to which Matthew will return as he closes his Prologue (see 4:14-16). The return *to Israel* (vv. 20-21) and the further specification of that return *to Galilee* (v. 22) continue Matthew's argument. Jesus is divinely directed to the two groups that formed part of the Christian community to which the Gospel was directed: Jews and Gentiles.

Joseph responds to God, and his response leads Jesus from one place to another, until "he dwelt in a city called Nazareth." In v. 23a Nazareth is given a title that hardly befits its status. It is a "city." This city becomes the place of Jesus' *permanent residence*. What is more important than the status of Nazareth, however, is the fact that Jesus' dwelling in Nazareth, the end of a long journey that has led from Bethlehem to Egypt to Israel to Galilee, fulfills the Scriptures. This final indication of the fulfillment of God's promises in the infancy narrative, however, differs from all other fulfillment formulae in the Gospel of Matthew. Jesus' settling in

Nazareth fulfills what was spoken – not by any single prophet – but *by the prophets*. Due attention must be given to this use of the plural, as scholars have long pondered *which particular passage* from the prophets is fulfilled by the fact that "He shall be called a Nazarene" (v. 23b).[40] Bringing this section of the Prologue to a close, Matthew has recourse to a number of passages in the Old Testament, and to the life of Jesus. They all play their part in understanding how Jesus' being known as a Nazarene fulfills "what was spoken by the prophets."[41]

a)   Jesus was, in fact, from Nazareth. The narrative that tells of Jesus' infancy ends at the place where he will begin his ministry (see 3:13).[42]

b)   In several places in the Old Testament the figure of a *Nazir* appears (see especially Judg 13:2-7 [Samson], 1 Sam 1:11 [Samuel]. See also Luke 7:33, with reference to John the Baptist). The *Nazir* was a person consecrated at birth to God, and made holy for God by means of a vow. There are two Old Testament passages that seem to have been formative of Matthew's claim that Jesus' being called a "Nazorean" fulfilled *the prophets*. Isaiah 40:3 ("He who is left in Zion and remains in Jerusalem will be called *holy*) and Judges 16:17 ("I have been a *Nazirite* to God from my mother's womb" [Samson's explanation to Delilah]).

c)   A further biblical text that plays into the Matthean use of "Nazorean" as a fulfillment of the prophets is Isaiah 11:1: "There will come forth a shoot from the root of Jesse (David's father), and from his roots, a branch (*Neser*)" This passage referred to a future Davidic king in Isaiah 11, but it was a text used by later Judaism as the promise of a future Davidic Messiah.

The Matthean infancy narrative began with an exalted Christological confession in 1:1. It closes with another in 2:23. Jesus' settling in Nazareth is the result of God's design, and all three possible backgrounds for "He shall be called a Nazoreon" (v. 23) play their role, as these words fulfill "what was spoken by the prophets" (v. 23a).[43] The man from Nazareth can be known as a "Nazorean" (v. 23b). But this expression also singles him out as a *Nazir*, a holy person set aside for God's service from his mother's womb and the *Neser*, the blossom from the Davidic branch of Isaiah 11:1. The Prophet Isaiah served Matthew when he wished to describe Jesus in the first fulfillment passage of 1:23: "They shall call his name Emmanuel" (Isaiah 7:14; 8:8-10). Isaiah is again called upon in this final fulfillment passage in the infancy story: "He will be called a Nazorean" (the *Neser* of Isa 11:1). The first citation brings to a close a narrative that dealt with the conception, birth, and identity of the promised child (1:1-23). The second concludes a narrative rife with hints of his mission and destiny (2:1-23). Joseph did what he was commanded by the angel of the Lord: he called the child by the name "Jesus" (1:18-23). The infancy narrative closes with Joseph's further act of obedience: he brings the child to Nazareth, so that he may be known as a "Nazorean."

Conclusion

Matthew 1-2 has provided the reader with the full identity of the son of David, the son of Abraham, the Son of God, the Emmanuel, known as "Jesus the Nazorean." It has also provided paradigms of true faith in Jesus in the figures of Joseph (from Israel, a descendent of David) and the wise men from the east (representing the Gentile world), side by side with characters who initiate the rejection of Jesus, Herod and Israel's leadership. The Christology and the contrasting responses to Jesus, the Christ, the Son of David and the Son of Abraham, will be played out until they are resolved in Jesus' death and resurrection, and his final commission to his fragile disciples. He will be with them till the end of the ages.

Notes

[1] For more detail on the function of a prologue to a Gospel, see above, Chapter Three: Reading Mark 1:1-13: A Prologue to the Gospel.

[2] On the threatening nature of these passages, see B. R. Gaventa, *Mary. Glimpses of the Mother of Jesus* (Studies on Personalities of the New Testament; Columbia: University of South Carolina Press, 1995), 30-32.

[3] The overall division of the material, and the suggestion that 1:1-25 deals with the questions of who Jesus is, and how he came to be born, and that 2:1-23 focuses upon the question of where Jesus is born and foreshadows his destiny, depends upon the epoch making study of R. E. Brown, *The Birth of the Messiah. A Commentary on the Infancy Narratives in the Gospels of Matthew and Luke* (New updated edition; Anchor Bible Reference Library; New York: Doubleday, 1993), 48-54.

[4] See R. R. Wilson, "Between 'Azel' and 'Azel.' Interpreting the Biblical Genealogies," *Biblical Archeologist* 42 (1979): 11-22.

[5] Various "messianic expectations" can be traced in first century Jewish thought. There was no standard "messianic hope." See J. J. Collins, *The Scepter and the Star. The Messiah of the Dead Sea Scrolls and Other Ancient Literature* (ABRL; New York: Doubleday, 1995).

[6] The change to the name "Abraham," in fact only a dialectical variant of Abram (meaning "the father is exalted"), is an exercise in popular etymology to associate artificially the new name to the Hebrew for "father of a multitude."

[7] As J. P. Meier, *Matthew* (New Testament Message 3; Wimington: Michael Glazier, 1979), 3, remarks: "The genealogies in Mt and Lk are to be understood as theological statements, not biological reports."

[8] For a survey, see W. D. Davies and D. C. Allison, *The Gospel According to Matthew* (3 vols.; International Critical Commentary; Edinburgh: T. & T. Clark, 1988-1997), 1:161-64.

[9] For a detailed presentation of these suggestions, see Brown, *Birth*, 71-74.

[10] E. Schweizer, *The Good News according to Matthew* (London: SPCK, 1975), 25.

[11] Davies and Allison, *Matthew*, 1:188.

[12] For a summary of this situation, admittedly based upon later rabbinic documents, but reflected here and elsewhere in biblical passages, see Brown, *Birth*, 123-24.

[13] Unlike Luke, where Mary's co-operation with God's design is described (Luke 1:26-38).

[14] D. Senior, *Matthew* (Abingdon New Testament Commentaries; Nashville: Abingdon Press, 1998), 41.

[15] The text says that Joseph decided to divorce her "quietly." What that means is hard to understand, as the pregnancy could hardly be kept "quiet." Following Brown, *Birth*, 128, and Davies and Allison, *Matthew*, 1:204-205, Joseph must be understood as interpreting Mary's pregnancy as the result of infidelity, and acting according to that judgment he applies the law as leniently as he can.

[16] The "angel of the Lord" is a figure who appears regularly across the Old Testament. The angel has no personal identity or significance, but bears the message of God, and is almost interchangeable with God. See C. A. Newsome, "Angels," *ABR* 1:248-53. She writes: "Yahweh's authority and presence in these encounters is to be affirmed, but yet it is not possible for human beings to have an unmediated encounter with God" (p. 250).

[17] For a detailed comparative study of the annunciation stories in both the Old and the New Testament, see Brown, *Birth*, 155-59.

[18] See Brown, *Birth*, 133-38.

[19] U. Luz, *Matthew 1-7* (trans. W. C. Linss; Edinburgh: T. & T. Clark, 1989), 1:121.

[20] An attentive reader will note that in my citation from Luz (see above note), the name was written "Immanuel," while I use "Emmanuel." This word

is transliterated from the Hebrew word meaning "God with us," and both transliterations are possible. I personally prefer "Emmanuel."

[21] Matthew's purpose is clear: there can be no shadow of doubt that Mary's child is not the result of intercourse between Joseph and Mary prior to the birth of the child. That is all the text wants to say. The Roman Catholic tradition concerning the perpetual virginity of Mary is often questioned by the use of this text. On the history of the interpretation of the passage, see Luz, *Matthew*, 1:124-25. Its most obvious meaning is that they had normal sexual relations after the birth of Jesus. However, it is not the only meaning possible. For a full discussion, see Brown, *Birth*, 132. He rightly concludes: "As for the marital situation after the birth of the child, in itself this verse gives us no information whatsoever." Such matters were not Matthew's concern.

[22] See Brown, *Birth*, 183.

[23] Josephus (*Antiquities* 15-17) reports his atrocities. His most violent reactions were against those whom he suspected were a threat to his authority. He killed the only wife he appeared to have loved, Mariamne, as he suspected that she was maneuvering her Hasmonean sons into a position where they could restore that line. He also executed several of his own sons (Alexander and Aristobulus in 7-6 B.C.E.), as he suspected they were becoming a threat to his authority.

[24] In English, one of the best-known witnesses to the idea of being born under a star is found in the song from Rogers and Hammerstein's musical, *Paint your Wagon*. The hero (famously recorded in the gravelly voice of Lee Marvin) sings: "I was born under a wandering star." For a survey of suggestions that have been made to explain the star as a natural phenomenon that occurred ca. 4 B.C.E., see Brown, *Birth*, 171-73. There is every likelihood that the memory of a phenomenon in the skies that took place at roughly the time when Jesus was born has been used in the Matthean tradition to develop this account. See Davies and Allison, *Matthew*, 1:235.

[25] An important Matthean theme emerges. The Christian community looks back to the Old Testament as a vital element in God's revelation. Israel was entrusted with this revelation, however difficult the relationships between the Matthean community and the Jewish community in Antioch may have been. See Brown, *Birth*, 182-83.

[26] The addition of (2) to the citation of Micah 5:1 is to indicate that in the MT the passage is found at 5:1 while in the LXX it is found in 5:2.

[27] For the following, including the translations, see Brown, *Birth*, 184-87.

[28] Matthew's reinterpretation is so pronounced (only eight words out of twenty-two found in the LXX remain) that some suggest he must have had a different Greek version. See the remark of Davies and Allison, *Matthew*, 1:242: "The differences are in fact sufficient to tempt one to speak of an 'interpretation' rather than a 'quotation' of Scripture."

[29] Davies and Allison, *Matthew*, 1:246, list biblical and secular examples of heavenly bodies that move and direct wanderers. Meier, *Matthew*, 12, suggests that the pillar of fire that led Israel during the Exodus may be background to the moving star.

[30] In Luke 2:1-7, the child is born in a manger as Joseph and Mary travel to Bethlehem for the census of Quirinius. In Matthew, Jesus is born in the home of his father, Joseph of the line of David. For Luke, Jesus is born on a journey, in a resting place by the side of the road. For Matthew, Jesus is born in the home of Joseph, a descendent of David, in Bethlehem, the city of David.

[31] See the important remarks of Davies and Allison, *Matthew*, 1:238: "Jerusalem is, in the first Gospel, the stronghold of Jewish leadership, and, despite its being 'the holy city' (4:5; 27:53), it represents corrupt political power and corrupt political authority. ... Jerusalem does not stand for the entire Jewish community. Instead she represents those in charge, the Jewish leadership (cf. 2:4)." Matt 2:1-12 is not focused upon a Gentile/Jewish contrast, but more upon a powerful/powerless contrast.

[32] For more detail, see Brown, *Birth*, 187-188.

[33] See W. Carter, *Matthew and the Margins. A Sociopolitical and Religious Reading* (Maryknoll: Orbis Books, 2000), 81-82, for a list of contacts between this passage and the story of Moses.

[34] Carter, *Margins*, 86.

[35] His last years brought to a culmination a reign of bloodshed (see Josephus, *Antiquities* 15-18). There are many accounts of innocents being slain (*Antiquities* 15:5-7, 50-87, 173-78, 232-36, 247-52, 260-66, 289-90; 16:361-94; 17:42-44, 167, 182-87). Five days before he died he had one of his sons (Antipater) executed, and ordered that, on his death, a large group of imprisoned leaders in society should be slain. Josephus reports the motive for this command: "So all Judea and every household weep for me, whether they wish it or not" (*Antiquities* 17:6,5-6). Happily, this mass slaughter was avoided (*Antiquities* 17:8,2).

[36] The identification of Bethlehem as the burial place of Rachel continues in the location of the modern site for Rachel's tomb, just outside Bethlehem.

[37] Brown, *Birth*, 217.

[38] See Josephus, *Antiquities* 17:342-44. It is not correct to call Archelaus a "king." He was an "ethnarch" (see Josephus, *Antiquities*, 17:317; *Jewish War* 2:93). The same problem emerges in Matt 14:9, where Herod the tetrarch is called "king." Matthew continues with the expression "king" because he "wishes to continue the theme of the conflict of kings" (Davies and Allison, *Matthew*, 1:273).

[39] For a presentation of stereotypical "dream visions," see Brown, *Birth*, 108.

[40] For a survey, from the patristic to the modern era, see Brown, *Birth*, 208-9.

[41] For what follows, see the more extensive treatment in Brown, *Birth*, 209-13.

[42] The Greek expression *Nazōraios* does not translate to "Nazarene," but rather to "Nazorean." But, in popular etymology, the word is close enough to be read as referring to the city of Jesus' origins. It is also open, however, to be understood as a reference to the *Nazir* and the *Neser* (see below).

[43] See Harrington, *The Gospel of Matthew* (Sacra Pagina 1; Collegeville: The Liturgical Press, 1991), 46: "It is likely that the readers were expected to keep all three connotations in mind rather than one alone. The latter two derivations would qualify the expression as a biblical quotation, and the first would tie them into the place where Jesus lived."

Commentaries on the Gospel of Matthew

The following list of single-volume commentaries on the Gospel of Matthew is not exhaustive. An interested reader could consult any one of them with profit. Bibliographical details for the outstanding multi-volume commentaries of U. Luz and W. D. Davies and D. C. Allison can be found in the notes of the preceding chapters.

Blomberg, C. L., *Matthew* (The New American Commentary 22; Nashville: Broadman Press, 1992).

Byrne, B., *Lifting the Burden. Reading Matthew's Gospel in the Church Today* (Collegeville: The Liturgical Press, 2004).

Carter, W., *Matthew and the Margins. A Sociopolitical and Religious Reading* (Maryknoll: Orbis Books, 2000).

Edwards, R. A., *Matthew's Story of Jesus* (Philadelphia: Fortress, 1985).

Garland, D. E., *Reading Matthew. A Literary and Theological Commentary* (Georgia: Smyth and Helwys, 2001).

Gundry, R. H., *Matthew. A Commentary on his Literary and Theological Art* (Grand Rapids: Eerdmans, 1982).

Harrington, D. J., *The Gospel of Matthew* (Sacra Pagina 1; Collegeville: The Liturgical Press, 1991).

Keener, C. S., *A Commentary on the Gospel of Matthew* (Grand Rapids: Eerdmans, 1999).

Kingsbury, J. D., *Matthew. A Commentary for Preachers and Others* (Philadelphia: Fortress, 1977).

Meier, J. P., *Matthew* (New Testament Message 3; Wilmington: Michael Glazier, 1980).

Senior, D., *Matthew* (Abingdon New Testament Commentaries; Nashville: Abingdon, 1998).

Senior, D., *The Gospel of Matthew* (Interpreting Biblical Texts; Nashville: Abingdon, 1997).

Schweizer, E., *The Good News according to Matthew* (trans. D. E. Green; London: SPCK, 1976).

Witherup, R. D., *Matthew. God With Us* (Spiritual Commentaries on the Bible; Hyde Park: New City Press, 2000).

PART IV

The Gospel of Luke

CHAPTER SIX

Reading the Gospel of Luke

Luke's Gospel is a unique story of Jesus. His lyrical telling focuses on much physical activity: Jesus' words are followed by scenes of him in action, and the whole Gospel is one relentless journey. But for Luke the story of the physical journey invites the reader to transcend its literal interpretation. Jesus' words are often full of warning, even in his great compassion for the lost, and the future is often threatening. In Jerusalem, the Holy City which for Luke is the fulcrum of God's saving history and where Jesus' Scriptural mission comes full circle, a new journey also begins, that of the disciples who will go on from Jerusalem spreading the Word to the ends of the Earth. This message, written for an early Gentile Christian community, is still issued by the Gospel to us today.

Chapter 6
summary

EVEN A FIRST READING OF THE GOSPEL OF LUKE indicates that this author wrote a unique story of Jesus. The impression that the third Gospel is somehow different strengthens when one draws some comparisons with the Gospels of Mark and Matthew. For example, only Luke portrays the image of Mary, the Mother of Jesus, in the fashion that many Christians have come to love and accept.[1] Our Christmas pageantry tells of the Annunciation, the Visitation, the Birth of our Lord, the Presentation and the Finding of the Child Jesus in the Temple. If we were to develop Christmas celebrations on the basis of the infancy of Jesus as told in the Gospel of Matthew, we would have: a genealogy, the suspicion of an illegitimate birth, Herod the Great's slaying of the innocent children in Bethlehem, the flight into Egypt, the return from Egypt to Israel, leading to a further flight to Nazareth, because of another wicked king, Archelaus.[2] Powerful images are found in both birth stories, but the Lukan version is the one that has captured popular imagination.

There are the many other narratives and parables found *only in Luke*: the restoration of the only son to a widow at Nain (Luke 7:11-17), John the Baptist, still wondering if Jesus is the one who is to come (7:18-23), the shock generated by Jesus' attention to, and forgiveness of, a sinful woman who enters the house of a Pharisee to perform an erotic ritual (7:36-50), the scandal of the women who journey with this itinerant preacher (8:1-3), the Good Samaritan (10:25-37), Martha and Mary (10:38-42), the parable of the great banquet (14:15-25), the parable of the lost sheep (15:3-7), the parable of the lost coin (15:8-10), the parable of the father with two lost sons (15:11-32), the parable of the cunning steward (16:1-9), the rich man and Lazarus (16:19-31) the one cured leper, a Samaritan, who returns to thank Jesus (17:11-19), the parable of the Pharisee and the tax collector (18:9-14), Jesus and Zachaeus (19:1-10), and Jesus' weeping over Jerusalem (19:41-44). These evocative Gospel stories, at the top of the list among the images captured by Christian iconography over the centuries are found *only in Luke*. And there is more. The Gospel of Luke tells the story of the passion of Jesus, but it has been transformed. Jesus' final words of despair in Matthew and Mark ("My God, my God, why have your forsaken me?" [Mark 15:34; Matt 27:46]), become: "Father, forgive them, for they know not what they do" (23:35), "Truly, I say to you, today you will be with me in Paradise" (23:43), "Father, into your hands I commend my spirit" (23:46). The Roman centurion does not say: "Truly this man was the Son of God"

(Mark 15:39; Matt 27:54), but he praises God, exclaiming, "Certainly this man was innocent" (Luke 23:47). Finally, Luke has his own way of seeing the resurrection, featuring the story of the journey to Emmaus (24:13-35), and Jesus' commission as Risen Lord: "Thus it is written, that the Christ should suffer and on the third day rise from the dead, and that repentance and forgiveness should be preached in his name to all the nations, beginning in Jerusalem. You are witnesses of these things. And behold, I send the promise of my Father upon you; but stay in the city, until you have been clothed with power from on high" (24:46-49).[3]

The ongoing story of the Acts of the Apostles is fundamental to a proper appreciation of the uniqueness of the Lukan story. The apostles do as they were commanded by the risen Jesus at the end of the Gospel. They stay in the city. After forty days, as Jesus ascends, he again instructs them: "You shall receive power when the Holy Spirit has come upon you; and you shall be my witnesses in Jerusalem and in all Judea and Samaria and to the end of the earth" (Acts 1:8). The story that follows tells of the gift of the Holy Spirit (2:1-4), the community in Jerusalem (2:5-8:1), the mission into Judea and Samaria (8:2-13:7), and by means of Paul's journeys, a journey to the ends of the earth. As the second volume of Luke's work comes to a close, indeed, in its very last line, Paul is in Rome "preaching the kingdom of God and teaching about the Lord Jesus Christ quite openly and unhindered" (28:31).

This overview of the Lukan storytelling about Jesus and the earliest Church uncovers an early Christian author using his imagination, reworking even earlier Christian tradition to tell Theophilus, in an orderly manner, the things that had been accomplished (see 1:1-4). Luke tells the story of the birth, life and teaching, death, resurrection and ascension of Jesus, followed by the journey of the earliest Church to the ends of the earth, to fire the imagination of his readers. The Gospel of Luke, with its focus upon the journey of Jesus from birth to ascension, via Jerusalem, is Luke's first volume. The Acts of the Apostles, focusing upon a further journey from Jerusalem, into Judea and Samaria, and eventually to Rome, is Luke's second volume. But the journey will go on to the ends of the earth (see Luke 24:47; Acts 1:8). It could be said that contemporary readers of the Gospel of Luke and the Acts of the Apostles are part of the as yet unfinished third volume. That story will be told till the end of time. As the two men in white robes say to the first disciples who stand gazing into the sky after Jesus' ascension: "Men of Galilee, why do you stand looking into heaven? This Jesus, who was taken up from you into heaven, will come back in the same way as you saw him go into heaven" (Acts 1:10-11). During the time of the Church, the in-between-time, there is a job to be done. Why are you standing motionless, looking into the clouds?[4]

As with all four Gospels, the Gospel of Luke is articulated across a carefully designed narrative with a dedication, a prologue, a ministry in Galilee, a journey to Jerusalem, and the subsequent events in Jerusalem. They culminate in Jesus' passion, death, resurrection and ascension. Reflection on the Gospel of Luke, following the unfolding design of the narrative, will guide us in our attempt to uncover an initial glimpse of the rich theological message of the creative author of the third Gospel.[5]

The Lukan Literary Design and Its Theological Message

There are places in the Gospel of Luke when the flow from one episode to another in the narrative can be somewhat hard to follow. However, it is widely accepted that the major elements of Luke's literary design of the story of Jesus can be traced in six major moments.[6]

1. The Dedication to Theophilus (1:1-4).

2. The Prologue (1:5-4:13).

3. Jesus' Ministry in Galilee (4:14-9:50)

    a) The mission begins (4:14-6:11)

    b) The Apostolic Community is gathered and instructed (6:12-9:6)

    c) A Christological turning point and the end of the Galilean ministry (9:7-50).

4. Jesus and the Disciples journey to Jerusalem (9:51-19:44)

    a) The prophet on his way to Jerusalem I (9:51-14:35)

    b) The search for the lost one – limitless compassion (15:1-32)

    c) The prophet on his way to Jerusalem II (16:1-19:44).

5. Jesus in Jerusalem (19:45-21:38).

    a) Jesus takes possession of the Temple (19:45-48)

b) Conflict with the Religious Leaders of Israel (20:1-21:4)

c) Jesus' discourse on the future of the Temple, Jerusalem, and the World (21:5-38).

6. Jesus' Passion, Death, Resurrection and Ascension (22:1-24:53).

1. *The Dedication (Luke 1:1-4)*

Luke 1:1-4 tells of a third-generation Christian, directing his book to a specific person, for a purpose. At the beginning of the Christian story there were eye-witnesses, and then ministers of the word (v. 3). As Luke belongs to the next generation, the author feels the need to write a narrative of the life of Jesus so that he can assure the person for whom the book is written, Theophilus, that he has been securely instructed in the truths about what God has done in and through the person of Jesus (vv. 1, 3-4).[7]

2. *Prologue (Luke 1:5-4:13)*

Luke opens the Gospel narrative with a lengthy prologue, introducing the reader to the person and mission of Jesus by means of an infancy narrative (1:5-2:52), and a series of related episodes (3:1-4:13). The infancy narrative spells out Jesus' origins in God and his relationship to another great figure, John the Baptist (1:5-25; 26-38 [two annunciations], vv. 39-45 [the two mothers meet], 57-80; 2:1-21 [two births]). Wonderful hymns praising God rise spontaneously from the lips of Mary (1:46-55), Zechariah (1:68-79), the angels and the heavenly host (2:14), and Simeon (2:29-32). A virgin mother, with unparalleled acceptance of the great things that God has done for her (1:26-28, 46-49), gives birth to a son (2:1-7) whose life and death will lead to the rise and fall of many in Israel (2:29-32). As the infancy narrative closes, Jesus speaks for the first time, telling his puzzled parents that he must be about the affairs of his Father (2:49).[8]

The reader follows further revelations in the preaching of John the Baptist. He tells of the coming of the Lord and the demands of a new quality of life. The Baptist prepares the way of one who will baptize with the Holy Spirit and fire (3:1-20). Jesus' baptism is accompanied by the heavenly proclamation of Jesus as God's "beloved Son" (vv. 21-22), further reinforced by a genealogy that runs from Jesus back to Adam, the son of God (vv. 23-28). But Satan tests this claim with the repeated rhetorical statement, "if you are the Son of God," only to be vanquished by Jesus' use of the Word of God (4:1-13). Luke has made mighty claims for Jesus in the infancy narrative and in his subsequent presentation of the Son of God. The living out of those claims will be told in the story of the life of Jesus that follows.

3. Jesus' Ministry in Galilee (Luke 4:14-9:50)

a) The Mission begins (4:14-6:11)

All three Synoptic Gospels open the ministry of Jesus with a lengthy account of his teaching and activity in Galilee. During this period Jesus calls and begins the formation of disciples and the Twelve, and experiences acceptance and refusal. Luke gathers the traditions that came to him to tell a carefully articulated presentation of this formative stage of Jesus' life-story. The ministry begins with a summary of his ministry in Galilee, full of the power of the Spirit, teaching in the synagogues, glorified by all (4:14-15). The following episode reports a single moment in a synagogue: the synagogue in his home town of Nazareth (vv. 16-30). This first detailed episode in the ministry of Jesus is a prophetic description of his life, teaching, death and resurrection. He interprets the Scriptures as fulfilled by his presence (vv. 16-21), and all speak well of him (v. 22). But some begin to wonder. They know his origins in this town of Nazareth, and Jesus tells them that one day they will say, "Physician heal yourself" (v. 23), and this will take place in the passion narrative (see 23:35-37). As Jesus points to the Gentile reception of God's prophets, all in the synagogue are now "filled with wrath" (v. 28). They attempt to slay him, but he passes through the midst of them and goes away. This episode is a paradigm for the Gospel that follows. It tells of Jesus' fulfillment of God's promises, the acceptance and rejection of his person and message, the attempt to slay him, and the thwarting of these designs through resurrection and ascension. Jesus leaves Nazareth, and will never return to the place of his origin.[9]

A collection of miracles, driving out an unclean spirit (vv. 31-37), a summary of his healing and exorcisms (vv. 38-41), and a summary of his widespread preaching (vv. 42-44), present Jesus' establishment of the reigning presence of God through his deeds (working wonders) and his words (preaching). Now that the mission is under way, Jesus calls his first disciples. Simon the fisherman recognizes his sinfulness, and is thus able to become Peter, a follower of Jesus laboring not for fish, but for the salvation of humankind (5:1-11). Accompanied by his disciples, Jesus continues to manifest the power of the kingdom as he works two further miracles (vv. 12-26: curing of a leper and the healing of the paralytic), adds a further disciple, the tax collector Levi, shares his table with sinners, and announces that the reason for his coming was to bring sinners to repentance (vv. 27-32). But such behavior and teaching cannot go unchallenged. The leaders of Israel challenge him about the lack of fasting among his disciples, their plucking grain on a Sabbath, and his curing of a man with a withered hand on a Sabbath. He reduces his opponents to silence (5:33-6:11). But opposition to who Jesus is and what he says and does has now become public. It will remain in the story until Jesus is crucified.

b) The Apostolic Community is gathered and instructed (6:12-9:6)

In 6:12-49 the narrative changes direction. Jesus goes out to "the mountain" to pray. The biblical image of the mountain, with its roots in the tradition of Sinai and the gift of the Law through Moses, is the background for Jesus' night-long prayer to God before he gathers his disciples, and from them chooses the Twelve, and they are named (6:12-16). This group "he named apostles" (v. 13). Up to this point in the story Jesus has called disciples, and they have followed. The Twelve, however, are not simply "disciples." They are "Apostles." The word comes from the Greek word "to send out" (*apostellō*). Among the Gospels, only Luke gives "the Twelve" the title of "Apostles." They are to be the foundational group of disciples who will form the next generation of Christians, in the period after Jesus. They are the founding figures behind the Gentile mission.[10] The Lukan community (or communities) is the fruit of that mission, and thus they are instructed that their origins can be found in this group of "Twelve Apostles" who were with Jesus from the beginning, and appointed by Jesus, after a long night of prayer.[11]

With these Apostles at his side, Jesus initiates their mission. He comes down from the mountain with them, to a level place where he offers new Torah instruction to people from Judea and Jerusalem (Jews) and from Tyre and Sidon (Gentiles) who are longing to hear his word and experience his authoritative power over evil (vv. 17-19). Jesus' instruction is directed primarily to the disciples, but also to the crowd (v. 20a). The blessings and the woes (vv. 20b-26), followed by radical ethical teaching on love, judgment and the source of good and evil in a human being,

172 The Living Voice of the Gospels

closes with instruction of the foundation of true commitment to Jesus and his message: "Everyone who comes to me and hears my words and does them" (v. 47), and the telling image of a house built on a rock or a house built on shifting sands (vv. 46-49).[12] As always, however, Jesus does not only instruct by word. This turning point in the story, Jesus' choice of the Twelve and their instruction *by word* is followed by two miracles (7:1-10: the cure of the Centurion's servant; 11-17: the raising of the widow's son). The first of these miracles is used to instruct the multitude (v. 9), and the second is directed at his disciples and the multitude (v. 11). The founding community is being formed and instructed by Jesus' words and deeds.

This process is heightened in the collection of traditions that follows. The closing episodes of this section, dedicated to the foundation and instruction of the Apostolic community (6:18-9:6), opens with John the Baptist's question from prison. Is Jesus the one who is to come? Jesus' answer is to point out that the messianic promises of Isaiah 35:5-6 (see also Isa 29:18) are being fulfilled, and turns to praise the Baptist as "among those born of woman none is greater than John" (v. 28a). A new period of history has opened, a period that follows the time of the prophets and John the Baptist (see 16:16). The reigning presence of God has broken into the human story in Jesus' person and message, and those least in the kingdom of God are greater than the Baptist (v. 28b). The Baptist has been rejected, and Jesus will be rejected, but in Jesus' new family, "wisdom is justified by all her children" (v. 35).

The members of the Lukan community must see themselves as children of wisdom, belonging to the reign of God established by Jesus. They are also to continue Jesus' practice of receiving and forgiving sinners, as a result of their love (vv. 36-50: the forgiveness of the sinful woman), and gathering other women, generally marginalized by society as second class citizens, into roles within the missionary community, essential for the mission (8:1-3).[13] This section of the narrative, devoted to the foundation and instruction of the apostolic community closes with considerable narrative force. Jesus instructs its members in their unique privileges and role (see 8:9-11) in the parable of the sower and its explanation (vv. 4-15) and the parable on the need for them to let their light shine (vv. 16-18). A new family of Jesus has been created. He no longer belongs only to his blood family (his mother and his brothers), because "My mother and my brothers are those who hear the will of

God and do it." The criterion of "belonging to Jesus" is always the same: putting into action the word of God, as Jesus' Mother had done: "Be it done unto me according to your word" (1:38).[14]

As so often in the Gospel of Luke, word is followed by deed. In a series of miracles Jesus shows his authority over nature (8:22-25: the calming of the storm) over the powers of the demonic (8:26-39: driving out the Legion of demons from the Gerasene) and over human sickness and even death (vv. 40-56: the curing of the woman with the flow of blood and the raising of Jairus' daughter).[15] The disciples witness and wonder at two of the miracles (the storm [v. 25] and the healing and raising of the women [v. 45, 51]), and the Gerasene is commissioned to act as an apostle: "Return to your home, and declare how much God has done for you" (v. 39). The chosen Twelve (see 6:12-16) are now sent out on mission (9:1-6). This is the only mission of the Twelve in the Gospel, but it will be repeated many times, beginning in the events reported in the Acts of the Apostles.

c) A Christological turning point and the end of the Galilean ministry (9:7-50)

The final section of the Galilean ministry opens with concerns of Herod. He asks the question that will be answered several times before 9:50: "Who is this?" (9:7-9. See v. 9 for the question). The answer is prefaced by the feeding of the five thousand, perfecting God's gift of bread during the Exodus (vv. 10-17). Who Jesus is, to be able to make such claims, is spelt out with great clarity in vv. 18-36. Jesus repeats Herod's question: "Who do people say that I am?" (v. 18), and after the stumbling report of general opinion, Peter confesses the faith of the disciples. Jesus is "the Christ of God" (v. 20). This simple confession is correct. Jesus is the Christ, but the Christ as willed and sent by God. But there is more to God's design. He is also the Son of Man who must be rejected, suffer, slain and be raised from the dead. Anyone who wishes to be a disciple of Jesus must be prepared to take up the cross daily, and follow the Christ, the Son of Man, down this way of suffering to ultimate vindication in resurrection (vv. 21-27). The demand that disciples follow Jesus into suffering and death raises the question of his person and authority even more powerfully. It is answered in the following scene, the transfiguration, where Jesus is seen by the disciples (Peter and those who were with him) transfigured in glory, discussing with Moses and

Elijah "his exodus, which he was to accomplish in Jerusalem" (v. 31).[16] Peter and the disciples are fearful and misunderstand, but the voice from the heavens commands them, in the midst of their confusion: "This is my Son, my chosen one. Listen to him!"

As the ministry in Galilee comes to an end, there should be no further misunderstanding about who Jesus is, and what he asks of them. But it continues. On descent from the mountain, Jesus cures the epileptic boy, as his disciples have not been able to do so. They are called a faithless and perverse generation (vv. 37-43a. See v. 41). Jesus again tells of his oncoming death (vv. 43b-44), but the disciples do not understand and are afraid (v. 45). They squabble over who will be the greatest, and they must be instructed that the least is the greatest (vv. 46-48). The Galilean ministry closes with a final misunderstanding. John forbids a man working in Jesus' name "because he does not follow with us." It is not the disciples who determine discipleship, but Jesus (vv. 49-50). At the transfiguration, Jesus, Moses and Elijah discussed the departure that would be accomplished in Jerusalem (v. 31). The Galilean ministry, with its high points and increasingly persistent low points, has come to a close.[17] Jesus now turns his face to Jerusalem (v. 51).

4. *Jesus and the Disciples Journey to Jerusalem (9:51-19:44)*
This section of the Gospel of Luke is unlike anything found in Mark or Mathew. Mark leads Jesus from Galilee through twenty-one verses (Mark 10:32-52), and the journey occupies only eighteen verses in the Gospel of Matthew (Matt 20:17-34). For Luke, the journey dominates a great part of the latter half of the Gospel, occupying ten chapters (Luke 9:51-19:44). We will consider the theme of "journey" below, but for the moment some literary elements present in this part of the Gospel need to be highlighted. In the first place, this section is largely (but not entirely) filled with encounters between Jesus and his disciples, Jesus and the crowds, and Jesus and the scribes, lawyers and Pharisees. Jesus raises his prophetic voice in a call to all who hear him to respond to the demands of God, his Father.[18] His words to his disciples are generally instructive in a positive sense. He is more threatening with the crowds as he calls them to repentance and conversion. He confronts the rejection and the hostility of the scribes, lawyers and Pharisees with probing, and sometimes punishing, prophetic utterances.[19]

But, whether instructing, calling to conversion or punishing, with very few exceptions the voice of Jesus always has a threatening edge. Some of the hardest sayings in the Gospels are found in this section of Luke's Gospel, as Jesus acts out his role as a prophet with his disciples, the crowds and the Scribes and Pharisees. Yet, at the heart of these sometimes stern demands that Jesus makes of all who would be his disciples, and his harsh criticism of those who reject him, one finds an almost lyrical passage on God's relentless search for the lost one: the lost sheep, the lost coin and the two lost sons in 15:1-32. This passage forms the centerpiece of 9:51-19:44, which can be broadly structured in three parts:

a) 9:51-14:35: The prophet on his way to Jerusalem I
b) 15:1-32: The relentless search for that which has been lost
c) 16:1-19:44: The prophet on his way to Jerusalem II.

These three major sections will serve as a guide in the outline of the literary structure that follows.

a) The prophet on his way to Jerusalem I

The journey begins as Jesus sets his face toward Jerusalem (v. 51), but the confusion of the disciples continues as they are sent ahead to prepare the way. James and John wish to bring fire down on an unwelcoming Samaritan town. Jesus rebukes them, and they journey on their way (vv. 52-56). As Jesus begins his journey (v. 57: "And as they were going along the road"), the future missionary journey of the Church is initiated as Jesus sends out the seventy-two disciples, instructing them how they are to travel, in the midst of both blessings and difficulties. They are to bring God's peace, but they will sometimes be rejected. This must not discourage them, as the kingdom of God is near, and the rejecting town will suffer grievously (10:1-12). Jesus condemns three such towns: Chorazin, Bethsaida and Capernaum, and assures the missionaries that as they are sent by Jesus, Jesus has been sent by God. The rejection of the missionary is the rejection of Jesus and God (vv. 13-16). The seventy-two return, able to report of the victories they have had over evil, and Jesus assures them that they have become "citizens of heaven."[20] The missionaries rejoice (v. 20) and Jesus sings his shared joy with these innocent ones (Greek: "infants") who have received the revelation of the Father from the Son, who have seen and heard what many prophets and kings have longed to see and hear (vv. 21-24).

This blessing is a cue for the question from a lawyer, attempting to test Jesus with the question concerning the gaining of eternal life, so

clearly promised to the missionaries. This leads to the parable of the
Good Samaritan, where Jesus insists that the true neighbor is the one
who shows mercy. Incredibly, the one who showed mercy was a despised
Samaritan, but the lawyer is told that if he wishes to gain eternal life, he
must behave as the Samaritan behaved (10:25-37). The journey goes
on, as Luke points out: "Now as they went on their way they entered
a village." The brief account of Martha and Mary follows. It must be
read in the light of the parable of the Good Samaritan. As Martha busies
herself, she is disturbed by Mary who sits at the feet of Jesus and listens
to his word. The parable and this brief report are to be read in tandem.
Martha is, in her own turn, being a "Good Samaritan" to Jesus, attending
to his needs.[21] But more is required. It is not enough to do merciful
things for one another. Such actions must be nourished by the word of
Jesus. For that reason, Mary has chosen the better part (vv. 38-42). The
attitude of "listening," and learning from the word of Jesus, moves easily
into a long section on true prayer, in response to the request from one
of his disciples "Lord, teach us to pray" (11:1). They are taught Jesus'
prayer to the Father (vv. 2-4),[22] and the need to pray with insistence (vv.
5-13), as "the heavenly Father will give the Holy Spirit to those who ask
him" (v. 13).

Opposition to Jesus emerges as some of the people claim that Jesus
has powers over the demonic because he is in league with Beelzebul, the
prince of demons. This accusation enables Jesus to open a theme that
lies behind many of the passages that lead into 15:1-32: a divided heart.
Divided kingdoms fall. Does Satan defeat Satan, or does Jesus cast out
demons by the "finger of God"? They must decide, as there cannot be
a divided allegiance to Jesus. He will not tolerate hypocrisy or a religion
that parades as religion, but is self-interested (11:14-23). The house
may be superficially put in order, but the unclean spirit returns, and the
situation is worse than before (vv. 24-26). The woman calling out from
the crowd about the blessedness of the body that bore and nourished Jesus
enables him to return to his fundamental requirement of the believer:
"Blessed are those who hear the word of God and keep it" (vv. 27-28).
Despite this reminder, superficiality continues: this generation, unlike
the generation of Jonah, will not read the signs of someone greater than
Jonah (vv. 29-32). They are not enlightened by an eye that sees, but are
in the dark because their eye is not sound (vv. 33-36). Jesus attacks the
hypocrisy of the Pharisees (vv. 37-44) and the lawyers (vv. 45-52). They

gather to plan a provocation that will lead him to utter a word they might use to condemn him (vv. 53-54). Hypocrisy is to be shunned (12:1-3), and the only one to be feared is the one who casts into hell. Believers have no need to fear physical danger, a threat close at hand for Jesus as his enemies plot (see 11:53-54). God cares for them (vv. 4-7). Only public and courageous acknowledgement of Jesus in this world will be acknowledged by Jesus before the angels. The charge that he overcame demons by means of the demonic still lingers, as Jesus points out that this is to blaspheme by the very authority that directs Jesus' life and mission: the Holy Spirit. Those who courageously follow Jesus will also be cared for in their suffering by the same Holy Spirit (vv. 8-12).

Episodes and words of Jesus tumble together, but the underlying sentiment is always prophetic warning.[23] Basic principles are taught: an undivided heart, hearing the word of Jesus and doing it, confessing Jesus publicly, but there is little or no narrative in this section of the Gospel that tells of people, disciples, crowds or Jewish leaders, who are responding to Jesus in this way. Thus the dire warnings continue. Those who covet this world's goods are rich fools (vv. 13-21), the disciples must not give in to anxiety in the face of dangers and suffering because they have so little. Their Father who nourishes the birds of the earth and beautifies the world with the lilies of the field knows their needs, and will care for them, but as yet they are "men of little faith" (vv. 22-31. See v. 28). They are to strike out boldly, forsaking both fear and the desire to gather the treasures of this world. Their Father will gladly give them the treasure of the kingdom of heaven, but where their treasure is, there will their heart be (vv. 32-34). All disciples are to be like watchful servants, performing their tasks faithfully in the time of the absence of the master, as they do not know when the Son of Man will come (vv. 35-40). Peter asks if this applies to just the disciples or for everyone, and he is told that even more will be asked of the privileged inner circle (vv. 41-48). Jesus' presence is a dividing fire. There can be no half-hearted response, as even the most intimate and established communities are divided by acceptance or rejection of his urgent word and person.[24] They must learn to read the signs of the times, and behave with one another as a people able to judge for itself what is right (vv. 49-59).

The report of Pilate's slaying of some Galileans leads Jesus to tell his audience that they will likewise perish, unless they repent. They will be given time, like the barren fig tree, but after the allocated time, the tree is cut down (13:1-9). The curing of a crippled woman on a Sabbath leads to more conflict. Jesus rails against the hypocrisy of the ruler of the synagogue, and puts all his adversaries to shame (vv. 10-17). In the midst of this opposition and anger, Luke has Jesus pause and issue words of comfort and courage in the light of unrelenting opposition. The mustard seed and the leaven are tiny and seemingly insignificant ... but they grow and produce growth. The reigning presence of God, so heavily opposed at this stage of the story, will likewise grow and produce growth (vv. 18-21). "He went on his way, through towns and villages, teaching" (v. 33). Many will lay claim to accepting Jesus as Lord, but many who may have expected positions of honor will not enter the narrow gate. They will be replaced at the table in the kingdom of God by others from the four corners of the world.

Jesus pauses in his relentless prophetic mission, and laments the hard-heartedness of Herod who wishes to kill him, and the inhabitants of Jerusalem who have long killed the prophets and those sent to them. Jesus desires a tender relationship of repentance and intimacy, but this will not happen "for it cannot be that a prophet should perish away from Jerusalem" (v. 33). They have lost their opportunity, despite the fact that they will shortly welcome him in triumph (vv. 31-35. See v. 35).

The prophetic voice is raised again as Jesus silences those who regard his actions on a Sabbath as unlawful (14:1-6), teaches humble acceptance of oneself as the way to be called higher, and asks that we bring the broken to our table. Such invitations bring blessings at the resurrection, where all human standards and expectations are reversed, as they cannot be repaid (vv. 7-14). The parable of the great banquet (vv. 15-24) is a concluding statement on the performance of Israel to this point in the Gospel. They have found superficial and hypocritical excuses not to attend the wedding banquet ... and their places will be filled by people from all quarters of the city, and then from the highways and the byways. But "none of those men who were invited shall taste my banquet" (vv. 15-24. See v. 24).[25] The disciples, who might regard themselves as invited to taste at the banquet of Jesus, are immediately reminded of the cost of this discipleship: leave all that they regard precious, assess carefully that they are prepared to pay the price of discipleship. "Whoever of you who does not renounce all that he has cannot be my disciple" (v. 33). If they are unable to accept and live the challenge, they become like worthless salt that has lost all saltiness, fit only to be cast out as refuse (vv. 25-35).

b) The search for the lost one – limitless compassion (15:1-32)

The relentless demands that Jesus has made upon his would-be disciples, the harsh words he has had with crowds and with Pharisees and lawyers, disappear for a brief section of the narrative. Or do they? The setting of the three parables on searching for the lost is important. Tax collectors and sinners are drawing near to hear Jesus. This situation leads the Pharisees and the scribes, continuing Jesus' portrayal of their superficial religiosity, and their inability to understand or accept who Jesus is and what he is doing, to exclaim: "This man receives sinners and eats with them" (15:1-2). Behind Jesus' prophetic words and actions from 9:51-14:35 lies the mystery of the one who sent him (see 10:16). The figure of the Father of Jesus is the thinly veiled background to the father who has two sons (vv. 11-32).

Two brief parables, constructed very similarly, and a further lengthy parable, are found in Luke 15. The brief parables ask the question that will be answered in the parable of the father with two sons. Jesus asks seriously: which one of you, if you had a hundred sheep, would leave ninety-nine of them in the wilderness, and go in search of the one that was lost? (v. 4). The answer to that question is – no one would do such a silly thing. But the search to bring the sinner to repentance goes to these crazy lengths, and leads to great rejoicing (vv. 5-7). Similarly, which woman, having ten coins, would turn her home upside down simply to find one that was lost? As with the lost sheep, the finding of the lost coin leads to great rejoicing (vv. 8-10). The Pharisees and scribes, questioning Jesus celebrating meals with sinners (vv. 1-2), are unwilling and unable to recognize what God is doing in and through Jesus through his compassionate search for the lost. The prophetic word spoken against them during the journey still stands.

The father with the two sons (see v. 11) stretches the message of the two briefer parables to the limit. He sets his younger son free, so that he can make his own choices, and bear their consequences (vv. 12-16). He is waiting for the son as he returns, and welcomes him back into the household with great joy and celebration (vv. 17-24). The real point of the parable, however, is found in its conclusion. This father runs the risk of losing his older son. One of them was lost and has been found, but as the parable comes to a close, the father is outside, away from the rejoicing, trying to save his second lost son, to whom he says: "My son, you are always with me. Everything I have is yours" (v. 31).

This may be read simply as the economic consequence of the younger son having squandered his half of the family inheritance. But that would be a superficial interpretation. Jesus points to a father who makes serious demands of all who would be his followers (see 9:51-14:35), but these demands must now be read in the bright light of a father who will always be found in unexpected places, searching for his lost sons and daughters (vv. 25-32). What is lost must be found (see v. 32. See also 5:31-32). This is the message that stands, in both the literary structure and the theological perspective, at the center of the Lukan presentation of Jesus' journey to Jerusalem (9:51-19:44).[26]

In the Gospel of Luke as a whole story, Jesus not only tells this parable. He lives it. As Luke tells Jesus' story, the crucified Jesus is abused: "He saved others, let him save himself" (23:35), and Jesus' first words to the people in Nazareth return to the reader: "Doubtless you will quote me this proverb, 'Physician, heal yourself'" (4:23). Jesus has been rendered powerless by his decision to love without condition. Nailed securely on solid wood he is powerless. For Luke, however, he lives out the parable in unconditional love. His last words forgive all who have rejected him (see 23:34). He invites them, in the person of the thief on the cross, to join him in the banquet prepared for all his lost sons and daughters in paradise (see 23:39-43). It is Jesus who has *told* and *lived* a parable of the powerless almighty God, his and our Father. Jesus knows his Father in heaven better than anyone else knows him (see 10:21-22). Should it not be true that this Father in heaven is to be found, first of all, where the father stands at the end of the parable – outside, away from the rejoicing, seeking his second lost son?

But the limitless compassion of Jesus as it is portrayed in the Gospel of Luke has a hard edge to it.[27] A proper understanding of Luke's use of this parable raises at least two concerns.

i) He revealed a different sort of God than the one expected and invented by the religions and culture of his own day. The message retains its power today, because we continue to look for God in the wrong places. The God revealed by Jesus is as much a surprise to us today as it was to Jesus' original listeners and Luke's original readers. We enthrone God on the altars, but he is more likely found out in the dark, trying to save his lost children.

ii) Jesus of Nazareth "lived" the parable; he did not just "tell" it. Jesus was and is the parable of God. In a unique way, therefore, Jesus reveals

God's presence in everything he says and does. The image of limitless compassion, as a manifestation of limitless love, has nothing to do with a cloying "being nice" to everyone. It is an imaginative proclamation of a God that we must seek out in the most unexpected places.

c) The prophet on his way to Jerusalem II (16:1-19:44)

The material gathered in the first section of the prophet's journey to Jerusalem (9:51-14:35) can be bewildering, and is held together only by the tone of warning, exhortation and promise that comes from the prophet who will die in Jerusalem (see 13:33). The second part of the journey, following the centerpiece of 15:1-32, is marked by collections of sayings, encounters and events that are more unified around a message. The movement toward Jerusalem becomes intense (see 17:11; 18:31; 19:11, 28, 41) and in 19:45: "He entered the temple."

The radical newness that Jesus brings into the world is stated at the center of chapter 16: "The law and the prophets were until John; since then the good news of the kingdom of God is preached, and everyone enters it violently" (16:16). This is the Lukan understanding of a turning point in human history. Jesus has introduced "fire upon the earth" (12:49). The Lukan Jesus calls for very radical measures to enter the kingdom. Across chapter 16, Jesus tells of the cunning steward who outwits his dishonest master (16:1-9), and the lesson disciples must learn from this worldly skill, as they cannot serve both God and mammon (vv. 10-13). The Pharisees are condemned as lovers of money (v. 14-15). The powerful attraction of possessions is then matched by Jesus' attack on those who allow the power of sexual desire to dictate their lives, as he condemns divorce (v. 18). The chapter ends with a memorable parable of the rich man and Lazarus (vv. 19-31). This folk-tale is rendered Christian by its final words, spoken by Abraham, and applied to all who will not accept Jesus' teaching: "If they do not hear Moses and the prophets, neither will they be convinced if someone should rise from the dead" (v. 31). Is Luke trying to rouse his community from their mediocrity by means of this warning? They know of someone who rose from the dead. What difference does that make to their lives?

Further prophetic instruction follows this ominous warning to readers who know of the one who has risen from the dead. Scandal leads to destruction (17:1-4), while the tiniest grain of faith can move trees and replant them in the sea (vv. 5-6). The disciple is called to recognize his or her role as an unworthy servant (vv. 7-10). "And on the way to Jerusalem, he was passing along between Samaria and Galilee" (v. 11). On the journey only one of the ten lepers, and that one a Samaritan, recognizes Jesus as the one who gives God's good gifts (vv. 11-19). The end time is never far away in Luke's presentation of Jesus. It will certainly come, and surprisingly. But that time is not yet with us, and no-one knows when it will come. Even this message, however, is part of Jesus' call for the disciple to be receptive to God's designs.

The theme of prayer returns (see 11:1-13) in the parable of the importunate widow, teaching that if even a wicked judge will eventually listen, how much more will God listen to those who "cry to him day and night" (vv. 1-8. See v. 7). It is the humble tax collector, on his knees and aware of his failure before God, who utters the prayer that is received by God (vv. 9-14).[28] Children are blessed because, like the tax collector, they are receptive to the gifts of God, and not full of themselves (vv. 15-17). The rich ruler who wishes to gain eternal life (v. 18), is unable to pay the price of total self-gift, and Jesus teaches that one can only do this when sustained by the power of God: "What is impossible for human beings is possible for God" (v. 27). He promises genuine riches, even now, and eventual eternal life to those who are open to the gift of God (vv. 18-30).

Jerusalem is now nearby, and in its proximity Jesus utters the third prediction of his forthcoming death and resurrection (vv. 31-33). As in the first part of his prophetic journey (see 13:33), also in the second Jesus promises that he will fulfill prophecy in Jerusalem: "Everything that is written of the Son of Man by the prophets will be accomplished (v. 32).[29] Like the recalcitrant Israelites under the prophetic direction of Moses, the disciples are unable to grasp what this means. Jesus "drew near to Jericho" (v. 35), a last port of call before arriving at Jerusalem. There a blind man shows the way to lay oneself unconditionally open to the gifts of God, made available in and through Jesus. Everyone gave praise (vv. 35-43). Positive examples of how one responds to Jesus bring the journey to an end. Hard on the heels of the radical self-loss of the blind man in Jericho, Zacchaeus strains to see Jesus, who calls him to share his table. As others complain at Jesus' preparedness to share with sinners, Zacchaeus shares his possessions, and Jesus announces that he has come to seek and save the lost (19:1-10). The motif of 15:1-32 returns as the journey comes to a close (see also 5:31-32). But the Lukan Jesus never allows this teaching to introduce complacency. It is followed by the parable of the ten pounds, carefully set within the journey theme, and returning to the question of the end time: "He proceeded to tell a parable because he was near to Jerusalem, and because they supposed that the kingdom of God was to appear immediately" (v. 11). The disciple is called to administer the gifts of God courageously and creatively in the long intervening time between Jesus' departure and his return. Not to do so leads to dire consequences, as there will be a final day when the disciples' attention to the gifts they have received will be assessed (vv. 11-27).

Finally, the arrival in Jerusalem is prepared as Jesus, the master of the situation, arranges his arrival. He is greeted with acclaim, "as he was now drawing near, at the ascent of the Mount of Olives" (v. 37). The disciples are unhappy with this acclaim, but Jesus insists that it must happen. However, the reader is aware that the acclaim will fade to hatred, as he has already announced in his lament over Jerusalem (see 13:35). Jesus weeps over Jerusalem, as he looks over the city from the Mount of Olives and laments the fact that the city will be destroyed "because you did not know the time of your visitation" (vv. 41-44. See v. 44). In v. 45: "He entered the temple." The prophet's journey to Jerusalem has come to an end. He will never again leave the city as "it cannot be that a prophet should perish away from Jerusalem" (13:33).

5. Jesus in Jerusalem (Luke 19:45-21:38)
On arrival in Jerusalem, after the unique concentration upon Jesus' prophetic journey to the city, Luke's report of Jesus' presence in Jerusalem returns to the traditional story of Jesus, as received from Mark. Of course, special Lukan concerns have shaped the way this part of the story is told.

a) Jesus takes possession of the temple (19:45-48)
The account of the purification of the temple, the dramatic opening of Jesus' arrival in Jerusalem in Mark 11:12-25, is reduced to a minimum. Jesus drives out "those who sold," insisting that the temple is his house, and that it shall be a house of prayer (19:45-46). Jesus has taken possession of his temple, and he teaches there every day. The leaders of Israel plot to destroy him, but the people hang on his words (vv. 47-48).

The scene has been set for this section of the Gospel, marked by conflict with the religious leaders of Israel, and avid listening to his preaching. Jesus will not leave the temple area or the city of Jerusalem until he sets out to journey with two disciples who are walking to Emmaus, about sixty stadia *away from* Jerusalem (24:13-25). But he will draw them back into the city (v. 33), and from the city he will ascend to heaven (vv. 50-53). The preaching of Jesus that dominates 20:1-21:38 takes place within the precincts of the Jerusalem Temple. For Luke, the city of Jerusalem is the end of his journey, and the place from which he will return to the Father. However, he will command his disciples not to leave the city so that their preaching can begin in Jerusalem (24:27. See Acts 1:4). Jesus' journey comes to an end, as another begins. The Acts of the Apostles begins in the city of Jerusalem, and there the risen Christ will instruct the disciples: "You shall be my witnesses in Jerusalem and in all Judea and Samaria and to the end of the earth" (Acts 1:8). Jerusalem is the center point of God's saving concern for human history. Jesus' journey leads there, and the Spirit-filled journey of the Church to the ends of the earth begins there.

b) Conflict with the religious leaders of Israel (20:1-21:4)

A series of episodes follow one another, during which Jesus and the religious leaders of Israel enter into bitter conflict. The chief priests with the scribes and the elders question Jesus' authority to take possession of the temple. He confounds them with a question about the origins of John's baptism. They will not answer, as they are afraid of the people who are listening to Jesus so enthusiastically, and thus Jesus does not respond to them (vv. 1-8). Jesus then tells the people the parable of the vineyard and the tenants who will not provide the owner of the vineyard some of its fruits, who slay his messengers, and finally slay his beloved son. The owner will slay these tenants and give the vineyard to others. The crowd, aware that the parable is about the vine that is God's holy people, finds this is a horrifying suggestion: "God forbid!" (v. 16). But Jesus will be a rejected corner stone, a crushing stone that will become the head of the corner. Simeon's prophecy about Jesus being the sign that is spoken against, yet the cause of the falling and rising of many in Israel will be fulfilled (vv. 9-18. See 2:34). Israel's leaders are aware that they have been accused, and would like to dispose of him, but are afraid of the people (v. 19).

The following passages systematically reduce the leaders of Israel to silence. Jesus silences them over paying due honor to God and Caesar

(vv. 20-26). He silences the Sadducees over the issue of life after death (vv. 27-40). He rejects the Jewish belief that the Messiah is the Son of David by means of a rabbinic interpretation of Psalm 110:1 (vv. 41-44), and turns on the scribes, attacking them for a parade of false religiosity, marked only by external signs. Each of these disputes closes with a statement that indicates Jesus' dominance of the situation: "they were silent" (v. 26), "they no longer dared to ask him any question" (v. 40), "they will receive the greater condemnation" (v. 47). Closing this series of condemnatory encounters, the story of the widow who puts two copper coins into the treasury contrasts true religion with the falsity of those who give from their wealth to parade their virtue. This woman, like any true follower of Jesus, puts in her whole life (Greek: *panta ton bion*).[30]

c) Jesus' discourse on the future of the Temple, Jerusalem, and the world (21:5-38)

Luke continues to follow Mark as he has Jesus proclaim his final discourse from within the temple precincts (see Mark 13:1-37).[31] Some point to the beauty of the building, its stones and its riches, but Jesus announces that it will be destroyed (21:5-6). This encounter opens a discourse that has three major sections. The issues dealt with in this discourse may not strike the contemporary reader as being especially relevant, but the fundamental teaching of Jesus found there is: there will certainly be an end time, when the Son of Man will come as judge.[32] However, that time lies in the future, and we cannot determine when that might be. *That* God will be the final Lord of all history is strongly affirmed. *When* that time will be is beyond our control and understanding. This is the question asked of Jesus: when will the destruction of the temple take place? (v. 7). Jesus does not answer the question. He warns his listeners of the many things that must happen before that time: false prophets, wars, natural disasters and sickness (vv. 8-9). But, most importantly, the Christian community will suffer trials, family division and hatred. Its members are to place their trust in God, and endure: "not a hair of your head will perish" (vv. 12-18. See v. 17). These things will come to pass *before* the destruction of Jerusalem, vividly described in vv. 20-24. The danger that the Lukan Jesus is facing here is that believers, aware of the urgent preaching of the proximate end time by Jesus and the earliest Church, must not read the tumultuous political and natural events, nor the sufferings they will experience, as indications that the end time has come. They must be courageous, and face an "in-between-time" that reaches beyond the destruction of Jerusalem to the final coming of the Son of Man. The destruction of the temple and the city of Jerusalem (vv. 20-24) is not the end of time. It will be tragic, but the end time is elsewhere. It is when "the times of the Gentiles are fulfilled" (v. 24). The mission must reach out to the ends of the earth (see Acts 1:8) before there can be any final establishment of the Son of Man as the eschatological judge.

However, that time will come. This is the content of the rest of the discourse (vv. 25-36). There will be extraordinary signs, as the world and the heavens will shake. Then the Son of Man will come. This will be the time for the believer to recognize that all they have suffered has its final vindication: "Look up and raise your heads, because your redemption is drawing near" (v. 28). One of Luke's major concerns was to open the minds and hearts of his readers and listeners to a long history, before Jesus returned as the Son of Man.[33] No doubt Luke did not imagine that we would still be waiting in the third millennium. Nevertheless, he instructs his readers and listeners to be aware of the signs of these final events. They can read the signs of nature; they should also read the signs that will announce the end of all history. In the meantime, they are to live according to the teaching they have received from Jesus for "heaven and earth will pass away, but my words will not pass away" (vv. 29-33. See v. 33). The "in-between-time" is a time to watch. The believers may not know *when* it will come, but they have been instructed *that* it will come, and thus they are to "watch at all times, praying that you may have strength to escape all these things that will take place, and to stand before the Son of Man" (vv. 34-36. See v. 36).

Jesus' presence as a teacher in the temple closes with a brief comment from the narrator, informing the reader and listener that all the encounters and preaching of 19:45-21:36 took place in the temple. He preached there every day, and the people came to hear him. At night, he went out to the Mount of Olives for his rest, but he never moved out of the region of Jerusalem (vv. 37-38).

6. Jesus' Passion, Death, Resurrection and Ascension (Luke 22:1-24:53)
The Lukan account of the final days of Jesus' story is shaped by a tradition, reaching back to the earliest days of the existence of a Christian community that had to explain the scandal of the cross. It is

unacceptable that the Messiah die on a cross (see Gal 2:13, with reference to Deut 27:26, 21:23); but history imposed upon early Christians the need to explain that the man they believed to be the Christ, had died on a cross. No-one expresses the difficulty of the early preaching of the Church better than Paul: "Jews demand signs and Greeks seek wisdom, but we preach Christ crucified, a stumbling block to Jews and stupidity to the Gentiles. But to those who are called, both Jews and Greeks, Christ the power of God and the wisdom of God" (1 Cor 1:22-24). The traditional passion narrative (Upper room, Gethsemane, betrayal, Jewish trial, Roman trial, way of the cross, crucifixion, death and burial) was a widely told story before Gospels appeared. The fact that all four Gospels follow this temporal sequence of events is a good indication that the "Christian telling" of Jesus' death and burial was one of the oldest coherent stories told by early Christians. Luke draws from that tradition, aided by the story as it is told in Mark. However, as we should expect after reading the Gospel of Luke thus far, this story tells these events and interprets the events in a very singular fashion.[34]

What follows is a brief sketch of the story and the overall message of Jesus' passion, death, resurrection and ascension in the third Gospel. It will be more fully developed in the following chapter, devoted to a detailed reading of Luke 22:1-24:53.

Judas joins the plot of the chief priests and the scribes to slay Jesus from the beginning, and the crowds are entirely absent (22:1-6). The description of the preparations for the celebration of the Passover, and the meal itself is unique (vv. 7-13, 14-23).[35] Unlike Mark and Matthew, Jesus shares two cups and the bread with the disciples. After a dispute over who is the greatest among the disciples, showing that they have not understood the significance of the words and gestures they have shared at the table, Jesus speaks to them in a long discourse, instructing them on the importance of service (vv. 24-30), telling of Peter's denial (vv. 31-34), and giving them instructions for the future mission (vv. 35-38). The prayer on the Mount of Olives, framed by warnings not to enter into temptation, is very brief (vv. 39-46). Jesus' arrest features betrayal and violence on the part of his enemies and one of those who were with Jesus. But Jesus heals the injured slave of the high priest, and allows the process to continue: "This is your hour and the power of darkness" (vv. 47-53. See v. 53). The account of Peter's denials, where he fails when tempted, is told in its entirety *before* the account of Jesus' suffering. His turning and looking at his failing disciple leads to Peter's bitter tears (vv. 54-62). The assault involved in the arrest is met with healing, and the betrayal of Peter is met with forgiveness and repentance.

Before the Jewish and Roman trials begin, Jesus is mocked, struck and reviled, as those who were holding him ask that he prophesy (vv. 63-65). This is high irony. What is about to happen is indeed the proclamation of Jesus as the prophet of God, a proclamation rejected by Israel and its leaders. At the Jewish trial, the irony continues, as Jesus, surrounded by falsity, accepts that he is the Christ, the Son of Man who will come as the final judge, and the Son of God. Unlike Mark and Matthew, the Jewish authorities do not condemn Jesus. They simply affirm that they need no further testimony (vv. 66-71).

The Roman trial follows, set around a visit to Herod. In the first part of the Roman trial, Jesus emerges as a King, and Pilate declares that he is innocent. He will eventually be handed over to death by one who declared him innocent (23:1-5). But when told that Jesus has been a problem in Galilee (v. 5), Pilate sent him to Herod. Jesus is silent before Herod, who wishes to be entertained by a miracle-worker. He is further reviled, and dressed in rich robes. Ironically, the truth about Jesus as the innocent, suffering King and Messiah is acted out, even as Jesus stands silent (vv. 6-12). Returned to Pilate, his innocence is even more vehemently affirmed by the Roman ruler. But Israel calls out for his death, and asks that Barabbas be released. A violent man is released, and the innocent bringer of peace (see 2:14) is "delivered up to their will" (vv. 13-25. See v. 25). Luke lengthens the report of the road to the Cross. Jesus is followed by Simon of Cyrene, a model of those who would carry the Cross of Jesus. He speaks words of compassion and warning to the women of Jerusalem. As Jesus entered Jerusalem, he wept over the city (see 19:41-44). As he is led out to die, women of Jerusalem weep over him, and he pronounces his last prophetic word about their future suffering (vv. 26-31).

Jesus, so often declared innocent, is crucified between two convicted criminals. From the Cross he forgives those who have crucified him. In their continued abuse of him, his enemies proclaim the truth. He is called "the Christ of God" (see 9:20), "the Chosen one" (see 9:35), and "King". They recall that he saved others, and ask that he save himself, and also that he save them. He welcomes the repentant sinner into paradise. He commends his spirit into the hands of his Father, and at his death, the Roman centurion announces what the reader has known all along: "Certainly this man was innocent!" All who had assembled return to their homes, beating their breasts. This death will indeed lead to his returning safely to the Father, and to the salvation of others (vv. 32-49). An unknown Joseph of Arimathea asks for the body, and it is buried in a new tomb on the day of preparation. Women who had been with him from Galilee (see 8:1-3) and who were at the Cross are with him still. They leave to prepare for his final anointing. For the Christian reader, the burial scene is full of promise. This is not the end of the story, but already in this carefully plotted passion narrative, Luke has instructed readers and listeners that Jesus has died as the humble and innocent suffering one who, even in his suffering and death, is God's prophet and God's Son, the bringer of pardon, healing and salvation.

We have already mentioned that once Jesus arrives in Jerusalem, he never leaves the city. This focus is heightened in the Easter story, as it all takes place on the same day. Luke makes this clear by his references to time: "on the first day of the week" (24:1), "that very day" (v. 13), "it is toward evening" (v. 29), "and they rose that same hour" (v. 33), "as they were saying this" (v. 36), "then he said to them" (v. 44), "then he led them out" (v. 50). At first light on that day the women find the empty tomb, and are sent away. They should not be seeking the living among the dead. Jesus will not be found in a cemetery (24:1-11). Disappointed disciples walk to Emmaus, but the presence of Jesus, teaching and breaking bread with them, reverses their walk. They return to Jerusalem (vv. 13-35). Gathered again in Jerusalem, Jesus appears to the disciples, and gives them their commission: they are to be witnesses of the fulfillment of the Scriptures in the death and resurrection of the Christ, and thus they are to preach repentance and forgiveness of sins to all nations, beginning from Jerusalem, clothed with power from on high (vv. 44-49). The Gospel closes as Jesus leads his disciples out to Bethany, and then leaves them. His journey is completed as he returns to his Father in heaven. The Gospel ends where it began: in the temple (see 1:5-24). But so much has been said and done between these two experiences in the temple. Now the disciples "returned to Jerusalem with great joy, and were continually in the temple blessing God" (vv. 50-53. See vv. 52-53). The journey of Jesus has come to an end. Clothed with the power from on high, however, the journey of the disciples is only about to begin.

Conclusion

We have already had occasion to follow the long physical journey that occupies almost half the Gospel.[36]   As we conclude this study of the Gospel of Luke, however, we must ask a further question. Is the theme of "journey" found only in 9:51-19:44? This *physical* journey is the most obvious indication of a major Lukan image aimed at a reader, inviting that reader into a journey that *transcends the physical*.[37]   If one keeps in mind the infancy narrative in Matthew's Gospel (Matt 1-2), we can already read the story of the birth of Jesus in Luke (Luke 1-2) as the story of a savior born on a journey, for a journey.

For Matthew, Jesus is born under a star in the home of Joseph, who followed the command of the angel of the Lord and took Mary to his home as his wife (Matt 1:18-25). There the Magi find them (2:1-12), and it is from there they must flee when death threatens Jesus, as it threatened the infant Moses. The family only arrives in Nazareth at the end of the story, again like Moses, coming out of Egypt. Jesus being known as a Nazarene is the result of a further flight. It is too dangerous to go back to Bethlehem, the city of David (2:13-23). For Luke, the story of Jesus *begins* with the annunciation to Mary *in Nazareth* (Luke 1:26-38). Proof of the fact that nothing is impossible to God demands that Mary *journey* to her aged cousin Elizabeth (vv. 36-37). There the incredible fruit of Elizabeth's womb recognizes the even more amazing work of God that is taking place in Mary: "How can it be that the mother of my Lord should come to me" (Luke 1:43). Mary's son is recognized as "Lord," and she sings her praises to God, who has done great things for her (vv. 46-55). The census of Quirinius calls for another *journey*, and the child is born while his parents are on that journey. There is no room for him in the usual wayside resting places, where travelers stop for the night. Jesus is born on a journey, for a journey (2:1-21). As the narrative closes, Jesus' parents come to learn that they have no hold on him. On yet another journey, they find their son is missing (vv. 41-52). When they find him, they learn he is about to go elsewhere. He must be about the affairs of his father (v. 49). The finding of Jesus in the temple opens the door to the public ministry, where Jesus sets out on a further journey, about the affairs of his Father.

The Galilean section of the Gospel (4:14-9:50), although influenced by Mark's presentation of Jesus' Galilean ministry, continues the Lukan theme of Jesus' relentless journey, in response to God. After the witness of the Baptist and his affirmation as the Son of God (3:1-4:13), Jesus leaves the area of the Jordan and, "returning in the power of the Spirit into Galilee" (4:14), comes to the synagogue in Nazareth where he reads from the Prophet Isaiah. The good news is to be preached to the poor, the captives freed, sight given to the blind, and the oppressed liberated by God's anointed (vv. 18-19). All speak well of him, but then some complain that this is Joseph's son. Jesus warns of the ultimate fruit of their unfaith – a chosen people abandoned, and a turn to the Gentile world. From here he moves on to Capernaum, and there performs many wonders (4:31-40), but he will not respond to the request – "What we have heard you did in Capernaum, do here also in your own country" (4:24). Jesus has moved on, from Nazareth to Capernaum, and from Capernaum he must journey further. His disciples want him to go back to the site of his marvelous miracles, but he responds, "'I must preach the good news of the kingdom of God to the other cities; for I was sent for this purpose.' And he was preaching in the synagogues *of Judea*" (4:44). He has journeyed a long way from his own town of Nazareth. After that paradigmatic scene of 4:16-30, he never returns, however much they would like to domesticate their local miracle man (see, by comparison, Mark 6:1-6a).

The promise of a journey that reaches beyond Galilee and Judea emerges in the Lukan version of Jesus' famous sermon. For Matthew, it is set upon a mountain (Matt 5:1-7:28). There Jesus instructs his disciples and a crowd on the perfection of the Law: "You have heard that it was said to the men of old … but I say to you" (6 times in Matt 5:1-48). This disappears in Luke's shorter version (see Luke 6:20-49). He goes to the top of a mountain, prays all night, then calls his Apostles, i.e. those who would be sent out on the mission (6:12-16), and then comes down with them on to a plain (v. 17a). There he is greeted by "a great crowd of people from all Judea and Jerusalem and the seacoast of Tyre and Sidon who came to hear him and be healed of their diseases … for power came forth from him and he healed them all" (vv. 17-19). The word and person of Jesus attract both Jew and Gentile. He addresses his beatitudes to disciples and the assembled gathering of both Jew and Gentile. His restless journeying goes on through Capernaum, Nain, the homes of Jews and Gentiles, the poor and the rich. And "he went on through cities and villages, preaching and bringing the good news of the kingdom of God" (8:1).

The *physical* journey, so clearly indicated across the journey from Galilee to Jerusalem is well under way in both the infancy narrative and the Galilean ministry. But it reaches a more sophisticated articulation in the story of Jesus' passion, death and resurrection. Once Jesus arrives in Jerusalem his journey, temporarily, comes to an end. He comes to the temple (19:45) and takes possession of it with authority (19:46). From then on – "He was teaching daily in the temple" (19:47). Jesus is always in the temple, and the discourse closes: "And every day he was teaching in the temple. …. And early in the morning all the people came to him in the temple to hear him" (21:37-38). For Luke, once Jesus comes to Jerusalem, he takes possession of the temple, and uses the Holy City and its Holy Temple as the location for his teaching. His journey is approaching its end, but another journey will begin from Jerusalem.

In Mark and Matthew, during the course of Jesus' passion and resurrection, the disciples are directed to return to Galilee (see Mark 14:27-28; 16:7; Matt 26:31-32; 28:7). There they will see him, and in Matthew, they encounter the risen Lord on the mountain in Galilee (Matt 28:16-20). But in Luke, the suffering and risen Jesus insists that the disciples *never* leave Jerusalem: "Stay in the city" (v. 49), for it is *in* Jerusalem that they will receive the power of the most high, and *from* Jerusalem they will be sent out to all nations, to Judea, Samaria and the end of the earth (v. 47; Acts 1:8). The disciples are, for the moment, to *stay in the city.* However, *Jesus' journey* started on the road from Nazareth to Bethlehem, crisscrossed Galilee and Judea, and eventually, once he set his face to go to Jerusalem (see 9:51), led relentlessly toward that city, where the temple became his pulpit. His journey comes to an end as, from Jerusalem, where all the Paschal events have taken place, he returns to heaven (Luke 24:51). The Gospel comes full circle as the disciples "returned to the Temple with great joy, and were continually in the temple blessing God" (vv. 52-53). The Holy City of Jerusalem is, for Luke, the fulcrum of God's saving history. It began in the Old Testament, is partially fulfilled in the journeying of Jesus to Jerusalem, and from Jerusalem back to the Father. But as Jesus' journey ends, another begins. The witnesses of the life, death and resurrection of Jesus are to proclaim repentance and forgiveness of sins to all nations (v. 47). The Acts of the Apostles takes up that story and another journey reaches out to the ends of the earth, even to that place, somewhere among Gentile converts, where this Gospel was first written read and heard.

How does this powerful image of "the journey" capture the Christian imagination? How did it strike those who heard and read it almost two thousand years ago, and what does it say to us today, as it has spoken to Christian readers for almost 2,000 years? I have mentioned that the Gospel of Luke was first heard among Gentiles. One of the understandable questions they asked had to be: how do we belong to this story of what God has done in and through the man, Jesus of Nazareth? Luke's two volumes connect them with that story. Where they are – at the ends of the earth, suffering from the tyranny of the distance they feel from Jesus, his life, his land, his culture, his religious practices, the founding Church – is all part of God's design. *They belong!* But that leads to a further problem. The message has reached out to the ends of the earth, and we are proof of that truth. Is this the time and the place to stop? The Gospel of Luke, with its relentless journeying, draws the believing Christian into God's journey to the ends of the earth.

Is it time to sit and be complacent about where we are? To develop a sense of Church as an institution that now has all the answers, a "rule of faith" that tolerates no further critical investigation, no attempt to re-articulate it in a Christian language and philosophical mind-set that respond to a post-modern and increasingly secularized world, is to reject a message central to the Gospel of Luke. To develop a preaching of the Gospel that encourages a Christian life that sits comfortably with where we are at the moment, a complacency that says we have done enough, is to reject a message central to the Gospel of Luke. The Lukan image of a journey is a thorn in the side to all who look back nostalgically to the comfortable securities of the past. The challenge the Lukan contribution to the New Testament offered to its first listeners remains urgently alive among the contemporary Christian Churches: You will be my witnesses to the end of the earth (see Acts 1:8).

Notes

[1] It is difficult to resolve this uncritical acceptance, on the part of many Christians, especially Roman Catholics, that the portrait of Mary in the Gospel of Luke is the way she was. This understanding of the Mother of Jesus continues to have ecumenical consequences in dialogue between Churches of the Catholic tradition and Churches of the Reform tradition. The recent study of E. A. Johnson, *Truly Our Sister. A Theology of Mary in the Communion of Saints* (New York: Continuum, 2003), is an attempt to do so. Her survey of theological approaches to Mary (pp. 3-134) is most instructive. In my opinion, the crowning achievement of this study is the situation of Mary in her own socio-economic, religious and socio-cultural world of Galilee in the first century (pp. 137-206). These pages deserve a wide readership, and should be used for the better education of Christians about "who Mary was."

[2] In many Christian celebrations of the Christmas Season, the only Matthean event that is recalled is the slaying of the Innocents on December 28 (the fourth day within the Octave of Christmas). It sounds a jarring note, in the midst of the widespread use of the Lukan pageantry.

[3] The Lukan passion story will be subjected to closer analysis in the following chapter.

[4] A trailblazing study of the Gospel of Luke, originally published in German in 1953, by H. Conzelmann, *The Theology of St Luke* (trans. G. Buswell; London: Faber & Faber, 1960), focused heavily upon this element in Luke-Acts. For Conzelmann, Luke faced the new problem in the early Church of the delay of the parousia. His Gospel places Jesus at the "middle of time" (the title of the book in German: *Die Mitte der Zeit*) and instructs throughout that followers of Jesus must face a "salvation history," i.e., a long period of time subsequent to the life, teaching, death and resurrection of Jesus, but determined by those events, during which God's saving actions are to be taught and discerned. There is much that is true in this important study, but the fascination with the delay of the parousia and the development of a theology of salvation history by Conzelmann leads him to miss many other important elements in the theology of Luke. However, the importance of Luke's instruction on the need for the Christian Church to face a long history before the final return of the Son of Man must certainly be affirmed.

[5] In the first chapter, "*Reading a Gospel Today*," we discussed the literary relationships that may have existed between the four Gospels. The Gospel of Matthew uses almost all and largely follows the order of the Gospel of Mark. This is not the case with Luke. As you will notice in the outline that follows, Luke has used Mark, Q and his own traditions (L), to produce a Gospel that has literary links with the other Synoptic Gospels. But Luke very often strikes out in a different direction, and contains much material unique to Luke. This has led many scholars to suggest that Luke may have used an already formed Gospel, independent of Mark and Matthew, called by the scholars "Proto-Luke." There is no need for this hypothetical reconstruction, however, once one credits Luke with finely tuned skills as a storyteller and a theologian.

[6] Not all commentators and scholarly discussions of the literary structure of the Gospel of Luke follow this structure's divisions of chapter and verse. However, most studies of the Gospel of Luke would agree with the general outline.

[7] We do not know whether Theophilus was a historical person, or if Luke opened his book in this fashion for literary effect. Both are possible. The name means someone who loves God, and this play on the Greek words indicates that he is a Gentile. The name is a first indication that the Gospel was written for a predominantly Gentile audience. The Acts of the Apostles is also directed to Theophilus (see Acts 1:1). See the outstanding study of L. Alexander, *The Preface to Luke's Gospel. Literary Convention and Social Context in Luke 1:1-4 and Acts 1:1* (First paperback edition; Society for the Study of the New Testament Monograph Series 78; Cambridge: Cambridge University Press, 2005).

[8] For a full-scale commentary, see the classical study of R. E. Brown, *The Birth of the Messiah. A Commentary on the Infancy Narratives in the Gospels of Matthew and Luke* (New updated edition; Anchor Bible Reference Library; New York: Doubleday, 1993), 235-499. For a briefer presentation, see F. J. Moloney, *Mary Woman and Mother* (Homebush: St Paul Publications, 1988), 15-29. Coming directly from a reading of Matthew's infancy narrative (Chapter Five), a reader is aware of the many differences between Matt 1-2 and Luke 1-2.

[9] For a fine study of Luke 4:16-30, see D. L. Tiede, *Prophecy and History in Luke-Acts* (Philadelphia: Fortress, 1980), 19-63.

[10] Only Luke and Paul use the expression "apostle" and "the Twelve Apostles"

in this way. For the significance of this, see the fine study of J.-A. Bühner, "*Apostolos*," in H. Balz and G. Schneider (eds), *Exegetical Dictionary of the New Testament* (3 vols.; Eerdmans: Grand Rapids, 1990-1993), 1:142-46. Some claim that the use of the expression in Mark 6:30 already has this meaning. But see F. J. Moloney, "Mark 6:6b-30: Mission, the Baptist, and Failure," *The Catholic Biblical Quarterly* 63 (2001): 647-50.

[11] Given the "missionary" nature of the Gospel of Luke, it is nowadays often suggested that the Gospel and Acts are directed to several Gentile communities. See, for example, R. J. Karris, "Missionary Communities: A New Paradigm for the Study of Luke-Acts," *The Catholic Biblical Quarterly* 41 (1979): 80-97.

[12] We have already noticed the different use of material that both Matthew and Luke would have found in Q for their presentations of Jesus' sermon on a mountain (Matt 5:1-7:28) and his sermon on a plain (Luke 6:20-49). For helpful further reflections, see R. E. Brown, "The Beatitudes According to Luke," in *New Testament Essays* (London: Geoffrey Chapman, 1967), 265-71.

[13] The Lukan interest in women characters, mostly without name, indicates both Jesus' original inclusion of women as active participants in the Jesus-movement, and Luke's desire to stress the inclusive nature of the earlier Church. On this, see the penetrating analysis of the emergence of the Jesus-movement from a feminist perspective in E. Schüssler Fiorenza, *In Memory of Her. A Feminist Theological Reconstruction of Christian Origins* (Tenth Anniversary Edition with a New Introduction; New York: Crossroad, 1994), 118-59. It is also an indication of Luke's consistent concern for the socially, religiously and economically marginalized. See below, note 27.

[14] My reference back to Mary's response indicates Luke's different approach to the mother and the brothers in this scene. In the Markan and Matthean parallels (Mark 3:32-35; Matt 12:47-50), the new family is presented as *replacing* his blood mother and brothers in an entirely new family. In Luke, Jesus' mother and brothers are *included* (necessarily, after Luke 1-2) among those who hear the word of God and do it.

[15] The pairing of these two miracles to form a unified narrative (the Jairus story acting as a frame around the account of the woman with the flow of blood) was already in place in Mark 5:21-43, and probably came to Mark in that form. It is

reported in the same way in Matt 9:18-26 and Luke 8:40-56. See F. J. Moloney, *The Gospel of Mark. A Commentary* (Peabody: Hendrickson, 2002), 106-111.

[16] The mention of the "exodus" in 9:31 prepares the reader, not only for Jesus' death, resurrection and ascension, but also for the prophetic presence of Jesus, leading his people to Jerusalem in 9:51-19:44. See the following note.

[17] On Luke 9:1-50 as the introduction to Jesus as a prophet like Moses, see D. P. Moessner, *Lord of the Banquet. The Literary and Theological Significance of the Lukan Travel Narrative* (Harrisburg: Trinity Press International, 1998), 60-70. On the Christology, formation of disciples, and the links with the events of the passion, see R. F. O'Toole, "Luke's Message in Luke 9:1-50," *The Catholic Biblical Quarterly* 49 (1987): 74-89.

[18] I am strongly influenced in all that follows by the work of Moessner, *Lord of the Banquet*. This is an unchanged paperback edition of an edition published in Minneapolis by Fortress Press in 1989, originally a doctoral dissertation defended in Basel, Switzerland, in 1983. For Moessner, the Lukan travel narrative is an example of the ongoing presence of the Old Testament deuteronomistic point of view in early Christianity. In Jesus the voice of a prophet like Moses (see Deut 18:18) is raised in warning against a fragile and sinful Israel (see Moessner, *Lord of the Banquet*, 56-60, on Moses as a prophet in Deuteronomy). For a study of the journey narrative (running from 9:51-19:46) that finds Moessner's study unconvincing, but is equally convinced that conflict is a major concern, see F. J. Matera, "Jesus' Journey to Jerusalem (Luke 9.51-19.46): A Conflict with Israel," *Journal for the Study of the New Testament* 51 (1993): 57-77. His disagreement with Moessner can be found on p. 60, note 10. In my opinion, Matera leaves a number of elements in the narrative unexplained (e.g., the centrality of meals, the miracles). This essay, however, provides excellent documentation for the long (and as yet unresolved) discussions over the structure, the literary function and the theological purpose of the journey narrative (see especially pp. 58-61, notes 7-11). Most recently, J. Severino Croatto, "Jesus, Prophet like Elijah, and Prophet-Teacher like Moses in Luke-Acts," *Journal of Biblical Literature* 124 (2005): 451-65, has added additional support to the position taken in my text.

[19] For this, see L. T. Johnson, *The Gospel of Luke* (Sacra Pagina 3; Collegeville: The Liturgical Press, 1991), 164-65, and B. Byrne, *The Hospitality of God. A Reading of Luke's Gospel* (Collegeville: The Liturgical Press, 2000), 93-94.

[20] This is the meaning of "names are written in heaven." It comes from the practice of cities and kingdoms in the ancient world drawing up lists of their citizens. The successful missionaries are thus "citizens of heaven." See J. A. Fitzmyer, *The Gospel according to Luke x-xxiv* (Anchor Bible 28A; Garden City: Doubleday, 1985), 863-64.

[21] Martha is doing what she should do. In Aramaic, her name means "the lady of the household," and she performs her duties as such. Her anxiety over these matters is the problem (see v. 41). All that she does should be learnt at the feet of Jesus (v. 42). See F. J. Moloney, *Woman: First Among the Faithful. A New Testament Study* (London: Darton, Longman and Todd, 1985), 61-62.

[22] The Lukan (Luke 11:2-4) and the longer Matthean version (Matt 6:9-13) of the prayer of Jesus (commonly known as the "Our Father," from the Matthean version), are markedly different. The Matthean version is most commonly known as "the Lord's Prayer." The briefer, and more direct version found in Luke may be closer to the original prayer of Jesus or of the prayer as it was found in Q, although one cannot be certain. On this, see the excellent study of R. E. Brown, "The Pater Noster as an Eschatological Prayer," in *New Testament Essays*, 217-53.

[23] As Moessner, *Lord of the Banquet*, xviii, caricatures it: "Luke seems to leave us with an odd pastiche of episodes and sayings of Jesus which are squeezed rather awkwardly into a journey framework." For a summary showing that this is not the case, see pp. 290-337.

[24] The divisions mentioned here may well have been the experience of people in the Lukan communities whose belief in the gospel had involved separation and opposition within their families. See C. F. Evans, *Saint Luke* (Trinity Press International New Testament Commentaries; Valley Forge: Trinity Press International, 1990), 541.

[25] Banquets, food and conflicts that arise in the sharing of meals are recurrent themes across the travel narrative (see 10:7-8; 12:19-22, 29; 45; 13:26; 14:1; 14:12, 15-24; 15:16; 17:8, 27-28; 19:1-9). Moessner, *Lord of the Banquet*, 268-84, links this theme with the exodus experience of a stiff-necked people seeking food other than that provided by the manna and the quail.

[26] See the excellent commentary on this parable in K. E. Bailey, *Poet and Peasant: A Literary-cultural Approach to the Parables in Luke* (Grand Rapids: Eerdmans, 1976), 158-212.

[27] It is beyond the possibilities of this chapter to elaborate Luke's concern to present Jesus' care for the marginalized. In the programmatic 4:16-30, he is the anointed one, sent by God to preach good news to the poor, to proclaim release to the captives and recovery of sight to the blind, to set at liberty those who are oppressed. He allows women into his life, raising the dead son of a widow (7:11-17). He forgives the sins of a woman who breaks through taboo and superficiality to shower her love upon him (7:36-50). He accepts women into his apostolic community, allowing them to journey with him on his mission, all the way to Jerusalem (8:1-3; 23:49, 55). He cures the woman with the flow of blood and raises the daughter of Jairus from the dead (8:40-56). Mary and Martha are used, in close association with the parable of the Good Samaritan, to show that one must not *only* be a good neighbor (as Martha and the Samaritan), but one must, *above all*, listen to the word of God and act upon it (Mary). In Jerusalem he singles out the widow who offers her all (21:1-4). On his way to the cross, he turns to the daughters of Jerusalem insisting that they weep not for him, but for themselves and their children (23:27-31). Other marginalized characters are drawn into his circle: fishermen (5:1-11), the tax collectors Levi and Zacchaeus (5:27-28; 19:1-10), with whom he shares his table (5:29-32; 19:5-10). The poor, to whom blessedness is promised (6:20), to whom the good news is preached (4:20; 7:22), for whom the banquet is prepared (14:13-14, 21) and whose representative, Lazarus, rests close to the bosom of Abraham, as the rich will not listen to the message of someone who has been raised from the dead (16:19-26). He points to the sinful tax collector as the one who is open to God's presence, and closer to the kingdom than the arrogant Pharisee (18:9-14). He asks that the little children, totally unconsidered in the society of Jesus' time, come to him (18:15-17). He reaches out to the untouchable lepers, of whom only a Samaritan returns to give thanks (17:11-19). A despised Samaritan is the example of a neighbor, and a Jewish lawyer is told: "Go and do likewise" (10:25-37). He forgives all who have so violently abused, tortured and slain him, and he welcomes a thief into paradise (23:32-43).

[28] For an important recent study of this passage, see T. A. Friedrichsen, "The Temple, a Pharisee, a Tax Collector, and the Kingdom of God: Rereading a Jesus Parable," *Journal of Biblical Literature* 124 (2005): 89-119.

[29] The introduction (9:7-50) and the journey narrative (9:51-19:44) refer consistently to prophets and prophecy (see 9:8, 19; 10:24; 11:47, 49, 50; 13:28, 33, 34; 16:16, 29, 31; 18:31).

[30] The Greek expression is deliberately ambiguous. It can mean "her whole livelihood." However, Luke is not primarily interested in economics here. He wishes to contrast the self-focused religiosity of all those he has attacked across 20:1-47 with the unconditional self-gift that is a genuine response to the demands of God. It is precisely in the gift of her entire livelihood that she gives herself, without condition.

[31] The Markan discourse also attempts to soften false ideas of the imminent end-time, and to point to a future, after the mission to all the nations (Mark 13:10) that only God will determine (vv. 31-32). However, Luke uses the Markan material to develop this message in a different fashion. One of the reasons for this is that Mark was probably written as Jerusalem was falling, or just after that event. Luke wrote well after that event. Mark is explaining the destruction of Jerusalem and its Temple (see Moloney, *The Gospel of Mark*, 248-73); Luke is using that past event for further exhortation.

[32] For a helpful presentation of what is meant by "eschatology" (and this passage is sometimes called "the eschatological discourse,") and what is "apocalyptic," (and there are some apocalyptic elements in Luke 21:5-36), see Byrne, *The Hospitality of God*, 163-66. In brief, "eschatology" refers to speculation about what will happen at the end of time and "apocalyptic" is an adjective applied to a vivid description, by means of revelatory imagery, of the overthrow of evil and the victory of good. Both are found in this discourse.

[33] See above, note 4.

[34] The Lukan passion narrative is so creatively different that it is especially here that scholars have suggested that Luke had a source different from the other Synoptic Gospels, known as Proto-Luke (see above, note 5).

[35] Some of the material used by Luke is found in the other Synoptic Gospels: the preparation for the meal, the dispute over greatness and Jesus' call to service. But they appear in this context only in Luke.

[36] See above, pp. 174-183.

[37] The all-pervading presence of the theme of "journey" across the Gospel of Luke, sketched in here by way of conclusion, is a further important contribution of the work of Moessner, *Lord of the Banquet*. See especially pp. 290-337.

Reading Luke 22:1-24:53:
Passion, Death, Resurrection and Ascension of Jesus

The Lukan story of Jesus' passion, death, resurrection and ascension is a subtle literary and theological achievement. Though using the traditional sequence of events as witnessed in the other Gospels, Luke is very bold in his creative interference, bringing about a unique reading of Jesus passion, death and resurrection. Themes that he establishes across the narrative of the Gospel come to a climax as the story of Jesus' life and departure ends in Jerusalem, the Holy City seen by Luke as the focal point of God's saving plan.

The passion narrative focuses strongly upon Jesus as the innocent, suffering Messiah and Son of God who will return as the Son of Man. The risen Jesus cannot be found among the dead. He journeys with his Church in the form of his disciples as they are sent to the ends of the Earth to witness until the end of time.

Chapter 7
summary

THE CLOSER READINGS OF SELECTED TEXTS from the Gospels thus far have concentrated on the prologue to the Gospel of Mark (Mark 1:1-13) and the infancy narrative in the Gospel of Matthew (Matt 1-2). This selection of texts guides us to understand better how the argument of a Gospel as a whole is applied to a specific text, and to different literary forms within the Gospel traditions. The passion narrative in the Gospel of Luke leads us to consider a long passage based upon a tradition that probably reached back to the earliest days of the existence of a Christian community. No doubt the most serious difficulty that faced the earliest Christians was that Romans executed the person they regarded as the Christ by crucifixion. This was an unacceptable understanding of "Messiah" (see Gal 2:13, with reference to Deut 27:26). The fact that the earliest Church could not avoid, however, was a fact of history: Jesus of Nazareth had been crucified. It was an enigma that the Christians had to explain to and for themselves, and also an enigma they had to face when they began their missionary activity among both Jew and Gentile. No one expresses the difficulty of the early preaching of the Church better than Paul: "Jews demand signs and Greeks seek wisdom, but we preach Christ crucified, a stumbling block to Jews and stupidity to the Gentiles. But to those who are called, both Jews and Greeks, Christ the power of God and the wisdom of God" (1 Cor 1:22-24).

It is widely accepted that the earliest Church grasped this nettle firmly, and *told the story of the passion, death and resurrection of Jesus* from its earliest days. It did not sidestep the issue.[1] The clearest evidence for this is found in the traditional sequence of events, found in all four passion narratives. Jesus meets with his disciples in a final meal, he prays in the garden of Gethsemane, one of the Twelve, Judas, betrays him, and he is arrested in the garden. Once he is arrested there are two so-called "trials": a hearing before the leaders of Israel, and a trial before Pilate, the Roman authority in Palestine. Condemned to death, he carries his cross to a place of crucifixion, is crucified, dies and is buried. All four Gospels then report an empty tomb, and all but the Gospel of Mark have various traditions of appearances of the risen Jesus.[2] Elsewhere in the Synoptic Gospels, episodes are brief and their sequence varies across the three Gospels. This does not happen with the passion story. Even the Fourth Gospel, so different in every way from the Synoptic Gospels, reports these events in their traditional order.

However, the telling of the passion and death of Jesus would never have been a straightforward story reporting the bare facts. From the beginning of this traditional storytelling it would have been told *to make sense of what God had done in and through Jesus.* The passion story, above all other Gospel stories, had to persuade readers and listeners that this horrific event made sense. This practice is found in the passion narratives in the four Gospels. This is not the place to describe the theological nature of each of the passion narrative in each of the four Gospels.[3] What follows will trace the Lukan use of that tradition to develop a particular theological and Christological point of view. As we should expect after our reflections on this Gospel in the previous chapter, Luke tells the events and interprets them in his own way. Indeed, Luke is very bold in his creative interference with the traditional sequence. At the meal with his disciples Jesus delivers a long discourse (22:24-38). Before the trials begin, Jesus is abused, and asked to prophesy (22:63-65). Instead of having the Jewish trial follow immediately on Jesus' arrest, he has the trial in the morning of the following day (22:6). He reports the Roman trial in two parts (23:1-5, 13-25), inserting a brief encounter between Jesus and Herod between those two parts (23:6-12). On his way to Golgotha, not only does he have the assistance of Simon of Cyrene, but the women of Jerusalem weep over him (23:26-31). Finally, he adds two new "events" to the resurrection narrative. As in the other Gospels (but with a special Lukan slant) Jesus has been raised from the dead, leaving an empty tomb (24:1-12). He is seen by many, and gives his disciples a commission (24:36-49). But one of the post-resurrection encounters takes place on a journey to Emmaus, unheard of elsewhere (24:13-35). Finally, the risen Jesus ascends into heaven (24:50-53), a physical description of Jesus' ascension into heaven only Luke narrates.[4]

The Lukan presentation of the passion and resurrection of Jesus, therefore, follows the traditional order of events, but Luke shapes them in his own way and inserts events that are not found in the other Gospels.

The Passion of Jesus

1. Judas joins the plot to kill Jesus (22:1-6)

2. The preparation for the celebration of a passover meal (vv. 7-13)

3. The meal (vv. 14-38)

    a) vv. 14-23: The meal and the betrayer

    b) vv. 24-38: The discourse:

i) Service and leadership (vv. 24-30)

ii) Peter's denials (vv. 31-34)

iii) The changed situation in the future mission (vv. 35-38)

4. The prayer on the Mount of Olives (vv. 39-46)

5. Betrayal and arrest (vv. 47-53)

6. Peter's denials (vv. 54-62)

7. Jesus is abused – "Prophesy!" (vv. 63-65)

8. The Jewish hearing (vv. 66-71)

9. The Roman hearing (23:1-25

a) vv. 1-5: Pilate's first meeting with Jesus

b) vv. -12: Pilate sends Jesus to Herod

c) vv. 13-25: Pilate's second meeting with Jesus

10. The crucifixion (vv. 26-49)

a) vv. 26-31: The way of the Cross

b) vv. 32-38: Crucifixion and abuse

c) vv. 39-43: A crucified criminal is promised paradise

d) vv. 44-49: The death of Jesus

11. The burial of Jesus (vv. 50-56).

The Resurrection and Ascension of Jesus

1. The empty tomb (24:1-12)

2. The journey to Emmaus and the return to Jerusalem (vv. 13-35)

3. The risen Jesus instructs and commissions his disciples (vv. 36-49)

4. The ascension of Jesus (vv. 50-53).

The Lukan passion and resurrection narrative is shaped by the older tradition, but from this outline alone it becomes clear that Luke tells the story in his own way, and for his own purposes.

The Passion of Jesus

1. *Judas joins the plot to kill Jesus (22:1-6)*

This first scene in the Lukan passion story is told in a way different to the other Synoptic Gospels. Judas is associated with the plot to kill Jesus from the start. In 4:1-13 Jesus overcame Satan, "and when the devil had ended every temptation, he departed from him until an opportune time" (v. 13). He now re-enters the story of Jesus, as he enters into Judas, one of the twelve apostles (22:3).[5] Judas is linked to the chief priests and the scribes who want to put Jesus to death, but they do not know how to go about this, for they feared the people. Luke always presents the crowds in a positive fashion. They maintain their sympathy for Jesus, even though during the passion they are drawn into the condemnation by their leaders (see 23:18). However, even through the passion of Jesus voices from the people are heard sounding a different tune: the women lamenting over Jesus during the way of the cross (23:27-31), the criminal on the cross (23:39-43), and the multitudes who return to their homes in sorrow after the death of Jesus (23:48).[6] They are not involved in the plot to kill Jesus. Only Judas and the Jewish leadership collude so that, after suitable payment of money, Judas can betray Jesus to them "in the absence of the people" (v. 6).

Luke has already foreseen the possibility of the final weakness of the people in his programmatic episode in the synagogue at Nazareth (4:16-30). An original response of wonder and excitement at Jesus' prophetic words turned hostile as he began to speak about the welcome God's word had received outside Israel. Luke is preparing the ground for the eventual pattern of the Christian mission. In the Acts of the Apostles, the mission to Israel meets with little acceptance.

2. *The preparation for the celebration of a Passover meal (vv. 7-13)*

A strong focus upon the period of the Passover marks the preparation for the meal. The word "Passover" is mentioned four times in this brief passage (vv. 7, 8, 11, 13). On the day of the unleavened bread, when the Passover lamb was slain, Jesus directs his disciples to prepare for the Passover meal. He gives details about their going into the city, following a man with a jar of water who will meet them. The householder of the house into which he will lead them is to be told that the Teacher is asking for the guest room, so that he might eat the Passover meal with his disciples. When shown the room, they are to make all the preparations. This improbable series of events, where unknown people follow an unknown person, and the master of the household acquiesces immediately to the request of "the Teacher," takes place exactly as Jesus said it would. The disciples make ready for the meal. Following hard on the description of the plot to kill Jesus, and Judas' association with that plot (vv. 1-6), Jesus is shown to be the master of the situation. His entering the city for the celebration of the Passover is the result of a deliberate decision on his part, and he directs his disciples through an elaborate series of events that lead to the preparation for the meal. For Luke, all that follows is not a tragic accident of fate. Jesus is lord of the situation as he takes the first steps toward the celebration of the Passover that will be highlighted by his death.

3. The Meal (vv. 14-38)

As we have seen in our earlier reflection on 9:51-19:44, Luke shows considerable interest in food and meals.[7] This theme comes to a climax in the final meal celebrated with his disciples before he dies. This section of the Lukan passion narrative is strikingly different from the Markan and Matthean accounts of the final meal. Luke may not be depending upon Mark for this part of his story, but blends his own theological concerns with the use of another source.[8] The account of the meal (vv. 14-23), and the subsequent discourse (vv. 24-38), are without parallel.

a) The meal and the betrayer (vv. 14-23)

The setting, provided by v. 14, links this meal with many other meals: "He sat at table, and the apostles with him." Across the Gospel, Jesus' shared meals have regularly questioned the *status quo*. He shared a meal with a tax collector (5:27-32), he draws a sinful woman into a meal setting, where her presence – generated by love – shocks all those present (7:36-50). At table with the Pharisees, he challenges them to recognize their lack of true justice (11:37-54), and to invite to table those who cannot repay (14:1-24). As he approaches Jerusalem, he again questions the *status quo* by sharing the table of Zacchaeus, another tax collector (19:1-10). As Jerome Neyrey has commented:

> Jesus' inclusive table fellowship mirrors the inclusive character of the Lukan Church: Gentiles, prostitutes, tax collectors, sinners, as well as the blind, lame, maimed and the poor are welcome at his table and in his covenant.[9]

Despite the crucial role the apostles must play in the period after Jesus' ascension, Luke tells his account of the meal to associate them with the long procession of fragile people who have shared meals with him during the ministry. "This final meal on the feast of the Passover crowns the meals ... which he has taken with his disciples and with sinners during his earthly life."[10]

Luke's unique account of the supper itself intertwines Jesus' teaching about the kingdom through the new covenant with the apostles, and all to whom they will be sent, established and sealed in his body and blood, and the explicit mention of the future betrayal of Judas. There is a deep bond between Jesus and the apostles, and he has longed for this meal with them, but it is a final meal before he suffers (v. 15). Luke reports more of the Passover meal, mentioning a first cup (v. 17) and a cup after the supper (v. 20). He associates this first cup with sharing, a symbol of the oneness of the future kingdom that will be established through Jesus' death and resurrection: the time when Jesus will again drink of the vine. This association of the disciples with Jesus in the initial sharing of the first cup, also carries the ominous warning of his oncoming suffering (v. 15), and the promise that the suffering will produce the fruit of the vine in the kingdom (v. 18). The eucharistic actions and words follow, no doubt reflecting the eucharistic practices of the Lukan Church.

Among the Synoptic Gospels, only Luke spells out that the bread is a symbol of a body broken for the apostles (v. 19b: "given for you") and that "this cup is poured out for you" (v. 20b).[11] And Luke is again the only Evangelist who adds the words of Jesus: "Do this in remembrance of me" (v. 19c), between the sharing of the bread and the wine (But see 1 Cor 11:23-25).[12] It is often suggested that these words come from early liturgical practice.[13] This may be the case, but poised as they are between Jesus' indication that he is breaking his body and pouring out his blood for the apostles, there is more to it. By the words "do this," they are urged to break their bodies and spill their blood in the future mission. It is not only in the cultic activity of the future Church that Jesus' death and resurrection will be proclaimed and thus "remembered," but especially in the broken bodies and the spilt blood of the apostles.[14] The Acts of the Apostles, and the history of the early Church indicate that such was the case. One hundred years after the appearance of Luke-Acts, Tertullian (ca. 160 – ca. 225) could write that the Church was born of the blood of the martyrs.[15]

But the passage comes to a close with the clear indication that these privileged and uniquely challenged apostles are marked by weakness and sin. The intimacy of the shared table will be shattered. One of the apostles, whose hand is on the same table, will betray him. This is tragic, and a puzzle to all who are at that table (v. 23), but a strange enigma of the fulfillment of God's design, despite the sinfulness involved, is being played out (vv. 21-22).

b) The discourse (vv. 24-38)

Judas is not the only failing disciple. As the discourse opens, the obtuseness of all the apostles is indicated by the dispute about who was to be the greatest. Jesus tells Simon that he will be called upon to "strengthen" his brethren (v. 32), implying that they will continue to fail. But even the one called to strengthen his brethren will fail: Peter will deny Jesus three times (v. 34). The discourse addresses the needs and the future of the foundational, but fragile apostles of Jesus Christ. Against this background, the discourse is to be understood as a New Testament example of a "farewell discourse." The practice of placing a "farewell speech" on the lips of a great man as he goes to his death is common practice in many religious writings in the first three centuries of the Christian era.[16] It is very widespread in the biblical literature. Jacob (Gen 47-50), Joshua (Jos 23-24), and Moses (Deut 31-34) deliver farewell speeches. Jesus (John 13-17), Paul (Acts 20:17-35), and Peter (2 Peter 1:12-15) continue this practice. Luke 21:14-38 is a further example of a farewell speech. The recently uncovered and critically examined document, *The Testament of the Twelve Patriarchs*, some of which dates from the second century BC, has provided even further examples of this literary form.[17] In the light of the biblical tradition, and the extra evidence provided by the *Testaments,* we are able to see that Luke has shaped Jesus' final words, using the pattern of the final words of a master, as follows.[18]

i) Prediction of death. This element has been provided in the description of the meal in vv. 15 and 22.

ii) Predictions of future attacks on the dying leader's disciples. Much of the discourse has this concern. It is most obvious in vv. 31-34: "Simon, Simon, behold Satan demanded to have you that he might sift you like wheat" (v. 31). It is also found in v. 36: "Now let him who has a purse take it, and likewise a bag. And let him who has no sword sell his mantle and buy one."

iii) Exhortation to ideal behavior. The setting of squabbling disciples provides Jesus the opportunity to challenge them not to be as the kings of the Gentiles, lording it over people and being called benefactors. The greatest is to be the youngest, and the leader as one who serves (vv. 24-27).

iv) A final commission. The blending of both blessing and fragility is skillfully handled by Luke. Within the context of the prophecy of Peter's future denials (vv. 33-34), Peter is commissioned: "I have prayed for you that your faith may not fail; and when you have turned again, strengthen your brethren" (v. 32)

The use of the setting of the meal has served Luke to show that Jesus shared his meal with fragile disciples, and involved them with him in the new covenant sealed in his body and blood. The use of the discourse, following the tradition of a "farewell discourse," establishes his apostles as his legitimate successors. Luke has composed 22:14-38 with great skill. Despite the brokenness of their table fellowship with the Lord, and the threat of future denials, betrayals and ignorance, they are his "apostles." They will continue his presence "to all nations" (24:47; Acts 1:8), breaking their bodies and pouring out their blood "in memory" of him (see v. 19).

4. *The prayer on the Mount of Olives (vv. 39-46)*

In the Garden of Olives (not Gethsemane), Luke does not report Jesus' sense of abandon, nor the three-fold going and coming to Peter, James and John. He tells the disciples who came out with him to pray lest they enter into temptation (vv. 39-40). The Greek word for "temptation" (*peirasmos*) means more than an inclination to sin. It refers to the return of Satan in power. Jesus drove Satan out of the story in 4:1-13, who left the scene "until the opportune time" (4:13). That time, the time of the *peirasmos*, is at hand, made clear by the explanation for Judas' joining the plot to kill Jesus: "Then Satan entered Judas called Iscariot, who was of the number of the twelve" (22:3). One of the apostles has succumbed to Satan. The others are to pray that they not enter into a similar pact with Satan. Jesus adopts a position of prayer, and prays that the Father's will be done (vv. 41-42). He rises from his prayer, and returns to his disciples who are so sorrowful that they have fallen asleep. Jesus has never collapsed to the ground (see Mark 14:35), and does not chide the disciples because they would not watch with him. He again tells them to be constant in prayer that they not enter into temptation (vv. 45-46). Gone is the agony. In its place we have the model of Jesus who shows the disciples what it means to pray to avoid temptation, the assaults of Satan that will be unleashed against Jesus and his followers.[19] There will be a struggle, but Jesus shows that openness to the presence of the Father will be found in its midst. The disciples, however, will show that they are not ready for this conflict.

5. Betrayal and arrest (vv. 47-53)

At his betrayal, Jesus remains in control of the situation. Judas, "one of the twelve," leads the crowd (v. 47). He was appointed as an "apostle" to be another type of leader, but he has fallen to Satan. Even before the betrayal, Jesus says to Judas: "Judas, would you betray the Son of Man with a kiss?" (v. 48). One of those with Jesus asks permission to use the sword, but then strikes the slave of the high priest without receiving that permission (vv. 49-50). Jesus intervenes vigorously, stopping the swordsman, and healing the injured slave. Jesus continues to call people to desist from what is wrong and to heal, as the passion begins. The arrest only takes place because Jesus allows it. He questions the motive of chief priests and officers of the Temple and elders. He has been among them in the Temple for many days, but only now they come to arrest him. He permits it because "This is your hour, and the power of darkness" (v. 53). In another important variation from the Markan and Matthean arrest scene, Luke makes no mention of the flight of the disciples (see Mark 14:50; Matt 26:56). The disciples will not be present during the trials, but they reappear at the Cross (see 23:49). The separation between the failing disciples and the forgiving Jesus is not so severe in the Gospel of Luke. Indeed, it will be fully restored in the meals with the risen Jesus that bring the Gospel story to a close (see 24:13-35, 36-43)

6. Peter's denials (vv. 54-62)

Unlike Mark and Matthew, who follow the Jewish trial with Peter's denials, Luke opens with this event. The reader is able to draw a comparison between the behavior of Jesus and Peter. Jesus has prayed that he might not enter into temptation, but Peter has not. Indeed, he is sitting among those who arrested Jesus (v. 55). On the Mount of Olives, Jesus allows the arrest (v. 53), but Peter now denies that he knows Jesus

(v. 57). Jesus does not fall in the face of temptation, and Peter, who has not prayed, does. Luke regards Peter's denials as a weak and almost tragic response to Satan's testing. He denies knowledge of Jesus (vv. 56-57); he denies knowledge of the rest of the disciples, by refusing to accept that he was "one of them" or that he has links with Galilee (vv. 58-59). Peter has denied three of the bedrock truths upon which the apostles were founded: adhesion to Jesus, beginnings in Galilee and belonging to the community. The crowing of the cock, however, proves that the word of Jesus is the only element of truth in these events. What Jesus said would happen, has happened (v. 60. See 22:34).

However, by placing Peter's denials *before* the cruelty and injustice done to the innocent Jesus during the trials, Luke is able to disassociate the chief apostle from the violence done to Jesus. It is *before* any of that violence begins that Jesus turns and looks at Peter (v. 61a). The silent look between the unjustly arraigned Jesus and his lying disciple breaks through Peter's frail defenses, and re-establishes a union that Peter had broken. Peter remembers the word of Jesus about his denials, and he repents with bitter tears of sorrow (vv. 61b-62). Simon Peter's repentance also recalls the words of Jesus at the supper: "Simon, Simon, Satan demanded to have you, that he might sift you like wheat, but I have prayed for you that your faith may not fail" (22:31-32a). Luke establishes yet another theological principle: all are capable of betrayal and denial, even leading apostles. By recalling the word of Jesus, repentance and salvation are made possible.

7. *Jesus is abused – "Prophesy!" (vv. 63-65)*

In another sequence unique to the Gospel of Luke, before the trials begin, "the men who were holding Jesus" mock him and beat him. They demand that he prophesy (vv. 64-65). Jesus' prophetic words to Peter in 22:34 have come true in 23:60. The reader knows that Jesus is a prophet, and that recalling his words bring healing and repentance. In an initial use of irony, a literary technique where the truth is proclaimed, despite the ignorance of those who utter the words, Jesus' opponents proclaim the truth. The Lukan Jesus has stressed the fact that Israel has rejected a long tradition of prophets (see 6:22-23; 11:47-50; 13:34-35). In the programmatic scene in the synagogue at Nazareth (4:16-30), Jesus has announced: "no prophet is acceptable in his own country" (4:24). The passion begins with the trials, but Jesus enters into his passion as the suffering and rejected prophet. The story thus far has made it clear that Jesus is God's Spirit-filled prophet, but that claim is rejected by Israel and its leaders.

8. *The Jewish hearing (vv. 66-71)*

In its general arrangement, Luke's version of Jesus' trials is different from those of Mark and Matthew. As we have seen, it is prefaced by the rejection of the prophet (vv. 63-65). Luke then times the Jewish hearing in the morning (22:66-71). This chronology probably represents more closely the correct sequence of these events. Luke also has two separate stages in the Roman trial (23:1-5, 13-25), separated by a visit to Herod (vv. 6-12). Across these trials, the irony already introduced in the abuse of the true prophet in 22:63-65 is used extensively. In the midst of insult and injury, the truth about Jesus is proclaimed.

In the trial before the Jewish authorities, Jesus is asked whether or not he is the Christ (v. 67a). The question, "If you are the Christ ..." repeats the form of the question asked by Satan at the first and third temptation (see 4:3, 9). There he responded to Satan with the word of God. Here he refuses by condemning his accusers: "If I tell you, you will not believe and if I ask you will not answer" (v. 67b-68). He then proceeds to instruct them on the authority of the Son of Man, that has its beginnings in these Passover events: "From now on ..." (v. 69). Since Jesus' other prophecies have come true, so will this promise. As a result of the passion, death and resurrection of Jesus, he will be enthroned as the Son of Man. As the Christ and the Son of Man, Jesus effects the salvation and the judgment of humankind. But this requires a unique relationship with God. The Jewish authorities understand this, and thus ask: "Are you the Son of God then?" (v. 70). Jesus' enigmatic acceptance of their ironic profession of the truth leads them to refuse all his claims. They have indeed heard from his lips that he is the Christ, the Son of Man and the Son of God, but they reject these truths. In Luke, however, there is no formal condemnation of Jesus by the Jewish authorities. The trials are used systematically to accumulate a series of christological truths that are rejected! Jesus' claims are true; those who reject them are in error.

9. *The Roman hearing (23:1-25)*
a) Pilate's first meeting with Jesus (vv. 1-5)

Taken to Pilate, three charges are leveled against him: perverting the nation, forbidding the people to give tribute to Caesar, and claiming to be Christ, a King (vv. 1-2). Jesus affirms Pilate's query about his being the King of the Jews (v. 3), but this only leads Pilate to tell the chief priests and the multitudes that Jesus is innocent (v. 4). The theme of Jesus' innocence will be stated repeatedly from this point on. Frustrated, the leaders add another accusation: stirring up the people from Galilee to Jerusalem (v. 5).

b) Pilate sends Jesus to Herod (vv. 6-12)

The mention of Galilee enables Pilate to send Jesus to Herod, the ruler of that region. This brief encounter between a vain man who is only interested in Jesus as a miracle worker, and a silent Jesus, may depend upon Isaiah 53:7: "He was oppressed and he was afflicted ... yet he opened not his mouth." There is no scourging and dressing as a king in Luke. This scene before Herod replaces it, as Herod dresses Jesus in a royal robe (v. 11), and ironically acts out the truth. Jesus is a king, and is dressed as such.

But Luke introduces a further subtlety by means of this scene. A corrupt Jewish ruler and a weak Roman governor become friends. The power of Satan works through the collusion of secular powers traditionally at odds with one another (v. 12). In his final discourse in the temple, Jesus had warned his disciples: "They will lay hands on you and persecute you, delivering you up to the synagogues and prisons, and you will be brought before kings and governors for my sake" (21:12-13). The future experiences of the Church and the disciples will be founded on the prior experience of Jesus.

c) Pilate's second meeting with Jesus (vv. 13-25)

Jesus' return to Pilate leads to a twofold insistence that Jesus is innocent (vv. 13-16, 22), but between the frame of these proclamations of innocence Barabbas, whose violent life-style is described in detail (vv. 17-19), is preferred to Jesus. A choice of violence over peace, prophecy, Christ, Son of Man and Son of God has been made. It is a wrong choice. Despite Pilate's repeated insistence that Jesus has done no evil, that he can find no crime in him, that he has done nothing deserving death (vv. 13-16, 22), he responds to the demand: "Away with this man" (v. 18). Barabbas is released, "but Jesus he delivered him up to their will" (v. 25). The evil and the corruption of the powers lined up against Jesus have been expertly summarized in vv. 1-25. An innocent person has been mocked, and condemned to death by Herod and Pilate. The violent man who has murdered has been given his freedom in the place of Jesus. The leaders of the people have had their way, and although they initially wished to avoid involving the multitude in the plot (see 22:2, 6), they have now led the people to demand the death of Jesus.

10. *The crucifixion (vv. 26-49)*

Luke tells the traditional sequence of events: Jesus carries his Cross to the place of execution, he is crucified and utters final words from the Cross, and he dies. But, as we have by now come to expect, Luke insinuates his own theological and Christological point of view throughout.

a) The way of the Cross (vv. 26-31)

On his way to the place of the skull (see v. 33), Simon of Cyrene is forced to carry the Cross of Jesus. In the Gospel of Mark, this is all that is said (see Mark 15:21). But Luke adds that they "laid on him the Cross, to carry it behind Jesus" (Luke 23:26). The passion of Jesus sets the pattern for discipleship, as Simon is a model of future Christians who will be called to follow Jesus on this final journey. He is also followed by many people, and women of Jerusalem who weep and lament over him (v. 27). Whatever may have been the cause for the decision of the multitude to ask for Jesus' death (see v. 18), there are still many who support Jesus and are in sorrow as he goes to death. There is never total opposition to Jesus. Jesus speaks to them, continuing his role as a prophet. As he drew near to Jerusalem he wept (19:42-43). In the temple he foretold the future destruction of the city and its temple (21:20-23). The women are both warned and challenged by the words of Jesus. If this is happening to me now, as I am slain by the Romans, how much more savage will be the experience of those who are guilty of his death? Readers of this Gospel, more than a decade after the destruction of the city (70 AD) sense the poignancy of Jesus' telling the women that they will ask the mountains to fall on them and the hills to cover them (vv. 28-31). As Jesus entered the city, he wept over it as he prophesied its destruction. As he leaves it, to be crucified outside the city walls, inhabitants of Jerusalem weep over him, and he again prophesies the destruction of the city.

b) Crucifixion and abuse (vv. 32-38)

Jesus, who has been thrice declared innocent by his judge (vv. 4, 14, 15), is led to the place of the skull and is crucified between two criminals

(vv. 32-33). Jesus may not be a criminal, but his concern on the cross is to offer salvation to those who are genuine criminals. His first words from the cross offer pardon and forgiveness to the "criminals" who have crucified him: "Father, forgive them, for they know not what they do" (v. 34). The response from the rulers (v. 35) and the soldiers (v. 36) ironically catches up truths proclaimed earlier in the Gospel: "If he is the Christ of God" (v. 35b. See 9:20), "his Chosen one" (v. 35c. See 9:35), "King of the Jews" (v. 36. See 23:3). The rulers scoff, "He saved others, let him save himself" (v. 35a), and the soldiers mock, "save yourself" (v. 37). Jesus' prophecy of 4:23 is acted out: "Doubtless you will quote me this proverb, 'Physician heal yourself'." Jesus, the innocent crucified one, is Christ of God, Chosen one, King of the Jews, Savior, and Prophet. Deep irony proclaims the central christological message of the Gospel of Luke.

c) A crucified criminal is promised paradise (vv. 39-43)
The theme of the innocence of Jesus is picked up by one of the crucified criminals. Jesus has forgiven all those who have created this "hour of darkness" (v. 34. See 22:53). As one of the criminals rails at Jesus, the other admits that he is receiving due reward for his wicked deeds (vv. 39-41). He asks Jesus to remember him when he comes into his kingdom (v. 42). No matter what his defects may have been, he is prepared to accept his sinfulness, and turn to Jesus for mercy and salvation. Jesus forgives the man and welcomes him into his company in paradise (v. 43). Following immediately on the charge from the rulers, "He saved others; let him save himself" (v. 35. See v. 37), the Lukan Jesus makes it clear that his mission is not to save himself, but to go on saving others. Through the saving event of the cross he returns to the Father, in the company of those he has saved.

d) The death of Jesus (vv. 44-49)
Signs that indicate the end of an era, and the tearing open of the veil of the temple indicating the end of God's former ways with Israel, greet the death of Jesus. In Luke's story, they *anticipate* the death, while in Mark and Matthew, they follow his death. With the turning point of the ages achieved, and the Holy of Holies open to the rest of the world, Jesus dies. His dying words show none of the anguish or terror of Mark and Matthew. He cries out, triumphantly: "Father, into your hands I commend my spirit." The response of the Gentile centurion is not the Markan/Matthean proclamation of Jesus as the Son of God,

but: "Certainly this man was innocent" (v. 47). Luke, who has never condemned the ordinary people, reports: "And all the multitudes who assembled to see the sight, when they saw what had taken place, returned home beating their breasts" (v. 48). Repentance begins immediately, as Jesus' death saves: he healed the severed ear of the high priest's slave (22:51), he reconciled Peter with a glance (22:61-62), he extended forgiveness to his executioners (22:34), he invited a repentant criminal to join him in paradise (23:43), and the crowds are moved to repentance at the Cross (23:48).

Mark and Matthew had dismissed the disciples from the passion story in Gethsemane: "They all forsook him and fled" (Mark 14:50. See Matt 26:56). Luke is not so harsh, as the disciples are his future witnesses. He reports: "And all his acquaintances and the women who had followed him from Galilee stood at a distance and saw these things" (Luke 23:49). In Luke's Gospel the disciples do not abandon Jesus, and Jesus does not die alone and forsaken. However peripherally ("at a distance"), the earliest Church is gathered at the Cross. In the events that have taken place at the Cross, disciples have witnessed the forgiveness of sins. They will soon be commissioned to preach repentance and the forgiveness of sins to the ends of the earth (see 24:46-49).

11. *The burial of Jesus (vv. 50-56)*
An unknown leader of the people, Joseph from the Judean town of Arimathea who had not consented to all that had been done, emerges and buries Jesus in a newly preserved tomb. Luke continues to indicate that there were many in Israel who were not party to the slaying of Jesus (vv. 50-53). People who had come from Galilee were present at the Cross (v. 49), and a man from Judea sees to his burial. Jesus is "King of all the Jews." It is the day of the Preparation, the eve of the Sabbath. Watched by women, Jesus is taken down and buried. The women know how and where he is buried, and return to the city to prepare the spices and ointments (vv. 54-56a). "On the Sabbath they rested according to the commandment" (v. 56b). The feverish pace of the passion story slows down, and comes to a stop, as the women rest and wait. The Christian reader, who knows that this is not the end of Jesus' story, also waits.

The Resurrection and Ascension of Jesus

The Gospels of Mark and Matthew both promise the reconstitution of a disbanded and failed group of disciples "on the other side" of Jesus' death and resurrection. They do this within the context of the Last Supper: "I shall not drink again of the fruit of the vine, until that day when I drink it new in the kingdom of God" (Mark 14:25. See Matt 26:29). Neither Mark nor Matthew report a scene after the resurrection when this promise is fulfilled. It was not needed, as the prophecy points to the celebration of the Eucharist as it was practised in both the Markan and the Matthean communities.

The Gospel of Luke maintains this tension that looks to a later moment when Jesus will again celebrate a meal with his disciples. Indeed, Jesus makes such a prediction on two occasions (Luke 22:16 and 18). The Gospel of Luke, however, goes further than either Mark or Matthew by reporting two occasions when the risen Jesus shares a meal with his disciples. The first of these meal scenes is recorded in Luke 24:13-35: the journey to Emmaus, and the second takes place in Jesus' final appearance to all the disciples (vv. 36-48). However, before these meal scenes, Luke respects the tradition, and reports the discovery, by women, of the empty tomb (vv. 1-12). All the episodes of the resurrection account are linked by an insistence that everything took place on the one day. The account opens with the naming of a given day: "On the first day of the week" (v. 1). The reader is next told, "That very same day two of them were going to a village named Emmaus" (v. 13). Towards the end of their journey Jesus' fellow-travelers say: "Stay with us for it is towards evening and the day is now far spent" (v. 29). After the breaking of the bread, "They rose that same hour and returned to Jerusalem." They make their report, but "as they were saying this, Jesus himself stood among them" (v. 36). This is the final presence of Jesus to his disciples in the Gospel as, at the end of the day, he leaves them in his ascension into heaven (v. 51). No other "day" has intervened across 24:1-53.

The whole of Luke's Gospel has been directed towards this "day." As Jesus began his journey towards Jerusalem in 9:51, the narrator commented, "When the days drew near for him to be received up, he set his face to go to Jerusalem." That "journey" comes to its close in Jerusalem through "the things that have happened there" (24:18). On this resurrection "day" we sense that we are at the end of a long journey. As we have seen in our reflection on the Gospel as a whole, one of the most important themes of the Gospel of Luke and its companion work, the Acts of the Apostles, is the theme of a journey.[20] Throughout the Gospel, a journey leads to Jerusalem, where the paschal events take place (see especially 9:51). At the beginning of Acts, the early Church is still in Jerusalem. The Spirit is given there, and it is from there that a second journey begins, reaching out to the ends of the earth. The center-point of Luke-Acts is the city of Jerusalem. The journey of Jesus leads him there. In Jerusalem the Paschal events take place, and he ascends to his Father from that city. Jerusalem is the end of the journey of Jesus and the journey of the apostles begins there. They are commissioned to go out to all the nations, but they are to "stay in the city" to await the gift of the Spirit (24:49). There they are given the Spirit (Acts 2:1-13), there they first become "church," one in heart and soul, celebrating the Lord's presence in their meals (2:42-47). However, it is from Jerusalem that they eventually set out, witnesses "in Judea and Samaria and to the ends of the earth" (Acts 1:8; see also 20:7-11; 27:33-36). The city of Jerusalem and the events of that "day" act as a fulcrum, around which God's saving history swivels.[21]

1. *The empty tomb (vv. 1-12)*

The essential elements of a resurrection account are found in Luke 24:1-12: the discovery of an empty tomb on the first day of the week, the appearance of heavenly figures who proclaim the Easter message, and the return of the women to report what has happened. Luke, however, has reshaped the telling of the story. The preparation of the spices has already taken place in the interval between the burial of Jesus and "the first day of the week" (23:56a; 24:1). The discovery of the empty tomb (vv. 2-3) only leaves them perplexed (v. 4a). Luke wishes to tell his readers and listeners that resurrection faith is not born at an empty tomb. In their perplexity, they are confronted with two men, dressed in dazzling apparel (v. 4b). The clothing is a traditional indication that these figures are messengers from heaven, and the response of the women, who bow their faces to the ground, confirms this (v. 5a). They do not wish to face the heavenly figures. The question the men pose to the women continues Luke's insistence that faith is not born at an empty tomb. They ask why they are seeking Jesus in a cemetery! If they wish to find Jesus, they will not find him among the dead (v. 5b). The men announce the Easter message: "He is not here, but has been raised" (v. 6a).[22]

There is a more profound basis for Easter faith. They may not have found the risen Jesus, but if they are seeking proof for the Easter message uttered by the men in v. 6b, they are to remember Jesus' word to them. They are to recall the message of Jesus, told them during their time with him in Galilee (see 8:1-3).[23] As with all the prophetic utterances of Jesus, what he, the Son of Man, said would take place has happened. His prophecies are true. He was delivered into the hands of sinful men, and they crucified him. But it is now the third day since he was slain, and the final part of Jesus' prophecy was: "and on the third day rise" (v. 7. See 9:22). The women must be regarded as coming to Easter faith. The men told them: "Remember" (v. 6), and the women "remembered his words." In this faith they leave the place of the dead. "Mary Magdalene, Joanna, Mary the mother of James and the other women with them" announce that Jesus' promises have come true to the eleven remaining apostles and everyone else. The apostles and everyone else regard such news as an idle tale (v. 11). Peter is reported to have gone to the tomb, found only the burial clothes and, like the women's initial response, wonders within himself what all this might mean.[24] Easter faith is not born at an empty tomb, but in remembering the words of Jesus.

2. The journey to Emmaus and the return to Jerusalem (vv. 13-35)

As Jerusalem is the center of God's history, and if the Lukan resurrection account centers its attention upon the "day" on which Jesus' journey comes to an end in Jerusalem, and eventually in his ascension into heaven, then the opening remarks of the journey to Emmaus are an indication of the situation of the two disciples. We are told that — in the midst of the paschal events — they were going to Emmaus, "about sixty stadia away from Jerusalem" (24:13).[25] They are walking *away from Jerusalem* (Greek: *apo Ierousalēm*), the central point of God's story; away from God's journey, making himself known in his Son, from Nazareth (Luke 1-2) to the ends of the earth (Acts 1:8; 28:16-31). Unlike Mark and Matthew, Luke never tells his readers that the disciples abandoned Jesus. They were even present at the cross, looking on from a distance (see 23:49). But these two disciples have broken that pattern, as they walk away from the place and the day of the Paschal events.

This impression is further reinforced once the reader notices the details of the account itself. In their sadness and disappointment the two disciples do not recognize Jesus (v. 15-17). They tell him of their expectations: "We had hoped that he was the one to redeem Israel" (v. 21). Jesus' way of responding to the Father has not fulfilled their expectations of the one who would redeem Israel. In fact, they know what one might be expected to know about Jesus, even the Easter message. They know of his life: Jesus of Nazareth, a prophet mighty in word and deed (v. 19).[26] They know of his death: "Our chief priests and rulers delivered him up to be condemned to death, and crucified him" (v. 20). They know of the events at the tomb: "it is now the third day" (v. 21), women have been at the tomb early in the morning, but "they did not find his body" (v. 23). They have even heard the Easter proclamation: there has been a vision of angels who said: "He is alive!" (v. 23). If, perhaps the witness of the women was not enough, "some of those who were with us" have been to the tomb, and found it empty. "But him they did not see" (v. 24). These disciples know everything ... but him they did not see, and thus they have had enough. Unlike the women, they have not remembered the words of Jesus, and thus they continue their walk away from Jerusalem.[27]

The practices of the Lukan Church meet the reader through the subsequent liturgy of the word, as Jesus chides them for their foolishness, and opens the word for them, explaining that it was necessary that the Christ should suffer many things to enter his glory (vv. 25-26). He "interpreted to them in all the scriptures the things concerning himself" (v. 27). Jesus journeys with these disciples who have abandoned God's journey that Jesus journeys, and he will eventually join with them at a eucharistic meal. After the liturgy of the word (vv. 25-27), and before the breaking of the bread (vv. 30-31), some initiative must come from the erring disciples themselves. Has the word of Jesus made any impact upon them? The Greek behind 24:28 reads: "He pretended (*prosepoiēsato*) to be going further." Jesus has unfolded God's plan through the explanation of the Scriptures. The disciples must now take some initiative. They respond generously: "Stay with us for it is toward evening, and the day is now far spent" (v. 29). As the Easter day draws to a close, the littleness of faith which led them to leave Jerusalem and the eleven is being overcome by the presence of the risen Lord (v. 15) and the instruction of his word (vv. 25-27). The process of repentance and forgiveness is under way (see v. 47).

At the meal the disciples recognized him in the breaking of the bread (vv. 30-31). Jesus has set out to follow and to journey with these failing disciples, as they walked away from God's designs for his Messiah (see

v. 26) and, implicitly, for those who would claim to be his followers. Yet he has come to meet them, to make himself known to them and to draw them back to the journey of God through opening the word of God to them, and through the breaking of the bread.[28] The memory of the many meals that Jesus has shared with them, and especially the meal he shared on the night before he died (22:14-38) opens their eyes. Touched by the word and presence in their failure, the immediate reaction of the failed disciples is to turn back on their journey: "And they rose that same hour and returned to Jerusalem" (v. 33).[29] The journey "away from Jerusalem" (v. 13: Greek: *apo Ierousalēm*) has been reversed as they turn back "to Jerusalem" (v. 33: Greek: *eis Ierousalēm*). Once they arrive back to the place they should never have abandoned and the eleven upon whom the community is founded, they find that Easter faith is already alive. They are told: "The Lord has risen indeed and has appeared to Simon" (v. 34).

The use of the name "Simon" calls for attention. As the Gospel opens, the reader comes to know of a man called "Simon" (4:38). Within the context of a miraculous catch of fish he is called to be a disciple of Jesus and Jesus introduces a new name for him "Peter" (see 5:8). The reader is reminded of this transformation in the Lukan list of the twelve apostles: "Simon, whom he named Peter" (6:14). From that point on, throughout the whole of the Gospel, he is called "Peter" (see 8:45, 51; 9:20, 28, 32-33; 12:41; 18:28). At the Last Supper, where the mingling of the themes of Jesus' sharing his table with the broken and the commissioning of his future apostles is found, he is still "Peter" (22:8, 34, 54, 55, 58, 60-61). Only in foretelling his future denials does Jesus emphatically revert to the name he had before he became a disciple: "Simon, Simon, behold, Satan demanded to have you that he might sift you like wheat" (22:31). The return to "Peter" at the end of Jesus' words is, in itself, a sign that all is not lost (v. 34). Yet, it is to the failed Simon that the risen Lord has appeared, to restore him to his apostolic role (24:34). The name "Simon," without any link with the apostolic name "Peter" appears only before this man's call to be a follower of Jesus (4:18) and at the end of the Emmaus story, when two failing disciples are restored to God's saving story which is taking place in Jerusalem. There another sinner, Simon, has also been blessed by the presence of the risen Lord (23:34).[30]

The failed disciples have come back home to another disciple who had failed his Lord. This return home, however, has happened because the Lord has reached out to them in their brokenness, and made himself known to them in the breaking of the bread:

> Here ... we find Jesus eating with outcasts, but this time the outcasts are two of his own disciples who have abandoned their journey of faith, fled Jerusalem, and embarked on their own journey. Jesus crosses the boundaries of disloyalty and breaks the bread of reconciliation with these disciples. Strengthened by the risen Jesus, Cleopas and his companion hasten back to Jerusalem and rejoin the journey of discipleship.[31]

Two disciples with inadequate faith had decided to walk "away from Jerusalem" (v. 13), and the Easter proclamation announced the presence of the risen Lord to the fragile Simon: "The Lord has risen indeed, and has appeared to Simon" (v. 34). In this return to the meal table, Jesus is eating with his disciples again (see 22:15), and drinking again of the vine (22:18). The kingdom of God has been definitively established through the death and resurrection of Jesus.

3. *The risen Jesus instructs and commissions his disciples (vv. 26-49)*

The return of the two disciples from Emmaus to Jerusalem leads into Jesus' final meal, celebrated with the eleven in the upper room (24:36-43).[32] Although "the scene is intended to stress the identity and the physical reality of the risen Christ who has appeared to his disciples,"[33] more is involved, as the close parallels between the experience of the Emmaus disciples and the experience of the eleven apostles indicate.

EMMAUS	JERUSALEM
Talking to each other (v. 14)	Talking to each other (v. 35).
Jesus appears (v. 15).	Jesus appears (v. 36).
He is not recognized (v. 16)	He is not recognized (v. 37)
Jesus asks a rhetorical question (vv. 25-26)	Jesus asks a rhetorical question (vv. 38-40)
Instruction based on Scripture (v. 27)	Instruction based on Scripture (vv. 44-49)
Revealing actions with bread (vv. 30-31)	Revealing actions with bread and fish (vv. 41-42).
Jesus disappears (v. 31).	Jesus disappears (v. 51).
The disciples return to Jerusalem (v. 33).	The apostles return to Jerusalem (v. 52).

The parallels between 24:13-35 and 36-52 suggest that the post-resurrectional, meals at Emmaus and Jerusalem are carefully constructed to bring to climax the many meals across the Gospel.[34] Fulfilling Jesus' promise at the meal before his death, his sharing table with his disciples (vv. 13-35) and apostles (vv. 36-49) announces that the kingdom of God has come (see 22:14-23). The use of fish in vv. 42-43 indicates that Jesus is physically present among them, but it also reminds the reader of an earlier episode. A link has been created across the Gospel between the final commission to the eleven in 24:36-39 and his initial formation of that same group in 9:10-17, where Jesus had earlier given them bread and fish (9:16).

Jesus drew the disciples who had lost their way at Emmaus back to Jerusalem through a eucharistic table. At another table, he commissions his apostles to witness repentance and the forgiveness of sins to all the nations (vv. 44-49). Jesus' suffering and death have interrupted fellowship at table. It has been re-established by his death and resurrection. The apostles have experienced failure, in the person of Peter. But Peter's denials have led him, in sorrow, to repentance (22:54-62). The disciples have experienced failure in the journey of Cleopas and his companion *away from Jerusalem*. But their disappointment with the way God has acted through his Christ, who had to suffer to come to glory, has been overcome by Jesus' journeying with them, and opening the scriptures. They experienced the presence of the risen Lord at their table leading them to the repentance and forgiveness of sins (24:13-35).

As this is the case, a double dynamic is at work in Jesus' commission to the apostles, and both elements will drive their future mission. All that Jesus has said is the fulfillment of God's design, as mapped out in the Law of Moses, the prophets and the psalms. The suffering, crucified and risen Christ has fulfilled God's design (vv. 44-46). Thus, in the first place, on the basis of their having witnessed the fulfillment of God's design in and through the words and deeds of Jesus, they are to preach repentance and forgiveness of sins to all nations (v. 47). However, as has been made obvious in the two meal encounters in vv. 13-35 and vv. 36-43, on the basis *of their own experience of repentance and forgiveness of sins,* the apostles are commissioned to witness to all the nations (v. 47).[35] They have witnessed the fulfillment of God's design in the words and deeds of Jesus. Luke's story tells of disciples and apostles who have experienced repentance and the forgiveness of sins in their own journeys with the Christ. Now they must wait in the city of Jerusalem. There the power from on high will be given to them, and from Jerusalem they will set out to preach repentance and the forgiveness of sins in the name of Jesus (vv. 47-49). They are eminently qualified to do so![36]

4. *The Ascension of Jesus (vv. 50-53)*

The Gospel closes as Jesus leads his disciples out to Bethany. They are still in the regions of the city of Jerusalem, as they were when he led them to the Garden of Olives, a place adjacent to Bethany. He says no words, but raises his hands in blessing (v. 50). His journey began in Nazareth and will conclude in heaven, via the events that have occurred in the city of Jerusalem. It came to an end as he was carried up into heaven (v. 51). But another journey is about to begin, and the apostles return to Jerusalem, obedient to the command of Jesus (see v. 49). The passion, death, resurrection, and ascension of Jesus produces great joy among these founding figures, who will preach repentance and the forgiveness of sin, in Jesus' name, to the whole world (v. 42). The Gospel ends where it began: in the Temple (see 1:5-24). But so much has been said and done between these two experiences in the Temple. Witnesses of all that has been said and done throughout this story, they will soon be clothed with the power from on high. The journey of the disciples is about to begin.

Conclusion

The Lukan story of Jesus' passion, death, resurrection and ascension is a remarkable literary and theological achievement. Themes that have appeared across the narrative of the Gospel come to a climax as the story of Jesus' life and departure ends. Other themes promise further expansion, as the Lukan story has not reached its conclusion. The passion account is prefaced with episodes that raise the issues of prayer, the role of Satan, the Eucharist and the eucharistic nature of the lives of disciples who must now be apostles of Jesus in the long period of time that lies between the departure of Jesus and the return of the Son of Man. The passion narrative focuses strongly upon Jesus as the innocent, suffering Messiah and Son of God who will return as the Son of Man. Even in his moments of greatest insult and injury, Jesus heals, forgives and promises salvation to fragile and sinful characters in the story, including his disciples and the apostles.

The risen Jesus cannot be found among the dead, but journeys with his Church, forgives its foundational members, and commissions them to be his witnesses. They have experienced repentance and forgiveness of sin from the Christ who had to suffer in order to fulfill the Scriptures. They are sent out to preach what they have experienced. As Jesus returns to his Father, the disciples joyfully return to the focal point of God's saving plan, the city of Jerusalem. There they will wait for the gift of God's power, and from there another journey will begin. They will witness to what they have seen and experienced to the ends of the earth.

Notes

[1] For a summary of the scholarly discussion of the question of a primitive passion narrative tradition, see D. Senior, *The Passion of Jesus in the Gospel of Mark* (The Passion Series 2; Wilmington: Michael Glazier, 1984), 7-11.

[2] We have already seen that Mark may not report appearances, but he promises one before bringing his story to a close in 16:8. For further reflections on this, see F. J. Moloney, *The Gospel of Mark. A Commentary* (Peabody: Hendrickson, 2002), 348-54.

[3] For a very good introductory study that does this, see F. J. Matera, *Passion Narratives and Gospel Theologies: Interpreting the Synoptics Through Their Passion Stories* (Theological Inquiries; New York: Paulist Press, 1986). For the Gospel of John, see F. J. Moloney, *The Gospel of John* (Sacra Pagina 4; Collegeville: The Liturgical Press, 1998), 481-515.

[4] In the Gospel of John Jesus speaks of his ascension to the Father (John 20:17), but there is no description of the event. Indeed, in the light of John 21, Jesus remains with the disciples. See Moloney, *John*, 547-68.

[5] H. Conzelmann, *The Theology of Luke* (trans. G. Busswell; London: Faber & Faber, 1960), 27-29, 156-57, has argued that between 4:13 and 22:3, the story of Jesus' presence (as the "middle of time") is free of Satan. This is not precise, as Satan does reappear in the narrative (see 10:18; 11:18; 13:16). Conzelmann is correct, however, in so far as Jesus is never again tempted by Satan (N. B.: "he departed *from him* until an opportune time"). The passion will provide the opportune time, but Jesus' prayer and unconditional openness to God (see 22:42) will overcome Satan, and he will exhort his disciples to prayer that they may also overcome the temptation of Satan (see 22:39-46). They sleep rather than pray (22:40, 45-46), and thus fail during the passion and resurrection narrative.

[6] For a helpful analysis of the relationship between Jesus, "the crowd" and "the people," see R. C. Tannehill, *The Narrative Unity of Luke-Acts. A Literary Interpretation. Volume One: The Gospel According to Luke* (Philadelphia: Fortress, 1986), 143-66.

[7] See, among many, R. J. Karris, *Luke: Artist and Theologian. Luke's Passion Account as Literature* (New York: Paulist Press, 1985), 47-78, and J. Neyrey, *The Passion According to Luke. A Redaction Study of Luke's Soteriology* (New York, Paulist Press, 1985), 8-11.

[8] For a detailed analysis of this issue, see J. A. Fitzmyer, *The Gospel According to Luke X-XXIV* (Anchor Bible 28A; New York: Doubleday, 1985), 1385-1406.

[9] Neyrey, *The Passion*, 10.

[10] X. Léon-Dufour, *Sharing the Eucharistic Bread. The Witness of the New Testament* (trans. M. C. O'Connell; New York: Paulist Press, 1987), 233.

[11] There is a difficulty with the original Greek text here. Some ancient manuscripts omit the second cup and the words over that cup. In defense of the longer reading (which I accept as original) see J. Jeremias, *The Eucharistic Words of Jesus* (trans. N. Perrin; London: SCM Press, 1966), 139-59, or the briefer treatment of Fitzmyer, *Luke X-XXIV*, 1387-89.

[12] Luke and Paul seem to be using the same tradition (sometimes called the Antiochene tradition), while Mark and Matthew share another tradition (sometimes called the Jerusalem or Palestinian tradition). For a detailed study of these variations and their origins, see Jeremias, *The Eucharistic Words*, 138-203.

[13] See Léon-Dufour, *Sharing the Eucharistic Bread*, 102-16.

[14] Paul expands on his version of the eucharistic words (very close to the Lukan version – see note 12) as follows: "As often as you eat this bread and drink the cup, you proclaim the Lord's death until he comes." For Paul, as for Luke, Eucharist is not only cult, it is also the grammar of a Christian life. See F. J. Moloney, *A Body Broken for a Broken People* (Revised Edition; Peabody: Hendrickson, 1997), 151-77. On liturgical "memory," see the precise and informative work of K. W. Irwin, *Models of the Eucharist* (Mahwah: Paulist, 2005), 122-44.

[15] This often cited passage, generally credited to Tertullian, had its origins there: "Semen est sanguis Christianorum" (*Apologeticum*, 50,13; *Corpus Christianorum Series Latina*, 1:171). This lapidary statement: "The seed is the blood of Christians," was developed and widely used by Augustine. See, for example:

"The seed of blood has been scattered, the harvest of the Church has risen" (*Sermon* 22,4,4: "Sparsum est semen sanguinis, surrexit seges ecclesiae. *Corpus Christianorum Series Latina* 41:294). See further development of the image by Augustine in *Sermon* 286,4,3 and *Sermon* 301,1,1.

[16] For a fuller discussion, with examples, see C. H. Dodd, *The Interpretation of the Fourth Gospel* (Cambridge: Cambridge University Press, 1953), 420-23.

[17] This is a troublesome document, as it has been transmitted by Christian scribes. Much of the material is pre-Christian, but there are many Christian interpolations. For an introduction and an annotated critical edition of this text (prepared by H. C. Kee), see J. H. Charlesworth, ed., *The Old Testament Pseudepigrapha* (2 vols.; London: Darton, Longman and Todd, 1983), 1:775-828.

[18] For a more detailed linking of these elements in the literary form of a "farewell discourse," along with many parallels drawn from *The Testaments of the Twelve Patriarchs*, see Moloney, *Body Broken*, 98-102.

[19] Later scribes, puzzled by the absence of an "agony in the garden" inserted a long passage about the appearance of an angel from heaven as Jesus sinks deeper into prayer, and perspiration like drops of blood falls to the ground as vv. 43-44. Many artistic presentations of Gethsemane add these details. They do not belong to the original text, and in fact betray Luke's purpose. See the detailed treatment of this question by Fitzmyer, *Luke X-XXIV*, 1443-45.

[20] See above, especially pp. 174-183.

[21] For detail, see R. J. Dillon, From Eye-Witnesses to Ministers of the Word (Analecta Biblica 82; Rome: Biblical Institute Press, 1978), 89-91.

[22] The Easter proclamation in v. 6a has long been omitted from the passage, as it was regarded as an interpolation from Mark 16:6. This is no longer judged to be the case. For the reason for this, and the inclusion of v. 6a in the original Lukan text, see Fitzmyer, *Luke X-XXIV*, 1542-43, 1545. The aorist passive indicative form of the verb "to rise" (Greek *ēgerthē*) should be translated as a passive: "he has been raised." God is the agent in raising Jesus from the dead. See Fitzmyer, *ibid.*, 1545.

[23] In both Mark (Mark 16:7) and Matthew (Matt 28:7) the women are to instruct the disciples that Jesus is going ahead of them to Galilee. This is impossible for Luke, as there can be no return to Galilee. All the saving events surrounding Jesus' passion, death, resurrection, and ascension take place in Jerusalem, and the Acts of the Apostles begins in Jerusalem. The Galilee tradition, however, is preserved in the command to the women to recall what Jesus said to them in Galilee.

[24] The tradition about Peter recorded in v. 12 is not found in a major textual tradition, and is insecure. It is very close to John 20:6-7, and may have been imported from there. However, it is consistent with Luke's general picture of the Apostle Peter, and it helps explain the report of the two disciples in the next episode: "Some of those who were with us went to the tomb, and found it just as the women had said; but him they did not see" (v. 24). I tend to accept v. 12 as authentic. See the more detailed discussion in Fitzmyer, *Luke –XXIV*, 1542, 1547. Fitzmyer supports its inclusion.

[25] Remarkably, commentators do not see the importance of the Lukan apo Ierousalēm. See, for example, I. H. Marshall, *The Gospel of Luke. A Commentary on the Greek Text* (The New International Greek Testament Commentary; Exeter: Paternoster Press, 1978), 892-893; E. Schweizer, *The Good News According to Luke* (London: SPCK, 1984), 370. There is a hint of it in Schweizer's passing parallel between the disciples' departure (vv. 13-14) and return (vv. 33-35) on p. 368. Fitzmyer, *Luke X-XXIV*, 1562, argues that Emmaus is mentioned because it is "in the vicinity of Jerusalem," and thus there is no journey away from Jerusalem. Similarly, see Dillon, *From Eye-Witnesses,* 85-86.

[26] For an excellent study of the Lukan Christology involved in the disciples' description of Jesus, see Dillon, *From Eye-Witnesses,* 111-145.

[27] Their knowledge of the "brute facts" of the resurrection story is widely recognized. For a suggestive analysis of what this means for Lukan thought, see Dillon, *From Eye-Witnesses,* 55-56; 110-111.

[28] For a fully documented discussion of the eucharistic character of 24:30, see J. Dupont, "The Meal at Emmaus," in J. Delorme and others, *The Eucharist in the New Testament* (London: Geoffrey Chapman, 1965), 115-121. See also Dillon,

From Eye-Witnesses, 149-155. Dillon has further pointed out that in both Luke and Acts "breaking of the bread" is associated with instruction concerning Jesus' person and mission.

[29] The fact that they "return to Jerusalem" in v. 33 further enhances the importance of their traveling "away from Jerusalem" in v. 13. Many scholars have seen the theological importance of this "return." For detail of this scholarship, see Dillon, *From Eye-Witnesses*, 92-94. Dillon finds himself in difficulty here. He has not appreciated the importance of the going "away from Jerusalem" in v. 13, and thus can only be "tentatively affirmative" (p. 93) to these suggestions.

[30] Most scholars see this return to "Simon" as an indication of the traditional nature of 24:34 (see 1 Cor 15:4). See, for example, Fitzmyer, *Luke X-XXIV*, 1569: "a stereotyped formula for appearances." I am suggesting that there is a more subtle Lukan point at stake. For a similar suggestion, see Dillon, *From Eye-Witnesses*, 100, note 88. See also Tannehill, *The Narrative Unity of Luke-Acts*, 292-293.

[31] R. J. Karris, "God's Boundary-Breaking Mercy," *The Bible Today* 24 (1986): 27-28. For a good study of the defects of the disciples in the Gospel of Luke, especially as they emerge over the passion narrative, see Tannehill, *The Narrative Unity of Luke-Acts*, 153-74.

[32] The importance of the table-fellowship in this passage has been shown by D. R. Dumm, "Luke 24:44-49 and Hospitality," in *Sin, Salvation and the Spirit. Commemorating the Fiftieth Year of the Liturgical Press* (ed. D. Durkin; Collegeville: The Liturgical Press, 1979), 230-239.

[33] Fitzmyer, *Luke X-XXIV*, 1575.

[34] See Tannehill, *The Narrative Unity of Luke-Acts*, 289-93.

[35] On this, see Dillon, *From Eye-Witnesses*, 197-203. See also Idem, "Easter Revelation and Mission Program in Luke 24:46-48," in *Sin, Salvation and the Spirit*, 240-270.

[36] On the Easter appearances as a restoration of failed discipleship, see Tannehill, *The Narrative Unity of Luke-Acts*, 277-301. As he writes: "What was closed can

be reopened" (p. 299). It must be, as the apostles are the main protagonists in the Acts of the Apostles.

Commentaries on the Gospel of Luke

The following list of single-volume commentaries on the Gospel of Luke is not exhaustive. An interested reader could consult any one of them with profit. Bibliographical details for the outstanding two-volume commentary of J. A. Fitzmyer can be found in the notes of the preceding chapters.

Byrne, B. *The Hospitality of God. A Reading of Luke's Gospel.* Collegeville: The Liturgical Press, 2000.

Danker, F. W. *Luke.* Proclamation Commentaries. Philadelphia: Fortress, 1976.

Danker, F. W. *Jesus and the New Age: A Commentary on St. Luke's Gospel.* Philadelphia: Fortress, 1988.

Ellis, E. E. *The Gospel of Luke.* New Century Bible. London: Oliphants, 1974.

Evans, C. F. *Saint Luke.* Trinity Press International New Testament Commentaries. Philadelphia: Trinity Press International, 1990.

Green, J., *The Gospel of Luke.* Grand Rapids: Eerdmans, 1997.

Johnson, L. T., *The Gospel of Luke.* Sacra Pagina 3. Collegeville: The Liturgical Press, 1991.

Juel, D. *Luke-Acts. The Promise of History.* Atlanta: John Knox, 1983.

Marshall, I. H. *The Gospel of Luke. A Commentary on the Greek Text.* The New International Greek Testament Commentary. Exeter: Paternoster Press, 1978.

Plummer, A., *The Gospel According to S. Luke.* 5th ed. International Critical Commentary. Edinburgh: T. & T. Clark, 1922.

Schweizer, E. *The Good News According to Luke.* Translated by D. E. Green. Atlanta: John Knox, 1984.

Stein, R. *Luke.* Nashville: Broadman, 1992.

Talbert, C. H. *Reading Luke. A Literary and Theological Commentary on the Third Gospel.* New York: Crossroad, 1982.

Tannehill, R. C. *Luke.* Abingdon New Testament Commentaries. Nashville: Abingdon, 1986.

Tannehill, R. C. *The Narrative Unity of Luke-Acts. A Literary Interpretation* 2 vols. Philadelphia: Fortress, 1986-1990. Volume 1.

PART V

The Gospel of John

CHAPTER EIGHT

Reading the Gospel of John

The Gospel of John is a much-loved document. Many of its passages "ring a bell" with any Christian. But this Gospel was not written as a collection of inspiring and comforting words. On the contrary, it came into existence to create crisis, not comfort.

This crisis is to be understood in the sense of the Greek word krisis meaning a call to judgment, or decision. The Gospel is written to throw down the gauntlet to the reader: believe in God and the Word made flesh, as witnessed in Jesus, and have eternal life, or perish. No middle course is possible. Stated simply, the Gospel of John will not settle for the established and safe. It is a challenge to think and think again about how Christians relate to God, to the Christ, and consequently, with one another. This Gospel presents a challenge at every turn.

Chapter 8
summary

THE GOSPEL OF JOHN IS A MUCH-LOVED CHRISTIAN DOCUMENT. Many of its passages "ring a bell" with any Christian. No scholarly training is needed for us to be moved by the proclamation "The Word became flesh and lived among us, and we have seen his glory, the glory as of the Father's only son, the fullness of a gift which is truth" (John 1:14). We share the belief expressed by the Samaritan villagers: "We know that this is truly the Savior of the world" (4:42), by Martha: "Lord, I believe that you are the Messiah, the Son of God, the one coming into the world," and Thomas: "My Lord and my God" (20:28). We respond with joy to Jesus' promises: "You will know the truth, and the truth will set you free" (8:32), "I am the way, the truth and the life" (14:6). But this Gospel was not written as a collection of inspiring and comforting words. On the contrary, it came into existence to create *crisis*, not *comfort*.

This *crisis*, to be understood in the sense of the Greek word *krisis* (a call to judgment), is not destructive. Stated simply, the Gospel of John will not settle for the established and safe. It is a challenge to think and think again about how Christians relate to God, to the Christ, and consequently, with one another. This Gospel presents a challenge at every turn. The Jesus of the Gospel of John summons the readers of the story to think again. Further decisions, more love and unconditional trust lie ahead. When characters in the story say "we know" there is almost always a shock in store for them. Their "knowledge" must be transformed if they hope to understand the God revealed by the Jesus of the Gospel of John (see, for example, 3:2; 4:25; 6:42; 7:27; 9:20, 24, 29, 31; 11:49; 16:30). This is the *krisis* of the Fourth Gospel: the call to engage in a never-ending quest for belief without sight (see 20:29). Jesus of Nazareth may not be present, but his story has been written to urge readers to reach deeper into the potential for love and belief. In this ever-deepening quest, one finds the exhilarating experience of life, both here and hereafter (see 20:31).[1]

Introductory Matters

Several documents in the New Testament have been regarded by Christian tradition as originating from a person named "John": the Gospel of John, the three Letters of John and the Apocalypse.[2] Only the Apocalypse refers to its author as "John" (see Apoc 1:1, 4, 9; 22:8). Scholarly opinion would regard this John, an elder writing from the island of Patmos (Apoc 1:9), as someone other than the author(s) of the Gospel and the Letters.

But tradition gradually associated all the so-called "Johannine" documents with the disciple of Jesus, John the son of Zebedee. In an addendum to the original Gospel (John 21), the narrator of the story identifies the Beloved Disciple found in the Gospel story as its author (see John 21:24: "This is the disciple ... who has written these things"). As early as 180 AD St. Irenaeus made the link between John, the son of Zebedee with the Beloved disciple.

All the Johannine Literature appears to have been written some time at the turn of the first century (100 AD). While the Apocalypse is generally associated with the persecutions of the Roman Emperor Domitian (81-96 AD), the Gospel and the Letters, although dated at about the same period, come from a different background.

1 The Gospel of John is marked by a strong conflict between Jesus and "the Jews" (see, for example, 2:13-25; 7:14-31, 40-44; 8:12-20, 48-59; 11:45-52), indicating a period when hostility between Christians and Jews was leading to a final separation. "The Jews" in the Gospel story are not the people of Israel but rather an expression used for those who have rejected Jesus as the unique revelation of God. Many of the original readers, and almost certainly the author, were Jews. For this reason, the expression is always placed between quotes: "the Jews."[3]

2 On three occasions in the Gospel of John, mention is made of the eviction of the Christians from the Synagogue. In the original Greek, a technical word (*aposunagōgos*) is used, and the eviction is associated with confession of faith in Jesus as the Christ (see 9:22; 12:32; 16:2). In the story of the man born blind (9:1-34) there is a gradual growth of faith in Jesus as the Christ that leads to the blind man being cast out of the Synagogue (see 9:34). The Gospel of John reflects a parallel process in an early Christian community.[4]

3 Any direct dependence of John's Gospel upon the Synoptic Gospels is not likely. Yet, behind the Fourth Gospel one senses traditions from the story of Jesus that are also found in the Synoptic tradition (the calling of disciples [1:35-51], the purification of the temple [2:13-25], the curing of a paralytic [5:1-9], the multiplication of the loaves and fishes [6:1-15], walking on the water [6:16-21], the curing of a blind man [9:1-7], the theme of Jesus as a shepherd [10:1-18], a woman washes Jesus' feet [12:1-8], the passion story [18:1-19:42], the resurrection story [20:1-29], the miraculous draught of fishes [21:1-14]). The Johannine community

began its history within Judaism, but was expelled from the Synagogue, and exposed to the wider world. The Gospel of John reflects its roots in the Jewish origins of the Christian Church, and also in its presence in the wider Greco-Roman world.[5]

The Letters of John depend upon the Gospel. While it is impossible to be certain of the author(s), the Gospel and the Letters come from the same Johannine community. However, the Letters were written in a situation of division, threat of conflict over the person of Jesus, and different understandings of the Christian life. These difficulties arose from divergent readings of the same foundational document: the Gospel of John. Without the Gospel there would be no Letters. The Gospel would have been written at the turn of the century and the Letters shortly after that time. They were written in a place where Judaism, early Christianity, the complex religions of the Hellenistic and Greek world, and incipient Gnosticism rubbed shoulders — often painfully.[6] The traditional site for the writing of the Gospel of John — Ephesus — remains one of the best locations for such a blend.

The identification of the Beloved Disciple who leaned on Jesus' breast at the Last Supper (see 13:23), was present at the foot of the Cross (see 19:25-27) and who saw and believed when he saw the clothes of death empty and folded in the tomb (see 20:3-10) and John, the son of Zebedee, is well attested in Christian art and history. This identification owes much to the work of St. Irenaeus (about 130-200 AD) who in many ways rescued the Gospel of John from the Gnostics of the second century. The Gnostics found the poetic, speculative nature of the Johannine story suited their myth of a redeemer who descended to give knowledge (Greek: gn sis) to the unredeemed, wallowing in the darkness of ignorance. A part of St. Irenaeus' defence of the Gospel of John was a link with an original Apostle. This story was not mere speculation; it went back to the first-hand witness of John, the son of Zebedee.

> Was St. Irenaeus right? It is impossible to give a certain answer one way
> or the other. The vast majority of contemporary scholars do not regard
> it as a significant question. Most who have pursued the matter conclude
> that the author was a founding figure in the community, probably
> a disciple of Jesus, but not the son of Zebedee or one of the Twelve.
> From the story of the Gospel itself, however, an interesting figure
> emerges. One of the active characters in the story is never named. He
> is generally called "the other disciple" (see 18:15, 16; 20:3, 4, 8), but

eventually becomes "the other disciple ... whom Jesus loved" (see 20:2). This is "the Beloved Disciple" (see 13:23; 19:26), the author of the Gospel (21:20, 23, 24). The narrative of the Gospel bears traces of its "author." He was a disciple of Jesus, a founding figure in a community whose Gospel we today call the Gospel of John. His desire to keep his name out of the account of the life of Jesus was respected, even after he had died.

His death is presupposed by 21:20-23. The addendum to the Gospel (chap. 21) provides information about the later situation of the Johannine Community. As Peter "follows" Jesus (21:19), he looks back to the Beloved Disciple who is, in turn, following (v. 20). He enquires about the destiny of this other important figure (v. 21). Jesus tells Peter that he is not to concern himself whether or not the Beloved Disciple will live on until Jesus returns (v. 22), but the narrator then adds a further explanatory comment to the words of Jesus (v. 23). Jesus did not say the Beloved Disciple would not die, but whether or not he would die was not Peter's concern. This comment is called for because "the rumour spread in the community that this disciple would not die" (v. 23), but that is not exactly what Jesus had said. The community had to be taught exactly what Jesus meant. What was the problem? The Beloved Disciple was no longer alive as chapter 21 was being written, and his death had to be explained.

St. Irenaeus might have been correct in identifying the Beloved Disciple with the Apostle John, but there is no way this can be proved. The weight of the evidence is against their being one and the same figure, but it should not worry us that we cannot be sure. The authority of this Gospel flows from its message, not from the apostolicity of its author. The most important thing about the Gospel of John is that it has stood the test of time. Today, after almost two thousand years of Christian history, we continue to read this life-story of Jesus. Whether or not John the Apostle was its author cannot alter that fact.[7]

The Johannine Literary Design and Its Theological Message

The Gospel of John, at first sight, is relatively simple to divide into a Prologue, two major sections, and a conclusion. The Prologue (John 1:1-18) is one of the most remarkable passages in the New Testament, and it stands alone, introducing the story of the life and teaching of Jesus. Immediately following the Prologue, a narrative about Jesus' public ministry begins. As with the other Gospels, we first read of John the Baptist's activity, but once Jesus enters the scene, he is the main focus of attention. He is in Jerusalem, by the Lake of Galilee, in discussions with Nicodemus, the Samaritan woman, the disciples, "the Jews," and many others from 1:19 to 12:36. There, after threatening darkness for those who reject him, he leaves the scene and hides himself (12:36b). In 13:1 the final evening Jesus spends with his disciples is introduced, and the account of those last days runs on till 20:29. Finally, as with the Prologue opening the Gospel, the author intervenes to bring his story to a conclusion. He tells us why he wrote the Gospel (20:30-31). However, a further chapter (John 21), added after the author had penned 20:30-31, has always been part of this story of Jesus. There was more to be said to the disciples, and all subsequent disciples who might read this Gospel. Our reading will follow those major divisions: John 1:1-18; 1:18-12:50, 13:1-20:31, and John 21.

Reading John 1:-18[8]

The Gospel of John does not begin with a birth story (see Matt 1-2; Luke 1-2). It reaches behind all time, behind "the beginning." The Word was turned from all time in loving union towards God, a union so intense that what God was, the Word also was (1:1-2). But this Word is, like all words, directed to others. Salvation is impossible without the Word, the light and life of humankind (vv. 3-4). This is a biblical way of saying that only in the Word can humankind find the answer to its hopes and deepest desires. However, there are powers of darkness opposed to the revelation of the Word of God. They attempt to overcome the light he comes to bring, but they fail. Although only a hint at this stage, the beginnings of a Johannine theology of the Cross is present in this succinct statement: "The light shines in the darkness, and the darkness did not overcome it" (v. 5).[9]

The argument thus far concerned God and God's Word. It now shifts into our experience through the intervention of John the Baptist, a figure from history. The Baptist points away from himself toward the true light (vv. 6-8). The light the Word brings, however, is neither recognized nor accepted, but to those who do receive it, a unique salvation is possible: they will become the children of God (vv. 9-13). The Word we must hear and accept as the light and the truth is not an abstract notion. The Word that is one with God has entered our history; he has dwelt among us, the fullness of the gifts of God. We are now able to see the revelation of God himself, "the glory of God," in the Word who has become flesh (v. 14).

But who is he? The Baptist re-enters, calling out in his own words that the one who may come after him in terms of chronological time, is greater than him because he has existed before all time (v. 15, recalling vv. 1-2). Israel regarded the gift of the Law as the greatest of all God's gifts. Now, claims the storyteller, there is an even greater gift. From the fullness of God we have all received a new gift that takes the place of a former gift (v. 16). The gift of the law to the Jewish people came through Moses, and it was a great gift. But now the perfect gift is among us: the gift of the revelation of the truth given to us through Jesus Christ (v. 17). No one has ever seen God but the life story of Jesus is not about Jesus; it is about God. Jesus' life will make God known (v. 18).

In v. 19 we begin a narrative linked to the Prologue: "And this is the testimony of John." Are the claims made in the Prologue for Jesus true? Answers to this question can only be found through a narrative matching the theory: a life-story of Jesus that shows he does reveal the glory of God (see 1:14). Well informed by the Prologue, we cannot be indifferent and we read the life-story of Jesus Christ in the light of the Prologue. They may or may not match. That remains to be seen. To be given information - however beautifully and profoundly that communication takes place - is not the end of the questioning. We emerge at the end of the prologue aware that the theology of the Word has become the theology of Jesus Christ. But how has this happened? Only the rest of the story can answer that question, and we must judge, and be judged, by the acceptance or refusal of that answer (see vv. 10-13). Herein lies the key to the *krisis* of the Gospel. We have been told all the answers to the mystery of Jesus Christ: his origins with God, his saving revelation, his relationship with God's former gifts. We have been told that *only Jesus* makes God known. But the characters we are about to meet in the story *have not read the Prologue.* As we make our way through the story, experiencing a variety of responses to Jesus, and listening to his words of revelation, do the claims of the Prologue still hold? That is the decision we must make as we read the rest of the story.[10]

Reading John 1:19-12:50[11]

1. *The First Days of Jesus (1:19-51)*
There is a deliberate setting of this first narrative section of the Gospel within the context of days (see vv. 29, 35 and 43: "the next day"). This leads into 2:1: "on the third day." There are four days behind the narrative from v. 19 through to v. 51, followed by the indication of "on the third day" for the first miracle at Cana. The background for these "days" comes from the Jewish celebration of Pentecost, which commemorates the gift of the Law on Sinai. In this celebration, there are four "days" of more remote preparation (vv. 19-51), the fourth day of which begins an intensive preparation for the gift of the glory of the Law (vv. 43-51), which takes place "on the third day" (see 2:1. See Exod 19:10-11, 16).

The days, therefore, are preparation for the revelation of the glory of God in Jesus, which will take place at Cana (see 2:11). On the first day we find a series of guesses about who John the Baptist might be, framed in terms of titles and hopes which were linked to first century Jewish messianic expectations:

◻ Who are you? (v. 19)

◻ I am not the Messiah (vv. 20, 25)

◻ Are you Elijah? (vv. 21, 25)

◻ Are you the prophet? (vv. 21, 25)

◻ What do you say about yourself? (v. 22).

The second day (see v. 29) finds the Baptist giving witness to Jesus. His words transcend Jewish hopes:

◻ Here is the Lamb of God, who takes away the sin of the world (v. 29)

◻ After me comes a man who ranks ahead of me, because he was before me (v. 30)

◻ The one who baptizes with the Holy Spirit (v. 33)

◻ This is the Son of God (v. 34).

On the third day (see v. 35) the Baptist points to Jesus of Nazareth as the Lamb of God, and the disciples of the Baptist set out to "follow" Jesus. However, the disciples, despite their having been instructed by the Baptist and having had a brief time with Jesus, express their own messianic hopes:

▫ Rabbi (v. 38)

▫ We have found the Messiah (which is translated Anointed) (v. 41).

On the fourth day (see v. 43), a day that begins the more intense preparation for the gift of the glory, Jesus enters the drama more actively. He calls Philip who calls Nathanael, but once again the disciples are unable to transcend their own expectations:

▫ We have found him about whom Moses in the law and also the prophets wrote (v. 45)

▫ Rabbi, you are the son of God! You are the King of Israel! (v. 49)

Jesus is dissatisfied, even with the exalted confession of Nathanael: "Jesus answered, 'Do you believe because I said to you I saw you under the fig tree? You will see greater things than these.' And he said to him, 'Very truly, I tell to you, you will see heaven opened and the angels of God ascending and descending upon the Son of Man.'"

As with all the other responses from the first disciples, something is lacking in Nathanael's confession of faith, based on his wonder at Jesus having seen him under the fig tree. Greater faith is required of him, and of all the disciples. They are promised, as a consequence of true faith, the revelation of the heavenly in Jesus, the Son of Man.[12] The incipient faith of the disciples is not wrong, but it does not go far enough. They are still locked within their own world. A faith based in what can be controlled and understood by the *disciples' expectation* is good, but not good enough. What more is required? It is to this question that the next section of the Gospel (2:1-4:54) turns.

2. *From Cana to Cana (2:1 - 4:54)*

The storyteller wants the reader to link two accounts of miracles performed by Jesus at Cana (2:1-12; 4:46-54). As he begins the second Cana story he comments: "Then he came again to Cana in Galilee where he had changed the water into wine" (4:46), and ending the story comments: "Now this was the second sign that Jesus did after coming from Judea to Galilee." This is a "frame" around a series of episodes recounting a variety of reactions to Jesus. But the reader of 2:1-4:54 has 1:19-51, which she or he has just read, in mind. The responses of the Mother of Jesus in 2:1-11 and the royal official in 4:46-54 set the atmosphere. Both trust completely in the efficacy of the word of Jesus. Even though Jesus questions his Mother (see 2:4), she simply says to the attendants: "Do whatever he tells you" (2:5). Similarly, the royal official is rebuked (see 4:48), but as Jesus promises health to his son, "the man believed the word Jesus spoke to him and started on his way (4:50). An unconditional acceptance of the "word of Jesus" is evident in the two examples of faith framing the narrative.

Between these two examples of perfect Johannine faith, there are two sets of possible reactions to the word of Jesus. There is more to these passages than the response of faith, but focusing upon that aspect of each episode we find that:

□ "The Jews" totally reject the word of Jesus (2:13-21. See vv. 18-21). They are to be judged as in a situation of no faith.

□ Nicodemus is prepared to admit that Jesus is a great teacher from God because he does great signs, but he is not prepared to let go of his categories when Jesus speaks of the need to be reborn from above (3:1-10. See vv. 2-9). He is in a situation of partial faith. There is a commitment, but within controllable categories.

□ John the Baptist is prepared to disappear totally from the scene, as he is only the friend of the bridegroom who listens for his voice (3:22-30. See vv. 27-30). His is a repetition of the complete commitment to the word of Jesus from the Mother of Jesus and the royal official that we found in the "frame." Here there is true faith.

All the characters in this series of responses to the word of Jesus come from the world of "the Jews" and a journey from no faith to true faith is possible within that world.

Once this cycle of a journey from no faith to partial faith to true faith is completed, we find that it starts again in the experience of the Samaritan woman and the Samaritan villagers.

□ In a first moment, the Samaritan woman is unable to go beyond her ideas of wells and water, and is incapable of grasping the words of Jesus as he promises a water that will give eternal life (4:1-15. See vv. 13-15). In this first stage she has no faith.

□ Jesus shifts the discussion to something she can understand (her marital situation) and she comes to see that he is a "prophet." She even suspects he may be the Messiah (4:16-30). She is responding with categories that come to her from her own religious and cultural circumstances, and she has moved into a situation of partial faith (see vv. 19, 25-26).

◻ Finally, the Samaritan villagers come to hear the word of Jesus himself, and on his word (not the woman's), they proclaim: "this is indeed the Saviour of the world" (4:39-42). We again encounter true faith.

Stories of a journey of faith from no faith to true faith in the non-Jewish world have been told. This episode is immediately followed by the second Cana miracle (4:43-54), and thus we find that there have been two movements from no faith, through partial faith into complete faith.

But there is more to it. The Mother of Jesus (2:1-12) is a Jew and the royal official (4:46-54) is a Gentile. The Mother's example is followed by stories that tell of the possibility of faith within Judaism, and the example of the Royal official is preceded by stories that tell of faith outside Judaism. As the first days of Jesus closed (1:19-51) we wondered what kind of faith Jesus demanded. We now have the answer: a complete and unconditional trust in the efficacy of the word of Jesus, in his person and in everything he has come to reveal. Such a journey is universally possible. Both Jew and Gentile have come to express their unconditional trust in the word of Jesus. Jesus has told the Samaritan woman, "Salvation is from the Jews" (4:22), and by the end of the series of encounters with non-Jews, the villagers can join "the Jews" in their proclamation: "This is indeed the saviour of the world" (4:42). The narrative, however, was not written to tell of what happened *in the past events of the life of Jesus*. It calls the readers of the Gospel into *krisis*: where do you stand in your response to the revelation of God which takes place in and through this story of Jesus?

3. *Signs and Shadows (5:1 - 10:42)*

The question posed by Jesus' response to the incipient faith of the first disciples generated the question: what is true faith? (1:19-51). The answer has been provided by the collection of episodes that mark 2:1-4:54, but that answer created a further question. As the Johannine Christians, the first people to be addressed by this Gospel, found themselves cut off forcibly from their traditional roots, cast out of the Synagogue (see 9:22; 12:42; 16:2), they had been told to place all their trust in the word of Jesus. Israel's celebration of its great feasts both recalled the great moments of God's saving intervention in the history of God's people, and made that God present to every community celebrating the feast. The feasts were a "memory" which made God present in the celebrating community. How were these saving moments still present to a community of Christians, excluded from the annual celebrations because they believed that Jesus was the Christ (see 9:22; 12:32)?

John 5:1 announces a new theme: "After this there was a festival of the Jews and Jesus went up to Jerusalem." From 5:1 on, there is a steady reference to Jewish feasts:

◻ 5:9b: Now that day was a sabbath.

◻ 6:4: Now the Passover, the festival of the Jews, was near.

◻ 7:2: Now the Jewish feast of Tabernacles was near.

◻10:22: At that time the festival of the Dedication took place in Jerusalem.

Jesus' presence at these feasts, and his teaching concerning the God of the feasts, dominate chapters 5-10.

a) The Sabbath: 5:1-47

After the general introduction to the theme of the feasts in 5:1, the setting for 5:1-47 is the celebration of the Sabbath (see vv. 9b-10, 26, 18). The miracle of the healing of the paralytic at Bethesda on the Sabbath (vv. 2-9a) leads, via the healed man, to a conflict between "the Jews" and Jesus. The key to an interpretation of the chapter is found in the reply of Jesus to the accusation that he has committed an unlawful act by working on a Sabbath. He claims: "My Father is working still and I am working" (v. 17). The prohibition of work on the Sabbath, well founded in the Torah (see Gen 2:2; Exod 20:11; 31:17), led to a difficulty for the Jewish theologians. People died, and infants were born on the Sabbath; time and history, especially the history of God's people, took its course on a Sabbath. God had to be working, even though the Torah said that God rested. Given these facts, the theologians allowed only God to work on a Sabbath, giving life and judging. Thus "the Jews" correctly interpret Jesus' claim to be working on the Sabbath, as his Father is working, as worthy of death: he broke the Sabbath, called God his Father and made himself equal with God (v. 18).

Jesus replies that as the Father could judge and give life on the Sabbath, so can the Son (see vv. 19-30). The witness that Jesus bears to himself is not really his own witness, but the witness of the God of Israel and of Moses, the very person who gave them the Torah, which they are using in their condemnation of Jesus (vv. 31-47). It is not that the celebration of the Sabbath is finished; it is transformed. As, at the end of the first century AD, the Synagogue continued to celebrate its form of Sabbath worship, the presence of Jesus in the Christian community made all such celebrations a thing of the past. By the end of the discourse, those who accused Jesus in the name of God and Torah, become the accused ones. The witness of the Father and of Moses are with Jesus, not with the Jewish Sabbath celebrations: "It is Moses who accuses you" (v. 47).

b) Passover: 6:1-71

After the indication that the feast of the Passover was near (6:4), Jesus multiplies bread and fish, but he is misunderstood as the crowd attempts to make him a king (see vv. 14-15). He comes to his disciples on the stormy sea and reveals himself to them as "I am he" (vv. 16-21), but the crowds who ate the bread had not been privileged with this revelation. They search for Jesus in confusion (vv. 22-24). Once they find him at Capernaum, Jesus warns them to seek the only true food, which will be given to them through the gift of the Son of Man. They are to leave their false pursuits and seek only to believe in the one whom God has sent (vv. 25-29).

This introduction leads "the Jews" into a question. They demand a sign from Jesus that will at least put him on a par with their fathers who ate manna in the wilderness. We are now at the center of the Passover theme, especially as "the Jews" quote their scriptures to him: "As it is written 'He gave them bread from heaven to eat'" (v. 31). The text, a combination of Psalm 78:24, Exod 6:4 and 15, reflects the Jewish Passover liturgy. A new interpretation of it is developed through the discourse that follows. Through vv. 32-51b the major theme is that of the gift of bread from heaven. Jesus spells out, using the background of Jewish Wisdom motifs, that there is a new "bread from heaven," a new nourishment which perfects the old gift from heaven: the revelation of the Father in his Son. He affirms: "For this is the will of my Father, that everyone who sees the Son and believes in him should have eternal life" (v. 40). Such a claim is possible for those who accept that only Jesus, the true bread from heaven, provides nourishment that produces eternal life (vv. 41-48).

But there is another dimension to bread, introduced as Jesus' discourse comes to a close: bread is eaten (vv. 48-51b). This theme introduces the final section of Jesus' words (vv. 51c-58) that insists on the eating of the body and the drinking of the blood of the Son of Man. Throughout the discourse Jesus asserted that the experience of God's freeing presence through the Passover celebrated in Judaism had been perfected by the revelation of the Father in the Son. But the question emerges: "Where do I see the revelation of the Father in the Son?" The answer lies in the celebration of the Eucharist. It is in the eating of the flesh and the drinking of the blood of the Son of Man (see vv. 53-54) that Christians of all ages can meet the revelation of God in the love of his Son. His broken body and spilt blood are the supreme revelation of a God who is love (see also 13:1; 15:13; I John 4:8, 16).

Not all his disciples, even though they have experienced Jesus' coming to them across the stormy waters, revealing himself as "I am he" (vv. 16-21), are able to accept such teaching (vv. 60-65). Indeed, there is even the possibility of failure among those who do (vv. 66-71). But the signs, symbols, biblical texts and theology of the Jewish Passover have been perfected by Jesus' revelation of the Father.[13]

c) Tabernacles: 7:1-10:21

The Feast of Tabernacles was one of the most spectacular feasts of the Jewish calendar. It was highlighted by three rituals. The first was the mounting of lights: four candelabra set in the center of the Temple area so that the Temple became the light of all Jerusalem. The second ritual was a solemn procession to the Pool of Siloam, where water was gathered, and taken back to the Temple area for ritual washings. Finally, the Priests recalled the apostasy of former generations by first moving towards the rising sun in the East, but turning away from it, they looked back to the Holy of Holies and professed faith in the one God.[14]

After a mysterious hesitation (7:1-9), Jesus goes to Jerusalem, only to be met with puzzlement and disbelief (vv. 10-13). This section of the Gospel deals with some key Johannine questions: the Messiahship of Jesus and the importance of the recognition of his origins for a correct understanding of him and all he came to reveal (vv. 14-36). The Priests' profession of their adherence to their one and only God is at stake! They fail as the hostility to Jesus mounts.

On the major day of the feast, Jesus stands up and proclaims: "Let anyone who is thirsty come to me, and let the one who believes in me drink. As the scripture has said, 'Out of his heart shall flow rivers of living water'" (vv. 37-38). To this, the narrator adds his own comment: "Now this he said about the Spirit, which those who believed in him were to receive; for as yet the Spirit had not been given, because Jesus was not yet glorified" (v. 39). The water quenching all needs is not the ritual water of the feast, but the water Jesus will give in his death and the gift of his Spirit (see 19:30).

In 8:12 another Tabernacle theme is taken up. The Temple was the "light of Jerusalem," but Jesus announces: "I am the light of the world; he who follows me will not walk in darkness, but will have the light of life." There is a mixed response to Jesus as the unique light and revelation of God for the whole of humankind (see also 8:24 and 28). Some of "the Jews" believe in him (see v. 30), but others hint that Jesus' origins are in doubt, whereas theirs are so perfect that they have all the "truth" that they need. This question of origins leads to Jesus' claim: "Before Abraham was, I am" (8:58), and they took up stones in order to kill him for such blasphemy. Once again, their profession of faith in God is at stake and they failed to recognize the Son of God.

The themes of Jesus as the light of the world and the living water are acted out dramatically through the experience of the man born blind. In 9:5 Jesus again proclaims, "I am the light of the world," and a miracle is effected through Jesus' sending the blind man to wash in the Pool of Siloam. A note explains that it is not the waters of Siloam which effect the cure ... it is Jesus "the Sent One" (see 9:7). But, as the man born blind progresses to a confession of Jesus as the Son of Man (see vv. 11, 17, 33, 35-38), the leaders of Israel move further into the darkness, away from the revelation of their God in the Son (see vv. 16, 24, 28-29, 34). They are accused of being blind with a blindness that refuses to accept Jesus. "The Jews" think they have all the answers in what they know already (9:39-41). This leads Jesus directly into the parable of the Good Shepherd. Against the falseness of the now "blind" shepherds of Israel (see Ezek 34:11-16), Jesus is the Good Shepherd, whose sheep know his voice, and who is prepared to lay down his life for his sheep (see 10:1-18).

The symbols of light and water have been perfected by the revelation of God in Jesus the light of the world, and the living water poured forth in his death, as he hands over the Spirit (see 19:30-34). The Christian author of the Gospel of John is convinced that the synagogue does not celebrate the *true* light and the *living* water. "The Jews" have lost contact with the one true God, the Father of Jesus. Only the community of Jesus Christ, full of the Spirit of life, living in the light and believing in Jesus, the Christ, the Son of God (see 20:31) can justifiably make this claim.

d) Dedication: 10:22-42
The final feast, Dedication, had come into existence in remembrance of Judas Maccabeus' restoration of the Temple to Israel in 164 BC.

Dedication, however, was more than a celebration of the restoration of a building. For Israel, the Temple was the dwelling place of God, the place where the "glory of God" dwelt among the chosen people. The loss of the Temple meant the loss of the place where the presence of their saving God could be seen and visited in the heart of the nation. During the Feast of the Dedication, "the Jews" reject Jesus' claims to be the Son of God, and again attempt to kill him (vv. 31 and 39). They do not belong to the Good Shepherd, as they do not respond to his voice (vv. 22-29). They do not recognise the Sonship of Jesus, and thus do not realise their own chance to become children of God (vv. 31-39). This violent refusal of the Son's revelation and the new possibilities of such a revelation takes place at the feast which commemorated the gift of the visible presence of God in their midst. It is during that feast that Jesus can point to himself — eliminating all further need to look to a temple — and claim: "I and the Father are one" (10:30).

The Christian community need not look to Jewish rites. The person of Jesus Christ embodies all that the feasts had celebrated. As Leo the Great put it:

> Lord, you drew all things to yourself so that all nations everywhere in their dedication to you might celebrate in a full, clear sacramental rite what was done only in the Jewish Temple and in signs and shadows (Leo the Great, *Sermon 8 on the Passion*, 6-8. PL 54:341B).

Jew or Christian, the gifts of God given through Moses and Jesus (see 1:17) are available to all who accept what has been done and made known in and through Jesus.

4. *The Turn toward the Cross (11:1-12:36)*

Twice in the account of the miracle of Lazarus, the narrator comments that the "glory of God" will shine forth through the miracle (11:4, 40). However, on one occasion he says more than that: "This illness is not unto death; it is for the glory of God, so that the Son of God may be glorified by means of it" (11:4). There are two issues here. The glory of God certainly shines forth in the raising of Lazarus (see 11:40), but there is a further glorification of the Son of God that will take place because of this event. This is a reference to "the hour of Jesus" set in motion by the Lazarus event. The raising of Lazarus leads to the decision that Jesus must die for the nation, and not for the nation only, but to gather into one the children of God who are scattered abroad (see 11:49-52). It is important to know that up to this point in the Gospel, the death of Jesus has never been mentioned. There have been hints of it in the use of the term "to lift up" (see 3:14; 8:28) and the ominous references to "the hour" which had not yet come (see 2:4; 4:21, 23; 7:30; 8:20). But the verb "to die" appears for the first time in 11:16. From this point on in the story, as Jesus turns toward the Cross, such references multiply (11:16, 50, 51; 12:24, 33). But his death will also be a gathering. "Caiaphas, who was High Priest that year, said to them, 'You know nothing at all; you do not understand that it is expedient for you that one man should die for the people, and that the whole nation should not perish.' He did not say this of his own accord, but being High Priest that year he prophesied that Jesus should die for the nation, and not for the nation only, but to gather into one the children of God who are scattered abroad" (11:49-52).

Lazarus is still present as his sister anoints Jesus, and Jesus' entrance into Jerusalem (12:12-16) leads to a decision that both Jesus and Lazarus must die (12:9-11, 17-19). But the Pharisees declare: "Look, the world has gone after him" (v. 19). The theme of the "gathering" around Jesus in his hour is unfolding. Some Greeks, representing those children of God who are scattered abroad (see 11:52), seek him (vv. 20-22). The hour for the glorification of the Son of Man has come (v. 23) and Jesus explains his own destiny and that of his followers through the symbol of the grain that must fall and die to give new life (vv. 24-26).

There is an emerging link between the glorification, the gathering of all peoples, the hour, and the death of Jesus (vv. 27-30). This is finally expressed in 12:31-33:

"'Now is the judgment of this world, now the ruler of this world will be driven out. And I, when I am lifted up from the earth, will draw all people to myself.' He said this to indicate the kind of death he was to die." The hour of Jesus is at the one time his being lifted up to glory and his crucifixion; it is the end of the rule of this world. The Cross of Jesus is the place where the glory of God will shine forth in a perfect way, as he gathers everyone to himself. He urges his grumbling audience to walk in the light while they have the light (vv. 34-36a). The public appearance of Jesus ends dramatically as the narrator comments: "After Jesus had said this, he departed and hid himself from them" (v. 36b).

5. *Conclusion to the public ministry (12:37-50)*
In 12:37-43 a question that plagued the early Church is asked: why did

Israel refuse the revelation of God in Jesus (see Rom 9-11)? The narrator first gives a traditional answer: the heart of Israel was "hardened," and this hardening was a part of God's plan so that the message might be preached to the Gentiles (12:37-41. See Isa 53:1; 6:10). However, the real reason, so clearly in evidence from the Johannine story of Jesus thus far, is given in 12:42-43. Playing upon the double sense of the Greek word *doxa* ("glory"), the narrator claims that the leaders of Israel loved the "*doxa* of men" rather than the "*doxa* of God." The secular meaning of the word *doxa* is linked to praise, esteem and honor, while the Johannine meaning, rooted in a long biblical tradition, refers to the experience of a saving God. For John this saving experience is especially evident in the event of the Cross. There had been a failure on the part of the people of Israel to abandon their total trust in the letter of the Law (see 1:16-17), the teaching of Moses (see 9:29) and their attempts to understand Jesus within a world-view that they could control (see 1:19-51; 3:2; 6:15 etc.). They preferred the praise (*doxa*) of men. Thus they failed to acknowledge the living presence of their God in Jesus of Nazareth. They did not see the glory (*doxa*) of God.

The public ministry closes with words of Jesus (vv. 44-50). He has come into the world as the unique revelation of light and truth. His coming leads to a judgment, but it is a judgment we bring upon ourselves. Those who believe in Jesus and all he has come to reveal will not remain in darkness ... but those who refuse the light and the truth of Jesus will finally be judged by the revelation they have rejected. The *krisis* is now very clear. We are not judged by God at the end of time. We judge ourselves now as we accept or refuse the God made known to us in and through the story of Jesus Christ. No one has ever seen God, but Jesus has made God known to us (see 1:18).

Reading John 13:1-20:31[15]

1. *The theme of glory (13:1-20:29).*
John 13:1-20:29 can be called "the book of glory." From the beginning of the ministry of Jesus, there is mention of an "hour" which is yet to come (see 2:4). The tension increases as, on two occasions during the Feast of Tabernacles, Jesus' opponents attempt to lay hands upon him (see 7:30 and 8:20). They are not successful, because his hour has not yet come. However, as Jesus turns towards the Cross (chaps. 11-12),

some Greeks come to see him, and he admits, for the first time, that the hour has come: "The hour has come for the Son of Man to be glorified" (12:23). There is an intimate link between the hour of Jesus, which is the Cross, and his glorification. Another prophecy of Jesus, throughout his public ministry, also makes this link. On three occasions he has foretold his oncoming death, speaking of it as his being "lifted up" (see 3:13; 8:28; 12:32). The Greek verb behind our English "to lift up" (*hupsōthēnai*) has two meanings, both of which must be retained in reading John: to be physically lifted up upon a stake, and to be exalted. The "hour of Jesus," his being "lifted up" on the Cross, is also his glorification.

It is not only Jesus who is glorified; God is glorified as Jesus fulfils the task that was given to him (see 4:34; 17:4; 13:31-32). By making God known through his loving gift of himself, Jesus comes to his own glory and glorifies God. We have been prepared for this, as Jesus explained the reason for the death of Lazarus: "This illness does not lead to death; rather it is for God's glory, so that the Son of God may be glorified through it" (11:4). The event that finally led to the decision to slay Jesus is the resurrection of Lazarus (see 11:49-50), but his death will be his glorification, and through it, he will glorify God by making God known.

How is it possible that crucifixion can also be glorification? A God who has loved the world so much that he gave his only Son (see 3:16) is made known, as that Son loves his own to the very end (see 13:1): "No one has greater love than this, to lay down one's life for one's friends" (15:13). John 13:1 - 20:29 tells the story of Jesus' death and resurrection (chapters 18-20), prefaced by the long discourse which explains the significance of Jesus' own and the revelation of God, so that "his own" might better understand all that they are about to witness (13:1-17:26). As Jesus explains: "I tell you this now, before it occurs, so that when it does occur, you may believe that I am he." (13:19). Thus, "the book of glory" that tells of Jesus' death and resurrection, also tells of the glory which comes from loving and being loved, and the revelation of the glory of God, who is love (see 1 John 4:8, 16).[16]

2. Footwashing, Discourse and Prayer (13:1-17:26)[17]

Jesus knows the hour has come for his return to the Father. Jesus has brought to perfection the work his Father gave him to do (see 4:34). Having loved his own on earth, he now returns to the Father (13:1). Without further ado, however, something dramatically new is introduced. We are told that the moment of "completion" has arrived in a love that is both the final act in a human story and a gesture of love which cannot be surpassed: "he loved them to the end."[18] Jesus' departure from this world to the Father, in a consummate act of love for "his own," will be *via* the Cross. Towards the end of this first part of Jesus' final moments with his disciples this awareness is further clarified in terms that are familiar. As the Greeks arrived, the hour of the glorification of the Son of Man was announced (12:23) and explained as a "lifting up" (12:32-33). Now, as Judas leaves the room to go into the darkness of the night, this theme returns. The Son of Man is now glorified and God is glorified in him (13:30-32).

The disciples are swept up into Jesus' love, despite their failure, ignorance, denial and betrayal (vv. 21-30; 36-38). They have part with Jesus (see v. 8), symbolized in the washing of the feet and the gift of the morsel (vv. 2-17; 21-38), accompanied by his words that link these gifts to the challenge of discipleship. Jesus gives an example, they are to do to one another as he has done to them (v. 15), and a new commandment, they are to be known as his disciples because they love one another as he has loved them (vv. 34-35). In this is Jesus glorified, and in him God is glorified (vv. 31-32). The love which is to be revealed in Jesus' self-gift will be continued in the lives of "his own," whom he leaves in the world (vv. 12-17; 33-35). Jesus tells these things to failing disciples, whom he has chosen and whom he will send out, so that when this moment of glorification takes place, they might believe that Jesus is the revelation of God: "so that you might believe that I am he" (vv. 18-20). *Jesus makes God known in the perfect love he shows for his fragile disciples. In and through his loving, Jesus is glorified, and God is glorified in him. The disciples are to be recognized as the sent ones of Jesus by the unity created by the love they have for one another.*

In John 14:1-31 Jesus explains that his departure is imminent. But the departure of Jesus, through his death (vv.1-6, 27b-31), is unlike any other departure. It is not a moment for either consternation or fear (vv. 1, 27b), as Jesus departs to return to the Father (vv. 2-3, 6, 28), to initiate an in-between-time, filled by the presence of another Paraclete who will be with the disciples forever (vv. 16-17, 26). Until this point in the story, Jesus has been the unique revelation of the Father. Now another character enters the story, continuing the revealing task of the earthly Jesus. Jesus is about to depart and leave the disciples (14:2-3a). His promise to come to them (see vv. 18, 28) will be fulfilled in the ongoing revealing mission of the Paraclete. But the earthly Jesus has opened the way to the Father (vv. 6; 20-21)

Once Jesus has begun his teaching on the gift of the Paraclete, this promise casts a light across the final discourse. There are now two characters sent by the Father: Jesus who is with the disciples now, but who is about to depart, and the Paraclete, who will remain with them forever. Prompted by Philip's request that Jesus show the disciples the Father (see v. 8), Jesus restates one of the fundamental messages of the Gospel: Jesus' oneness with the Father makes his words and his works the unique revelation of God (14:7-11. See 1:3-4, 14, 18). His going away from the disciples does not end this revelation. The gift of the Paraclete will ensure that the oneness that exists between the Father and the Son will be revealed in the disciple who loves Jesus and keeps his commandments, now swept into that same oneness (vv. 18-21). This promise of an in-between-time undermines all expected response to a departure by death. In place of consternation and fear (see vv. 1, 27b), the Spirit-filled disciples will experience love (see vv. 15, 21, 23-24, 28), further belief (see vv. 15, 21, 23-24, 29) and joy (see v. 28). The gift of the departing Jesus to the disciples is his peace, which cannot be matched by anything the world can provide (v. 27a).

But the hostility of the world to Jesus (see 14:17, 19, 22, 24, 30) has not disappeared, despite Jesus' claim that the prince of this world has no power over him (v. 30c). There is a tension in the closing sentences of this first discourse. Jesus announces that he will no longer talk much (v. 30a), but that the prince of this world is coming (v. 30b). We are caught in this tension between the revelation of God in the word of Jesus, now no longer spoken, but available through the gift of the Paraclete (see v. 26), and the ongoing presence of the prince of this world. This is the tension which lies behind Jesus' summons to rise and face the prince of this world (14:31c), and the need for further words from Jesus which will guide all disciples of Jesus through the conflicts and hatred of the in-between-time (see 15:1-16:3). *Jesus instructs his failing disciples on his departure, and the conditions and challenges which they will face. Guided by the Paraclete in his physical absence, love, faith, joy and peace should be theirs, swept up into the love which unites the Father and Jesus, the sent one.*

The focus of Jesus' argument changes in 15:1-11. The use of the symbol of the vine, and Jesus' claim to be the *true* vine, is linked to traditional Israel's claim to be a vine or a vineyard (see Hos 10:1-2; Isa

5:1-7; Jer 2:21; Ezek 15:1-5; 17:1-21; 19:10-15; Ps 80:8-18). But more important than the image of the vine is Jesus' command to his disciples "to abide," and his explaining what this abiding will mean for them. Some form of the verb "to abide" appears ten times in vv. 1-11. Jesus' command asks that disciples take on a new and deeper reciprocity with one who is about to come to his glory through a Cross. The metaphor, based on the every-day experience of a vine and the vinedresser (vv. 1-2), is the springboard for the call to abide, maintaining and deepening the uniqueness that the disciples have been granted: they are already made clean by the word of Jesus (v. 3. See 13:10). Jesus speaks of the creative and fruitful unity flowing between the reciprocity of love between Jesus and the Father, and the disciples' being swept up into that love by their abiding in Jesus (vv.4-10). The disciples' oneness with Jesus leads them into the oneness existing between the Father and the Son. The joy of Jesus' oneness with the Father will also fill the lives of the disciples (v. 11). *Oneness and joy are generated by abiding in Jesus, the true vine, and by being swept up into his abiding oneness of love with the Father.*

In v. 12 the new commandment of love returns: "This is my commandment, that you love one another as I have loved you" (v. 12. See 13:34). The Cross is behind Jesus' statement of the principle that the greatest act of love is the gift of one's life for one's friends (v. 13). The new commandment is not something that the disciples do of their own ability. They are now in a new situation, where slavery has disappeared because Jesus has made the Father known to them (vv. 14-15). This has been made possible because of the initiative of Jesus, summed up with words which look back to the image of the Good Shepherd: "Greater love has no one than to lay down one's life for one's friends" (v. 13; see 10:11, 16), and others which remind us of the use of the metaphor of the vine : "You did not choose me, but I chose you and appointed you that you should go and bear fruit" (v. 16). The love Jesus has for his own surpasses all paradigms of love for one's friends (see 13:1-38). John 15:12-17 forms the centrepiece of 15:1-16:3, and is highlighted by Jesus' command that *the disciples love as he has loved, as a consequence of all he has done for them.*

The tone changes in v. 18, as the world's hatred, rejection and expulsion become the subject of Jesus' discourse. As Jesus has been hated, so also will the disciples be hated, rejected and even murdered because they are the chosen ones of Jesus, no longer part of this world's system (vv. 18-19). The rejection of the word of Jesus continues in the rejection of the word of his disciples (v. 20). The problem arises because those who have hated Jesus will also hate, reject and kill the disciples, "because they do not know him who sent me" (v. 21) ... "they have seen and hated both me and my father" (v. 24) ... "they will do this because they have not known the Father nor me" (16:3). Thus, they stand condemned, rejecting the revelation of God brought by Jesus, and fulfilling the Scriptures by hating without reason (vv. 22-25). But, as the pain created by the separation that flows from Jesus' departure is to be enriched and guided by the Paraclete, so also the Spirit of truth, who is sent from the Father, will comfort the pain of rejection. The witness of the Spirit will make clear the truth of the Father and Jesus. Even in the midst of conflict the disciples will have the responsibility to continue this witness to later generations (vv. 26-27).

Balancing Jesus' insistence that he is the *true* vine (v. 1), the disciples are told that they will be cast out of the Synagogue, and even killed (16:2) by people who do not accept the word of Jesus, and who refuse to believe that Jesus is the sent one of the Father (vv. 20-21, 23-24; 16:3). We recognize "the Jews" from the story of 1:19-12:50 as the *false* vine (see Jer 2:21). The teaching on the love and joy flowing from abiding in Jesus, the *true* vine (15:1-11), is reversed as Jesus tells the disciples of their future treatment by the *false* vine in 15:18-16:3. The fruits of abiding in Jesus and the Father are matched by *the hatred, rejection, expulsion and slaying of the disciples which will result from the actions of "the Jews," the false vine which has rejected Jesus and the Father.*

The disciples have remained silent throughout 15:1-16:3. They return as interlocutors in 16:4-33 as the theme of departure and the form of a discourse interspersed with words from the disciples reappear. Jesus again addresses the theme of his departure to the Father (16:4b-6, 25-28), and of his coming back to the disciples (vv. 16, 21). As in 13:1-38 and 14:1-31, the disciples fail to understand (vv. 16-19). Jesus promises the presence of the Paraclete to expose the failures of the world and to guide and instruct the disciples in the time of his physical absence (vv. 7-15). This aggressive presence of the Paraclete over against "the world" (vv. 8-11) is different from the teaching and remembering role described in 14:26-27, and developed further in 16:12-15, but these roles — one internal and the other external —are two aspects of the same reality. The theme of prayer to the Father in the name of Jesus, present in the earlier discourse (see 14:12-14), returns as a central motif (vv. 21-24).

The allegory of the woman in labour is based on a pattern of "before and after." *Before* the hour of birth, she has tribulation; but by passing through the hour, *after* the birth, she has great joy, as a child has been given to the world (v. 21). The disciples are now sorrowful over the departure of Jesus, but they will finally come to a time when they will be seen by Jesus in joy which no one can take from them, and they will no longer have need to ask for anything (vv. 22-23a). But they must live through an in-between-time in the fullness of joy, given in the name of Jesus when they turn to the Father in prayer (v. 23b-24). The disciples are assured that their prayer will be answered. The Father will give them anything asked in his name (v. 23b), as they live through the in-between-time, after which they will no longer need to ask anything of Jesus (v. 23a).

As the disciples have believed that Jesus comes from the Father, the Father loves them (vv. 25-27). Jesus' return to the place of oneness with the Father (v. 28), leads the disciples to a final glimmer of understanding. They see that Jesus' origins assure the uniqueness and authority of his revelation (v. 29). But they make no mention of his departure. Their confession is limited by their present circumstances. Between the "now" of the upper room and the "then" of perfect faith among the disciples there are to be moments of suffering and loneliness. Jesus is about to experience suffering, but his oneness with the Father overcomes all loneliness. Jesus has overcome the world, and the disciples' awareness of this victory should bring them joy in the midst of tribulation (v. 33). The themes of 14:1-31, however much developed, return in 16:4-33. *Jesus instructs his failing disciples on his departure, and the conditions and challenges they will face. Guided by the Paraclete in his physical absence, joy and confidence should be theirs, as they are loved by the Father who sent Jesus.*

The narrator's comment that Jesus adopts a traditional position of prayer (17:1a), and Jesus' words of prayer directed to the Father (vv. 1b-2) initiate a change in literary form. It soon becomes clear that words and themes from the footwashing and the gift of the morsel return. Jesus prays for himself (v. 1b-8). He then prays for "his own" (vv. 9-19). They are the foundational disciples, still present with him at the table. Finally he prays for the generations of believers who will believe through the word of the disciples (vv. 20-26). Themes that were central to 13:1-38 return: "the hour" (v. 1. See 13:1), the glorification of the Son and the Father

(vv. 1, 4-5. See 13:31-32), Jesus' self-gift having brought to perfection the task given him by the Father (vv. 3-4. See 13:1), his ongoing love for his fragile disciples (vv. 9-19. See 13:4-17; 21-31a), and the disciples as the fragile sent ones of Jesus who will reveal the one who sent Jesus by the unity which their love for one another creates (vv. 11b, 21-23. See 13:18-20, 34-34). He has revealed God in his life (and death) in a unique and authoritative way (v. 4) and now seeks a return to glory with the Father (v.5). The disciples have believed in Jesus' revelation of the Father, and in the basis for the truthfulness of that revelation: Jesus comes from the Father. They are presented to the Father as the worthy successors of Jesus (vv. 5-8).

However, as Jesus turns to pray explicitly for them, their fragility is recalled. Jesus asks his Father to care for them and to sanctify them. He first asks his Father, who is holy (v. 11b), to be Father to them, that he care for and keep them (vv. 11b, 15) in the hostile world. They are not of the world, as Jesus is not of the world (vv. 12-16). They have succumbed to the attractions of the world on more than one occasion, and Judas has already gone out into the darkness (v. 12. See 13:30). Jesus next asks the Father to make them holy (v. 16) so that they may perform the same sanctifying mission as Jesus (vv. 16-19). The disciples are in need of greater holiness, as a gift from God, if they are to parallel the saving action of Jesus' self-gift (see v. 19). This is what he wants from them: to be one as Jesus and the Father are one, and to be filled with the perfection of the joy of Jesus (v. 13).

The seriousness of their mission (vv. 18-19), and the mission of future generations of followers (vv. 21-23) makes this even clearer. The oneness of love which marks the unity between the Father and the Son is to be repeated within the community of believers, so that the world may believe that Jesus is the sent one of God (vv. 21, 23a), and that God loves the disciples just as he has loved the Son (v. 23b). The prayer closes with a request that disciples of all generations be swept up into the oneness of love that exists between the Father and the Son (v. 26). As the theme of love opened 13:1-38 (see 13:1), it closes 17:1-26 (see 17:24-26). In and through this love God has been glorified, and the Son is glorified (vv. 1b, 5, 24). The unity of love granted to the disciples, aware of the truth about God in a way unknown to the world, will enable them to contemplate that glory (v. 24-25). *Jesus makes God known in the perfect love he shows for his fragile disciples. In and through his loving, Jesus is glorified, and God is glorified in him. The disciples are to be recognised as the sent ones of Jesus by the unity created by the love they have for one another.*

This brief outline of the first part of the book of glory shows that the author has gathered traditions about the footwashing, discourses, and a final prayer, to state and re-state his message (13:1-38 = 17:1-26; 14:1-31 = 16:4-33; 15:1-11 = 15:18-16:3 [in a contrasting fashion]).[19] At the center is the crucial teaching on the new commandment of love (15:12-17). See Table 2 opposite.

The stage is set for the story of Jesus' glorification, "the hour" when he is "lifted up" to draw everyone to himself, making known the love of God.

3. The Passion of Jesus (18:1 - 19:42)

Up to this point, the word "kingdom" has only been used twice in the Gospel, and both times in a traditional passage, referring to "the kingdom of God" (see 3:3, 5). In the passion account it appears three times in one important verse (18:36). Thus far in the Gospel the title "king" has been found four times (1:49; 6:15; 12:13, 15). On each occasion people who would like to make Jesus a king have addressed him in a way that reflects false messianic hopes. Throughout the passion narrative the term "king" appears ten times. Jesus is crowned and dressed as King, and he acts out his role as King, "lifted up" from the earth. Thus, although the story of an arrest, a Jewish and a Roman trial, a crucifixion, a death and a burial is told, it is told in a way which ironically proclaims that Jesus is a king.[20]

i) Jesus in a Garden: With his Enemies (18:1-11)

Jesus is not arrested in this scene (see v. 12). His opponents, representing the darkness, arm themselves with lanterns and torches as they to seek "the light of the world" (v. 3. See 8:12; 9:5). Jesus is the master of the situation from the beginning of the passion story. He asks them whom they seek, and he reveals himself to them as "I am he" The use of the expression "I am he," which we have met regularly during the course of our reading, reaches back to God's revelation to Moses at Sinai (see Exod 3:14). But for our author it is especially the Prophets who inspired him. They spoke of YHWH, the one and only true God among many false Gods (see, for example, Isaiah 43:10; 45:18; 46:4; 48:12). Here, as throughout the Gospel (see especially 6:26; 8:24, 28, 58; 13:19), Jesus applies the expression to himself. His opponents fall to the ground impotent ... but Jesus calls them to their feet, insists that his disciples

Table 2: Outline of John 14:1-17:26, the first part of the book of glory.

13:1-38: Jesus makes God known in the perfect love which he shows for his fragile disciples. In and through his loving, Jesus is glorified, and God is glorified in him. The disciples are to be recognised as the sent ones of Jesus by the unity created by the love they have for one another.

14:1-31: Jesus instructs his failing disciples on his departure, and the conditions and challenges they will face. Guided by the Paraclete in his physical absence, love, faith, joy and peace should be theirs, swept up into the love which unites the Father and Jesus, the sent one.

15:1-11: The oneness and joy created by abiding in Jesus, the true vine, and being swept up into his abiding oneness with the Father.

15:12-17: The disciples of Jesus are to love as he has loved, as a consequence of all he has done for them.

15:18-16:3: The hatred, rejection, expulsion and slaying of the disciples which will result from the actions of "the Jews," the false vine which has rejected Jesus and the Father.

16:4-33: Jesus instructs his failing disciples on his departure, and the conditions and challenges they will face. Guided by the Paraclete in his physical absence, joy and confidence should be theirs, loved by the Father who sent Jesus.

17:1-26: Jesus makes God known in the perfect love which he shows for his fragile disciples. In and through his loving, Jesus is glorified, and God is glorified in him. The disciples are to be recognized as the sent ones of Jesus by the unity created by the love which they have for one another.

go free and prevents violence from Peter. On the one hand the Church must flow from the events that are about to take place, and on the other, Jesus has come to drink the cup that his Father has asked him to drink (v. 11. See also 4:34 and 12:27).

ii) The Jewish Hearing (18:12-27)
Peter denies Jesus and draws near to the fire, set by those who had come with lanterns and torches to take Jesus (vv. 15-18). One who has lived with the light draws near to the false light, set by the darkness that opposes and rejects Jesus. Meanwhile, Jesus is inside, interrogated about his disciples and his teaching (v. 19). He refuses to answer, as his time of public manifestation and teaching is over (see 12:36b). The message has been made known and it is now the era of the Church, the time for the disciples to preach what they have heard (vv. 20-21). A soldier's slap rejects this message, but its "rightness" cannot be questioned (vv. 22-23). However, one of the disciples is outside, denying Jesus a second and a third time (vv. 25-27). Jesus is the great witness to the Truth, and the Church has the task of continuing that witness (see vv. 20-21). That the disciples, the bearers of that message, often deny such knowledge does not alter the situation.[21]

iii) The Roman Trial (18:28 - 19:16)
In the trial before Pilate Jesus is both proclaimed (see 18:33-38a, 38b-40; 19:13-15) and crowned as King (19:1-3). But the trial story is told around a series of changes of place. At times the trial goes on inside the praetorium with Pilate, and at other times Jesus is presented before the crowds and "the Jews" outside. There is only one scene without a change of place: the central scene, where Jesus is crowned (19:1-3). A more detailed outline of the flow of this passage shows the dramatic alternation between Jesus and Pilate where the King of Truth overcomes the political powers of this world, and Jesus is presented to the people as their King, and rejected (see Table 3 opposite).

The Roman trial has been placed at the center of the Johannine passion story so that, even before he goes to his Cross, Jesus is ironically proclaimed and crowned as King. Indeed, his ironic coronation lies at the center of the Roman trial (19:1-3). The Cross scene can now follow, where Jesus will act as a King, but in a way most unlike the kings of this world: "My kingdom is not from this world. If my kingdom were from this world, my followers would be fighting to keep me from being handed over to the Jews. But, as it is, my kingdom is not from here ... For this I was born

Table 3: Outline of John 18:28-19:16, The Roman Trial.

Introduction: 18:28 The actors and the place Pilate, Jesus and "the Jews" at the Praetorium	*Conclusion: 19:16* "He handed him over to them to be crucified."
1ˢᵗ Scene: 18:29-32 "Pilate went out." "The Jews" accuse Jesus as a malefactor and ask for crucifixion.	*7ᵗʰ Scene: 19:13-15* "Pilate brought Jesus out." "Behold your King!" "Crucify him!"
2ⁿᵈ Scene: 18:33-38a "Pilate entered …" Jesus proclaims that he is the King of truth. Pilate waves Jesus away with the retort: "What is truth?"	*6ᵗʰ Scene: 19:8-12* "Pilate entered …" Jesus tells an arrogant Pilate that all authority comes from above. Pilate has lost his opportunity to know the truth.
3ʳᵈ Scene: 18:38b-40 "Pilate went out …" He declares Jesus innocent and calls him "King of the Jews." They ask for Barabbas.	*5ᵗʰ Scene: 19:4-7* "Pilate went out …" He declares Jesus innocent and says, "Behold the Man!" They ask for crucifixion.

4th (Central) Scene: 19:1-3
No change of place mentioned.
Jesus is crowned and dressed
as a king. He is acclaimed:
"Hail, King of the Jews!"
But this truth is rejected
by slaps.

and for this I came into the world, to testify to the truth. Everyone who belongs to the truth listens to my voice" (18:36-37).

iv) The Crucifixion of Jesus (19:17-37)

The crucifixion of Jesus is rapidly reported (v. 18), as the focus of the account is still upon Jesus' Kingship. He is universally proclaimed as King with the plaque, written in the languages of the Jews, the Greeks and the Romans, nailed to the Cross. But "the Jews" refuse to accept the proclamation (vv. 17-22). Jesus' Kingdom will never be torn apart, even in the hands of the enemy. The symbol of Jesus' seamless robe, that will not be torn apart (vv. 23-26), makes this clear. The central scene (vv. 25-27) indicates the nature of the new Kingdom of the crucified King. The first of all believers, the Mother of Jesus (see 2:1-11) and the Beloved Disciple (see 13:23; 20:2-10) are given to one another as Mother and Son (vv. 25-27). "And from that hour" (the Greek would perhaps be better translated "because of that hour") they become one (see v. 27). The central scene in the Johannine account of the crucifixion of Jesus reports the foundation of the new community of Jesus, the formation of a new family, based on faith and love, which cuts through all bonds of flesh and blood. It is, however, important to notice that the term "mother" is mentioned five times in vv. 25-27. The "Mother" of Jesus becomes the "Mother of the disciple" at the Cross of her son.

As Jesus dies, he claims to have brought to perfection the task he was given (see 4:34 and 17:4). He thus "pours down" his Spirit on the newly formed community. In the Fourth Gospel, the gift of the Spirit takes place at the Cross (vv. 28-30). Finally, the narrator tells of the blood and the water flowing from the side of the elevated Christ (vv. 31-37). Through this message he addresses his own community at the end of the century, so that its members also may believe (see v. 35). This was not to be understood as simply an event reported from the past. The revelation of the love of God on the Cross must go on in the life of the community of Jesus. It takes place among Christians in the sacraments of the blood and the water, flowing from the side of the crucified Jesus: in Eucharist and Baptism. The Cross of Jesus challenges the Christian community to look upon the crucified one as the ultimate revelation of a God who is love: "They shall gaze upon him whom they have pierced" (v. 37).

v) The Burial of Jesus (19:38-42).

As the passion began with a garden scene where Jesus met his enemies (18:1-11), it concludes with a further garden scene as Jesus is laid to rest by his friends (19:38-42). These friends are named as Joseph of Arimathea and Nicodemus. We recall that Nicodemus came to Jesus in secrecy (see 3:1-2), that he tried, at one stage, to defend Jesus' rights, only to wilt under abuse (see 7:50-52). Joseph of Arimathea has not appeared earlier in the Gospel of John. But the Synoptic Gospels (see Mark 15:43; Matt 27:57; Luke 28:51) present him as a leading Jew who moved from secrecy into light as a result of the death of Jesus. The community of Jesus is now in action, as once-hidden disciples publicly ask for the body of Jesus. They bury his body with a large quantity of myrrh and aloes, a burial fit only for a King. He is buried in a new tomb, and we wait for the proclamation of a new day. A passion story that began in a garden in the midst of hatred and darkness, closes in another garden where love and light are in evidence.[22]

The passion account has once again been structured in a familiar literary pattern as shown in Table 4:

Table 4: Outline of John 19:38-42, The Burial of Jesus

> 18:1-11: Jesus in a garden, with his enemies
>
> 18:12-27: The Jewish Hearing: The Church as the bearer of the Word
>
> **18:28-19:16: The Trial before Pilate: Jesus as King**
>
> 19:17-37: The Crucifixion of Jesus: The Church is founded and nourished
>
> 19:38-42: Jesus in a garden, with his friends.

4. *The Resurrection of Jesus (20:1-29)*

Given the theology of the Cross developed throughout the Gospel of John, it is sometimes asked what point there is in having a resurrection story. The Johannine account of the resurrection and the appearances of Jesus agrees with the traditions of an empty tomb discovered by women (here one woman: Mary Magdalene [20:1-2]), an account of appearances

(vv. 11-18, 19-23, 24-29) and a final sending out of disciples on a mission (vv. 21-23). But those themes are used in a different way. Three features of this resurrection account appear only in the Gospel of John: the experience of Peter and the Beloved Disciple in their journey to the empty tomb (vv. 2-10), the appearance to Mary Magdalene (vv. 11-18) and the episode of doubting Thomas (vv. 24-29). The Gospel of John opened with the indication of the possibility of a journey of faith from no faith to complete faith in the experiences recounted in the journey from Cana to Cana (2:1-4:54).[23] Now it ends with further indications of such a journey.

At the end of the Gospel, however, there is a difference. Original members of the Christian community, Peter and the Beloved Disciple, Mary Magdalene and Thomas all begin in a situation of unbelief (see vv. 2-3 [the disciples], 13-15 [Mary], 24 [Thomas]). However, they are led by the risen Lord, through their various experiences of little and partial faith (vv. 9-10 [the disciples], 16-17 [Mary], 25 [Thomas]), into a final total commitment in faith (vv. 19-22 [disciples], 18 [Mary], 28 [Thomas]). What must further be noticed is that the Beloved Disciple "saw and believed" (v. 8), without *seeing Jesus*. The initial responses of Mary Magdalene and Thomas are very physical. Mary wishes to cling to Jesus (v. 17), and Thomas will only believe if he can physically penetrate Jesus' wounds (v. 25). In the end, they overcome these limitations, and come to faith. But the risen Jesus reminds Thomas that he believed *because he saw Jesus* (v. 29a). Jesus' final words are: "Blessed are those who have not seen yet believe" (v. 29b). As the Beloved Disciple believed without seeing, all who follow the way of the Beloved Disciple are specially blessed. The Gospel of John, at the end of the first Christian century, points back to the foundational experience of the Church. The encounter with the risen Jesus has led the very first believers from the poverty of their unfaith to true belief. In his final words, the risen Jesus blesses in a special way those who do not have the experience of seeing Jesus himself, but yet believe (v. 29). They will all be Beloved Disciples. The story of people struggling to come to a deeper faith in Jesus must not be limited to the characters in the story. The author wishes to touch our experience, as readers of the story. Jesus' final words are addressed to all of us, reading and listening to the Gospel.

5. *Conclusion to the Story (20:30-31)*

The fourth Gospel closes with words from the narrator: "Now Jesus did many other signs in the presence of the disciples, which are not written in this book; but these are written that you may believe that Jesus is the Christ, the Son of God, and that believing you may have life in his name" (vv. 30-31). We have been led to a point of decision (*krisis*). "God so loved the world that he gave his only Son, that whoever believes in him should not perish but have eternal life" (3:16). No middle course is feasible; there are only two possibilities: to perish or to have eternal life. This Gospel sees humankind as inexorably caught between two cosmic forces. On the one side there is the darkness (blindness, evil, this world, the Prince of this world) and on the other is light (life, sight, the Spirit). To choose darkness means death, but the possibility of light and life has now been revealed in Jesus Christ. We judge ourselves by our own decision for or against the God revealed in and through Jesus Christ.

The fourth Gospel exhibits a passionate belief in the saving power of a decision for Christ. The appearance of Jesus in history is the irruption of light from the divine realm into the created order where darkness and evil are rampant. The struggle is fought out but in the historical events of the life of Jesus. This is why the Gospel of John tells the story of God's ways with the world through the story of his Son, Jesus of Nazareth. At the heart of the struggle that marked the life of Jesus, the cross is central. It is "the hour" (12:23; 13:31-32) when, at the level of human history, the powers of darkness appear to have brought their enemy down. Yet, with an irony so typical of this Gospel, we learn that it is precisely in "the hour" that the Son of Man is glorified. He has revealed God so that men and women of all times - living in the presence and under the guidance of the Paraclete, sent by the glorified Jesus (14:16, 26; 15:26; 16:7, 13-15) - might gaze upon him and be saved (3:13-14; 8:28; 12:32; 19:37). Do you believe this?

Reading John 21:1-25

The Johannine story has come to an end, but it is a story told by a group of men and women who, as time passed, needed to face further questions about their identity, their mission and those among them entrusted with authority.[24] These questions were addressed by the episodes told as part of the Gospel in John 21:1-25. As disciples gather at the Sea of Tiberias, and set out upon their normal occupation of fishing, the risen Jesus appears to them, and a large catch of fish results from his directions. At the miracle the Beloved Disciple recognizes Jesus, and he tells Simon Peter: "It is the Lord" (v. 6). Although the main theme of this section of the narrative concerns the Church, the disciples and their mission as sent ones of Jesus, the question of the relationship between the Beloved Disciple and Simon Peter is also present. It is the Beloved Disciple who recognizes Jesus and confesses that he is "the Lord."

We are not told of Simon Peter's faith, but of his action as he leaps into the sea (v. 7). The other disciples bring the boat to shore, but on Jesus' command that some of the freshly caught fish be brought, it is again Simon Peter who acts, hauling the heavy net ashore. A large number of fish is in the net — one hundred and fifty three of them — but the net is not torn. Although the numbers may baffle us, the symbolism is clear. Peter leads, enthusiastically taking action at the word of the Beloved Disciple and at the word of Jesus, but the Church is a boat under the direction of its Lord, Jesus. It draws into its net people of all tribes and places, but is never damaged (see v. 11). Lord and disciples share a meal. The person who shared many meals with them during his ministry, is still with them at the table (vv. 12-13). The identity and the mission of the Johannine community have been sketched, but what of Simon Peter and the Beloved Disciple?

If Peter is the leader, what is the reader to make of his earlier failures? True to the criterion of authentic discipleship demanded by Jesus throughout the Gospel (see 13:34-35; 15:12, 17), Peter must three times confess his love for Jesus. His three-fold profession of love (21:15-17) overcomes his three-fold denial (see 18:15-18, 25-27). On the basis of his love he is entrusted with the task of shepherding the sheep, of being to the community what Jesus was: a good shepherd (see 10:1-18). Indeed, Peter is told that he will, like Jesus, lay down his life for his sheep (21:18-19. See 10:18). But the members of the community looked back to the Beloved Disciple with great respect and reverence. How does Peter relate to him? Peter asks the question: "Lord, what about him?" (21:21). The Beloved Disciple is no longer alive, and the community of Christians are informed that they should not be surprised at this (vv. 22-23). He provided the link between the community and Jesus. He was at the cross, as the disciple whom Jesus loved, as the Christian community was founded in the gift of the Mother to the Disciple and the Disciple to the Mother (see 19:25-27). It is his witness that is recorded in the Gospel story of this particular Christian community. He may have died, but his Gospel is alive and life giving. The Beloved Disciple remains the authority behind the community's story of Jesus: "This is the disciple who is bearing witness to these things" (21:24).

Conclusion

The Johannine Community has a strong awareness of two important foundational disciples: the Beloved Disciple and Simon Peter, the shepherd of the flock. Peter may not be the best of all disciples but he has committed himself to the love of Jesus. As a consequence he is the appointed shepherd of the flock of Jesus (vv. 15-17). Throughout the Johannine Community's story of Jesus, The Beloved Disciple recognizes Simon Peter's position of primacy. At the supper table, Peter sat on the right (see the indications of 13:23-24), and even though the Disciple arrived at the empty tomb first, he stood back and allowed Peter to enter (see 20:5). Authority has been entrusted to Peter. Summoned to love more, Peter commits himself to that loving (21:15-17) and is told that his ministry to the flock will cost him his life (vv. 18-19).

Authority rests with Simon Peter, but the test of true discipleship does not lie in one's dignity or authority. Intimacy is granted to the Beloved Disciple: at the table (13:23-24), at the cross (19:25-27) and at the tomb (20:2-10). It is his memory of Jesus that has just been told. The true disciple is the one who loves, is loved, and who tells the story of Jesus. In this - at least for the Johannine community - the Beloved Disciple remains the model. A Christian understanding, distinguishing authority and discipleship, was established in the earliest years of the Christian Church. Attention to the story of Jesus and love are the measure of discipleship, not where one stands in the line of authority.

Notes

[1] This brief description of the overall rhetorical purpose for the writing of the Gospel of John, stated in John 20:30-31, presupposes that the Gospel was written for a community that already believed in Jesus as the Christ, but was being asked to go deeper and further in its life of faith and love.

[2] For a more complete and up to date treatment of the issues discussed in this section on introductory matters, see R. E. Brown, *An Introduction to the Gospel of John* (ed. F. J. Moloney; Anchor Bible Reference Library; New York: Doubleday, 2003).

[3] This is a very difficult issue in reading John. It is most important that "the Jews" are not read as the Jewish people. They represent those who have decided that Jesus is not the sent one of God, and they reject him and subsequently, the Johannine community, many of whom are also Jewish. Much has been written on this question. See especially R. Bieringer, D. Pollefeyt, and F. Vandecasteele-Vanneuville, eds., *Anti-Judaism in the Fourth Gospel* (Louisville: Westminster John Knox, 2001); F. J. Moloney, "'The Jews' in the Fourth Gospel: Another Perspective," in *The Gospel of John. Text and Context* (Biblical Interpretation Series 72; Boston/Leiden: Brill, 2005), 20-44.

[4] The threefold reference to being "cast out of the synagogue," with the use of the Greek *aposunagōgos*, found only in John (9:22; 12:42; 16:2), has led to a very popular understanding of the Gospel as the fruit of the community's expulsion from the synagogue following the development (in the 80's of the first century) of a synagogue ban of Christians by means of the so-called "the blessing of the heretics" (*birkat ha-minim*). The work of J. L. Martyn, *History and Theology in the Fourth Gospel* (3d edition; Louisville: Westminster John Knox, 2003) has been crucial in this debate. Subsequent debate has asked whether the "blessing" should be dated in the first century, and whether it referred to Christians. The Fourth Gospel was probably not the result of a universal "ban" of Christians from the synagogue (by means of the *birkat ha-minim*), but the community behind the Gospel (most clearly in 9:22; 12:42 and 16:2, but elsewhere in the conflict with "the Jews") has experienced a separation from their synagogue "home." This may have been a very local experience. On this, see P. W. van der Horst, "The *Birkat ha-minim* in Recent Research," *The Expository Times* 105 (1994): 363-68.

⁵ For a magisterial study of these questions, see D. Moody Smith, *John among the Gospels* (2d ed.; Columbia: University of South Carolina Press, 2001).

⁶ On the Letters of John, and their relationship to the Gospel, see R. E. Brown, *The Epistles of John* (The Anchor Bible 30: Garden City: Doubleday, 1982), 46-115.

⁷ On this question, see R. A. Culpepper, *John, the Son of Zebedee. The Life of a Legend* (Studies on Personalities in the New Testament; Columbia: University of South Carolina Press, 1994); F. J. Moloney, *The Gospel of John* (Sacra Pagina 4; Collegeville: The Liturgical Press, 1998), 6-9.

⁸ I will not document everything that follows. I apologize in advance for the repeated reference to my own publications. The reading of the Gospel found in the remainder of this chapter, much of which is found only in my interpretation of John, has been distilled from my many years of work with the Fourth Gospel. Further discussion and references to a wide range of opinions can be found in these works. Fuller explanations of my reading of John 1:1-18 can be found in F. J. Moloney, *Belief in the Word. Reading John 1-4* (Minneapolis: Fortress, 1993) 23-52; Moloney, *John*, 33-48.

⁹ For the argument that the Prologue already deals with the incarnation in 1:1-5, and that v. 5 refers to the cross, see Moloney, *John*, 34-37.

¹⁰ The form and content of John 1:1-18 is unique in the New Testament. However, it still plays the role of a "prologue." On this, see Chapter Three .

¹¹ For more detailed study of this section of the Gospel, see Moloney, *Belief in the Word*, 43-199; Idem, *Signs and Shadows. Reading John 5-12* (Minneapolis: Fortress, 1996); Idem, *John*, 48-369

¹² See F. J. Moloney, *The Johannine Son of Man* (2d ed.; Rome: LAS, 1978), 23-41.

¹³ For a more detailed reading of John 6:1-71, see the following chapter.

¹⁴ John 7-8 are the most difficult chapters in the Gospel. Set during the celebration of the feast of Tabernacles, the passage is marked by bitter debates

and mutual insult. For a study that attempts to explain this section of the Gospel in the light of its setting during Tabernacles, see F. J. Moloney, "Narrative and Discourse at the Feast of Tabernacles," in *The Gospel of John. Text and Context*, 193-213.

[15] For a full explanation of this section of the Gospel, see F. J. Moloney, *Glory not Dishonor. Reading John 13-21* (Minneapolis: Fortress, 1998), 1-181; Moloney, *John*, 370-545.

[16] See F. J. Moloney, "Telling God's Story: The Fourth Gospel," in *The Gospel of John. Text and Context*, 93-111.

[17] Critical scholarship has made much of the temporal and literary tensions that exist across John 13-17. See, most famously, 14:31. Jesus tells his disciples that he will no longer talk much with them (v. 30), and invites them to rise and go forth (v. 31). Three further chapters of discourse (chaps. 15-17) and the prayer of Jesus (17:1-26) follow. On these tensions, and the need to resolve them, see F. J. Moloney, "The Function of John 13-17 within the Johannine Narrative," in *The Gospel of John. Text and Context*, 260-283.

[18] The Greek expression *eis telos* is open to both a temporal meaning (he loved them till the very end of his life) and a qualitative meaning (he loved them in a consummate fashion). As often in the Gospel of John, in 13:1 *both* meanings are to be retained: Jesus manifested his consummate love for his own in his death on the cross.

[19] In recent German and French Johannine scholarship, a helpful interpretation of one passage as a "re-reading" of another passage that had been produced earlier in the life of the community has been developed. This practice in the Johannine community appears to be particularly in evidence here. For a description of this approach, see Brown, *Introduction*, 291-292, and the references to Dettwiler, Scholtissek and Zumstein in the bibliography (pp. 295-97).

[20] On this, see F. J. Moloney, "The Johannine Passion and the Christian Community," *Salesianum* 57 (1995): 25-61.

[21] See F. J. Moloney, "John 18:15-27: A Johannine View of the Church," in *The Gospel of John. Text and Context*, 313-29.

22 The Church Fathers, and traditions associated with the Holy Sepulchre in Jerusalem, make a link between the two gardens in the Johannine passion narrative, and the Garden of Eden in Genesis. As innocence was lost in a garden, it is restored in a garden. Once hesitant to accept such suggestions, after 30 years of involvement with this subtle Gospel, I now suspect that the Fathers may have been right.

23 See above, pp. 245-247.

24 See Moloney, *John*, 547-68.

Reading John 6:1-71:
Bread from Heaven

The Johannine community, excluded from their traditional Jewish ritual celebrations, developed a story which told of Jesus' presence at the Sea of Galilee at Passover time. John 6 shows that in Jesus, the Passover God of Israel has not been lost, but rendered incarnate.

Jesus does not deny the Jewish Passover memory of the gift of the manna, present in the nourishment provided by the Law that makes God known in Israel. But the revelation of God in the Law is not the end of God's action in history.

The Johannine community is asked to accept Jesus' claim: "I am the bread of life" (6:35). There is no longer need to celebrate the former gift of the bread from heaven given through Moses. Such a tradition was a sign and a shadow of what has taken place in and through Jesus Christ.

Chapter 9
summary

A S WE READ THROUGH THE GOSPEL OF JOHN in the preceding chapter, we found that John 5-10 reported Jesus' presence and teaching within the context of four major feasts of "the Jews." This section of the Gospel responds to both pastoral and theological issues that had emerged within the Johannine community as its members gradually established their self-identity separated from post-war Judaism. The first people to be addressed by this Gospel had been separated from their traditional roots, cast out of the Synagogue (see 9:22; 12:42; 16:2). In the "Cana to Cana" section of the Gospel (John 2-4) they had been instructed on true faith; they were to put all their trust in the word of Jesus. But they looked back on the faith of Israel, and wondered if their being separated from their former community among the Jews, also led to the loss of their adhesion to the God of Israel.

For this reason, John presents Jesus at the Jewish feasts. Israel's celebration of its great feasts recalled the great moments of God's saving intervention in the history of God's people in a way that made God present to the Jewish community celebrating the feast and to the nation as a whole. The feasts were a "memory" which did not merely look back in wonder at events from the past, but which made the God of the Sabbath, Passover, Tabernacles, Pentecost and Dedication present in the celebrating community.[1] How were these saving moments still present to a community of Christians, excluded from the annual celebrations because they believed that Jesus was the Christ (see 9:22; 12:32)? They were no longer able to celebrate with their former friends in the Synagogue. Had they lost touch with the God of the Sabbath, the God of the Passover, the God of Tabernacles, and the God of Dedication?

John 5:1 announces a new theme: "After this there was a festival of the Jews and Jesus went up to Jerusalem." From 5:1 on, there is a steady reference to Jewish feasts (5:9b: "Now that day was a Sabbath," 6:4: "Now the Passover, the festival of the Jews, was near," 7:2: "Now the Jewish feast of Tabernacles was near," 10:22: "At that time the festival of the Dedication took place in Jerusalem"). John 6 is dedicated to Jesus' deeds, and especially his words spoken in a long discourse, within the setting of the celebration of the feast of the Passover.[2]

The events in chapter 5 took place in Jerusalem. Chapter 6:1-4 introduces a new place (v. 1: the Sea of Galilee which is the Sea of Tiberias), a new set of characters (v. 2: a multitude; v. 3: the disciples) and a change of time (v. 4: the Passover). The reason for this gathering is also given: "because they saw the signs which he did on those who were diseased" (v. 2).[3] The celebration of Passover contains elements commemorating the passage from winter to spring and the liberation of the Jewish people from Egypt. It affirms liberation from every form of enslavement. Two independent feasts, Passover (originally associated with the slaying of a sheep or a goat in a pastoral community) and Unleavened Bread (originally associated with eating unleavened bread in a community producing a barley harvest) were joined soon after Israel's settlement of Canaan. These feasts were then historicized and associated with God's deliverance of Israel from Egypt, and elements of the celebration recalled the biblical record of that event. The slaying of the Passover lamb recalled God's action in protecting the first born of the Israelites in Egypt (see Exod 11:1-10; 12:29-51), and the eating of unleavened bread recalled God's nourishing of Israel with the manna in the wilderness (see Exod 16:1-36), regarded as the gift of a "bread from heaven" (see Exod 16:4; Neh 9:15). After the loss of the Temple, and its associated ritual sacrifices, post-war Judaism was gradually adapting and domesticating these rituals.

The Johannine community, now excluded from the Jewish ritual celebrations, yet equally the product of a post-war Jewish world, developed a story which told of Jesus' presence at the Sea of Galilee at Passover time in the following fashion:

a) *Verses 1-4:* An introduction: where? when? who? why?

b) *Verses 5-15:* The miracle of the loaves and fishes

c) *Verses 16-21:* Jesus comes to the disciples across the stormy sea

d) *Verses 22-24:* A second introduction: where? when? who? why?

e) *Verses 25-59:* The discourse on the bread from heaven

f) *Verses 60-71:* The crisis created by the word of Jesus:

   i. *Verses 60-66:* Many disciples leave Jesus

   ii. *Verses 67-71:* Peter's confession leads Jesus to warn of Judas' betrayal.

The chapter is a coherent piece of skilful Christian reflection upon Jesus and the Jewish Passover, and shows that in Jesus the Passover God of Israel has not been lost, but rendered incarnate.

An Introduction: 6:1-4

The introduction to the passage answers four questions: Who? Where? When? and Why? The people involved in all that follows are: Jesus (v. 1), the disciples (v. 3) and a multitude (v. 2). They are on the mountain (v. 3) on the other side of the Sea of Galilee (v. 1). The time of the year is Spring, as the feast of "the Jews," the Passover, approaches (v. 4). The multitude follows Jesus because the people have seen the signs which he did on the sick (v. 2). Jesus ascends an unnamed mountain and seats himself there with his disciples. The use of the definite article to describe "*the* mountain" may be a first hint that Jesus is adopting a position parallel to Moses who received the Law on a mountain (see Exod 19:20; 14:1-2; Isa 34:2-4).[4] The critical stance Jesus has taken with other characters in the story who came to him because of the signs he did (see 1:49-51: Nathanael; 3:1-11: Nicodemus; 4:16-26: the Samaritan Woman) and the narrator's comment in 2:23-25, that Jesus did not entrust himself to those who believed in him because of his signs, indicate that the multitude still has much to learn.

The Miracle of the Loaves and Fishes: 6:5-15

If we incorporate the introduction (vv. 1-4) into this section of the narrative, the following shape emerges:

a) *Verses 1-4:* Setting the scene and the characters

b) *Verses 5-9:* A problem posed by Jesus cannot be solved by the disciples

c) *Verses 10-11:* A miracle takes place through the words and actions of Jesus

d) *Verses 12-15:* The aftermath of the miracle.

1. *The story (vv. 1-5)*
Found in the Synoptic Gospels (Mark 6:31-44; 8:1-10; Matt 14:13-21; 15:32-39; Luke 9:10-17), a traditional miracle story is told. However, a unique Johannine point of view has been insinuated into its telling that leads into the long discourse that will dominate John 6.

2. *The problem (vv. 5-9)*
The distinction between the participants in the scene (see vv. 1-4) is carefully maintained. Lifting up his eyes, Jesus sees the multitude coming to him, and he speaks to one of the disciples, Philip. Unlike the synoptic

accounts of this miracle (see Mark 6:37; 8:4; Matt 15:33), Jesus takes the initiative, indicating his concern that the people be fed (v. 5). A question which Moses asked of YHWH in the desert returns: "Where am I to get the meat to give all these people?" (Num 11:13), but Jesus' concern is rhetorical. In an aside, the narrator informs the reader that Jesus knew what he would do (v. 6b). The question tests the faith of the disciples (v. 6a). Moses, bread, and a moment of "testing" form the background for a story which takes place as "the Passover, the feast of the Jews, was at hand" (v. 4). Philip's response is limited to the material bread which one would need to feed such a multitude (v. 7). Andrew joins Philip in pointing to the paucity of their supplies: a lad is at hand with five barley loaves and two fish (vv. 8-9). Andrew and Philip have been with Jesus from the first days of the Gospel (see 1:43), but they have not learnt from their master's attempt to draw them beyond the limitations of their expectations (cf. 1:35-51), in this case the need for a large sum of money to buy quantities of bread. Nevertheless, the raw material for the events that follow have been provided: the loaves and the fish, and the reader waits for Jesus' action, as "he himself knew what he would do" (v. 6b).

3. *The miracle (vv. 10-11).*
Jesus commands the disciples to have the people lie down, taking up a formal position for a meal. In v. 3 Jesus "sat down," but he asks that the people take up a position that prepares for a meal (v. 10). The narrator adds two details: there was much grass in the place, and the men who arranged themselves for the meal were about 5,000 in number.[5] The latter detail indicates the immensity of the crowd, and heightens the impact of the feeding. The green grass, however, recalls Ps 23:2: "He makes me lie down in green pastures." Jesus takes the loaves, gives thanks, and distributes them to the people, stretched out for the meal (v. 11a). The distribution of the loaves recalls the formal setting of a eucharistic celebration. He also distributes the fish (v. 11b) and all are satisfied (v. 11c). The promise of Ps 23:1 is fulfilled: "The Lord is my shepherd, I shall not want."

Jesus commands the disciples again: "Gather up the fragments (Greek: *ta klasmata*) left over, that nothing perish (Greek verb: *apoleō*)" (v. 12). Eucharistic language colors this command. Early Christian authors use the verb "to gather" to speak of the gathering of the faithful for Eucharist, and "the fragments" is the term used for the eucharistic fragments.[6] Jesus has fed a vast multitude in a way that recalls a Christian celebration of Eucharist, and this feeding takes place at Passover time, which celebrates the gift of the manna. The disciples are commanded to gather the fragments from this original meal so that they might not perish (Greek: *apoleō*). The Passover and Eucharist blend as the practice of the Exodus people is recalled. They gathered the manna each day, eating till they had their fill (see Exod 16:8, 12, 16, 18, 21). However, Moses commanded that the manna was *not to be stored,* and any manna that was hidden away perished (Exod 16:19-20). Jesus' gift to people who come to him in search of bread (see v. 5) must not be lost, and the disciples are to see to its preservation.

An abundance of "fragments" is still available. Unlike the manna given by God in the desert to the ancestors of Israel (Exod 16), the "fragments" given by Jesus on the occasion of the Passover feast have not perished; they are still available. Much that happened in the desert (Exod 16) is repeated beside the lake (6:1-13), but there are some important Christian developments of that tradition. The traditional number 12 indicates a collection complete in itself (cf. Mark 6:43; Matt 14:20; Luke 9:17), and the fragments are gathered by the disciples, obedient to the word of Jesus (v. 13). They are commissioned to care for the fragments that they may be available for future believers wishing to share from the bread which Jesus distributed on the occasion of the feast of the Passover. As throughout the miracle, there is a blending of Passover traditions and the Christian traditions which surround the ongoing celebration of Eucharist.

4. *The aftermath (vv. 14-15).*
The sight of the miracle leads the people to a profession of faith: "This is indeed the prophet who is to come into the world" (v. 14). Like the disciples (1:35-49), Nicodemus (3:2) and the Samaritan woman (4:19, 25, 30), a sign has led to a limited faith. They have not progressed from v. 2: "A multitude followed him, because they saw the signs which he did." They are looking for a figure who will satisfy their expectations and see Jesus as a Moses-like prophet, based on the word of YHWH to Moses in Deut 18:15-18: "The Lord your God will raise up for you a prophet like me from among you, from your brethren—him you shall heed ... I will raise up for them a prophet like you from among their brethren; and I will put my words in his mouth, and he shall speak to them all that I command him." They associate themselves with another Jewish hope, which awaited a second gift of the manna to mark the

opening of the messianic era: "And it shall come to pass at that self-same time that the treasury of manna shall again descend from on high, and they will eat of it in those years, because these are they who have come to the consummation of time" (*2 Baruch* 29:8).[7] Jesus is not prepared to accept their acclamation, nor their desire to impose their messianic criteria upon him. He sees that they wish to force him into a royal role (v. 15a). He leaves them, retiring to the mountain from which he had descended to feed the multitude (v. 15b).[8] His departure marks the end of the episode.

The Miracle on the Sea: 6:16-21

A second miracle story now follows (vv. 16-21), matching the shape of the account of the multiplication of the loaves and fishes (vv. 5-15). Although briefer, the same elements, common to most miracle stories, return.

a) *Verses 16-17:* Setting the scene and the characters

b) *Verse 18:* The problem of the storm is reported

c) *Verses 19-20:* Jesus comes to the disciples across the stormy waters

d) *Verse 21:* The aftermath of the miracle.

1. *Setting the scene (vv. 16-17).*
As evening comes, the disciples go down to the sea (v. 16). The characters of vv. 1-4, who had been together in vv. 5-15, have been separated. Jesus has returned to the mountain (v. 15), the disciples are at the seashore (v. 16) and the multitude has not moved. The disciples struggle across the lake. The narrator specifies that the night had fallen, and then comments that "Jesus had *not yet* come to them" (v. 17b). The introduction to the episode indicates that Jesus will come to the disciples, as they struggle with the storm.

2. *The storm (v. 18).*
The narrator briefly states that a storm arose: turbulent wind and rising seas. The eastern coast of the normally placid Sea of Galilee is formed by high country split by deep gorges. Sudden changes of weather can tunnel strong winds through the gorges, and create difficult conditions on the lake.

3. *Jesus comes on the waters (vv. 19-20).*

About half way across the lake, the disciples see Jesus walking upon the lake, drawing close to their boat. They are struck with fear. The drama of a difficult sea journey in the night (vv. 16-17), the storm (v. 18) and the fear of the disciples (v. 19) prepare for Jesus' words to them which provide the setting for an Old Testament literary form for a manifestation of the divine (see Gen 15:1; 26:24; 46:3; Isa 41:13-14; 43:1, 3) and the Old Testament theme of YHWH's unique authority over the terror of the sea (e.g. Exod 14-15; Deut 7:2-7; Job 9:8; 38:16; Pss 29:3; 65:8; 77:20; 89:10; 93:3-4; Isa 43:1-5; 51:9-10). It is as Lord that Jesus comes across the waters, reveals himself to the disciples with the formula "I am he" (Greek: *egō eimi*), and tells them not to fear (v. 20).

4. *The aftermath (v. 21).*

The multiplication of the loaves and fish did not advance the crowds' understanding of Jesus (cf. vv. 2, 14-15). Jesus' self-revelation to the disciples leads them to receive him gladly, and they find themselves "at the land to which they were going" (v. 21). As earlier in the story the acceptance of the word of Jesus led to a miracle (cf. 2:1-12; 4:46-54; 5:2-9a), the seemingly insurmountable problem of the journey to Capernaum on a stormy sea (cf. vv. 17-19a) is solved as the disciples "receive" Jesus. Where they will go from here, however, remains an open question.

The narrative has reached a point where the characters in the story have been separated (vv. 15-16). As a result of this miracle, Jesus and the disciples are reunited (v. 20). The reunion is marked by Jesus' coming to the disciples as Lord, revealing himself as "I am he," and being received by them (v. 21). None of this has happened to the crowds, who remain at the place of the miracle of the loaves and fish. The false messianic hopes of the crowds (vv. 14-15) have been corrected by Jesus' self-revelation (v. 20), and the disciples are willing recipients of that revelation (v. 21). But the crowd has not received this revelation. The crowd, the disciples and Jesus will shortly gather once more (vv. 22-24), and Jesus will deliver his discourse on the bread from heaven (vv. 25-59). The disciples, who have accepted Jesus' self-revelation with joy, will strangely disappear from the action as Jesus speaks to the multitude and "the Jews" (vv. 25-29). But they will return to the action in vv. 60-71, and the quality of their faith will be tested.

A Second Introduction (6:22-24)

In a passage which matches vv. 1-4, the narrator establishes who is present, and where, when and why a further gathering takes place.

a) Jesus (vv. 22, 24), the disciples (vv. 22, 24), and "the people who remained on the other side," who had eaten the bread (vv, 22, 23) are brought together again

b) They gather at Capernaum (v. 24)

c) It is "the next day" (v. 22)

d) The multitude was "seeking Jesus" (v. 24).

In a changed situation, the questions of who, where, when, and why, are resumed from vv. 1-4, and given answers which fit the changed circumstances.

"The people who remained on the other side" (v. 22), those who "ate the bread after the Lord had given thanks" (v. 23), are aware that Jesus and the disciples have been separated. They had observed on the day before that there was only one boat, but that Jesus had not departed with his disciples (v. 22). Yet neither Jesus nor his disciples are "there." They are left wondering and confused. Has another miracle happened? Anxious to find their miracle-working provider of the messianic manna (cf. vv. 14-15), they hail boats passing by from Tiberias and set off for Capernaum "seeking Jesus."

An atmosphere of hustle and bustle is created as people crowd into boats to find their miracle-man (vv. 14-15). The eucharistic hints of the bread miracle (cf. esp. v. 11) have reappeared in v. 23: "where they ate the bread after the Lord had given thanks." The issue of the preserved "fragments" (v. 13) remains open. The place for the assembly is Capernaum (v. 24. See vv. 16, 21), and it is "the next day," after the disciples' night encounter with Jesus (vv. 16-17). The next day brings the discourse and the events which are about to be reported closer to the celebration of the Passover feast (see v. 4).

The Discourse on the Bread from Heaven(6:25-59)

We come now to the lengthy discourse on the bread from heaven that has been prepared by the two miracles, and the re-gathering of Jesus, the disciples, and the crowds who had eaten bread beside the lake at Capernaum. The rich interplay of theological themes and the complexity of the ongoing discussion with Jewish Passover traditions have made this section of the Fourth Gospel one of the most discussed texts in the New Testament. The interpreter faces a number of critical problems. Closely related questions concern the literary unity of the passage as we now have it and the possibility that at least part of the discourse reflects the Johannine celebration of the Eucharist.[9] The relationship between these two questions arises from the fact that vv. 51-58 are widely accepted as overtly eucharistic, and some suggest that v. 51c may even reflect the eucharistic formula used in the Johannine community.[10]

My reading of this discourse understands the passage as a Christian use of a Jewish practice of reading the Scriptures, called "midrash." This means that it is a long homiletic explanation of the Old Testament text provided to Jesus by his interlocutors in v. 31: "He gave them bread from heaven to eat." The discourse is formed by a repeated play upon words which come from this text. The first part of the discourse (vv. 32-48) is an interpretative and homiletic paraphrase and development of the words from Scripture: "He gave them bread from heaven." The latter part (vv. 49-58) continues to use expressions plundered from "He gave them bread from heaven," but devotes particular attention to a commentary on the words "to eat."[11] The rhythm of question and answer determines its shape.

a) *Verses 25-29:* "Rabbi, when did you come here?" (v. 25). This trivial question leads Jesus to instruct the crowd on the need to search for the food which endures to eternal life: belief in the one whom God has sent.

b) *Verses 30-33:* "Then what signs do you do?" (v. 30). Jesus is asked for miracle-working credentials which surpass Moses' gift of the manna (vv. 30-31). He points to another bread, *the true bread from heaven.*

c) *Verses 34-40:* "Lord give us this bread always" (v. 34). Jesus presents *himself as the true bread from heaven,* the only one able to make God known and give eternal life.

d) *Verses 41-51:* "Is not this Jesus, the son of Joseph, whose father and mother we know? How does he say, 'I have come down from heaven'?" (v. 42). Jesus discusses the question of origins.

e) *Verses 52-59:* "How can this man give us his flesh to eat?" (v. 52). A final question leads Jesus to instruct "the Jews" on the need to eat the flesh and drink the blood of the Son of Man.

The discourse unfolds around these questions and answers, each section developing a new thought around the single theme of the bread from heaven.

1. *Introduction to the theme (vv.25-29).*
The people's question, "Rabbi, when did you get here?" (v. 25), shows they understand Jesus in their terms ("Rabbi." See 1:28, 49; 3:2), and they have trivialized his presence by asking the time of his arrival. The question is logical, after the puzzlement of v. 22, but when last with Jesus they wished to make him king (see v. 15). They seem to have gone backwards in their understanding of Jesus, and his response to their question accuses them of seeking him for baser reasons. A double use of "amen" introduces Jesus' words in vv. 26-27. This expression is only found in the Gospel of John (the Synoptic Gospels have Jesus introduce solemn sayings with one "amen"). Jesus interprets their search for him (see v. 24) as no longer even motivated by the sign of the miracle, but because they enjoyed the bread that he provided. He instructs them to work, not for the bread that fills their bellies, not for the food that perishes (Greek verb: *apoleō*), but for the food that endures. There is a form of nourishment that transcends earthly bread, and this must be the goal of the people's searching; it is for this that they must work (v. 27a). The final event in the miracle of the loaves and fish also returns. The disciples have gathered the fragments "that nothing may perish (Greek: *apoleō*)." There is a link between the need to abandon the search for the food which perishes and the disciples' gathering of the fragments (ta klasmata) so that they would not perish (Greek: *apoleō*). Although by no means the main focus of the discourse at this stage, a subtle hint of the gift of the Eucharist is still present.

The food which endures to eternal life will be given to them by the Son of Man (v. 27b). The reader knows from earlier uses of the expression "the Son of Man" by Jesus that he is referring to the only revealer from God (see 3:13) who makes God known (see 1:51) by means of a "lifting up" (see 3:14). The acceptance or refusal of the revelation brings about judgment (see 5:27). Questions multiply: what is this food and where can it be found? A further important question arises from the future tense of the verb: "which the Son of Man *will give* to you." When might this be? There will be a moment further on in the story when the revelation of God in the lifting up of the Son of Man will provide a food which will endure for eternal life. The promise of a nourishment that provided life matched Israel's belief that the Law provided life for those who lived by it (see Sir 17:11; 45:5), and they "labored" upon the Law so that they might have this life. Jesus points to an alternative nourishment as the source of eternal life: the future gift of the Son of Man. There can be no questioning this promise, however veiled its final significance might be at this stage of the story, for God the Father has set his seal upon the Son of Man (v. 27c). The nourishment that the Son of Man will give is unique because it is "God the Father who attests the authority and the truth of Jesus."[12] As an author puts his seal upon a missive to show its authenticity and to give it authority, so has God the Father done with the Son of Man, his unique mediator between heaven and earth. He is the one who has come down from heaven (cf. 1:51; 3:13), bearing the credentials of God the Father (6:27c).

The crowd attempts to bypass the promise of the Son of Man, asking: "What must we do to be devoting ourselves to the works of God?" (v. 28). The question depends upon the Jewish belief that the Law, given through Moses, allows them direct access to God. Doing the works of the Law is doing things which please God. Jesus' response indicates that the way to God by means of the works of the Law is but a shadow of the possibility he offers them. Access to God is only through the Son who makes God known (see 1:18). The only way to do the work of God is to believe in the one whom God has sent (v. 29).

As the Passover approaches (cf. vv. 4, 22) Jesus teaches that there will be a gift of God, made available through the Son of Man (v. 27), the one sent by God (v. 29), which surpasses all human nourishment (v. 26). Laboring for the possession of this nourishment (vv. 28-29), believing in the one whom God has sent (v. 29) will produce eternal life (v. 27). The program for the rest of the discourse has been established. "The whole discourse is summarized here,"[13] and it is closely linked to important themes from the celebration of the Passover: nourishment, bread from heaven, and the revelation of God in the Law.

2. The true bread of God from heaven (vv. 30-33)

Two questions open the next stage in the discourse, "Then what sign do you do that we may see it, and believe you? What will you do?" (v. 30). They show that the crowd recognizes Jesus' words on belief in the sent one of the Father (v. 29), mean belief in him. The people tell Jesus why they trust in the Mosaic tradition: "Our ancestors ate the manna in the desert; as it is written: 'He gave them bread from heaven to eat'" (v.

31). Judaism was familiar with the tradition of requiring what can be called "confirmatory miracles."[14] A religious figure who makes serious claims is required to provide some miraculous proof that "confirms" his association with God. The crowd asks that Jesus respond to their requirements. Ironically, Jesus' interlocutors provide him with the text (v. 31b) he will use for the backbone of his response. They also maintain the focus upon the Passover background central to John 6.[15]

When Israel looked back to the foundational experience of the Exodus, a link was made between Moses and the gift of the manna, understood as a bread from heaven (see Exod 16:4; Pss 78:24; 105:40; Neh 9:15; Wis 16:20). This never-failing nourishment from God was identified, in both the wisdom and Jewish interpretative traditions, with the gift of the Law.[16] Despite Jesus' warnings and promise (vv. 25-29), the people attempt to force Jesus into their Mosaic model: Moses, the manna and Torah give life to Israel. What sign can Jesus do to surpass the sign of the gift of bread from heaven in the desert, and all that this has come to mean: the life-giving presence of the Torah to God's people? Within the context of the Jewish celebration of Passover, when the gift of the manna was recalled and celebrated, Jesus has summoned the crowd to labor for the bread that does not perish (v. 27. See vv. 12-13). Aroused by these words, the people demand that he offer them a sign which authorizes him to challenge the unique authority of Moses and the Torah, the ongoing presence of the manna, God's nourishment for the Jewish people.

Another double "amen" (v. 32) opens Jesus' words that warn the people against setting too much store by Moses. Moses did not give the bread from heaven; God did. But that gift *once given*, is surpassed by a bread which God *now gives*: the true bread from heaven. However wonderful the former gift of God, once given, the true bread from heaven is the gift that the Father of Jesus (see 5:17) is now giving (v. 32). It comes down from heaven and gives life to the world (v. 33). The use of "true" (Greek: *alēthinos*) sets this bread over against all other breads, even the bread given to the ancestors of Israel through Moses. This is the authentic bread which is and does all that it claims to be and do.[17] The present gift of God comes down from above and, unlike the Torah, which gave life to Israel, gives life to the whole world. Both contrast and continuation are found here. In the past it was God who gave the bread, not Moses (see v. 32). Now this same God, the Father of Jesus, gives the true bread from heaven. The Mosaic manna provided nourishment for

Israel; the true bread from heaven gives life to the whole world.

3. Jesus is the bread of life (vv. 34-40).

The response of the crowd to Jesus' words on the true bread from heaven opens the next section. The people ask, "Sir, give us this bread again and again" (v. 34). They misunderstand the nature of the bread and ask Jesus to give the bread from heaven repeatedly.[18] Jesus responds by identifying himself with the once-and-for-all gift of the bread: "I am the bread of life" (v. 35a). Jesus is not describing who he is, but what he does: he nourishes with a bread that produces life. Jesus claims that he is perfecting the former gift, the life-giving nourishment provided by Torah. Gone are the limitations of a chosen people, as Jesus promises that *anyone* who would come to him will not hunger and that *anyone* who believes in him will not thirst. Set in close parallel, to come to Jesus and to believe in Jesus mean the same thing. Those who come to Jesus and believe in him will find rest from the never-ending search for Wisdom: "Those who eat me (Wisdom) will hunger for more, and those who drink me will thirst for more" (Sir 24:21. See also Isa 49:10). No longer will Moses, the manna, Wisdom or Torah provide sufficient nourishment. Jesus, the bread of life (v. 35a) will satisfy the deepest needs of humankind, all hunger and all thirst (v. 35b).

But the words of Jesus are *in the future tense*. Those who come and believe shall not hunger and they shall not thirst. Some time in the future Jesus will provide never-failing food and drink. The links with Jewish tradition indicate that the revelation of God in and through Jesus will surpass the revelation of God in and through the Law, but when might this happen? This promise of some future moment in which God will be made known recalls other unresolved promises. When will "the fragments" (*ta klasmata*) gathered by the disciples so that they might not perish (v. 13), be consumed? When will the never-perishing food provided by the Son of Man (v. 27) be given? There will be some moment in the future when a food will be provided by the Son of Man which will explain the fragments and provide never failing food and drink to those who believe (vv. 13, 27, 35).

Jesus claims he has told them of their lack of belief, even though they have seen (v. 36). These words are not found earlier in the Gospel, but they refer back to Jesus' revelation through the miraculous gift of the bread which the crowd has interpreted in terms of their Mosaic traditions. The key to a correct reading of v. 36 is v. 26. They have seen

(vv. 5-15), but they have not believed (v. 26). Jesus is the nourishment of Israel and of the whole world (v. 35). He perfects God's gifts of the manna and Torah, but the people have not believed in this revelation, even though they have seen it. The Father sends those who come to Jesus in faith, and Jesus willingly accepts "everyone." He will not "cast out" anyone or anything given to him by the Father. As well as continuing the theme of universality broached in v. 35, the text addresses the Johannine community. Its members have been "cast out" (see 9:34) because of their faith in Jesus as the Christ. Their "coming to" and "belief in" Jesus places them in a new situation where such violence will never again be done to them.

As the word of God (see Isa 55:10-11) and the Law of God were understood as a gift of God come down from heaven (see Exod 19:11, 20), Jesus presents himself as the perfection of the former gift of the Law. Like the Law, his presence is a reflection of the will of the Father (see 4:34; 5:36). The Father gives (v. 37), the Father sends (v. 38a), and the one who is sent responds unconditionally to the will of the one who sent him (v. 38b). How this relates to and perfects the former understanding of the gift of the Law needs some further explanation. As the Law was to lead a chosen people to belong forever to YHWH, so it is with Jesus. In the new situation, where the Law has been perfected and universalized by Jesus, and the new people of God includes whomsoever the Father gives to him, the will of the Father is that not one of these be lost, neither now nor hereafter (v. 39). These words on life both here and hereafter are essential for a third-generation Christian church, facing the mystery of the death of its members (v. 39b; 16:2; 21:23).

In the light of what he has claimed concerning his being the true bread, the gift of God from heaven which brings nourishment and life to those who come to him and believe in him, Jesus promises eternal life to those who would perfect their adherence to the Law by believing in the Son sent by the Father (v. 40a). It was through the concrete reality of the Law, words of God that spoke to the lived situation of a chosen people, that Israel would find the will of God. This "living presence," the visible assurance that God cares for and guides his people, has been perfected. It is to be seen and to be believed in the presence of the Son: "*All* who see the Son and believe in him may have eternal life" (v. 40b). The *universal* and *never-ending* promise of life is made to *all* as Jesus will "raise them up at the last day" (v. 40c). Both the temporal dimensions of the Law, guarding and directing a people during its earthly pilgrimage, and the ethnic limitations of the Law, an exclusive covenant between God and the people of Israel, have been perfected in Jesus. He promises life to *all,* both *now* and *forever.* The former gift of the bread from heaven has been perfected in Jesus, the true bread from heaven.

4. The question of origins (vv. 41-51)

The unspecified crowd, Jesus' interlocutor thus far, suddenly becomes "the Jews." Once this group emerges from the crowd, hostility increases. Their "murmuring," recalling the behavior of the Israelites in the wilderness (see Exod 15:24; 16:2, 7; 17:3), indicates rebellion. Jesus' claim to be the bread from heaven in vv. 35-40 is challenged. How can he make that claim (vv. 41, 42b) when his human father and mother are known (v. 42a). The theme of this section of the discourse has been struck: Jesus has made claims that can be understood only in terms of his origins: a descent *from his Father above.* His opponents will not consider such a possibility; they know *his father Joseph.* Moses had warned the murmuring people of Israel, "Your complaints are not against us, but against the Lord" (Exod 16:8). Jesus repeats this process as he reproaches the murmuring of "the Jews" (v. 43) by pointing to the Father, and explaining his role in terms of his origins with the Father. The Father sends Jesus, the Father draws believers to him, and the response of those drawn to the revelation of the Father in the sent one will be the measure of their everlasting life. It is Jesus who will raise up the believer on the last day (v. 44). While God determines the process, the encounter between the human being and the revelation of God in Jesus determines life, death and everlasting life. This is only possible because Jesus is not the son of Joseph (vv. 41-42), but the Son of the Father.

The prophets had foretold that "they shall all be taught by God" (v. 45a, freely citing Isa 54:13). Thus Jesus asks that "the Jews" listen to God that they might be instructed. God taught Israel through the gift of the Law, but Jesus claims that all who have truly learned from God will come to him (v. 45). The instruction God gives to *all peoples* (v. 45a) draws them to Jesus (v. 45b). Continuing the theme of universality of vv. 35-40, Jesus now claims that in fulfillment of the prophetic promise (v. 45a) a process is in motion which leads to the true believer's coming to Jesus. No longer is Israel the object and the Law the source of God's instruction. It is aimed at all believers, without limitation of race or nation, and it comes through Jesus.

Jesus is the one who makes the Father known. No one has ever seen the Father (see 1:18), but the one who has come from the Father makes him known (v. 46). As in 1:16-18, the relationship between Jesus and Moses is in question. However exalted were the claims of Moses, the Son who throughout his human story gazes toward the Father is the only one who has ever seen God.[19] The difference between Moses and Jesus is their respective origins. Jesus' origins with God (1:1) give him a unique authority to make God known (1:18). Because this is the case, the one who believes in the revelation of Jesus, the true bread who has come down from heaven, has eternal life. The comparison continues between the manna of the Law and Jesus, the true bread from heaven. It is no longer the Law that produces life. Jesus, the true bread from heaven, came to make the Father known and, in doing so, surpasses the former gift of a bread from heaven (cf. vv. 32-33). He is the bread of life (v. 48).

As the comparison of two "breads" draws to a conclusion, Jesus recalls the experience of Israel's ancestors who ate the bread that came down from heaven in the form of manna: they all died (v. 49).[20] The bread that comes down from heaven in the person of Jesus promises a life that is eternal: there will be no death for those who consume that bread (v. 50). There is a close parallel between the words of Jesus in v. 50: "This is the bread that comes down from heaven," and in v. 51: "I am the living bread that came down from heaven." As once Moses pointed to the manna and said, "This is the bread that the Lord has given you for food" (Exod 16:15), Jesus points to himself and says, "This is the bread" (v. 50). The Mosaic bread did not produce life (see v. 49), and even Moses is dead (see Deut 34:5-8). Now there is a bread which surpasses the bread given by Moses: "This is the bread that came down from heaven (v. 50) ... I am the living bread that came down from heaven" (v. 51). Jesus' identification of himself with the bread of life which came down from heaven looks back to the basis for his claims: the moment when the Word became flesh (1:14).

There has been an intensifying concentration upon the person of Jesus: "This is the bread ... I am the bread" (vv. 50, 51). The one who is the bread now makes a further surprising promise: "The bread which I shall give for the life of the world is my flesh" (v. 51c). The true bread that has come down from heaven *will* make God known in an unconditional gift of himself for the life of the world. When will this be? How will it happen? As in earlier statements which point to a future encounter between the darkness and the light (1:5), the hour of Jesus (2:5) and his being "lifted up" (3:14), much is still shrouded in mystery. But there are already clear hints that Jesus will be slain by "the Jews" in their rejection of him at the Temple in 2:13-23, and their plot to kill him in 5:18. The mystery does not lie in the *fact* that Jesus will die at the hands of "the Jews." The Johannine community and all subsequent believers have known that before they began reading or listening to the Gospel of John. But *how* does Jesus' experience of death provide nourishment for the life of the world?

This is not the first time Jesus has promised a future gift. In vv. 12-13 the disciples were commanded to gather the fragments so that they might not be lost. In v. 27 Jesus urged the crowds not to labor for a food which perishes, but for a food which endures, which would be provided by the Son of Man. In v. 35 Jesus' claim to be the bread of life leads to a further promise: all who come to him *will not* hunger, and all who believe in him *will not* thirst. The mounting impression is that there will be a definitive nourishment which will forever satisfy the needs of all who believe in Jesus. Jesus has outraged "the Jews" by telling them that he *will give* his flesh for the life of the world (v. 51). Their horrified question, asking *how* this is possible (v. 52), sheds light upon when and how Jesus' promise of the bread that surpasses all that the Passover celebrated will be given.

5. Jesus gives his flesh to eat (vv. 52-59)

The question that emerges from the dispute among "the Jews" is a rejection of Jesus' outrageous suggestion: "How can this man give us his flesh to eat?" (v. 52). But it allows Jesus to conclude his discourse on his perfection of the Mosaic gift of bread from heaven through his gift of himself as the true bread from heaven. Unable to go beyond the physical, "the Jews'" question misunderstands Jesus' promise. Jesus insists upon a gift of flesh and blood for life by stating negatively (v. 53) and positively (v. 54) that whoever eats the flesh and drinks the blood of Jesus, the Son of Man, has eternal life now and will be raised up on the last day. The play upon the verb "to eat" provided by the Exodus passage in v. 31 has reached its high point. Flesh and blood emphasize that it is the incarnate life and very real death of the Son which is life-giving food. Only the physical body of a human being produces flesh and blood. The argument of vv. 25-51 continues into vv. 52-59, especially in Jesus' words which point to the resolution of a series of promises (see vv. 12-13, 27, 35,

51c). Jesus will provide a food for the life of the world, and that food is his flesh and blood.

As the ancestors of Israel were nourished by the gift of the Torah, Jesus will nourish the whole world with the gift of himself. The people of Israel were nourished by eating the manna, perennially recalled in the nourishment provided for them by their total receptivity to and absorption of the Law. Now "the Jews" are told of the absolute need to eat the flesh and drink the blood of the Son of Man. Unless they eat the flesh and drink the blood of the Son of Man they have no life (v. 53); whoever eats the flesh and drinks the blood of Jesus has eternal life (v. 54). The shift from the more respectable verb "to eat" (Greek: *phagein*) to another verb which indicates the physical crunching with the teeth (Greek: *trōgein*) accentuates that Jesus refers to a real experience of eating. Hints of the Eucharist continue to insinuate themselves into the words of Jesus. Flesh is to be broken and blood is to be spilled. Violence has been in the air since Jesus' behavior on the Sabbath led "the Jews" to initiate a process that would lead to his death (5:16-18).[21] Jesus now associates the separation of flesh and blood in a violent death as the moment of total giving of himself. Jesus, the Son of Man, will give of his whole self for the life of the world (6:51c) by means of a violent encounter between himself and his enemies (1:5, 11; 2:18-20; 3:14; 5:16-18) in which his body will be broken and his blood will be poured out (6:53-54).[22] This is the ongoing presence of Jesus in the gathered "fragments" (vv. 12-13), the enduring gift that the Son of Man will give, the food that will not perish (v. 27), but will forever satisfy all hunger and thirst (v. 35).

The Passover context must not be forgotten. As once Israel ate of the manna in the desert, and was nourished by adhesion to the Law given at Sinai, now the world is summoned to accept the further revelation of God in the broken body and spilled blood of the Son of Man. In this way all will have life, now and hereafter (vv. 53-54). These claims are further developed through vv. 55-57. Earlier parts of the discourse are recalled as Jesus insists that his flesh really is food and his blood really is drink. This play upon words recalls Jesus' promise of the food that the Son of Man would give (v. 27), and his claim that over against all other bread from heaven, and especially the gift of the Law from heaven, the Father gives "the true bread from heaven" (v. 32). Jesus is the true bread from heaven (v. 35).

Jesus claims that his flesh and blood are authentically food and drink. The interpretive explanation of v. 31 continues: through a total absorption (*trōgein* is again used) of the revelation of God made available through the bloody death of Jesus, believers will come to a mutuality where they live in Jesus and Jesus lives in them (v. 56). This mutual indwelling flows from the union that exists between the Father and his Son (v. 57). Jesus' words play upon the verb "to live." He refers to the Father as "the living Father" who has sent his Son who has life in him because of the intimacy between the Father and the Son. If the one who sends is "living," then the one who is sent lives because of the one who sent him. He thus has authority to pass on life to those who accept the revelation of the Father in the Son (v. 57). The idea of the reception of the revelation of God in and through his Son is not new (see, for example, 3:11-21, 31-36),[23] but the imagery has been changed by the Passover context. No longer does Jesus speak of "belief in" (cf. 3:12, 15, 18, 36), but "the one who eats me" (v. 57b). The expressions are parallel. As throughout the Gospel, unconditional commitment to the revelation of God in and through Jesus leads to life here and hereafter: the one who eats the flesh of Jesus will live because of him (v. 57b). As Jesus lives because of the Father (v. 57a), the believer lives and will live because of Jesus (v. 57b).[24]

The discourse closes as it opened, comparing the bread that Israel's ancestors ate in the desert and the bread which comes down from heaven (v. 58. See vv. 30-33). All former gifts from heaven have been surpassed. Playing upon the two possibilities of life — physical life which the manna could not provide, and eternal life which the true bread of life does give (cf. vv. 49-50) — Jesus points to the death of Israel's ancestors and promises everlasting life to those who eat of the true bread from heaven. A new possibility has entered the human story. The Law was a gift of God (see 1:17), but it has been surpassed by Jesus, the bread from heaven (v. 35), promising his abiding presence (v. 56), communicating the life of the Father to all who consume this true bread (v. 57). On the occasion of the celebration of Passover Jesus announces that there is another bread from heaven that eclipses all the original bread offered to the ancestors of Israel (v. 58). "This he said in the synagogue, as he taught at Capernaum (v. 59). Jesus has not moved. The discourse ends where it began: at Capernaum (vv. 24, 59). The narrator closes the discourse with a comment which reminds the reader that Jesus is in a Jewish center of worship during Passover time, uttering a message that presupposes, fulfils, and transcends a Jewish Passover tradition.

6. *The Eucharist in vv. 51c-58.*

The major concern of this final part of the discourse on the bread from heaven is not eucharistic, but the commentary upon the verb "to eat" (see v. 31) summons up a rich tradition of eucharistic language: "bread," "food," "flesh," "blood," "to eat," "to drink," "will give," "for your sakes." The discourse, from v. 25 down to v. 59, presents Jesus as the true bread from heaven, perfecting the former gift of bread from heaven, the manna of the Law. The believer must accept the revelation of God that will take place in broken flesh and spilled blood (vv. 53-54), a never-failing nourishment (v. 35) that the Son of Man will give (v. 27). But at the end of the first century, Johannine readers, and the Christian readers of subsequent centuries, have every right to ask: where do we encounter this revelation of God in the flesh and blood of the Son of Man? The author's insinuation of eucharistic language into the final section of the discourse provides the answer: one encounters the flesh and blood of Jesus Christ in the eucharistic celebration. The use of the expression "fragment" (*klasmata*) to refer to the bread consigned by Jesus to his disciples (vv. 12-13) has lurked behind the discourse, reminding the reader of such celebrations.

The author is working at two levels. The main thrust of the discourse is to point to Jesus as the revelation of God, the true bread from heaven, perfecting God's former gift, the bread of the manna. However, the use of the expression "fragments" (*klasmata*) in vv. 12-13, the promise in v. 27 of a future gift of food that the Son of Man would give, the reference to the satisfying food and drink in v. 35, and the further promise in v. 51c of the gift of the flesh of Jesus for the life of the world, keep the eucharistic question alive. The unfolding interpretation of the verb "to eat" (see v. 31) in vv. 49-58 naturally led to the use of eucharistic language to insinuate a secondary but important theme. The Eucharist renders concrete, in the eucharistic practice of the Christian reader, what the author has spelled out throughout the discourse. The Eucharist is a place where one comes to eternal life. Encountering the broken flesh and the spilled blood of Jesus, "lifted up" on a cross (vv. 53-54), the believer is called to make a decision for or against the revelation of God in that encounter (vv. 56-58), gaining or losing life because of it (vv. 53-54).[25]

The Crisis Created by the Word of Jesus (6:60-71)

The form of a discourse disappears as a two-fold response to Jesus' words is reported:

a) *Verses 60-66:* "Many of his disciples" find Jesus' word hard (v. 60), and Jesus addresses their difficulties (vv. 61-65), mentioning a future betrayal (v. 64). However, "many of his disciples" no longer go with Jesus (v. 66)

b) *Verses 67-71:* The Twelve, represented by Peter, confess belief in the word of Jesus (vv. 68-69), but Jesus foretells that even from among these believing disciples, one will betray him (vv. 70-71).

The possibility of acceptance or rejection of the word of Jesus has been canvassed regularly, from the Prologue (cf. 1:11-13) onward (cf. 3:11-21; 31-36), and various examples of how one might respond to the word formed the core of the journey from Cana to Cana (2:1-4:54).[26] As Jesus' discourse on the bread from heaven concludes, some of the disciples who had seen him on the waters, heard his self-revelation of "I am he" and came safely to land (cf. vv. 16-21), leave him (vv. 60-66). Others are told that failure is always possible, even among those who believe (vv. 67-71).

1. *The disciples no longer go with Jesus (vv. 60-66).*
Many disciples have *heard* what Jesus said (v. 60a). The disciples have reached a crucial moment. They have been the privileged recipients of Jesus' self-revelation on the stormy sea: "I am he; do not be afraid" (v. 20). They, more than the other characters in the story, the crowd and "the Jews," have been shown (vv. 5-13, 16-21) and told (vv. 25-59) *who it is* who speaks to them. But they regard Jesus' discourse as unacceptable, harsh, offensive (v. 60). They find that it is not possible to "listen" to this word.

Jesus challenges them with a further word, directed specifically to them. Do they take offense at what he has said? He has claimed to make God known in a way that transcends the revelation of God in the gift of the Torah; he is the true bread from heaven. Thus, he suggests to his disciples that they may be looking for further support for his claim to be the definitive revelation of God. Jesus' unfinished question, "What if you were to see the Son of Man ascending to where he was before" (v. 62), is high rhetoric. Understood is the conclusion: "would that satisfy your doubts?" The question presupposes all that has been said so far about the Son of Man, but especially Jesus' words in 3:13: "No-one has ascended into heaven but one has descended from heaven, the Son of Man." Throughout the discourse of vv. 25-59 Jesus has pointed to himself as the bread that has come down from heaven (vv. 32-33, 35, 38, 51). When "the Jews" questioned his origins (vv. 41-42) he affirmed that he is from God (vv. 46-47). The Son of Man has come from heaven (3:13), but perhaps the disciples would like to see him ascend to heaven, matching the ascent of traditional revealers, Abraham, Moses, Isaiah and Enoch. Within the Passover context, it is particularly the Jewish tradition of the ascent of Moses to receive the Torah which lies behind this half-asked question. But Jesus transcends all that Moses said and did. To make God known Jesus has no need to ascend from earth to heaven (v. 62a). He comes from there; he has been there before (v. 62b), and on the basis of his previous union with God (1:1) his words have ultimate authority.[27]

The disciples fail because they are attempting to assess Jesus' words and actions by the superficial judgment of human expectation. Such an approach to Jesus is "fleshly," and "the flesh is of no avail" (v. 63b).[28] Jesus warns the disciples against a "fleshly" lack of courage and understanding when they are faced with his words. The words of Jesus are spirit and life (v. 63c), but the disciples want Jesus to conform to their expectations (v. 62). He rejects their pretensions as worthless, as only the spirit gives life (v. 63a), not the superficiality of the flesh (v. 63b). What matters is the life-giving power of the Spirit, made available to the disciples in and through the revelation of God in and through the word of Jesus (v. 63). But Jesus is aware that, no matter how much has been revealed to the disciples, some do not believe, and one among them would betray him (v. 64). The relationship between Jesus and the disciple is crucial, but the initiative of God is the ultimate explanation for the disciple who comes believingly to Jesus, and who never turns away (v. 65).

The disciples have seen the miracle of the loaves and the fish (vv. 5-15), witnessed Jesus' coming across the waters announcing "I am he" (vv. 16-21) and heard the discourse on the true bread from heaven (vv. 25-59). But many of them have found the word of Jesus impossible (v. 60), and because of this rejection of the word of Jesus "many of his disciples" drew away from him (v. 66). The true disciple is the one to whom discipleship is given by the Father, and who believes in the Son (vv. 64-65). It is not information that makes a disciple, but a Spirit-filled response to the Father made known in the word of Jesus. Behind this negative response to the word of Jesus lies the experience of early Christians, and Christians of all times. The word of Jesus is the essential nourishment of the community, its spirit and life. However, many are unable to accept this, and would prefer that Jesus conform to their ideas. Some members of the Johannine community would rather have had Jesus conform to the Mosaic pattern of a heavenly revealer. When he refused to accommodate their expectations, they "drew back and no longer went with him" (v. 66).

2. *The belief and the possibility of failure (vv 67-71)*

But another response is possible, and Jesus challenges the Twelve, a restricted group within the larger crowd of disciples.[29] He asks if they too would like to leave him, to return to the world of their own securities (v. 67. See vv. 62-63). Simon Peter answers for them all, indicating that the Father does not fail to draw believing disciples toward Jesus (cf. v. 65): "Lord, to whom shall we go? You have the words of eternal life" (v. 68). Reflecting the unconditional openness to the word of Jesus that marked certain characters in the Cana to Cana journey (cf. 2:5: the Mother of Jesus; 3:29: John the Baptist; 4:42: the Samaritan villagers; 4:50: the royal official), Simon Peter tells Jesus that Jesus is the only possible focus for the Twelve (v. 68a). The Father has drawn them to him, and they recognize that his earlier statement to the larger group of disciples is true: "The words that I have spoken to you are spirit and life" (v. 63. See v. 68b).

Peter's confession goes further. Looking back across the story thus far, his next words tell of the experience of the Twelve: "we have believed and we have come to know" (v. 69a). They have arrived at belief in Jesus and are living from that faith and knowledge. Thus, in the name of the Twelve, Peter can confess, "You are the Holy One of God" (v. 69b). For the first time in the narrative a character has expressed faith in Jesus for the right reason: *his origins*. The holiness of Jesus comes from the fact that he is *of God*. But even among this group, failure is possible. Jesus responds to this confession of authentic belief by announcing that there will be a betrayer, Judas Iscariot (vv. 70-71). Jesus has chosen the Twelve, but there is a larger design in God's leading some to Jesus (cf. v. 64), and each believer is free to accept or refuse this gift. The fragility of the human response remains, even among believers. More than a confession of faith is called for. If there is a betrayer, then there will be a betrayal. The shadow of a violent death, which has fallen across much of the celebration of the Passover (cf. vv. 12-13, 15, 27, 51, 53-54), again emerges as the account of Jesus' activity on the occasion of the feast comes to a close (vv. 70-71). The confession of Simon Peter is excellent ... so far! How will this expression of faith survive in the difficult moments that will bring this story to an end? How will the believers respond to the "lifting up" of the Son of Man (cf. 3:14) that will provide a food which will endure to eternal life (6:12-13, 27, 35, 51, 53-54)?

Conclusion

The Passover provides the essential chronological, literary and theological background to John 6. Jesus does not deny the Jewish Passover memory of the gift of the manna, present in the nourishment provided by the Law that makes God known in Israel. But the revelation of God in the Law is not the end of God's action in history. "The Jews" and many of the disciples are unable to go any further than the Mosaic traditions in their response to God. For them Moses, the manna, and the Law exhaust all possibilities. At the end of the first century, deprived of their traditional priesthood, cult and Temple, "the Jews" focus upon the gift of the Law, but the Johannine community is asked to accept Jesus' claim: "I am the bread of life" (6:35. See vv. 41, 48, 51). There is no longer need to celebrate the former gift of the bread from heaven given through Moses. Such a tradition was a sign and a shadow of what has taken place in and through Jesus Christ. Christians are asked to accept that Jesus is the true bread from heaven, the one who gives life to all who believe in him. Jesus is the perfection of the Mosaic gift of the bread from heaven: he is the *true bread* from heaven.

As the final verses of this section of the Gospel reveal (cf. vv. 60-71), this Christian reinterpretation of the Mosaic traditions brought pain and division to the Johannine community. Not only were "the Jews" outraged by the words of Jesus; so were "many of the disciples" (vv. 60, 66). It is one thing for a Christian community to establish a theology and a Christology that respond to the crises created by faith in Jesus Christ (see 9:22; 12:42; 16:2). It is another for everyone in the community to accept these notions, and to live by them. Many could not accept that Jesus' words were spirit and life (v. 63), and thus "drew back and no longer went about with him" (v. 66).

Notes

[1] All these feasts are represented in the Gospel of John. Across John 5-10 Jesus is present at the celebration of the Sabbath, Passover, Tabernacles and Dedication. My interpretation of John 1:19-2:11 regards the "days" of preparation (1:19-51) and the vision of the glory of God "on the third day" (2:1-11) as a reflection of the celebration of Pentecost. See F. J. Moloney, *The Gospel of John* (Sacra Pagina 4; Collegeville: The Liturgical Press, 1998), 48-74. Passover is also the context for the beginning of Jesus' ministry (see 2:13, 23) and the end of his life (see 11:55-57; 12:1; 13:1; 19:14, 31, 42).

[2] The Roman Catholic Lectionary, and other Lectionaries, read John 6:1-71 during Cycle B, from the Seventeenth till the Twenty First Sunday of the Year.

[3] Many scholars have suggested that the present location of chapter 6 creates geographical difficulties which can only be resolved by rearranging chapters 4-7. If 6:1-71 is placed immediately after 4:43-54, Jesus' presence in Galilee is explained. The following events of chapters 5, 7, 9 and 10 all take place in Jerusalem. This suggestion, which has no support from textual traditions, focuses too strongly on geography. The issue that determines the order of events in John 5-10 is the celebration of the feasts of "the Jews" (cf. 5:1). After the general indication of the theme of feasts in 5:1, the fundamental observance of the Sabbath follows logically (cf. 5:9b). Other Jewish feasts then follow, in the correct sequence of the Jewish year: Passover (celebrated for 7 days in the first month of the year), Tabernacles (celebrated for 7 days in the seventh month of the year), and Dedication (celebrated for 8 days in the ninth month of the year).

[4] In support of this first hint of a link between Moses and Jesus, see the important commentaries of R. Schnackenburg, *The Gospel according to St John* (trans. C. Hastings; 3 vols.; Herders Theological Commentary on the New Testament; London: Burns & Oates; New York: Crossroad, 1968-82), 2:18; R. E. Brown, *The Gospel according to John* (2 vols.; The Anchor Bible 29-19A; Garden City: Doubleday, 1966-1970), 1:232. See also J. M. Perry, "The Evolution of the Johannine Eucharist," *New Testament Studies* 39 (1993) 23-25.

[5] In singling out "men" for the very large number of 5000, in contrast to "people" who are asked to adopt a physical position in readiness for a meal, the passage

shows the patriarchy of the times. Greek has words to distinguish between a man (*anēr*) and a person (*anthrōpos*), but the author uses the former.

[6] Christian documents from the earliest period repeat this language: *The Didache* (9:4), *1 Clement* (34:7) and Ignatius (*Letter to Polycarp* 4:2). These texts can be found in K. Lake, ed., *The Apostolic Fathers* (2 vols.; Loeb Classical Library; Cambridge: Harvard University Press, 1959). The exact references (English translation with the Greek on the facing page) can be found on pp. 323, 67, and 273 respectively.

[7] The Jewish writing known as 2 Baruch was written after the destruction of the Temple. It is roughly contemporaneous with the Gospel of John. For the text, see J. H. Charlesworth, ed., *The Old Testament Pseudepigrapha* (2 vols.; London: Darton, Longman & Todd, 1983), 1:630-31.

[8] There is no indication of Jesus and the disciples and the crowd coming down from the mountain. It must be presupposed that the miracle took place beside the lake, as the narrator indicates that he returns to the same mountain, but this time alone. The next sections (vv. 16-21; vv. 22-24) situate the disciples and the crowd beside the lake. Both groups embark on separate journeys across the lake (vv. 16-17; vv. 23-24). Only Jesus is separated from the lake, on the mountain.

[9] My words "as we now have it" may call for some explanation. As with the Synoptic Gospels, so also with John, various earlier traditions, maybe some oral and some written, have been assembled over a long period of time to produce the Gospel "as we now have it." The setting that produced these passages may have varied, but once the narrative is composed in its present form, it takes on a life of its own. This is the Gospel "as we now have it."

[10] See, for example, Brown, *John*, 1:287. For further discussion of this question, see below, p. 296.

[11] In this, I am very dependent upon the work of P. Borgen, *Bread from Heaven: An Exegetical Study of the Conception of Manna in the Gospel of John and the Writings of Philo* (Supplements to Novum Testamentum 10; Leiden: E. J. Brill, 1965), 28-57. For more detail of my application of Borgen's rich analysis, see F. J. Moloney, *The Johannine Son of Man* (2d ed.; Biblioteca di Scienze Religiose 14; Rome: LAS, 1978), 94-98.

[12] C. K. Barrett, *The Gospel according to St John* (2d ed.; London: SPCK, 1978), 287.

[13] Barrett, *St John*, 282.

[14] For more on this, see Schnackenburg, *St John*, 2:39-40.

[15] No Old Testament text states explicitly, "He gave them bread from heaven to eat" (v. 31). Borgen (and others) claim that it comes from the Passover text found in Exod 16. It is a combination of Exod 16:4 and 15. See Borgen, *Bread from Heaven*, 40-42. Others find the text in Ps. 78:24. See, for example, C. K. Barrett, "The Flesh of the Son of Man," in *Essays on John* (London: SPCK, 1982), 39-40. Most likely the Exodus text lies behind Ps 78:24 (and also Neh 9:15). Thus, both Exodus and the Psalm provide the "Scripture" for the citation of v. 31 ("as it is written").

[16] For the texts that show this, see Borgen, *Bread from Heaven*, 148-64.

[17] For further discussion of the Greek word for "true," an expression that does not only indicate the facts are correct, but what is "true" is exactly what it should be, see Moloney, *John*, 213, and the references there. In English we speak of a "true blade" in this sense. In Australia we speak of a genuine human being as a "true blue." These uses of "true" carry some of the biblical sense of the Greek word *alēthinos*.

[18] The Greek word I have translated "again and again" (*pantote*) is generally translated "always." The crowd has not understood Jesus' promise of a true bread from heaven, and are seeking ordinary bread, and they want it to be given to them on a regular basis.

[19] On this very important passage for understanding the Gospel of John (1:16-18), where the Prologue points out that the great gift of God given through Moses is perfected in the fullness of the gift that comes through Jesus Christ, see Moloney, *John*, 40-41.

[20] The verb "to eat" appears for the first time since v. 31. It marks the beginning of the interpretative treatment of the verb provided in v. 31: "He gave them bread from heaven *to eat.*"

[21] On this passage, and its indication that Jesus is being put on trial for his claims of oneness with God, whom he calls "Father," see Moloney, *John*, 169-71, 174-75.

[22] For a detailed study of v. 53, arguing that its primary reference is the crucifixion, see F. J. Moloney, "The Function of Prolepsis for the Interpretation of John 6," in *The Gospel of John. Text and Context* (Biblical Interpretation Series 72; Boston/Leiden: Brill, 2005), 169-92. One of the best clarifications of the meaning of this passage is found in E. C. Hoskyns, *The Fourth Gospel* (ed. F. N. Davey; London: Faber & Faber, 1947), 297: "First, redemptive significance is assigned to the death of the Son of God, who is to offer His Flesh as a sacrifice for the life of the world; secondly, sacrificial significance is assigned to the Eucharist, which is at once the concrete commemoration of the sacrifice once offered and the guarantee of its efficacy."

[23] On these important early passages that present Jesus as the revelation of God, see Moloney, *John*, 94-97, 106-108.

[24] The idea that the Law was consumed and absorbed like food is common in Jewish thought. For a collection of many Jewish texts that make this point, see H. Odeberg, *The Fourth Gospel. Interpreted in Its Relation to Contemporaneous Religious Currents in Palestine and the Hellenistic-Oriental World* (Chicago: Argonaut, 1968), 238-47.

[25] See F. J. Moloney, "John 6 and the Celebration of the Eucharist," *The Downside Review* 93 (1975): 243-51.

[26] See above, pp. 245-47.

[27] The question: "What if you were to see the Son of Man ascending where he was before?" requires completion. It is a question beginning with "if" (a protasis) and therefore requires completion, i.e. "then ...." (an apodosis). Interpreters must supply the apodosis, and there are three main solutions. Some suggest that if the disciples were to see Jesus ascend to where he was before their difficulties would be greater. Others say that the use of "ascend" refers to the cross, and similarly suggest that the offense would be greater. A third group claims that if they were to see him ascend where he was before their problems would be diminished, as they would know that he had authority to make such statements.

See the survey in Moloney, *Son of Man* 120-21. I have developed the third option, linking it to Jewish speculation that surrounded the ascensions of the great revealers of Israel. If the disciples were to see Jesus ascend — just as they believed the greater revealers from Israel's sacred history, and especially Moses, had ascended - then would they be prepared to accept his "hard word"? For the Jewish background to the tradition of great revealers who "ascended," especially Moses, see F. J. Moloney, "The Johannine Son of Man Revisited," in *Theology and Christology in the Fourth Gospel. Essays by Members of the SNTS Johannine Writings Seminar* (Bibliotheca Ephemeridum Theologicarum Lovaniensium 184; Leuven: Peeters, 2005), 190-93.

[28] Some major scholars conclude that vv. 51c-58 have been added to the original discourse, as there is a contradiction between the positive use of "flesh" in vv. 51c-58 and the negative use of it in v. 63. This is not called for. One must determine *whose flesh* is being spoken of. The flesh of Jesus is the place where the glory of God can be seen (1:14), while the flesh of human beings leads them into superficial judgment (see, as well as 6:63; 7:24 and 8:15).

[29] This is the only mention of "the Twelve" in the Gospel of John. They are an important group of disciples in Mark and Matthew, and "apostles" in Luke, as we have seen. John shows here that he is still in contact with early traditions. This tradition no doubt reaches back to the pre-Easter life of Jesus.

Commentaries on the Gospel of John

The following list of single-volume commentaries on the Gospel of John is not exhaustive. An interested reader could consult any one of them with profit. Bibliographical details for the outstanding two-volume commentary of R. E. Brown and the three-volume commentary of R. Schnackenburg, can be found in the notes of the preceding chapters.

Barrett, C. K. *The Gospel According to St John*. 2d ed. London: SPCK, 1978.

Beasley-Murray, *John*. 2d ed. Word Biblical Commentary 36; Nashville: Nelson, 1999.

Brodie, T. L. *The Gospel According to John. A Literary and Theological Commentary*. New York/Oxford: Oxford University Press, 1993.

Bruce, F. F. *The Gospel of John*. Basingstoke: Pickering & Inglis, 1983.

Carson, D. A. *The Gospel According to John*. Grand Rapids: Eerdmans, 1991.

Culpepper, R. A. *The Gospel and Letters of John*. Interpreting Biblical Texts. Nashville: Abingdon, 1998.

Hoskyns, E. C. *The Fourth Gospel*. Edited by F. N. Davey. London: Faber & Faber, 1948.

Kysar, R. *John*. Augsburg Commentary on the New Testament. Minneapolis: Augsburg, 1986.

Lightfoot, R. H. *St. John's Gospel. A Commentary*. Oxford: Clarendon Press, 1956.

Lindars, B. *The Gospel of John*. New Century Bible. London: Oliphants, 1972.

Marsh, J. *Saint John*. The Pelican New Testament Commentaries. Harmondsworth: Penguin Books, 1968.

Moloney, F. J. *The Gospel of John*. Sacra Pagina 4; Collegeville: The Liturgical Press, 1998.

Sloyan, G. *John*. Interpretation. Atlanta: John Knox Press, 1988.

Smith, D. M. *John*. Abingdon New Testament Commentaries. Nashville: Abingdon, 1999.

Stibbe, M. W. G. *John*. Readings: A New Bible Commentary. Sheffield: JSOT Press, 1993.

Talbert, C. H. *Reading John. A Literary and Theological Commentary on the Fourth Gospel and the Johannine Epistles*. New York: Crossroad, 1992.

PART VI

The Gospels Today

CHAPTER TEN

Modern and Contemporary
Gospel Criticism

This introduction to the Gospels illustrates modern and contemporary methods of reading and interpreting the four Gospels. In conclusion, readers may find useful a presentation of these methods. Four major moments in modern and contemporary Gospel study are described: the earliest stage (source criticism), the second moment that led to the study of the literary forms and their history (form criticism), the turn toward an interest in the theological motivation of each Evangelist as he redacted the traditions to articulate a theological point of view (redaction criticism), and the contemporary interest in the narrative as such (narrative criticism).

This section also traces the three quests for the historical Jesus. It concludes with an examination of the relationship between the person of Jesus and the Christian disciple in the light of an understanding of Jesus as the Son of God and the Son of Man.

Chapter 10
summary

THIS INTRODUCTION TO THE GOSPELS, and the chapters dealing with Mark, Matthew, Luke and John, illustrate modern and contemporary methods of reading and interpreting the four Gospels. As a conclusion to this book, readers may find useful a presentation of these methods. Although the chapters of the book have focused on the message of each Gospel, references have been made throughout to "earlier traditions." Thus, I will also discuss the so-called "three quests" for the historical Jesus that have accompanied the last 150 years of critical interest in Mark, Matthew, Luke and John. My conclusion, and the conclusion to the book as a whole, will take the form of a biblical and theological meditation on the importance of the human Jesus for a better understanding of the Christian life.

The Search for History

The fifteenth and sixteenth-century Renaissance led to a rebirth of interest in the great achievements of the classical world. This led to a Reformation of the European Church in the sixteenth-century, and the birth of a new spirit of freedom and confidence in the limitless capacity of the human mind. The philosophical systems of the seventeenth-century generated a period across the seventeenth and eighteenth-centuries that celebrated this new spirit of freedom, known as "the Age of the Enlightenment." Hand in hand with serious, inquiring minds and exciting scientific experimentation that produced some spectacular inventions, much European culture came to accept that claims to truth had to withstand the critique of the human mind. Unless an affirmation could be shown to be true by means of experimentation and the strict application of logical principles, then it should be regarded as belonging to the uncertain and the improvable. Such uncertain affirmations were increasingly regarded as irrelevant for the progress of humanity. Many positive aspects of contemporary culture flow from this period: humanitarian concerns, toleration of differences, better legal systems and their administration, education, social welfare, critical scholarship in all areas of learning, and the rapid development of serious and objective scientific experimentation. However, there were also some damaging results, especially the overestimation of the intellect, and the underestimation of that which could not be proved as true by rational processes. Religions based on a book that received its authority from an improvable affirmation that it was divinely inspired were soon to come under fire.

This new spirit led to a movement, beginning among the so-called English Deists (e.g., Lord Herbert of Cherbury, John Toland and Matthew Tindal), and spreading to France (e.g., Voltaire, Jean Jacques Rousseau and Denis Diderot), Germany (e.g., King Frederick II and Gotthold Lessing), and the United States (e.g., Benjamin Franklin and Thomas Jefferson). Such influential figures were either skeptical of a biblically revealed religion, or condemned it completely. A critical generation found unacceptable the many imaginative narratives of the Bible, the lack of obvious logical sequences, especially in narratives, the repetitions, and especially many of the doctrines and ethical principles that flowed from a literal reading of the Bible. In general, they did not reject the need for some form of religion. Nevertheless, the increasing disrespect for and lack of interest in traditional religion, regarded as irrelevant by some today, have their roots in nineteenth century skepticism. It was motivated by a desire to locate all worthwhile knowledge in the identifiable principles that directed nature and were articulated according to the principles of human reason.

There is a close connection between this post-Enlightenment age and the birth of what was called, at that time, "higher criticism," and has since come to be known as historical-critical biblical scholarship. The Christian Religion, especially as it was understood and practiced in the Protestant traditions in Germany at that time, was deeply dependent upon the Bible. The catch phrase of Martin Luther, *sola Scriptura* (Scripture alone), was taken very seriously. The attack upon the religious value of the Bible had to be challenged; an enduring sense of the Bible as a revealed Word of God, despite its obvious oddities, had to be pursued. Thus, it needs to be kept in mind, the critical approach to the Bible, which led to so much turmoil in nineteenth-century Europe, was born from a desire *to defend the biblical basis of the Christian Religion.* To do so, the tools of the post-Enlightenment had to be taken up, and applied to the Bible. A closer analysis of the relationships between the various biblical texts (source criticism), a deeper study of the original languages, and the worlds that lie behind the Bible (historical criticism) and eventually, a comparative study of the religion of the Bible and the religions of other Ancient Near Eastern cultures (history of religions), were the major tools of the first century of "higher criticism." Many of the early scholars fell away from mainstream religious traditions and practice as they exposed the biblical text to severe historical criticism. Aggressively anti-Christian scholars joined the fray, and the Christian Churches and their beliefs were subjected to severe rationalist criticism, much to the dismay, fear and pain of religious leaders and believers.[1] But this should not distract us from recognizing the Christian motivation that led to the desire among many of the original historical critics to defend the biblical basis of the European religious traditions.

Source Criticism

An important feature of burgeoning critical biblical scholarship during the nineteenth-century was an attempt to show that the books of the Bible did not drop out of the skies, directly handed to an author by God, or by some inspiring angel. They may have been the Word of God, but they were products of human experiences, and were eventually written down in the words of men and women.[2] Thus, it became increasingly clear that the books had their "sources." This was most obvious in the first five books of the Old Testament: the Pentateuch of Genesis, Exodus, Leviticus, Numbers and Deuteronomy. This collection of books was regarded by Israel, and subsequently by Christianity as writings left by Moses. Even before the rise of critical biblical scholarship, scholars had searched for the different popular traditions lying behind this collection of authoritative texts. They were seen as a blend of narratives (some of them telling the same story twice, but in different ways [most famously, the account of the creation in seven days Gen 1:1-2:4, and the second, more imaginative account of Gen 2:5-3:24, highlighted by the creation of Adam and Eve and the beginning of sin]), folk-tales, liturgical settings (Jewish Feasts), laws, genealogies, exhortations to faithfulness, and much other material. Scholars of the Old Testament had long questioned the possibility that Moses had personally written all five books, and entirely from his own experience.

The same questions were simultaneously asked of the Gospels by an emerging group of New Testament scholars. One of the problems generated by the Gospels of Matthew, Mark and Luke was the acceptable repetition of the same stories (they were, after all, about the same man), but the unacceptable differences found in the three accounts of the same episode. For example, at Caesarea Philippi, did the encounter between Jesus and Peter run as it was reported in Matt 16:16-20, with Peter's complete understanding of Jesus' person, followed by Jesus' blessing of Peter before his warning not to speak of his Messianic status? Or was it a briefer recognition on the part of Peter that Jesus was "the Christ" followed by Jesus' warning not to make this truth known, as is found in Mark 8:27-30? Maybe the encounter happened in an unnamed place, after Jesus had prayed alone, where Peter simply answers Jesus' question about their understanding of his identity with the words: "You are the Christ of God," as Luke reports (Luke 9:18-20). Did Jesus deliver the Beatitudes to his disciples, on a mountain (Matt 5:1-11), or did he speak them to a large crowd, including Gentiles, on a level place, after he had come down from a mountain where he had chosen the Twelve Apostles (Luke 6:12-26)? Close analysis of the Gospels of Matthew, Mark and Luke soon showed that these issues emerged in almost every episode reported by all three (Matthew-Mark-Luke), or by any two of the Evangelists (Mark-Matthew, Mark-Luke, material common to Matthew and Luke, generally called "Q").[3] As these questions were being asked about Mark, Matthew and Luke, the uniqueness of the Gospel of John became more obvious, and many scholars of this period (and since) expressed deep doubt about the historicity of the Johannine narratives.[4]

Nineteenth-century post-Enlightenment criticism wanted to know "what had actually happened" so that the "real Jesus" could be identified. The best way to discover that information was to trace the "source" of the three Synoptic Gospels. Thus, early Gospel criticism developed what came to be known as "source criticism." It did not take long to decide that Mark, the shortest, and least used of the Gospels, was the major source for Matthew and Luke. Ongoing work on the three Synoptic Gospels continues to lead most contemporary scholars to agree with the majority position from the nineteenth-century: Mark was the first of all the Gospels.

However, this general agreement (it was not universal, nor is it today) that Mark was the major "source" for all the Gospels, led to a further understandable development in the study of the Gospels. We will return to this question in more detail in our later overview of "the search for Jesus." But the decision that Mark was the first of the Gospels, and thus the most "historical," generated widespread reflection upon the life and teaching of Jesus of Nazareth. For fifty years scholars developed a series of "lives of Jesus" on the basis of Markan priority. But it was this "historical" reading of Mark as the clearest evidence for the life of Jesus that led to the demise of the first stage of critical Gospel study. Early in the twentieth century Wilhelm Wrede, in a deeply flawed but nevertheless important and passionate study, showed that Mark was not primarily interested in telling the story of Jesus "as it actually happened." Wrede was the first to point out that Mark developed a *theology* of Jesus as Messiah and Son of God. Indeed, Wrede called it a "dogma." Shortly after Wrede's work appeared, Albert Schweizer produced a remarkable survey of nineteenth century "lives of Jesus," proving conclusively that this search for Jesus, on the basis of the Gospel of Mark as a primary "source," led the search for Jesus into a blind alley where it found a "Jesus of history" that was often a mirror image of the searcher.[5] The contributions of these two giants in the history of the study of the Gospels will be considered in more detail in the section devoted to the search for Jesus,[6] but the work of Wrede and Schweizer showed that a study of the Gospels that limited itself to "sources" was too narrow.[7] It was time to move beyond the question on "sources."

The Search for Religious Parallels

The Form Critics

As biblical scholarship became increasingly obsessed with the rediscovery of historical issues, it lost touch with the beauty and message of the narratives themselves.[8] The problem was accentuated by a turn toward the other religions of the time, and a desire to "classify" the documents of the New Testament, and the constituent parts of those documents, by finding parallels with other religions.[9] Between World War I and World War II, Karl Ludwig Schmidt, Martin Dibelius, and Rudolf Bultmann founded a new approach to the Synoptic Gospels that focused upon the identifiable prehistory of each individual passage in the Gospels.[10] These passages, carefully divided into smaller literary units called "pericopes," were subjected to intense scrutiny, compared with parallel literature from other ancient religions, and classified. The early so-called "form critics" had different names for the various "forms" of pericopes in the Gospels and identified parallel "forms" in the literatures of other contemporary religions and cultures. A certain common form and structure could be found in miracle stories, conflict stories, legends, pronouncement stories, parables, and so on. Once each passage had been "classified" according to its literary form, the historical quest of the source critics was applied. Did this passage come from a "setting in the life of Jesus" (*Sitz im leben Jesu*) or from a setting in the emerging Christian Church, as it developed its founding narratives (*Sitz im Leben der Kirche*: "setting in the life of the Church")?

Over a period of some fifty years, Mark had been regarded as the first and most important *historian* to provide a framework for the life of Jesus. Further reflection upon this now crucial text led to the conclusion that Mark was an author who devoted little attention to history. The form critics took the process one step further, and came to regard him as an editor who assembled pieces of material that came from the historical Jesus (very little) and from the creativity of the early Church (a great deal). As Rudolf Bultmann commented in 1921:

> In Mark we can still see clearly, and most easily in comparison with Luke, that the most ancient tradition consisted of individual sections, and that the connecting together is secondary. ... Mark is not sufficiently master of his material to be able to venture on a systematic construction himself.[11]

Not only had the historian *par excellence* been reduced to an editor, but — if Bultmann's assessment were correct — to a rather poor editor!

However, something of lasting value emerged over those years, hand in hand with shifts of direction in the study of the Gospels. The work of the source critics and their opponents eventually led to an appreciation of the theological creativity of the Gospels. The form critics showed that, as authors, the Evangelists received material from prior traditions and shaped it into a story of Jesus. The form critics, however, have not won the day in the assessment of Mark (or any of the Gospels) as "not sufficiently master of his material to be able to venture on a systematic construction himself."[12] While Wrede and Schweizer destroyed any suggestion that the Gospels provided reliable history, they also insisted that the writing of the Gospels was not driven by a desire to write history, but by a desire to communicate a theological point of view.

But even here we must be wary. The post-Enlightenment era assessed good or bad history by judging, according to its own criteria, whether or not the historian under scrutiny reported the past "exactly as it had happened." This is not the only responsibility of a historian. Modern historiography insists that good history is *at least as concerned* to report not only a well-researched order of events, but also to provide some interpretation of *what these events meant*.[13] It had been established that Mark was primarily interested in theology, not a correct sequence of events that might serve as a "framework" for the rediscovery of the life of

Jesus. But perhaps the Evangelists, in their compilations of narratives shot through with a theological agenda, did make an honest attempt to pass on to later generations *what the events of the life, teaching, death and resurrection of Jesus meant*. My earlier chapters indicate that I have learnt much from the source critics and the form critics. The Gospels are not primarily history books. The Evangelists do gather from their sources and assemble them in a way that suits their purposes. But what are those purposes?

The Search for Theologians

After the Second World War (1939-1945) two major moments signaled the deepening scholarly appreciation of the Gospels as works of theology. In a first moment, several scholars, who depended upon the work of the form critics and accepted that Mark, Matthew, Luke and even John were editors of sources, began to ask why each author edited sources to produce the works that became known as the Gospels of Mark, Matthew, Luke and John, and eventually accepted as Sacred Scripture in the Christian tradition. This approach to the Gospels has been given the name "redaction criticism."[14] Redaction criticism was generated by asking the logical question left unanswered by the form critics: they may have been editors, but what was the principle driving their editorial work? In the last decades of the twentieth-century, and into the twenty-first-century, a second major development has taken place within Gospel criticism. The Evangelists consciously chose to adopt the practice of writing *narratives*. Increasingly, Mark, Matthew, Luke and John are being appreciated as more than editors; they are theologically motivated storytellers. This approach to the Gospels has been called "narrative criticism."[15] As we have seen in our study of the Gospels of Mark (chapters 2-3), Matthew (chapters 4-5), Luke (chapters 6-7) and John (chapters 8-9) the Evangelists are nowadays understood as creative theologians. Each "history" of Jesus is not *primarily* concerned with "what actually happened" during the life of Jesus and at his death and resurrection, but with what these words and events meant and still mean.

Redaction Criticism
The period across the 1950's and 1960's was marked by an increasing number of scholars who accepted the conclusions of the form critics. Each Evangelist received many traditions, oral and written, and acted

as an editor to assemble our present Gospels. But, they began to insist, there were further questions to be asked of the activity of the Evangelist. Once Markan priority was established as a basic working hypothesis, it was relatively easy for scholars to follow how Matthew or Luke had taken words of Jesus, or an account from the life of Jesus they found in Mark, and adapted them for their own ends. The acceptance of a common source called "Q" also enabled them to trace the different use of the same material that is common to Matthew and Luke, even though not found in Mark. The project has been well described by Hans Conzelmann, whose work on the theology of the Gospel of Luke is widely regarded as a founding study in the development of redaction criticism:

> Our aim is to elucidate Luke's work in its present form, not to enquire into possible sources or into the historical facts which provided the material. A variety of sources does not necessarily imply a similar variety in the thought and composition of the author. *How did it come about that he brought together these particular materials?* Was he able to imprint on them his own views? It is here that the analysis of the sources renders the *necessary service* of helping to distinguish *what comes from the source and what belongs to the author.*[16]

The stressed passages highlight Conzelmann's programmatic statement, originally published in German in 1957, for all subsequent redaction critics. The form critics had determined that the authors of the Gospels worked with sources, and worked largely as editors. The redaction critics asked further: "How did it come about that he brought together these particular materials?" It must be taken for granted that Mark, Matthew, Luke and John had a great deal of material, some oral, some written, some perhaps embedded in the community's Christian rituals (e.g., hymns, prayers) and each Evangelist *made a selection* from these sources (see John 20:30, where the Evangelist admits that he has selected from among the "many signs"). What were the overarching literary and theological agendas that drove such a selection? This important question, however, depended upon the work of the form critics. The redaction critics did not ignore the sources that had been uncovered by the form critics, but "the analysis renders the *necessary service* of helping to distinguish what comes from the source from what belongs to the author." The methods and the conclusions of the form critics were essential for the redaction critical approach to the Gospels.

The principles of redaction criticism are easier to apply to Matthew and Luke than to Mark and John. The critic takes it for granted that Matthew and Luke had Mark and probably Q (a common source, now lost to us, but available to Matthew and Luke) in front of them.[17] It was easy, especially with the aid of a *Synopsis*, to see the alterations made to their sources. This was not possible with Mark, as we have no literary text, upon which Mark might depend, that was in existence prior to Mark. The same can be said of the Gospel of John, although some would still argue that John knew and even used Mark, Luke, or even all three Synoptic Gospels. The absence of an obvious literary source that may have been "redacted" by Mark and John, however, has not stopped the redaction critics. Starting from the *correct insight* that both Mark and John were primarily theologians and not historians, the critics have developed methods to determine what passages in these two Gospels came to them from prior traditions. Although not as precise as tracing the use that Matthew and Luke make of Mark and Q, a careful interpreter can sense when Mark or John is working with prior traditions.

Some examples of redaction critical work will serve to indicate the value of this important approach to Gospel texts. Let us look at some familiar passages, some of which we have already discussed. Peter's confession of faith at Caesarea Philippi is a celebrated passage, well known – generally in the words found in Matthew – by all Christian readers of the Gospels. But the earliest report of this confession is found in Mark 8:27-33. After Jesus' question, "Who do people say that I am?" (v. 27), he asks the disciples, "But who do you say that I am?" (v. 29a). Peter replies: "You are the Christ" (v. 29b). Jesus commands his disciples to say nothing to anyone about this (v. 30), and moves on to reveal himself to the disciples as the suffering Son of Man (v. 31), a revelation that Peter will not accept (v. 32). Peter is rebuked, called "Satan," and told to go to his correct place, following Jesus: "Get behind me" (v. 33). For Mark, this passage marks a turning point in his story. For the first time in the Gospel, Jesus is recognized as "the Christ." However, there is a danger that this might be misunderstood. It must be filled out by Jesus' prophecy of his forthcoming suffering, death and resurrection. The Messiah, for Mark, is also the suffering Son of Man who will be finally vindicated by the action of God in the resurrection.

Matthew and Luke have the Markan account of this episode before them as they write their Gospels. Matthew develops it into a major statement about Jesus and about Peter (Matt 16:13-23). At Caesarea

Philippi, Jesus asks who people think the Son of Man is, and after the response, like Mark, asks who the disciples think he is (vv. 13-15). Peter replies with his well-known words: "You are the Christ, the Son of the living God" (v. 16). Jesus praises this superb confession of faith as having come to Peter through heavenly inspiration. On the basis of this confession, Peter is commissioned as the rock upon which the Church will be built, and he is given authority to teach and interpret within the community. None of this is in Mark.[18] But Matthew returns to Mark, has Jesus tell of his forthcoming death, and Peter refuses to accept this prophecy. He is called both a stumbling block to Jesus on his path, and Satan (vv. 22-23). Peter is a central figure in the Gospel of Matthew. He articulates the faith of the Church, and is to be seen, already in the story of Jesus, as the bedrock upon which the Church is built. Over against the Jewish interpreters and leaders in the synagogue, the Matthean community also has someone who will authoritatively interpret the Scriptures for them. However, as in all the Gospels, Peter is not perfect. He still makes mistakes. The portrait of Peter in the Gospel of Matthew is an elegant balance of a portrait of a leader who is courageous and generous. He sometimes gets everything right, and at other times he fails, especially in his denials of Jesus. The Church is built upon a rock, and it has an authoritative interpreter. But sinfulness is always possible.

Luke deals with this episode very briefly (Luke 9:18-22). He does not locate the passage at Caesarea Philippi. At this stage of the Gospel, Luke is preparing the disciples for the journey to Jerusalem. People who have been well instructed by the events of 9:1-50 must make the journey. Who is it they are following to Jerusalem? As Jesus is praying alone, the disciples approach, and Jesus asks the questions about the people and then the opinion of the disciples (vv. 18-20a). Peter answers: "The Christ of God." For the Lukan understanding of Jesus, this is a fine confession. Jesus is the Christ, but the Christ who corresponds to God's design. The episode ends there, as there is no correction of Peter or passion prediction. Jesus goes on to speak about the cost of "following" him (vv. 23-27), and reveals himself on the mountain in the transfiguration, talking to Moses and Elijah about the "exodus" that he would accomplish in Jerusalem (vv. 28-36).

Looking back to our earlier studies of Mark, Matthew and Luke,[19] one can see that the use of this single episode from the life of Jesus has been shaped by each Evangelist to respond better to the overall Christological and theological message of the Gospel. Following the "redaction" of this single passage across Mark, Matthew and Luke, we can trace the creativity of each Evangelist. Our earlier reflection on the Matthean and the Lukan use of Q material for their *different* settings and interpretations of Jesus' sermon on the mountain/plain, shows how these two Evangelists have "redacted" Q in their own way.[20]   Similarly, our study of John 6 looked at the bread miracle, a journey in a boat and a confession of faith. These episodes, in exactly this sequence, are found in Mark (8:1-30) and Matthew (15:32-16:23). John was not *using* the Synoptic Gospels, but he was no doubt shaping received tradition in order to communicate his understanding of Jesus as the perfection of all God had done for Israel at the Passover.[21]   The work of the redaction critics, because of the difficulties in determining sources objectively and with precision, must be treated with respect, but care. Despite these difficulties, they have uncovered a clearer understanding of the theological development of the early Christian Church, as it is reflected in the Gospels.

Narrative Criticism

Contemporary narrative criticism has its roots in the study of narrative literature in general. Rather than trace various sources, and see how each storyteller has arranged these sources to develop a particular point of view, narrative criticism insists that the story must be understood as a whole. An author writes a narrative from beginning to end, and it must be approached as a *unified utterance*. The narrative critics continue the process of the redaction critics as they look for an author's point of view, but the narrative critics' main concentration is upon the world in the text. They attempt to show how the story has been designed and told in order to influence the world in front of the text. Biblical scholarship has gradually come to appreciate more fully that there are more than two "worlds" involved in the interpretation of an ancient text. Historical-critical scholarship has devoted almost 200 years to the rediscovery of the *world behind the text*, so that no contemporary agenda might be imposed upon the *world in the text*. Redaction critics focused more intensely upon the world *in the text*. Contemporary narrative critics are devoting more attention to the world *in front of the text* as there is now a greater interest in approaching each single document, however limited and flawed it might be, as a work of art. [22]

Behind any "story" there is a *real author* who has a definite person or group of people in mind as he or she speaks or writes. Thus, there is an intended *real reader* for whom the story was originally written. Neither of these figures can be found *in* the story itself. One produces it and the other takes it in hand to read it, or listens to it. The Gospels must be regarded as four such writings, but they are something more. The real author of each Gospel story, whoever he might have been, is long since dead, as are the original recipients of the book. However, the Gospels still have a widespread readership. There is something about this book that has generated interested readers for almost 2000 years, however little we may know of the original authors and readers.

Although the real author and the real reader(s) do not play an active role in the events of any narrative, they leave their traces. Narratives have deliberately contrived plots and characters that interact throughout the story along a plotted time line, through a sequence of events. An author devises rhetorical features to hold plot and character together so that the reader will not miss the author's point of view. These rhetorical features are *in* the narrative. One can broadly claim that the communication between a real author and a real reader who are *outside* the text takes place through elements that can be found *inside* the text. The details of the concrete situations of the original real author and the original real reader(s) may be obscure. We know little or nothing about the "historical Mark, Matthew, Luke or John," the original authors of the Gospels (the real authors). We can only speculate, in the light of the evidence of the Gospels themselves, on the concrete situation of the people for whom these texts were originally written (the real readers). Nevertheless, *we have the text*, and much can be gleaned from it. This reflects everyone's reading experience. The following example of a possible "reading experience" may clarify what I mean by the above theory.

A lost letter picked up by a disinterested third party quickly tells the reader something of the person writing the letter. The rhetoric of the letter also reveals something of the author's understanding of and approach to the reader. The person who has found the letter knows neither the real author nor the original intended reader, but the real reader — the person who picked up the letter from the pavement — is able to identify the communication attempted by the letter. The person who found the letter traces an author "implied" and a reader "implied" by the letter. Indeed, a very beautiful letter may even move the "eavesdropper." When that happens, mutuality is established between the reader "implied" by the letter and the real reader of the letter. One does not have to be part of the original communication process between the original writer of the letter and its original reader to be moved and inspired by the power of the emotions expressed by the letter. The literary form of a letter is different from the sometimes complex literary shape of a narrative, especially one (like the Gospels) that was written almost 2000 years ago. However, the process of communication between an author and a reader takes place in both. Contemporary narrative approaches to the Gospels attempt to enter into the process of communication between an author and a reader whom we do not know, and who are long since dead, so that the contemporary reader might be moved and inspired by the passionate convictions of the author.

Narrative critics focus upon the literary features found in the Gospel narratives. Attention is devoted to the literary shape of each section of the story; the way each section follows logically from what went before and leads directly into what follows; the roles of the various characters in the story; the passing of time; unresolved puzzles which emerge, forcing the reader to look further into the narrative to tie these puzzles together; the consistency of the underlying point of view of an author who has shaped and told a story of the life of Jesus. Like the reader who "eavesdropped" on the letter found on the pavement, and was moved by the sincerity and power of the emotions communicated by the letter, we are "eavesdropping" on an ancient story of Jesus as we read a Gospel. "Eavesdropping" on this particular story, however, has been going on for a long time, and it has served as an inspiration for Christians from all walks of life for almost 2000 years.

Just as we cannot be certain of the identity and the hopes of the original author, nor do we have concrete evidence of the response of the original readers. Nevertheless, the ongoing existence of the Gospels demonstrates that they were received, treasured, and passed on. Already in the second-century, later generations of Christians had, in their own turn, both received them and honored them. *Within the narrative* there is a reader addressed by an author, as there was an identifiable reader implied by the letter described above.[23] As the narrative unfolds, the reader is gradually provided with information and experiences. This reader is shaped by the desires of the author and emerges as the text unfolds. The literary critic Stanley Fish has described the experience of the reader as follows:

The basis of the method is a consideration of the *temporal* flow of the reading experience, and it is assumed that the reader responds in terms of that flow and not to the whole utterance. That is, in an utterance of any length, there is a point at which the reader has taken in only the first word, and then the second, and then the third, and so on, and the report of what happens to the reader is always a report of what happened *to that point.*[24]

As we have seen in the readings of Mark, Matthew, Luke and John, as each page of a Gospel is opened, more is learnt about Jesus, his activity, his teaching, his disciples, his reception and his rejection. At times he utters words that point to the future, for example in his predictions of his passion and resurrection and his foretelling the betrayal of Judas and the denials of Peter. These forward looking words and prophecies add tension to the narrative, as one is urged to read further into the story to see these promises resolved. Whether they are resolved, and how they are resolved, makes for a satisfactory reading experience. Narrative texts keep promising the great prize of understanding – later.[25] There is still more to learn from those parts of the story that lie ahead.

But the Gospels belong to our texts of Sacred Scripture. Because of this, it is impossible that the reader in a Christian Gospel has no knowledge or experience of the story of Jesus of Nazareth and Christian life and its practices. Christian faith can be born from these stories, and is nourished by them. The authors of the Gospels take it for granted that the reader knows Greek, and also understands Jewish titles of honor that are applied to Jesus, especially Son of God, the Christ and the Son of Man. Allusions to the celebration of the Lord's Supper in the bread miracles and at the meal on the night before he died show that the original readers were already practicing this ritual. In the Gospel of John, the reader also picks up allusions to baptism at John 3:3-5, 13:21-30 and 19:34.

Above all, however, the readers of the Gospels lived in a believing community, based upon a shared understanding of the saving significance of the death and resurrection of Jesus. Much more than knowledge of the Greek of the Gospel texts is presupposed of its reader. The reader in the stories of the Gospels may be credited with a basic knowledge of the story of Jesus. But *the way it is told* by Mark, Matthew, Luke and John can bring surprises. For example, the reader of the Gospel of Mark knows that Jesus died on a cross, and Mark insists that this death is both a cruel and humiliating descent into abandon (see Mark 15:33-37).

Nevertheless, the establishment of Jesus as Messiah and Son of God, the rejected corner stone, upon whom a new temple of God will be built (see Mark 12:10-11; 14:58; 15:29-30, 37-38), takes place at the Cross. As we have seen, the reader of the Gospel of Luke will learn of an innocent, forgiving Christ and Son of God, while for John the crucifixion is the moment when Jesus is glorified, lifted up on the Cross (see John 3:14; 8:28; 12:32), bringing to perfection the task that the Father had given him (see 19:30).

But we must recognize that every word of the Gospel is historically and culturally conditioned. The fact that it is written in *koiné* Greek is clear evidence of this truth. There is inevitably something "strange" and "foreign" about the biblical text which demands that we wrestle with it. First century history and culture must play a part in Gospel interpretation. The Gospels, like all biblical texts handed down to us by Jewish and Christian tradition, is a foreign text when read in translation in our present cultural context. The worlds that produced the Gospels are an important point of reference in following the interplay between author and reader in the text. Adela Yarbro Collins has rightly insisted that we:

> [G]ive more weight to the original historical context of the text. This context cannot and should not totally determine all subsequent meaning and use of the text. But if ... all meaning is context bound, the original context and meaning have a certain normative character. I suggest that biblical theologians are not only mediators between genres. They are also mediators between historical periods. ... Whatever tension there may be between literary- and historical-critical methods, the two approaches are complementary.[26]

The use of narrative criticism for Gospel interpretation must devote attention to *the world behind the text*, to understand its distance from our world and our concerns. A narrative approach should also ask: how does the reader *in the text* who emerges as this ancient story of Jesus unfolds speak to the knowledge and experience of the twenty-first century Christian reader *of the text*? There is, of course, a context that unites the original and all subsequent readers of the Gospels: a context generated by Christian faith. Both the original readers and the contemporary readers believe that Jesus is the Christ, the Son of God, the Son of David, the *Logos* of God (see Mark 1:1; Matt 1:1; Luke 1-2; John 1:1-18).

The secret of the lasting value of a narrative lies in the mutuality that is created between the implied reader *in the text* and the real reader *of the text*, and the common context of Christian belief helps this mutuality. A story that tells of Jesus the Christ, the Son of God, Son of David and *Logos* should appeal to Christians. Nevertheless, there are libraries of Christian books that have not! What is it in the Gospels that has generated their ongoing readership? There must be an understanding and respect for the world behind the text, which shaped the reader *in the text*, but there is more. When I read a good novel for the first time, I become the implied reader. I become part of the story, caught in its characters, events, time and places as the pages turn. This is the case with any good book, but in a classic there is an even deeper relationship between the reader in the text and the reader of the text. A classic is not simply a narrative that catches my imagination during my reading, only to be forgotten as I pass on to my next activity. A classic generates a deeper mutuality between the implied reader *in the text* and the real reader *of the text.* As David Tracy has said: "The classic text's real disclosure is its claim to attention on the ground that an event of understanding proper to finite human beings has here found expression."[27] As Honoré de Balzac's narrator informs the reader at the beginning of *Père Goriot*: "You may be certain that this drama is neither fiction nor romance. *All is true*, so true that everyone can recognise the elements of the tragedy in his own household, in his own heart perhaps."[28] For Balzac, the issue was human tragedy, but there are many other profound expressions of experience and belief, "events of understanding proper to finite human beings," that can be communicated by means of classical narrative writing.

We can claim that the Gospels are Christian classics. As we continue to read them after nearly two thousand years of reading, in a variety of contexts, we can be sure that there has been mutuality between the Gospel stories and their myriads of real readers. The unfolding narrative of the Gospels raises problems the reader will solve through the ongoing reading of the story of Jesus. Did these solutions speak to the members of the early Christian communities, the original intended readers of Mark, Matthew, Luke and John? They were part of the world of the narrative of the Gospels in a way that the contemporary real reader can never be. They read Greek, or at least understood it as it was read; they caught the subtleties of references to messianic claims, their celebration of the Lord's Supper and the ironies found across the story, especially in the Passion Narrative. None of this can be taken for granted for many contemporary readers of the Gospels. Do the questions raised and the solutions offered by the Gospel stories still speak to real readers at the beginning of the third millennium? Is this text a classic? Does its ongoing claim to a readership rest upon "the ground that an event of understanding proper to human beings has here found expression" (Tracy)? One hopes that two thousand years of reading the Gospels, and perhaps the guidance offered by this introduction to the four Gospels suggests a positive answer to these questions.

The Search for Jesus

We have considered four major moments in modern and contemporary Gospel study: the earliest stage (source criticism), the second moment that led to the study of the literary forms and their history (form criticism), the turn toward an interest in the theological motivation of each Evangelist as he *redacted* the traditions to articulate a theological point of view (redaction criticism), and the contemporary interest in the narrative as such (narrative criticism).[29] In this section, dealing with the search for Jesus, we must look back across the history of Gospel study traced to this point. The "first quest for the historical Jesus" had its beginnings in the widespread (but not universal) conviction, in the second half of the nineteenth century, that Mark was the earliest and simplest of all the Gospels. Once the historical issue was resolved, scholars suggested they were then in a position to claim a bedrock account of the life of Jesus. The authentic "source" for all subsequent "lives of Jesus," including those of Matthew, Luke and (to a lesser extent) John had been found. The source critics, especially (but not only) H. J. Holtzmann, argued that the Gospel of Mark, the most primitive of all the Gospels, took us back to a reliable historical "framework" for the life of Jesus. On the basis of the Gospel of Mark, one could be certain that Jesus' life-story evolved as follows: Jesus' messianic consciousness developed over a period of preaching in Galilee, and reached its high point at Caesarea Philippi. There he made known to his followers his belief that he was the expected Jewish Messiah. His journey to Jerusalem and his end there were the result of the Jewish leadership's rejection of his claim.[30] Thus, it could be concluded that the Evangelist Mark, on the basis of the Gospel that bears his name, was the first to write *a history of Jesus*. Once that was established, so-called "lives of Jesus" proliferated.

This conclusion was systematically demolished by two epoch-making studies that we have already mentioned in our consideration of the stage of critical Gospel scholarship that searched out "sources."[31] In *The Messianic Secret* Wilhelm Wrede made clear that Mark was, *above all* a theologian,[32] and Albert Schweitzer's *The Quest of the Historical Jesus* reviewed the "lives of Jesus" to expose the fundamental problem of all nineteenth century interpretation. Each "life of Jesus," so important to nineteenth-century criticism, reflected more the mind, heart and setting of the scholar than a first-century Palestinian Jew. In his own inimitable prose (even in translation) Schweitzer describes the accepted Christian understanding of the person of Jesus, Messiah and Savior, as follows:

> The Jesus of Nazareth who came forth publicly as the Messiah, who preached the ethic of the kingdom of God, who founded the kingdom of heaven on earth, and died to give His work its final consecration, *never existed.* He is a figure designed by rationalism, endowed with life by liberalism, and clothed by modern theology in a historical garb.[33]

In the end, Schweitzer was iconoclastic when it came to the development of his own portrait of Jesus. He viewed the Gospels as prejudiced sources, most unreliable as historical documents. For Schweitzer, the preaching of the kingdom of God marked Jesus out as a figure who preached the imminent end of time. As such, as a historical character, he had to be judged a failure. Jesus believed, taught and died because he understood his God-ordained mission as the proclamation of the end of time. The failure of the eschatological hopes of the historical Jesus, however, did not render Christianity irrelevant. It was overcome in the growing Christian Church and its understanding and preaching of Jesus. The four gospels and the rapid development of a Christian people and culture reinterpreted his person and message. Thus, largely as the result of the work of Wrede and Schweitzer, the use of the Gospels, and especially the most primitive Gospel, Mark, as sources to reconstruct history was buried, and along with that, the "first quest" came to an end.

The emergence of form criticism took it for granted that it was impossible to rediscover anything of the Jesus of history. The elements that had been gathered together by (rather clumsy?) editors had never intended to portray Jesus as he actually lived, taught and died. But in the middle of the twentieth century, students of the father of form criticism, Rudolph Bultmann, raised the question of Jesus once again. As the redaction critics began to trace the theological tendencies of each of the Gospel narratives, they asked: what was behind the development of the traditions used by the Evangelists to develop their narrative? Equally important was their further question: what inspired these early Christian authors to develop their subtle theological combination of pre-existent traditions? These questions led Günther Bornkamm and Ernst Käsemann to re-open the question of the Jesus of history. The so-called "second quest" for the historical Jesus was born.[34] These scholars, and the others who joined this quest, regarded the task of recovering something of the story of the man, Jesus of Nazareth, and his impact on his contemporaries, as a necessary element in the study of the Gospels. To ignore this historical figure, the person behind all Gospel traditions, was regarded as dishonest. However, they had learnt from Schweitzer and Bultmann that there could be no romantic return to the earlier quest, where the Jesus produced by the scholar was often a mirror image of the scholar! Objective criteria that could be applied to the narratives had to be established.

Most important was what has come to be known as the *criterion of dissimilarity*. The words and deeds of Jesus, as reported in the Gospels, that were dissimilar from the Judaism of Jesus' time, and also dissimilar from the teachings of emerging Christianity could be regarded as certainly coming from Jesus. Other supporting criteria emerged: if the same words and deeds were found across a number of different sources (for example: Mark, M, L, Q and John), they most likely reached back to Jesus. This came to be known as the *criterion of multiple attestation*. Yet another guide was whether one could find the same message, even though expressed in different ways, across many traditions. This is nowadays called the *criterion of coherence*. Recently, a further important criterion has emerged: *the criterion of embarrassment*. Such things as the denials of Peter, the betrayal of Judas, the ignominy of Jesus' insults and suffering must have happened, as no early Christian would invent such embarrassing episodes. Other less decisive, but helpful, techniques were applied to the Gospel texts. For example, the retroversion of Jesus' words into Aramaic, the language of the time of Jesus, may also indicate that it came from Jesus.[35]

These criteria, and others, are used to uncover a body of material that could then be used to develop a portrait of Jesus. This was a very positive step, but the criteria (especially that of dissimilarity) tended to set Jesus apart from everything and everyone. He emerged as someone who had little to do with the Judaism of his time – yet he was a product of that world. He also emerged as someone who had little to do with the teaching of the early Church – yet it found its source and inspiration in him. This "second quest" has never come to a close. The criteria, however, have been subjected to intense criticism, and the ongoing study of Jesus of Nazareth is providing more and more information that helps us come closer to an understanding of the man, Jesus of Nazareth. Studies continue to be published, most of them too technical for the general reader.[36]

A small group of contemporary scholars known as "the Jesus Seminar" claims to have opened a "third quest." The group has meetings, discussions, publications, and various processes (e.g., a system of "voting" for the authenticity of texts and episodes) that decide what is historical and what is not. It disregards some of the central discoveries of the "second quest" as inadmissible (e.g., Jesus' preaching of the kingdom of God, and its eschatological element, anything that smacks of a contact with the world of the divine, etc.). Their work produces a rather colorless, wandering charismatic "wisdom figure." The group has gained notoriety, as its work tends to be iconoclastic, ridiculing the results of scholars who have continued "the second quest." The sometimes startling suggestions about the teaching and the person of Jesus from this Seminar can regularly be found in the pages of the popular press and in television programs. They arouse interest and perplexity for many Christians.[37] Mainstream biblical scholarship, however, disregards their methods and their conclusions. [38] Much of this may sound sophisticated, and some of it is! Yet, as I hope to point out in the following reflection, and in conclusion to this chapter, the figure of Jesus remains crucial for all who claim to be his followers. Reflection upon Jesus can and should enrich the life of the Christian disciple and the Christian Church.

Jesus: Son of God and Son of Man

It is beyond the scope of this book to embark upon a study of the human Jesus whose life, teaching, death and resurrection produced the Christian Church. I must refer my readers elsewhere for my own argument that Jesus understood himself as a "Son of God" in the sense of his being unconditionally open to the will of God, and as "the Son of Man" who was prepared to accept the consequences of such radical obedience.[39] There is more about the historical Jesus that deserves our attention: his preaching in parables, his message concerning the reigning presence of

God as King, his miracles, the "historicity" of the descriptions of his birth, death and resurrection. The discussion of these questions can be found in the work of other fine scholars.[40] For the moment, allow me to close this book with a reflection upon Jesus as a person unconditionally open to God, whom he called Father.[41] Radical obedience gave him a freedom that led him away from himself into a loss of himself in love: an obedient suffering love that led to a cross and, ultimately to the action of God in the resurrection. Jesus did not know or speak of Cross and resurrection, but he was convinced that God, whom he regarded as his Father, would have the final word. History has told us that this "last word" was resurrection.[42] If Christian discipleship is an *imitatio Christi* believers are asked to "walk behind Jesus of Nazareth" (see Mark 1:16-20) or, as Paul would put it, "to put on Christ" (see Gal 3:27-28; Col 3:10). Jesus is the first-born from the dead and the slavery that sin and the desire to control the world have brought (see 1 Cor 15:20-28; Gal 5:1). For the New Testament, Christology and reflection upon the Christian vocation to discipleship are intimately related. But what is the relationship between the person of Jesus and the Christian disciple? It is an element of that relationship I would now like to pursue, in the light of my understanding of Jesus as the Son of God and the Son of Man.

Jesus, Son of God and Son of Man

For almost five centuries, the early Church struggled with the question of the balance between the divinity and the humanity of Jesus. Already at the Council of Nicea (325 AD), an Ecumenical Council had formulated the doctrine of the Trinity, in which Jesus, the Son of God, was understood as the second person of the Trinity. If such were the case, the debate raged, how could he possibly be human? Yet, the evidence of the New Testament speaks for his profound human experience and sentiment: "Although he was Son, he learned obedience through what he suffered" (Heb 5:8). Modern and contemporary research has further uncovered the crucial importance of Jesus' humanity.[43] This debate divided Christians in both the Eastern and the Western Churches, and led inevitably to the Council of Chalcedon (451 AD). There another Ecumenical Council defined that Jesus was both divine and human. Indeed, the major thrust of the Council of Chalcedon was to defend the humanity of Jesus. But the Fathers of the Council went further than simply affirming that Jesus was both human and divine. Equally important in their definition of faith was the insistence that the divinity of Jesus did not impinge upon the human experience of Jesus, and that the human experience of Jesus did not alter his divine status. This is the faith and teaching of our Christian and Catholic Tradition. The Council of Chalcedon did *not* define *how this is possible*. Chalcedon insists upon the *fact* of the humanity and divinity of Jesus, but does not tell us *how* Jesus could be both human and divine. It could be claimed that theological debate over the person of Jesus since the Council of Chalcedon has always circled around this question: how can Jesus of Nazareth be – at one and the same time – both human and divine? Chalcedon did not bring debate over the person of Jesus to an end … it opened the door to centuries of further debate.[44]

What follows depends upon my lifetime of involvement with the New Testament, and the Christology of one of the great theologians of the Twentieth century, Karl Rahner.[45] It questions the usefulness of a long-held explanation of the *way in which* the humanity and divinity of Jesus has been explained. Theological speculation is not Christian truth! Chalcedon told us *that* Jesus was both human and divine, but did not tell us *how* he was both human and divine. There is no formal "teaching of the Church" on *how* Jesus is both human and divine. That has long been left to theological speculation, but the speculation that follows starts and ends with the teaching of the Christian Church: *that* Jesus of Nazareth is both human and divine, and *that* this apparent nonsense lies at the heart of Christian discipleship.

Over recent centuries theologians started from the Johannine presentation of Jesus as the entry into the world of someone who comes *from above*, destined eventually to ascend again to *where he was before* (see John 1:1-18; 3:13; 6:62; 20:17). The Incarnation has been taught in theology classes, and in the communication of the Christian Faith to generations as the inbreak of the divine into the human sphere. The classical presentation of this mystery can be presented with the following:

The divine   The immensity of the Godhead

↓

The human   Jesus of Nazareth (the presence of all that can be said
of the divine, but in the human story).

The difficulty with this classical position has always been to explain how Jesus of Nazareth had genuine human experiences: faith, hope, love, trust, fear, sexual desire, pain, laughter, tears, and a myriad of other experiences that are fundamental to the human condition. If Jesus did not have such experiences, trying to hold them all in balance during the course of his life, then he cannot be regarded as truly human. The experience that must be questioned is the cross. Did he really suffer as any other human being would suffer? Or all through that experience was he able to call upon his divine nature to overcome human pain? Did he go through the motions, knowing that he would be raised from the dead and established at the right hand of his Father? If he did, do the suffering and death of Jesus lose something of their salvific significance? The great theologians who have held to this classical view over the centuries have been aware of these difficulties. They generally explained the tension created between the contemporaneous presence of the human and the divine in the figure of Jesus of Nazareth by speculating that Jesus had several levels of consciousness. Using the stories of the Gospels as if they were all factual descriptions of what had happened, they speculated that Jesus switched in and out of his levels of consciousness at various moments in his life and ministry. His suffering and death was lived entirely at the level of his human consciousness, and thus it continues to bear the full salvific significance given to it by the Christian tradition.

A different theological speculation begins, following Rahner, not with the inbreak of the divine into the human, but with a closer look at the depths and richness of all that is human. Those aspects of "being human" mentioned above may be listed again: faith, hope, love, trust, fear, sexual desire, pain, laughter, tears. Why is it so important to love and to be loved, to feel pain at the loss, through death or physical separation, of a loved one? What makes people rise every day and face hopeless situations, yet struggle and suffer to bring about good for others? What is perhaps the more important truth is that our capacity to live, to love and to die in this fashion is what makes each one of us the unique being that we are. Only once in the history of humankind have I, or you, existed. There is only one history of each one of us, and we bear ultimate responsibility for it. We also bear responsibility for the way we have allowed others to shape it in love or hatred, and for the way we have shaped other histories in love or hatred, and the many other possible relational possibilities between those two extremes. None of this is theological speculation. This is the way things are! A moment's quiet reflection proclaims loudly deep inside each one of us: what matters is loving and being loved, and the only unconditionally free action that we will ever perform is the gift of ourselves into the mystery of death. Our abilities as scholars, writers, preachers, teachers, athletes, musicians, etc., are not the final measure of who we are.

After a long and profound look at the human condition, which he calls "spirit in the world," Rahner makes a theological leap. He points to those things that are deepest in us, and which make or break us as human beings, and suggests that they transcend us. They are bigger than us, and they overwhelm us, yet determine us as human beings. In short, they are the experienced signs of the presence of the divine within every single human being. Thus, to be authentically human means to recognize the reality of the divine within us. To be authentically Christian, is to respond to the divine that makes or breaks us, in the light of Jesus Christ and the Gospel. We are all divine, and we yearn for the divine home, for which we were created. The words of St Augustine continue to ring true: "You have made us for yourself, and our heart is restless until it rests in you."[46] Our humanity is not something negative. It is wrong to say: "Oh well, I am only human!" That is the best thing about us, not our weak point. We sin when we do not respond properly to the presence of the divine in our humanity, and we begin to act selfishly, arrogantly, jealously, proudly, satisfying the hungers of our basic urges. These responses are not "human." They belong to the instinctual response world of the animal kingdom. However, we know that our lives are often marked by such sinfulness.

This was *never the case* with Jesus of Nazareth. Again, as the Letter to the Hebrews says: "We have not a high priest who is unable to sympathize with our weaknesses, but one who *in every respect* has been tempted as we are, *yet without sin*" (Heb 4:15). With this in mind, let us return to our diagram, and suggest another possibility.

The divine The only human being who has ever unconditionally realized the divine potential that is in *every* human being: The exalted Jesus

↑

The human Jesus: bringer of the Kingdom in word and person, Son and Son of Man (unconditionally open to the divine potential present in all of us).

Rather than understanding the union of the human and the divine as a divine invasion of the human, that took place only in Jesus, this model works in the opposite direction. The Gospels lead us to suggest that in Jesus the full potential of humanity has been totally realized. This means that, in and through Jesus of Nazareth, the human invaded the divine. Problems remain, as with the traditional model. How can the divine be caught up in the human? A lifetime of searching will not answer that question, and I too must fall back on the truth that here we are dealing with the mystery of the design and action of God. However, this suggestion places "mystery" where it belongs, in the divine Godhead, and not in the humanity of Jesus, something which he shares with us, and which we can experience and understand. It is here that the life of Jesus of Nazareth and the life of the Christian disciple intersect.

Conclusion

We must be careful not to claim that Jesus was no more than a human being who did not sin, who always said "yes" to God, and thus *became* divine. That is a false understanding of the Christian tradition. Jesus brought in the reigning presence of God, and as Son responded unconditionally to God, costing the Son of Man no less than everything. But he did not do this simply because he was a good human being. While there is truth in claiming: "One of us made it!" … it is not the whole truth. Jesus realized the fullness of the divinity possible for all human beings *because he was Son*. It is his being the Son of God that engenders his response to God. Does this mean that we can never hope to do the same? On the contrary, and this is the point of this concluding reflection. We are all capable of repeating the life-style of Jesus and, in our own time, realizing our divinity in its fullness. However, we do this not because we *are* sons and daughters, but because we are *made* sons and daughters by means of our Baptism. We have been *graced* with discipleship. To say it in somewhat technical language: Jesus was son of God *by nature*; we are sons and daughters of God *by grace*. This was what Paul was trying to convey to the Galatians and the Romans when he told them how blessed they were to be able to cry out, in the Spirit, *Abba* Father! (Gal 4:4-7; Rom 8:14-15). As we all so sadly know, the reality of sin is powerfully present in our lives, and we fall short of our full potential; we are less "human" than we could be! We are potentially "another Christ," but this, for a variety of reasons, sometimes lies beyond us.

Finally, these reflections call us to recognize our vocation as disciples to "life in Christ." We are to "put on Christ" so that we might recognize our dignity. All that is noble in us: our loving, our laughter, our play, our mission as preachers, our dancing, our eating and drinking, our praying, alone or with others, our search for justice and peace, and the many other things that we do in response to that which is deepest within us, is part of our journey to be as Jesus Christ was (see Phil 2:5-11; 4:8-9). Like Jesus, Christian disciples reach beyond themselves into the mystery of the divinity that is, at one and the same time, constitutive of our being, yet the object of our search. As Rahner puts it:

> I encounter myself when I find myself in the world and when I ask about God; and when I ask about my essence, I always find myself already in the world and on the way to God. I am both of these at once, and cannot be one without the other.[47]

Notes

[1] John Updike, describing the loss of faith of Clarence Arthur Wilmot, a Presbyterian minister and the founding figure of the dynasty traced in his novel, brilliantly caricatures the impact of this radical criticism: "He (Clarence) had plunged into the chilly Baltic Sea of Higher Criticism – all those Germans, Semler and Eichhorn, Baur and Wellhausen, who dared to pick up the Sacred Book without reverence, as one more human volume, more curious and conglomerate than most, but the work of men – of Jews in dirty sheepskins, rotten-toothed desert tribesmen with eyes rolled heavenward, men like flies on flypaper caught fast in a historic time, among myths and conceptions belonging to the childhood of mankind. They called themselves theologians, these Teutonic ravagers of the text that Luther had unchained from the altar and had translated out of Latin, and accepted their bread from the devout sponsors of theological chairs, yet were the opposite of theologians, as in the dank basement of Greek and Aramaic researches they undermined Christianity's ancient supporting walls and beams" (J. Updike, *In the Beauty of the Lilies* [New York: Fawcett Columbine, 1996], 15). Explanatory parenthesis added.

[2] This is the background to Updike's caricature: "the work of men – of Jews in dirty sheepskins, rotten-toothed desert tribesmen with eyes rolled heavenward, men like flies on flypaper caught fast in a historic time, among myths and conceptions belonging to the childhood of mankind."

[3] On the theoretical source for the material common to Matthew and Luke, called "Q" (from the German word "Quelle" = source), see above, pp. 19-22.

[4] For further discussion, and some suggestions about the strength of the historical underpinning of some Johannine traditions, see F. J. Moloney, "The Fourth Gospel and the Jesus of History," in *The Gospel of John. Text and Context* (Biblical Interpretation Series 72; Boston/Leiden: Brill, 2005), 45-65.

[5] The epoch making works were: W. Wrede, *Das Messiasgeheimnis in den Evangelien. Zugleich ein Beitrag zum Verständnis des Markusevangeliums* (Göttingen: Vandenhoeck & Ruprecht, 1901). The book, reprinted four times since then (last reprint 1969), is available in English (translated from the 1969 reprint): *The Messianic Secret*, (trans. J. C. G. Grieg; Cambridge & London: James Clarke, 1971). The work of Schweizer had two major editions. The first

edition appeared in 1905, and a second, much enlarged, edition, appeared in 1913. The earlier edition was translated into English (A. Schweitzer, *The Quest of the Historical Jesus* [trans. W. Montgomery; London: A. & C. Black, 1910]), but not the revision. Only recently has the complete edition of Schweitzer's contribution been provided in English. See A. Schweizer, *The Quest of the Historical Jesus* (First Complete Edition; ed. J. Bowden; Minneapolis: Fortress, 2001).

[6] See below, pp. 326-29.

[7] For further discussion of the contributions of Wrede and Schweizer, see below, pp. 326-29.

[8] An important, but difficult, study of this turning point in reading the Bible is H. Frei, *The Eclipse of Biblical Narrative: A Study of Eighteenth and Nineteenth Century Hermeneutics* (New Haven: Yale University Press, 1974).

[9] This scholarly activity was not limited to biblical studies. New archeological and literary discoveries opened up a world of ancient religions hitherto unknown. There were different methods, but this movement was called "The History of Religions School."

[10] K. L. Schmidt, *Die Rahmen der Geschichte Jesu: Literarkritische Untersuchungen zu ältesten Jesusüberlieferung* (Damstadt: Wissenschaftliche Buchgesellschaft, 1964 [original 1919]). There is no translation. The title reads "The Framework of the History of Jesus: Literary Critical Investigations of the Oldest Traditions concerning Jesus." M. Dibelius, *From Traditon to Gospel* (trans. B. L. Woolf; Library of Theological Translations; Cambridge & London: James Clarke, 1971 [original German: 1919]); R. Bultmann, *History of the Synoptic Tradition* (trans. J. Marsh; Oxford: Basil Blackwell, 1968 [original German: 1921]).

[11] Bultmann, *History*, 338, 350.

[12] Ibid., 350.

[13] Much has been written on this topic. For a brief, but first-class, treatment, see E. H. Carr, *What is History?* (New York: Knopf, 1962).

[14] See N. Perrin, *What is Redaction Criticism?* (Philadelphia: Fortress, 1969).

[15] For an introduction to narrative criticism, see F. J. Moloney, "Narrative Criticism of the Gospels," in *"A Hard Saying": The Gospel and Culture* (Collegeville: The Liturgical Press, 2001), 85-105; M. A. Powell, *What is Narrative Criticism?* (Minneapolis: Fortress, 1990).

[16] H. Conzelmann, *The Theology of St. Luke* (trans. G. Buswell; London: Faber & Faber, 1961), 9. The stress is mine.

[17] On "Q," see above, pp. 19-22.

[18] This does not necessarily mean that Matthew "invented" the famous Petrine passage. In fact, Matt 16:17-19 shows all the signs of being pre-Matthean. Matthew drew it from his tradition, and added it to the material he edited from Mark. See the excellent study of R. E. Brown, "The *Pater Noster* as an Eschatological Prayer," in *New Testament Essays* (London: Geoffrey Chapman, 1967), 217-53. On the passage itself, and its Petrine implications, see B. Byrne, *Lifting the Burden. Reading Matthew's Gospel in the Church Today* (Collegeville: The Liturgical Press, 2004), 127-32.

[19] See above, pp. 46-70 (Mark), 94-126 (Matthew), 166-201 (Luke).

[20] See above, pp. 22-26.

[21] See above, pp. 277-305.

[22] See S. M. Schneiders, *Interpreting the New Testament as Sacred Scripture* (2d ed.; Collegeville: The Liturgical Press, 1999). For what follows, see also F. J. Moloney, *The Gospel of John* (Sacra Pagina 4; Collegeville: The Liturgical Press, 1998), 13-20.

[23] We have already had occasion to insist upon the fact that in Gospel "prologues" (Mark 1:1-13; Matt 1-2; Luke 1-2 and John 1:1-18) an author addresses readers. In the Gospel of John, the author directly addresses his readers ("you") in 19:35 and 20:30-31.

[24] S. Fish, *Is There a Text in This Class? The Authority of Interpretative Communities*

(Cambridge: Harvard University Press, 1988), 26-27.

[25] See S. Rimmon-Kenan, *Narrative Fiction: Contemporary Poetics* (New Accents; London: Methuen, 1983), 125.

[26] A. Yarbro-Collins, "Narrative, History and Gospel," *Semeia* 43 (1988): 150, 153.

[27] D. Tracy, *The Analogical Imagination: Christian Theology and the Culture of Pluralism* (New York: Crossroad, 1981), 102.

[28] H. de Balzac, *Old Goriot* (Penguin Classics; Harmondsworth: Penguin Books, 1951), 28. Stress in original.

[29] It must be pointed out that once critics began to focus upon the impact that the text made upon the reader, many "contemporary criticisms" emerged: narrative criticism (considered here), reader-response criticism, feminist criticism, post-colonial criticism, various forms of radical post-modern criticism, etc. The shift away from a primary focus upon *the text* to the *situation of the reader* leads to many possible interpretative approaches. See The Bible and Culture Collective, *The Postmodern Bible* (London and New Haven: Yale University Press, 1996). As a contemporary literary critic puts it: "Once you take seriously the notion that readers 'construct' (even partially) the texts that they read, then the canon (any canon) is not (or not only) the product of the inherent qualities of the text; it is also (at least partly) the product of particular choices of the arbiters of choice who create it – choices always grounded in ideological and cultural values, always enmeshed in class, race, and gender" (P. J. Rabinowitz, "Whirl without End: Audience-Oriented Criticism," in C. D. Atkins and L. Morrow [eds.], *Contemporary Literary Theory* [London: Macmillan, 1989], 94). Not all such readings are helpful, and not all serve in the responsibility of the Christian interpreter to read the text within the contours of the Christian tradition. I have limited myself to a consideration of what is called "narrative criticism." I regard this approach to the text as a reading that can be done *in* the Christian community, *by* the Christian community, and for the *building up of* the Christian community. However, it is not the *only* contemporary reader-oriented approach to the Gospels. For a balanced collection of studies that deal with many of these approaches, see E. V. McKnight and E. S. Malbon (eds.), *The new literary criticism and the New Testament* (Valley Forge: Trinity Press International, 1994).

[30] H. J. Holtzmann, *Die synoptischen Evangelien: Ihr Ursprung und geschichtlicher Charakter* (Leipzig: Wilhelm Engelmann, 1863). This book has no English translation. Its title reads "The Synoptic Gospels: Their Origin and Historical Character." For a fuller discussion, see S. Kealy, *Mark's Gospel: A History of Its Interpretation* (New York: Paulist, 1982), 58-89.

[31] See above, pp.312-14.

[32] Wrede focused upon the continual commands to silence that surrounded Jesus messianic deeds. He mistakenly explained them all away as the consistent theological activity of the early Church, to explain why some knew Jesus as the Messiah, but others did not. He was correct, however, in pointing out that the Gospels were not primarily interested in reporting the brute facts of *history*, but the Church's understanding of the ultimate *theological* significance of the life, teaching, death and resurrection of Jesus. For a fuller assessment of Wrede's contribution, in my opinion the forerunner of what was to become "redaction criticism," see F. J. Moloney, *Mark. Storyteller, Interpreter, Evangelist* (Peabody: Hendrickson, 2004), 23-25.

[33] Schweitzer, *The Quest of the Historical Jesus*, 478. Stress mine.

[34] Crucially important for the birth of this "second quest" were G. Bornkamm, *Jesus of Nazareth* (trans. I. and F. McLuskey with J. M. Robinson; New York: Harper & Row, 1960), and E. Käsemann, "The Problem of the Historical Jesus," in *Essays on New Testament Themes* (trans. W. J. Montague; Naperville: Allenson, 1964), 15-47; Idem, "Blind Alleys in the 'Jesus of History' Controversy," in *New Testament Questions of Today* (trans. W. J. Montague; Philadelphia: Fortress, 1969), 23-65. Both Bornkamm and Käsemann were Bultmann's students.

[35] See, on this, the work of J. Jeremias, *New Testament Theology: The Proclamation of Jesus* (trans. J. Bowden; London: SCM Press, 1971), 1-37.

[36] For a very fine, and readable, survey of the question, see M. A. Powell, *Jesus as a Figure in History. How Modern Historians View the Man from Galilee* (Louisville: Westminster John Knox, 1998). Powell offers a fine study of the various "criteria" on pp. 31-50. Two powerful books that should be considered by any educated reader are: E. P. Sanders, *The Historical Figure of Jesus* (Allen Lane: The Penguin Press, 1993), and L. Keck, *Who is Jesus? History in the Perfect Tense* (Studies in

Personalities in the New Testament; Columbia: University of South Carolina Press, 2001). The most comprehensive, convincing, and still unfinished study is J. P. Meier, *A Marginal Jew. Rethinking the Historical Jesus* (3 vols.; New York, Doubleday, 1991-2001). Meier's work is a sophisticated use of the historical critical approach and the various "criteria" developed in the "second quest." In Meier, the "second quest" is very much alive. See his own valuable comments on the "quests," in J. P. Meier, "The Present State of the "Third Quest" for the Historical Jesus: Loss and Gain," *Biblica* 80 (1999): 459-87.

[37] On this, see the stern words of L. T. Johnson, *The Real Jesus. The Misguided Quest for the Historical Jesus and the Truth of the Traditional Gospels* (New York: HarperSanFrancisco, 1996), 1-27. This chapter is entitled: "The Good News and the Nightly News."

[38] For a stinging critique, see Johnson, *The Real Jesus*. See also B. Witherington III, *The Jesus Quest. The Third Search for the Jew of Nazareth* (Downers Grove: Intervarsity Press, 1995). For a less passionate rejection of the methods of the Seminar, and a presentation of the work of two of their major representatives (John Dominic Crossan and Marcus Borg), see Powell, *Jesus as a Figure in History*, 65-112.

[39] For more detail, see F. J. Moloney, *Mark. Storyteller, Interpreter, Evangelist* (Peabody: Hendrickson, 2003), 136-43 (Son of God); 143-51 (Son of Man).

[40] See especially the work of Sanders, Keck and Meier, mentioned above in note 22.

[41] What follows is taken from F. J. Moloney, "The Son of Man and Christian Discipleship," *Lutheran Theological Journal* 39 (2005): 117-21.

[42] We are on delicate theological and hermeneutical ground here, associating "history" and "resurrection." This is not the place to resolve the issue, but by "history" I do not mean the brute facts of what can be measured (in German: *Historie*, e.g. the number of soldiers Napolean took to Austerlitz), but an event from the past that "took place" but escapes our control or measurement (in German: *Geschichte*, e.g. the "event" of falling in love). We cannot "measure" the event of the resurrection, but we live as Christians because of it.

[43] For an excellent study of this research, leading to a personal presentation of a Christology based upon Jesus' humanity, see J. Macquarrie, *Jesus Christ in Modern Thought* (London: SCM Press, 1990). On Karl Rahner, see pp. 304-308 ("The most illustrious of this new breed of Catholic theologians" [p. 304]). For his own Christology, see pp. 348-422.

[44] For a brilliant and precise presentation of the achievements of Chalcedon and the conflicts it generated, see Robert L. Wilken, *The Spirit of Early Christian Thought: Seeking the Face of God* (New Haven: Yale University Press, 2003), 110-35.

[45] Rahner's theological writings are voluminous and difficult to read. His seminal work on Christology can be hard to trace, as it was scattered through a number of volumes with the title *Theological Investigations*, some of which continued to appear after his death in 1984 (Volume 21 appeared in 1988). The best synthesis of his thought can be found in K. Rahner, *Foundations of Christian Faith. An Introduction to the Idea of Christianity* (trans. W. V. Dych; London: Darton, Longman & Todd, 1978), 176-321.

[46] Augustine, *Confessions*, I, I. Translation from Henry Chadwick, *Saint Augustine Confessions* (World's Classics; Oxford: Oxford University Press, 1991), 3.

[47] K. Rahner, *Spirit in the World* (trans. W. V. Dych; London: Sheed and Ward, 1968), 406.

About the author

FRANCIS J MOLONEY WAS BORN IN MELBOURNE, AUSTRALIA, and joined the Australian Province of the Salesians of Don Bosco in 1960. He was awarded a Doctorate of Philosophy in 1976 from the University of Oxford, UK, for his study of the use of the term "the Son of Man" in the Fourth Gospel.

In 1976 he returned to Australia and was the Professor of New Testament at Catholic Theological College within the ecumenical Melbourne College of Divinity from 1976 till 1994. During that period he was the Visiting Professor to the Salesian Pontifical University, Rome (1978, 1982), to the Ecole Biblique, Jerusalem (1989-90), and to the Pontifical Biblical Institute, Rome (1993-94). In 1992 he was elected a Fellow of the Australian Academy of Humanities. 1994 saw him made a member of the Order of Australia, a State Honor in recognition of his services to Australian religion and culture. In 1994 he was appointed the Foundation Professor of Theology at Australian Catholic University. He was appointed the Professor of New Testament at the Catholic University of America in Washington, DC, in January, 1999. In August, 2001, he was elected the President of the Catholic Biblical Association of America, the first non-United States citizen ever to hold this prestigious position. Pope John Paul II appointed Professor Moloney to the International Theological Commission to the Holy See in 1984, an appointment he would hold for 18 years. In April, 2002, he was appointed to the endowed Chair at the Catholic University of America: the Katharine Drexel Chair of Religious Studies. In October of 2003 he was elected Dean of the School of Theology and Religious Studies. In June, 2005, he was appointed the Provincial Superior of the Salesians of Don Bosco in Australia and assumed that ministry in January 2006.

Professor Moloney's major writings and publications are listed on the next page.

Major writings and publications

PROFESSOR MOLONEY, A FOUNDING EDITOR of the Australian theological journal *Pacifica*, and an associate editor of *The Catholic Biblical Quarterly*, is the author of 36 books and a large number of articles, both scholarly and popular, in journals from all parts of the world. Of particular pastoral interest are: *A Body Broken for a Broken People. Eucharist in the New Testament* (Peabody MA: Hendrickson, 1997) and his three volumes on the Sunday Gospels, *The Gospel of the Lord,* Years A, B and C (Homebush: St Paul). Other major writings are his commentary on the Fourth Gospel, *The Gospel of John* (Sacra Pagina Series 4; Collegeville MN: Liturgical Press, 1998), *"A Hard Saying." The Gospel and Culture* (Collegeville: Liturgical Press, 2001), a large-scale study of the Gospel of Mark, entitled *The Gospel of Mark. A Commentary* (Peabody MA, Hendrickson Publishers, 2002). He has recently updated, edited and rewritten posthumous material, left by Raymond E. Brown: *Introduction to the Gospel of John* (ed. Francis J. Moloney; Anchor Bible Reference Library; New York: Doubleday, 2003). His most recent books are a further study of the Gospel of Mark, *Mark: Storyteller, Interpreter, Evangelist* (Peabody: Hendrickson, 2004) and *The Gospel of John: Text and Context* (Biblical Interpretation Series 32; Boston: Brill, 2005).